DRIVEN OUT

DRIVEN OUT

THE FORGOTTEN WAR AGAINST CHINESE AMERICANS

JEAN PFAELZER

RANDOM HOUSE  NEW YORK

Published in the United States by Random House, an imprint of The Random House Publishing Group, a division of Random House, Inc., New York.

RANDOM HOUSE and colophon are registered trademarks of Random House, Inc.

ISBN 978-1-4000-6134-1

LIBRARY OF CONGRESS CATALOGING-IN-PUBLICATION DATA

Pfaelzer, Jean.
Driven out : the forgotten war against
Chinese Americans / Jean Pfaelzer.
p. cm.
Includes bibliographical references and index.
ISBN-13: 978-1-4000-6134-1
1. Chinese Americans—California—History—19th century. 2. Chinese Americans—Crimes against—California—History—19th century. 3. Chinese Americans—Relocation—California—History—19th century. 4. Racism—California—History—19th century. 5. Violence—California—History—19th century. 6. Forced migration—California—History—19th century. 7. California—Race relations—History—19th century. 8. Ethnic neighborhoods—California—History—19th century. 9. California—History, Local. I. Title.
F870.C5P48 2007
979.40045'1—dc22 2006051031

Printed in the United States of America on acid-free paper

www.atrandom.com

2 4 6 8 9 7 5 3 1

FIRST EDITION

Designed by Stephanie Huntwork

for

PETER PANUTHOS

SOPHIA PFAELZER PANUTHOS

JOHANNA PFAELZER

JONATHAN PANUTHOS

CONTENTS

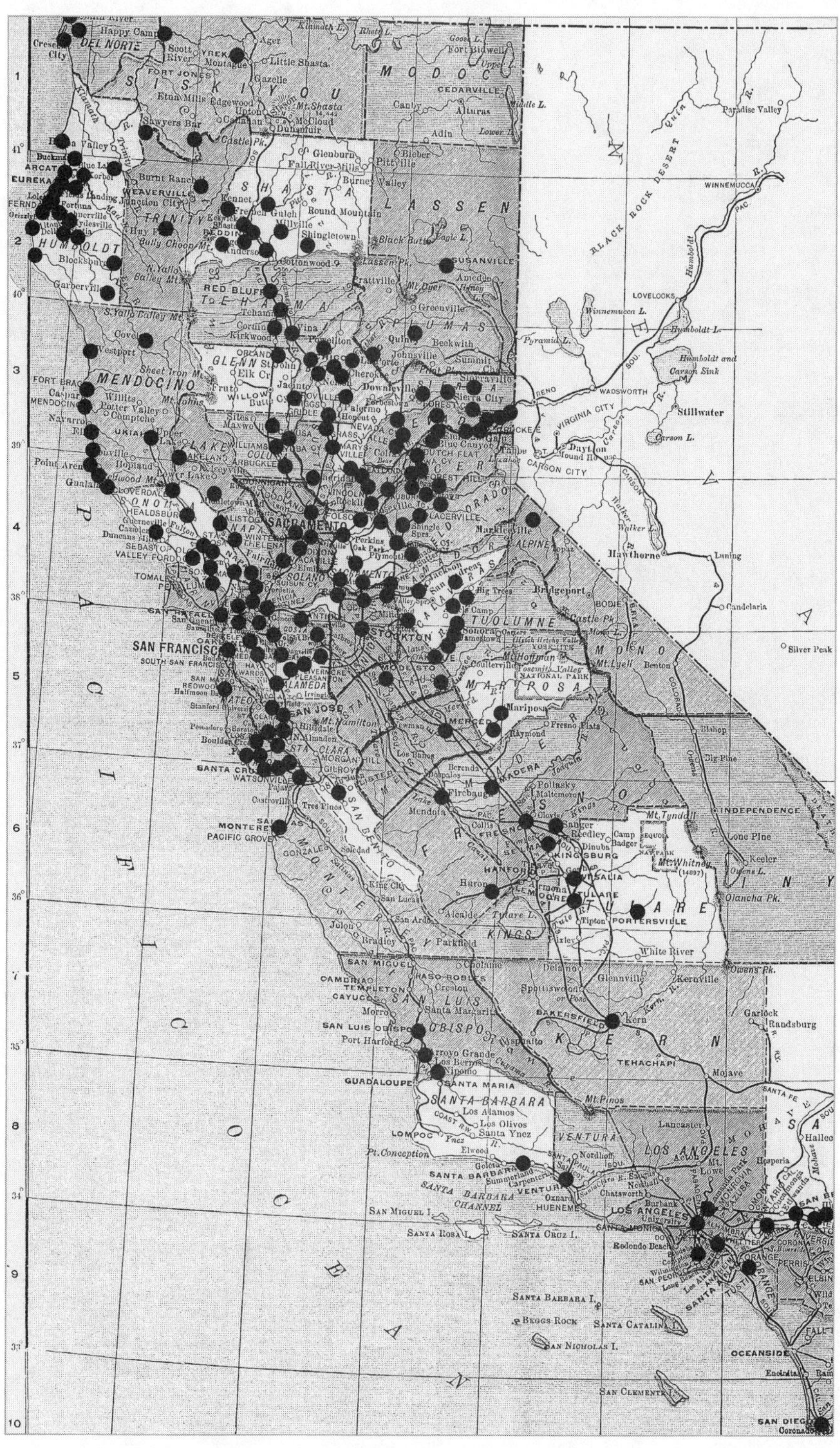

Roundups of Chinese Americans in California, 1849–1906.

There were more than two hundred such roundups.

LIST OF ILLUSTRATIONS

INTRODUCTION

THE CHINESE CALLED IT *PAI HUA*, OR *THE DRIVEN OUT*

At nine o'clock on the morning of November 3, 1885, steam whistles blew at the foundries and mills across Tacoma, to announce the start of the purge of all the Chinese people from the town. Saloons closed and police stood by as five hundred men, brandishing clubs and pistols, went from house to house in the downtown Chinese quarter and through the Chinese tenements along the city's wharf. Sensing the storm ahead, earlier in the week, about five hundred Chinese people had fled from Tacoma. Now the rest were given four hours to be ready to leave. They desperately stuffed years of life into sacks, shawls, and baskets hung from shoulder poles—bedding, clothing, pots, some food. At midday, the mob began to drag Chinese laborers from their homes, pillage their laundries, and throw their furniture into the streets. Chinese merchants pleaded with the mayor and the sheriff for an extra twenty-four hours to pack up their shops.

Early on that cold Tuesday afternoon, armed vigilantes corralled two hundred Chinese men and women at the docks. The governor of the Washington Territory, Watson C. Squire, ignored telegrams from Chinese across the Pacific Northwest urging him to intervene. The mayor and the sheriff hid out at city hall as the mob marched the Chinese through heavy rain to a muddy railroad crossing nine miles from town. The merchants' wives, unable to walk on their tiny bound feet, were tossed into wagons.

Lake View Junction was a stop on the Northern Pacific Railroad, which had been built by Chinese laborers. A few of the evicted Chinese found damp shelter in abandoned storage sheds, in stables, or inside the small station house. Most huddled outside. During the cold and rainy night, two or three trains stopped at the station. People with cash paid six dollars to board the overnight train to Portland, Oregon. Others crammed onto a passing freight train. The rest began the hundred-mile trek south to the Chinatown in Portland, where they hoped to find sanctuary in a community that had just refused the town's orders to leave. For days they were seen following the tracks south. Others fled the country for Canada.

Two days later, Tacoma's Chinatown was destroyed by fire.

LUM MAY

Territory of Washington
County of King
June 3, 1886

Lum May being duly sworn on his oath saith:

I was born in Canton, China, and am a subject of the Chinese Empire. I am aged about 51 years. Have been in America about eleven years and have been doing business in Tacoma for ten years. My business there was that of keeping dry goods, provisions, medicines and general merchandize store.

On the third day of November I resided with my family in Tacoma on the corner of Railroad Street some little distance from Chinatown. At that time I would say there were eight hundred or nine hundred Chinese persons in and about Tacoma who . . . were forcibly expelled by the white people of Tacoma. Twenty days previously to the 3rd of November, a committee of white persons waited upon the Chinese at their residences and ordered them to leave the city before the 3rd of November. I do not know the names of [the] white persons but would recognize their faces. The Committee consisted of 15 or 20 persons . . . who notified the Chinese to leave.

I asked General Sprague and other citizens for protection for myself and the Chinese people. The General said he would see and do what he could. All the Chinese after receiving notice to leave were frightened lest their houses should be blown up and destroyed. A rumour to that effect was in circulation. Many of them shut up their houses and tried to keep on the look out.

About half past 9 o'clock in the morning of November 3, 1885, a large crowd of citizens of Tacoma marched down to Chinatown and told all the Chinese that the whole Chinese population of Tacoma must leave town by half past one o'clock in the afternoon of that day. There must have been in the neighborhood of 1000 people in the crowd of white people though I cannot tell how many. They went to all the Chinese houses and establishments and notified the Chinese to leave. Where the doors were locked they broke forcibly into the houses smashing in doors and breaking in windows. Some of the crowd was armed with pistols, some with clubs. They acted in a rude boisterous and threatening manner, dragging and kicking the Chinese out of their houses.

My wife refused to go and some of the white persons dragged her out of the house. From the excitement, the fright and the losses we sustained through the riot she lost her reason, and has ever since been hopelessly insane. She threatens to kill people with a hatchet or any other weapon she can get hold of. The outrages I and my family suffered at the hands of the mob has utterly ruined me. I make no claim, however, for my wife's insanity or the anguish I have suffered. My wife was perfectly sane before the riot.

I saw my countrymen marched out of Tacoma on November 3rd. They presented a sad spectacle. Some had lost their trunks, some their blankets, some were crying for their things.

Armed white men were behind the Chinese, on horseback sternly urging them on. It was raining and blowing hard. On the 5th of November all the Chinese houses situated on the wharf were burnt down by incendiaries.

I sustained the following losses through the riot, to wit: 2 pieces silk crape trowsers female, 2 pieces black silk, 6 silk handkerchiefs, 2 crape jackets, 10 blue cotton shirts, 8 pieces black cotton trowsers, 12 Pairs Chinese Cotton Stockings, 2 Leather trunks (Chinese), wool great dress female, 4 flannel jackets, 3 pairs embroidered shoes, 1 dressing case, 6 white cotton shirts, 1 carpet bag, 2 white woolen blankets, 2 red woolen bed covers, 1 feather mattress, 1 spring bed, 2 tables, 6 chairs, 2 stoves, 4 pictures and frames, 1 large mirror, 2 woolen trowsers (male) and solvent debtors (Chinaman), 1 business and good will, loss of perishable goods, total $45,532.

A few of the Chinese merchants I among them were suffered to remain in Tacoma for two days in order to pack up our goods or what was left of them. On the 5th of November, after the burning of the Chinese houses on the wharf I left Tacoma for Victoria where I have since resided. . . . No Chinaman has been allowed to reside in Tacoma since November 3rd.

Mayor Weisbach appeared to be one of the leaders of the mob on the 3rd of November. I spoke to him and told him that Mr. Sprague had said the Chinese had a right to stay and would be protected. He answered me: "General Sprague has nothing to say. If he says anything we will hang him or kick him. You get out of here." I cried. He said I was a baby because I cried over the loss of my property. He said, "I told you before you must go, and I mean my word shall be kept good."

I desire to add to this that . . . it is ten years since we began business there.

Lum May[1]

Tacoma's Chinese residents did not go quietly. On November 5, 1885, aided by China's consul in San Francisco, they compelled the U.S. attorney to arrest the mayor of Tacoma, the chief of police, two councilmen, a probate court judge, and the president of the YMCA. Then they filed seventeen civil claims against the U.S. government, for a total of $103,365.

The Tacoma roundup was one of a hundred Chinese pogroms that raged across the Pacific Northwest in the late nineteenth century. In the winter of 1885–86, the raids and arson in Chinatowns reached Portland, and the Chinese refugees from Tacoma fled again—some to San Francisco, some back to rural hamlets in the Washington Territory closer to their old homes, some to the East Coast, and some to work on plantations in the South.

Word of the raids resounded in newspapers, in state capitals, in the boardrooms of railroad companies and lumber mills, in Congress, and across the Pacific Ocean. Defying protests from both Republicans and Democrats, President Grover Cleveland decided to accede to the refugees' demands for reparation, with the hope that this might cause China to revive trade talks with the United States. China's population of four hundred million people, he believed, could purchase America out of its deep economic depression, and China's government might open trade routes for a nation come lately to foreign expansion.

Congress was ambivalent. It understood that whichever party controlled California would likely control the House of Representatives, the

Senate, and the next presidency. The firestorm of roundups in California was compelling evidence of the sentiments in the golden state.

The violent raids were bannered in the press—in the local *Tacoma Register* and the *Eureka Times-Telephone,* and nationwide in *The New York Times* and *Harper's Weekly.* Most Americans knew of the Chinese purges in California, Oregon, Washington, Wyoming, Nevada, and Colorado. But before Congress complied with Cleveland's request, it wanted to know the economic value of a Chinese life.

In 1886, at the order of Congress, Governor Watson Squire desperately sought to track down the two hundred Chinese men and women who had been driven out of Tacoma so that they could bear witness to the public violence done against them in his name. Ultimately, he could locate only a few. Most were unable or unwilling to be found.

Lum May had fled to Victoria, Canada. He and his wife had legally entered the United States in 1874, before the Page Act of 1875 banned the entry of almost all Chinese women and before the Chinese Exclusion Act of 1882—the first immigration law to exclude people based on their race—banned the thousands of immigrants who crisscrossed the Pacific each year from reentering the United States.

Governor Squire found Lum May, but as a subject of the Chinese Empire, he was barred from testifying in a U.S. court. Through his written affidavit, Lum's is one of the Chinese voices that speaks across the silent years since being Driven Out.

TUCK NAN

Governor Squire also located Lum May's close friend and business partner, Tuck Nan. On the night of the purge, Tuck Nan had fled to Portland, where he had decided to remain despite the ongoing anti-Chinese violence in the area. It was there that Squire was compelled to listen to and record Tuck Nan's story.

Now fifty years old, Tuck Nan had come to the United States at age sixteen, arriving in San Francisco with the first wave of Chinese immigrants who came in the gold rush. Within two years of the discovery of gold on January 24, 1848, at a sawmill on the American River in California, more than 150,000 men—from the eastern United States and across the globe—

poured into San Francisco. Driven from their homelands by poverty and political repression, and now dreaming of gold, they quickly made their way to the creek beds of the Sierra Nevada. Arriving in 1852, Tuck Nan was one of seven hundred Chinese émigrés.[2] Within the next eighteen months, twenty thousand more Chinese miners entered California. And thousands more were waiting in China's port cities to board ships bound for San Francisco.[3]

Ten of the early Chinese immigrants were women, kidnapped to work as enslaved prostitutes in California. Soon the ships would also carry baby girls, seized in China for the same fate. Most did not survive. Some Chinese prostitutes, however, escaped from the locked "cribs" and brothels in San Francisco, only to be forced to return to their owners after the purges in Tacoma, Eureka, Antioch, and Truckee.

White Americans, many unemployed, spread onto lands stolen from indigenous Americans, "inherited" from Spain by Mexico in 1821, governed by "joint occupancy" with Britain, which had handed over its rights to the United States in 1846, and seized by the United States in the Mexican War in 1848. These white miners led the first purges of the Chinese, sparking a wave of violence that raged over the next four decades—north to Tacoma, south to Los Angeles, east to Wyoming and Colorado. After the Civil War, the new trade-union movement took up the anti-Chinese cause and the Knights of Labor spread the racist message through the Workingmen's Party. White boot makers, cigar rollers, cooks, and woodcutters who were competing with lower-paid Chinese workers joined in the brutality.

The Driven Out was spurred on by Irish and German immigrants fearful of job competition and by destitute, unemployed white migrants from the East Coast who felt betrayed by the false promises of new industry in eastern cities. When these men came to the American West, they were enraged to discover that the railroads and new land barons, such as Miller and Lux Co., which owned an empire in California as large as Belgium, had a stranglehold on land and timber along the Pacific coast.[4] West Coast Jews, too, participated in the anti-Chinese violence: in San Francisco in the 1880s, the Anti-Coolie League met at B'nai B'rith on Friday nights, at the start of the Jewish Sabbath.

The roundups were also led by mayors and governors, judges and newspaper editors, wealthy timbermen and ranchers willing to betray their need for cheap labor in order to mark their common whiteness and stitch together the raw communities that were quickly emerging in the fields, at river junctions, in fishing ports and lumber towns.

The purges of the Chinese followed two other paths toward racial purity converging in the West. First, along the Pacific coast, the American military and armed irregulars were murdering Native Americans or forcing them off their traditional lands, making way for white settlement, agriculture, mining, and logging. In Northern California, native people were driven onto reservations, along the Klamath River, at Nome Lackee, at Round Valley, and at Hupa (now known as Hoopa). African Americans, too, were being dispossessed of the land on which they had worked. Both before and after the Civil War, ideas of racial inferiority and white purity moved West. By the 1880s, the southern Democrats had taken over California's governor's mansion, state legislature, and many county boards, and were eagerly implementing versions of the southern Black Codes, passed after the Civil War in order to restrict the new political freedom of emancipated slaves. Now the southerners were targeting the Chinese by implementing special taxes, "cubic air" ordinances limiting how many Chinese could inhabit one room, and city ordinances banned laundries built of wood.

Tuck Nan was a link in a global migratory chain of immigrants who came to California for gold yet remained tied to family, foods, tools, clothes, and ideas from their homeland. He had faced tremendous obstacles in leaving China. Indeed, for centuries Chinese émigrés who tried to return were punished as deserters by the Qing emperors.[5] Political turbulence and famine were stretching China's cords of loyalty, but Tuck Nan's early emigration still betrayed affiliation and authority—to family, clan, and village.

Tuck Nan left his homeland amid the chaos of war and starvation. In the mid-nineteenth century, China, burdened with a population of four hundred million, faced waves of insurrections, invasions, and internal ethnic wars. In 1839, sensing this moment of vulnerability, Britain launched the Opium Wars, which sought to balance its compulsive purchase of Chinese tea and silk by forcing China to buy opium, grown in India but brokered and transported by England. In the Treaty of Nanking, which ended the war, Britain opened China's doors to the addictive drug and to the economic, military, shipping, and missionary presence of the West.

China's first treaty with the United States, the Treaty of Wanghsia, followed in 1844, and the British and Americans sailed in force into the southern ports of Canton, Shanghai, Ningbo, Amoy, and Foochow.[6] By the early

1850s, Russia's army had invaded China's eastern border and seized Manchuria, leading the foreign efforts to carve up the Chinese Empire.

Many Chinese chose to sail to the United States; thousands of others fled or were kidnapped to work on plantations in Cuba or Mexico or in the deadly guano pits of Peru.

Tuck Nan never made it into the mines of the Sierra Nevada. He remained in San Francisco, where he watched his countrymen return from the gold fields and new mountain towns, quickly forced onto barges heading down the rushing western rivers. He stayed in San Francisco for thirteen years, likely working as a launderer, a waiter, a house servant, or a peddler, sending some of his small earnings back to China. In 1865, he moved north to Portland, where he opened a supply shop for miners leaving for the new gold fields. But violence followed him.

In 1876, Tuck Nan "removed" farther north to Tacoma, in the Washington Territory. There he went into partnership with Lum May. Nine years later he became one of the Driven Out when several hundred "angry and excited white persons" broke into his store and shoved his friends out the door. The mob told him, "'Oh the Chinese you must go—every one.'" Tuck Nan recounted that he "begged them to leave me remain a few days to settle our business," but the vigilantes said, "Take your goods and go. You had notice on the 9th October to leave before 1st of November—and the time is up. You've had time enough to get ready." Tuck Nan added, "They would listen to nothing but told us to be ready at 2 o'clock in the afternoon when they would carry away our goods." And just at two the mob returned, armed with weapons and clubs. "Some had poles and they used these to drive us like so many hogs, if any of us went slow or stopped. I was very much afraid."

In June 1886, Tuck Nan demanded fifteen thousand dollars in reparations from the U.S. government and signed his own affidavit in English.[7]

YOKE LEEN

Despite the roundups and the fears of enslaved prostitution, many Chinese women in America insisted that the local government protect their right to live where they chose. One Chinese woman refused to submit to sexual slavery. In 1910, Yoke Leen marched into the courthouse in Sonora and demanded that her deposition be taken and preserved in the county records:

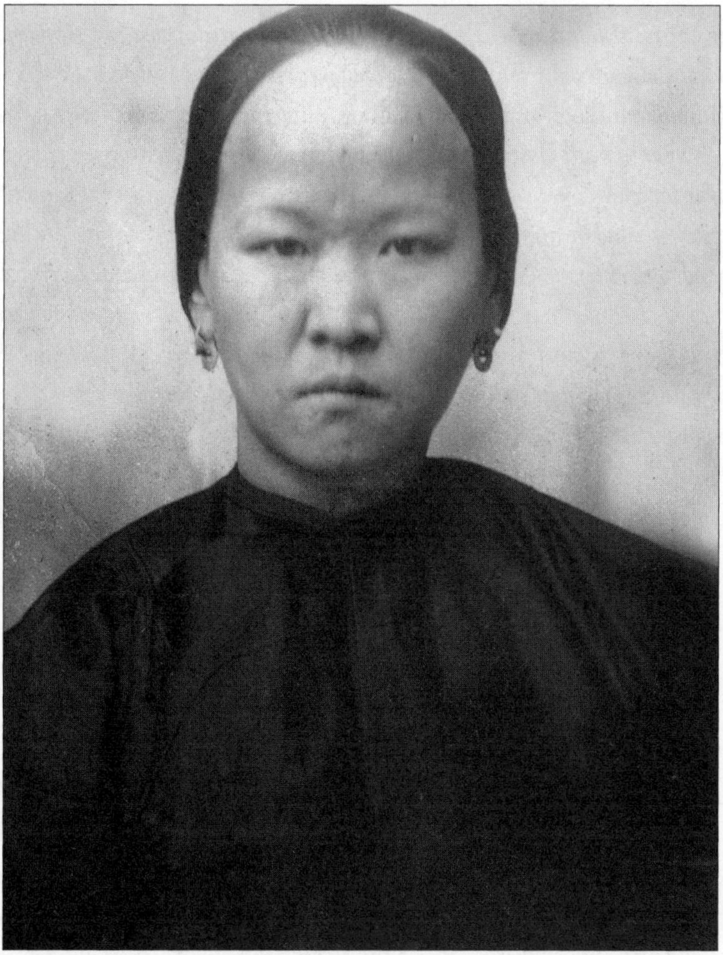

Yoke Leen from Sonora

State of California
Sonora, County of Tuolumne
21 day of February, 1910

YOKE LEEN, being first duly sworn, deposes and says:

I reside in the city of Sonora, State of California, and am the age of 36 years. That I am a native of the State of California, having been born in San Francisco, California. That I am about five feet tall and weigh about 110 pounds. That I have a scar on my face on the right side of the nose near the right eye and also a large scar on the right side of the mouth, also a small raised scar at the base of the index finger of the right hand and a small scar

on the right hand about an inch below the wrist at the base of the thumb. That the annexed photograph is a photograph of myself taken by William Harrington, Photographer, at Sonora, California, in January, 1910.

That this affidavit with the annexed photograph is made for the purpose of identifying me in case I should be kidnapped or in case any criminal charge should be brought against me and by reason of the fact that my husband, Charlie Jones, is now in jail charged with a criminal offense and I fear that his enemies may try to do away with me either by bringing some fictitious charge against me or by kidnapping and imprisoning me. The annexed signature is my name written in English and also in Chinese.

Yoke Leen[8]

SPEAK, MEMORY

In August 1974, I moved with my six-year-old daughter into a cabin in the woods of remote Humboldt County to begin my career as a professor of American studies. Each morning I would drive south from Big Lagoon, a little community of beach cottages, damp and empty in the chilled fog and gray light of the north coast, past the jagged rocks at Patrick's Point, through the redwood forest above the fishing village of Trinidad, past sober white egrets guarding the green fern prairies (oblivious to the sixty-five inches of rain that fall each year in the county), and finally cross the Mad River to climb the hill to Humboldt State University in Arcata. Nestled in the redwoods between Oregon and the lumber and fishing town of Eureka, California, Arcata borders the marshes and dunes that fade into Humboldt Bay.

The week that we moved to this isolated corner of the Pacific Northwest, President Nixon resigned. The following spring, the last American soldier was killed in Vietnam. That April the last Americans were evacuated by helicopter from the roof of the U.S. Embassy in Saigon. The Vietnam War was ending, and I danced with my students around the statue of President McKinley in Arcata's town square. Our spirits were hopeful.

Humboldt State University had an unusual mix of white and tribal students. But in my classes, in the corridors of Founders Hall, at meetings demanding that Native American myths and history be included in a sequence called "The American Frontier," and at the nightly peace rallies, I noticed the complete absence of Asian American students.

When I asked around about this, I was told by a local poet that Chinese parents would not send their kids to HSU because ninety years earlier all the Chinese had been driven from Eureka. Her answer came from Humboldt lore and collective memory. Troubled, I went to the library, where I found one brief article, written more than fifty years ago, that verified the fact that Eureka, Humboldt's county seat, had indeed expelled all its Chinese residents in 1885.

A year later I left Humboldt State University to take a job at the University of California, San Diego. But with a few friends, I bought a tiny cabin in Big Lagoon, twenty miles north of Arcata. For hundreds of years before the lumber companies arrived, the Yuroks had lived in small clans along the lagoon and called the place Oketo, or "there where it is calm." Some translate it "there where we dance." Then, as now, I was haunted by the power of the redwoods, the storms that blow across the ocean, the fern forests, the Roosevelt elk foraging in the placid lagoons, the light slicing under the fog banks over the Pacific. But the image of the Chinese roundup remained in me. As I returned each year to Big Lagoon, where the redwood forests meet the harsh surf of the Pacific coast in a scene of great beauty, I was disturbed by the history of violence embedded in the landscape, by the dissonance between the land and its history.

Thirty years later, I decided to find the story of the missing Asian students. But on the first day of my quest, sitting at a cloudy microfilm reader in the Bancroft Library on the UC Berkeley campus reading the *Daily Alta California,* I discovered that the story was much larger. I began to follow the footsteps of thousands of Chinese people who were violently herded onto railroad cars, steamers, or logging rafts, marched out of town, or killed. They were expelled from towns from the Pacific coast to the Rocky Mountains, from Seattle and Portland, from hamlets along the Klamath River and up into the Siskiyou Mountains, down through the arid Central Valley to "Nigger Alley" in Los Angeles. Between 1850 and 1906 there were close to two hundred roundups, all designed to rid the United States of the Chinese.

During the past five years I have traveled to most of these cities and towns. I have talked with librarians, local historians, archivists, collectors, police officers, and tribal leaders. Some people seemed eager, even relieved, to tell their town's story; librarians, county clerks, and researchers for county museums and historical societies delved into archives, maps, court records, clipping files, leather wallets, private photo collections, scrapbooks, and old safes to expose the purges that had occurred in their counties. Others denied the story I already knew. I was discovering firsthand how the preservation, cataloguing, and even the filing of historical documents work toward exposure or erasure, revelation or repression.

One day, nearing the end of my research, I visited historian Connie Young Yu at her home in Los Altos Hills, near San Jose. We'd never met before, and I walked into a living room cluttered with piles of loose white tissue paper and cardboard boxes and silken robes. Connie dressed me in the clothes of her ancestors, merchants in San Jose, to help me understand the emotional path of my discoveries. I had brought her a copy of a lawsuit filed in 1891 by the Chinese residents against the mayor of San Jose, who had hired thugs to pose as policemen and drive the Chinese from town. There, in this early lawsuit, Connie found her grandfather's firm, Kwong Wo Chan, listed as a plaintiff.

Connie's grandfather, Young Soong Quong, and the other parties to the suit were some of the Chinese voices from the nineteenth century who spoke this story. From the writings, legal pleadings, photographs, and clothing of the nineteenth-century Chinese, I learned of the pogroms and of massive and diverse resistance. The Chinese fought every effort to expel them, first from the gold diggings, then from rural towns, and finally from the orchards and vineyards of the Central Valley. In *Wing Hing* v. *the City of Eureka* (1885), they filed the first lawsuit for reparations in the United States. In San Jose they used trespass law to design an early suit against police harassment. In Truckee they ordered muskets from China to defend their Chinatown. The "overseas Chinese" pressured the government of China to intervene with governors, legislators, and the president of the United States on their behalf.

In many hostile towns, the Chinese refused to sell their vegetables, starving white households and hotels of fresh food. In the summer of 1883, Chinese workers in Shasta County declared a general strike. In Truckee they formed their own fire brigades. In Amador County they organized an armed militia of more than fifty members to protect themselves. They mutinied on the American slave ship the *Norway*. In Monterey and San Jose, they flatly refused to leave. Elsewhere they returned laundry, neatly folded but still dirty. In 1893, answering the call of red posters that were pasted on walls, gates, and barns from California to New York, 110,000 Chinese people refused to wear photo-identity cards required by the U.S. government to verify their immigration status. They paid for this mass civil disobedience with lynchings, night raids, and deportation.

The Chinese fiercely and tenaciously fought for their right to live and work in the United States, to travel back and forth between China and the United States, to testify in court, to own property, to marry, and to have their children receive public education.

Historians, librarians, archivists, filmmakers, and fiction writers have repressed a story whose evidence is in fact not hard to find. Photographs, advertisements, placards, local newspapers, court records and testimony, campaign documents, songs, business cards, and diaries fabricate a history of docile but wily Chinese invaders—dirty, diseased, and exotically enticing—even as they record the expulsions and reveal how Chinese immigrants fought back.

Different countries have disclosed lost historical memories to different effect. In the former Yugoslavia, memories of ethnic violence coexist with memories of shared neighborhoods and interethnic marriages. The historian Jacquelyn Dowd Hall reminds us that in Rwanda and in the Balkan countries the history of community was repressed when ethnic violence was unleashed, inciting ongoing hatred. In Ireland, the telling of ancient grievances provoked even more brutality. The "tellings" knit people together in imagined communities of pain, communities that could exclude and kill, again and again.[9] The people of South Africa have staked their hope for reconciliation on the conviction that their history of atrocities must be released; if the perpetrators are forced to hear the victims' testimony, they will admit what they have done and national healing can begin.

The roundups in the Pacific Northwest occurred from 1850 to 1906. The actors have passed away, and their living imaginations and memories are no longer with us. With most Chinese women then barred from entering the country, descendants from the generations who endured the roundups are few. I thought that the existential memory must be lost. And, indeed, it was hard to find the Chinese voices from the nineteenth century. A people on the run did not stop to record violence as it happened. Chinese newspapers burned in the fires following the 1906 San Francisco earthquake. Because the Chinese were barred from testifying in court, there is no record of their side of many conflicts. Thousands of Chinese letters home, letters sometimes hand-carried by *shuikes*—"water guests" or returning émigrés—have been lost in the waves of war, famine, and the Cultural Revolution.[10]

At first I had no idea how to solve the mystery of the missing students. Yet quickly I found that county libraries, private collections, local historical societies, and state archives are bursting with all sorts of uncatalogued evidence of the violence and the resistance. An institutional internment of documents, it seems, was part of the expulsion, part of the Driven Out, and it has sustained images of the Chinese as a disempowered people.

Yet the fact is that Chinese families still rarely send their sons and daughters to Humboldt State University. Collective memory reaffirms the reality of the past.[11]

But I was still seeking Chinese voices that tell of the Driven Out. There were a few Chinese letters to newspapers and to state and local legislators protesting the vigilante violence. In desperate telegraphs Chinese men search for one another and for the women who have run away. Passionate letters and diplomatic correspondence, songs and poems about the roundups, slowly surfaced. The lawsuits give voice to entitlement and assertion.

Some Chinese people have found their ancestors in this project. When I talked publicly about the roundups, white or Chinese descendants came forward, and their family histories have helped me reconstruct a past in which memory and documents cohere. Hanging out is good historical methodology.

Finally, again sitting at a microfilm reader, this time at the National Archives, where I was reading the correspondence from the Chinese legation to the Department of State, I suddenly heard the voices of "expulsed" Chinese men. Lum May, Tuck Nan, and others describe the brutal roundup in Tacoma to Governor Squire. They tell of the long trek in the mud and rain to the railroad crossing, and they demand money, reparations—justice that repairs.

The purges of the Chinese in the American West bring to my mind *Kristallnacht,* the night in 1938 when Nazi Germany violently exposed its intention to remove the Jews. That night became embedded in historical memory as the shattering of glass and windows—the German *kristall*—of Jewish homes and stores, images of my own family's diaspora. The expulsions of the Chinese from California towns in the nineteenth century anticipated the history of Poland and Greece in the 1930s and 1940s and, more recently, of Rwanda, Indonesia, and Bosnia. Now, as I write, millions of refugees in Nigeria, Eritrea, Iraq, and Darfur are being driven out of their homes and villages.

Today thousands of women and young girls are being unloaded from the holds of ships, from packing crates and container cars, to work in San Francisco and Silver Spring and Kansas City as enslaved prostitutes, while communities such as Herndon, Virginia, pass housing codes and loitering laws to drive them out. Today thousands of immigrants, thousands of people born in the United States to parents born abroad, and thousands of others are marching through the streets of Los Angeles, Houston, and New York, refusing to be temporary people, transients, *braceros,* guests, or sojourners.

Surely the term *expulsion* doesn't fully represent the rage and violence of these purges. What occurred along the Pacific coast, from the gold rush through the turn of the century, was ethnic cleansing. The Chinese called the roundups in the Pacific Northwest *pai hua*—the Driven Out.

Jean Pfaelzer
Big Lagoon, Trinidad, Humboldt County
January 2007

DRIVEN OUT

1

GOLD!

"PEACEABLY IF WE CAN, FORCIBLY IF WE MUST"

On February 2, 1848, a vanquished Mexico signed the Treaty of Guadalupe Hidalgo and ceded California to the United States, unaware that just nine days earlier, nuggets of pure gold had been found in a creek at a sawmill in the foothills of California's Sierra Nevada range. The discovery of gold did not make the front page of the San Francisco papers until March 15, but sailing vessels quickly carried the news to countries that bordered the Pacific Ocean. Word soon spread from Mexico to Panama to Chile.[1] In April, the Pacific Mail Steamship Company launched five side-wheel steamships to carry eager South American miners north to San Francisco.

At the dawn of 1848, 150,000 native people and a few thousand Mexicans and Californios lived in the northernmost corner of Mexico. Yuroks, Miwoks, Nisenan, Yokuts, and Karuks were among fifty tribes or nations who first inhabited the area.[2] Mestizos, rancheros, peons, Spanish priests, and runaway African American slaves were the first settlers. Their worlds were about to collide.

Word of gold traveled across the Pacific to the Sandwich Islands and from there to China. In port cities across Asia, captains and crews altered their routes, sailed for California, and abandoned laden ships in San Francisco Bay. Many ships rotted and sank in its cold waters as officers and sailors headed for the Sierra mountains. Other ships anchored at the docks and were promptly rebuilt as saloons or restaurants to serve the tide of gold seekers. In San Francisco and Sacramento, stores and offices closed, houses were boarded up, crops were abandoned, and Mexicans, Californios, and white laborers, merchants, artists, and physicians all rushed into the Sierra foothills. They traveled any way they could, on burros, horses, or wagons, sometimes hiking, sometimes buying overpriced tickets on steamships to carry them up the Yuba, Bear, and American Rivers.

From the East Coast, unemployed veterans, just home from the Mexican War, returned to the West—back overland by carriage, on horseback or foot, across the mountains and jungles of the Isthmus of Panama, where they desperately awaited ships to finish their voyage up the Pacific coast. These new "argonauts" joined mechanics, ranchers, laborers, merchants, and professional men and stormed up California's mountains, sharing an expansionist vision and a military determination. None was interested in laboring as a waiter, servant, mill worker, or field hand, even at wages of ten to twenty dollars per day.[3]

When news of gold reached the newly "open" port cities in China, shipmasters in Hong Kong and Canton had little difficulty convincing Chinese men to sail for California. In rice-growing and fishing villages in Guandung Province, shipping companies circulated broadsheets and maps urging men to forswear country and clan for gold. Facing warlords, destitution, and British battleships, villagers read ads promoting America as a haven of plenty and equality:

> Americans are very rich people. They want the Chinaman to come and will make him welcome. There will be big pay, large houses, and food and clothing of the finest description. You can write your friends or send them money any time, and we will be responsible for the safe delivery. It is a nice country, without mandarins or soldiers. All alike; big man no larger than little man. There are a great many Chinamen there now, and it will not be a strange country. China God is there, and the agents of this house. Never fear, and you will be lucky. Come to Hong Kong, or to the sign of this house in Canton and we will instruct you. Money is in great plenty and to spare in

"A Chinaman en Route for the Mines"
GLEASON'S PICTORIAL DRAWING ROOM COMPANION, 1852

America. Such as wishes to have wages and labor guaranteed can obtain the security by application at this office.[4]

Dreaming of wealth on "Gold Mountain," as California came to be known, Chinese villagers sold their fields or fishing boats, or borrowed money to sail to California. They landed in a raw new territory, a land without traditions of nationhood, authority, ethnic commonality, or even clear geographic borders.

Few Chinese women journeyed across the Pacific. Unlike their brethren, most Chinese women who entered California in the mid-1800s were slaves. Kidnapped for prostitution from the southern ports of China, they were brokered and owned by Chinese merchants who also emigrated to San Francisco.

The Chinese arrived as California was growing from a cluster of harbor

Chinese miner by creek (1849)

towns and mining camps into a national financial and political force. From San Francisco up through the Sacramento delta and north to Crescent City, fishing villages and small towns built to trade in hides and tallow rapidly became staging and supply centers for miners eager to move into the mountains.[5] Ninety percent of California's workforce was tied to gold.

California's new leaders promptly abandoned the area's ties to Spanish priests and Mexican ranchers. They identified with the Anglos and debated how to govern thousands of Chinese, Chilean, French, Mexican, and Peruvian prospectors. In the Sierra Nevada the Chinese argonauts encountered Native Americans and Mexican Americans who were facing death, enslavement, or violent pogroms by white men eager to quickly gather the golden ore that had lain sparkling in California's rivers for thousands of years.

The gold rush also offered a serendipitous finale to a war premised on national expansion and the extension of slave territory. By 1845 abolitionists had lost their decadelong struggle to prevent the annexation of Texas.[6] The Washington *Union,* a paper of southern Democrat views, wrote, "Who can arrest the torrent that will pour onward to the West? The road to California will be open to us. Who will stay the march of our Western people?"

That year John O'Sullivan, editor of the *Democratic Review,* declared that it was "our manifest destiny to overspread the continent allotted by Providence for the free development of our yearly multiplying millions."[7]

Ideas of white superiority bracketed the image of white expansion, "free development" and industrial inevitability in California and the West. The *Illinois State Register* insisted, "Shall this garden of beauty be suffered to lie dormant in its wild and useless luxuriance? . . . myriads of enterprising Americans would flock to its rich and inviting prairies; the hum of Anglo-American industry would be heard in its valleys; cities would rise upon its plains and sea-coast, and the resources and wealth of the nation be increased in an incalculable degree." Mexicans, wrote the *American Review,* must yield to "a superior population, insensibly oozing into her territories, changing her customs, and out-living, out-trading, exterminating her weaker blood."

At the same time, the final push for the abolition of slavery was taking hold. The American Anti-Slavery Society declared that the Mexican War was "waged solely for the detestable and horrible purpose of extending and perpetuating American slavery through the vast territory of Mexico." The poet and abolitionist James Russell Lowell, through his character Hosea Biglow, a New England farmer, announced,

> *They just want this Californy*
> *So's to lug new slave states in*
> *To abuse ye, an' to scorn ye,*
> *An' to plunder ye like sin.*

Newly organized workingmen in New England well understood that despite the military's promises to enlistees of plunder, pay of seven dollars per month, and a land grant of 160 acres, territories seized from Mexico "would be giving men that live upon the blood of others an opportunity of dipping their hand still deeper in the sin of slavery. . . . Have we not slaves enough now?" As the war began, a convention of the New England Workingmen's Association announced that its members would "not take up arms to sustain the Southern slaveholder in robbing one-fifth of our countrymen of their labor."

The young labor movement had reason to be fearful. Under the Treaty of Guadalupe Hidalgo, the vast territory seized by the United States could extend southern slavery to the Pacific coast. And so, in the Compromise of 1850, in return for admitting California as a free state, the United States would absorb remaining territories without "any restriction or condition on the subject of slavery." That year Congress also passed the Fugitive Slave Law, which stated that any federal marshal who did not arrest a runaway slave could be fined one thousand dollars; any person suspected of being a runaway slave could be arrested without a warrant and turned over to anyone claiming to be the owner; a suspected slave could not ask for a jury trial or testify on his or her behalf; and any person who aided a runaway slave by providing shelter, food, or transportation faced six months' imprisonment and a one-thousand-dollar fine. The law also offered a "fee" or bribe for every slave remanded back into slavery. The presumptions of the treaty, of the law, of national entitlement, and of race would soon shape the history of Chinese America.

At the end of the Mexican War, most returning veterans could not hold on to their allotments of land, but they still clung to the myth of white possibility and expansion in the West. Wrote a young naval officer, "Asia . . . will be brought to our very doors. Population will flow into the fertile regions of California . . . public lands . . . will be changed from deserts into gardens, and a large population will be settled."

This "large population" was to come to the Pacific Northwest from all over the globe. From 1845 to 1849, the Great Hunger in Ireland, caused by Britain's long interference with Ireland's agriculture and also by a potato fungus, killed between five hundred thousand and a million people from 1845 to 1849 and destroyed the Irish economy. Some two million desperate Irish refugees immigrated to England, Canada, Australia, and the United States—and thousands hopefully made their way west.

In France, Austria, Hungary, Italy, and Germany, between February and June 1848, radical movements of working people and students erupted. These seemingly spontaneous protests demanding liberty and revolution were soon crushed, and many dissidents fled to the United States. Some went west.

The cry "California for Americans!" soon boomed across the foothills of the Sierra Nevada and the lower Siskiyou Mountains. In 1849 a mob of white miners in Mariposa County declared that any "Chinaman" who

Chinese gold miners in Tuolumne

mined for gold must "leave on twenty-four hours notice, otherwise the miners will inflict such punishment as they deem proper."[8] In Marysville, demonstrators proclaimed that "no Chinaman shall hence forth be allowed on any mining claim in the neighborhood."[9]

Rain had finally come to the arid creek at Camp Salvado, washing down the dry dark dirt to expose clusters of golden nuggets to Chinese miners working for an English stock company.[10] News of the Chinese discovery quickly spread. A gang of white miners promptly rode down to Salvado and assaulted the Chinese, who fled from their prosperous claim. Stunned by this first mass purge, the English investors abandoned the diggings, and the sixty remaining Chinese miners trekked over the mountain into Tuolumne County. There they built Chinese Camp, likely the first all-Chinese town in the United States. The roundup at Camp Salvado ignited the brutal firestorm of purges that burned in the West for fifty years.

Like white miners, the Chinese built bunkhouses or boardinghouses or pitched tent camps—rough male villages. During the gold rush, the proportion of both Chinese and white women to men was low, about three to one hundred. Few miners of any nationality asked their wives or fiancées to join them in the gold fields.[11] Across the country, abandoned white wives exercised their new rights under California's liberal laws and divorced the men who had rushed to the diggings. Until the end of the nineteenth century, the divorce rate in California was the highest in the world.[12]

The low number of Chinese women probably made the Chinese communities in America particularly vulnerable to persecution. Chinese women would have foretold family, civilization, and permanence, and their very presence would have stood as a barrier to the idea that the Chinese had come to the United States as "sojourners"—temporary and enduringly foreign.

The first Chinese woman in the gold town of Sonora was an enslaved young girl who worked in a bar selling drinks and sex to white miners.[13] Known to whites as "China Lena," she grew vegetables in a large garden and peddled them on the hilly streets, carrying them in two baskets hanging from a pole across her shoulders. But Lena was forced to live in China Camp, supervised by a Chinese pimp. In an era when southern whites warned that abolition would lead to interracial sex and "amalgamated" races, the California State Legislature banned marriage between Chinese and whites. But the enslaved prostitution of Chinese women grew quickly into a tolerated and profitable business.

"CALIFORNIA FOR AMERICANS!"

In the spring of 1852, sixty white miners, accompanied by a brass band, rode through a chain of Chinese diggings along the sandy shore of the American River. They assaulted two hundred Chinese men who shared a claim at Mormon Bar, then rode a few miles down the river and attacked four hundred Chinese miners camped along Horseshoe Bar. Although the Chinese miners greatly outnumbered the vigilantes, they abandoned their river claims, no doubt fearful for their lives. The white miners boasted to the press that they helped the Chinese dismantle their tents.[14]

Early that summer, white miners in El Dorado County barricaded the dusty stage road and turned back all wagons and coaches carrying Chinese

"Pacific Chivalry"

HARPER'S WEEKLY, AUGUST 7, 1869

passengers and freight. At nearby Weber Creek, vigilantes set fire to the tents and tools of Chinese miners, burning out the Chinese camp.[15]

In Columbia, white miners facing Chinese competition along the riverbeds blamed capitalists, shipowners, and merchants, men who "engaged in the importation of these burlesques on humanity," thus "fastening . . . a system of peonage" in the gold fields. These greedy investors "would crowd their ships with the long-tailed horned and cloven-footed inhabitants of the infernal regions, and contend for their introduction in the mines on an equality with American laborers, if they could add one farthing to the rates of freight, or dispose of one pound more of pork or for a few shillings of rice by the operation."[16] The Columbia miners announced that they were "empowered to take such steps as they may deem necessary" to make sure that "no Asiatic or South Sea Islander . . . be permitted to mine any longer in Columbia, or any where else in California . . . either for himself or for others."[17]

But more and more Chinese flocked to Tuolumne County, and in September 1852, white miners called the first Jamestown Miners Convention and demanded that no immigrant from Asia, Polynesia, or South America be given citizenship. They agreed to vote only for state legislators who would "drive the coolies from some of our mining districts."[18] Their demand, wrote the *Daily Alta California,* was "harsh and unlawful in design and dangerous in tendency" and was conceived in a spirit of "hatred and hostility" without parallel in California.[19]

Yet the mob's decrees traveled up the rivers and along the lupine valleys where few lumps or even grains of gold still shimmered in the green waters. Pioneer Alfred Jackson wrote in his diary that whenever white miners found a group of Chinese miners along the sandbars of the Yuba River, they would quickly make a law that the Chinese could not "take up or hold ground." Some "thought it would be a good thing to sell them claims, as it was an easy way to make money," but most "were for driving them out of the country entirely."[20]

Without women in the gold fields, both Chinese and white miners did their own domestic work—they cooked, sewed, and washed their own

"Chinese Sleeping Accommodations"

FRANK LESLIE'S ILLUSTRATED SUNDAY MAGAZINE, MARCH 1881

clothes. But in songs, sermons, plays, cartoons, speeches, and advertisements, Chinese men were depicted as lacking virility. In this mostly male world, Chinese men became targets of white men's fears of homosexuality or the objects of their desire.

The ruthless evictions went on. On January 21, 1854, at an open meeting at Watles and Granger's General Store in Placer County, miners unanimously voted that "no Chinaman shall be allowed, from this date, to hold any mining claim, or to work upon any claim in the district of Green Valley."[21] Late on the evening of August 21, during that hot and dry mountain summer, a hundred white men roamed through Nevada City's Chinatown, breaking into the Chinese brothels, dragging frightened women into the streets, and pitching their furniture into the dirt. By the next morning, the Chinese men and women had disappeared from town. But when many returned, frustrated white miners turned to the state legislature to drive the Chinese off the mountain and bar them from registering claims at rich spots along the crowded narrow shores and sandbars of the Sierra rivers.

In the cold and snowy January of 1855, Chinese miners in Shasta's "Hong Kong" heard that hundreds of Anglo miners were coming into town on foot, on horseback, and in wagons to hold an anti-Chinese convention. Frustrated, greedy, and cold, the white miners bitterly complained that the state had failed to rid Shasta of its Chinese residents: "We the miners of Shasta County forbid Chinamen from working in the mines of this county." After February 25, 1855, they decreed, no white man in Shasta County could ever again employ a Chinese person.[22]

A RACE WAR IN THE GOLD FIELDS

In the winter of 1858–59, a race war began. The Chinese had refused to leave the gold fields, and a mob of two hundred white men rode out from Shasta City armed with rifles, shotguns, and ropes. Following the twisting trail above the rocky canyons of the McCloud River, they came upon a Chinese camp at Lower Springs and ordered the Chinese at gunpoint to forsake their claim and never return. Grabbing their pans, shovels, and clothes, the Chinese took flight. The aroused white mob then found another group of Chinese miners a few miles down the rough river gorge and forcibly expelled them too.

Unbeknownst to the mob, a young new county sheriff was in pursuit. Thin, wiry, and determined, Clay Stockton, a twenty-five-year-old Kentuckian, had been chasing the gang along the stage road and, even as white runners scattered to remote diggings to announce that the purge from Shasta County had begun, he arrested seven or eight vigilantes. He forced them back to Shasta City and locked them in the jail. At sundown, several hundred white men burst into the courtroom where the trial was about to begin and demanded that Stockton hand over their friends. The frightened judge quickly dismissed the trial and "yielded up" the sheriff's prisoners.

Defiant, Shasta's Chinese miners bought arms and returned on foot to their claims. A few, however, remembering brutal evictions at Middle Creek and Lower Springs, abandoned the diggings.

Over the next three years the purges of Chinese miners—the threatening conventions and propaganda, the night raids, the destruction of their camps, and the forced marches—spread farther into the gold fields, up the

Sheriff Clay Stockton

riverbanks, and into the makeshift mining towns in the Siskiyou Mountains. In 1859, white miners convened at Brannan's General Store on Middle Creek in the Siskiyous. Amidst the barrels of crackers, coffee, and dried meat, the Shasta Miners Convention determined to expel the Chinese from the surrounding mines once and for all. On February 5, the convention gave the Chinese three weeks to wind up their business. After that date, "if any Chinese are found working in our claims we will . . . assemble and expel such Chinese, peaceably if we can, forcibly if we must."[23]

On a cold mountain night three weeks later, hours before the deadline, two hundred armed white miners hiked up the ice-crusted trails to the remote Chinese claims at the mouth of Rock Creek. Disobeying the convention's order to leave, the Chinese miners had remained by the frozen rivers to protect their claims, sleeping in tents and lean-tos. Suddenly the gang of white miners burst into their camp and ordered them off the mountain. Rushing across the creek and scaling the high canyon wall, most of the Chinese escaped, but about seventy-five Chinese were seized, and their tents, sluices, tools, and clothing were destroyed.

At daylight, the mob forced the Chinese men to parade through Shasta City. Townspeople lined the dirt road, jeering and pelting them with stones. Sheriff Stockton met the march with his armed deputies, freed the Chinese captives, and arrested fifteen vigilantes. Again a mob threatened to storm the jail as news of the Rock Creek roundup spread to the coarse new towns.

Four days later, gangs of white miners, packing rifles and shotguns, attacked the rich Chinese claims close to Shasta City. Riots broke out in the small mountain towns of Horsetown, Middletown, and Oregon Gulch, where white miners vowed to behead or crucify the Chinese. Many Chinese miners were badly wounded; many were seized and paraded through Shasta City. Sheriff Stockton dispersed the mob and freed two hundred Chinese men. The vigilantes scattered.[24]

Stockton knew that he was losing control of the county and desperately wired Governor John Weller: "An armed body of men, 300 strong and increasing, is organized for the purpose of driving the Mongolians out, in defiance of the law and its officers."[25] He pleaded for a large posse, two hundred rifles, and one thousand pounds of ammunition from the state armory. Weller balked—he was saving California's munitions for the wars against the Indians. Stockton flooded Weller with telegraphs, and finally, fearing a civil war, the governor sent one man to Red Bluff, partway up the river, on the steamer *Uncle Sam,* to deliver 113 rifles. Worried that the mob could easily seize these few guns—indeed, sensing that this was a setup to arm the vigilantes—Stockton and his deputies rode thirty-eight miles to meet the boat, hauled the weapons back up the mountain, and made themselves ready.

All through the night of March 2, as saloon brawls and hotel fights spilled into Shasta's streets, Stockton arrested rioters. At noon the next day, he called a town meeting in Excelsior Hall; there he announced to the overflowing crowd that the law had been "broken and trampled underfoot by large bodies of armed men" and that he would end the Chinese purges "at all hazards and all costs." As more hostile miners poured into town, Stockton deputized two hundred men into his "law and order ranks," with more at the ready. For the moment, he had restored order.

As the riots raged on, Chinese miners from claims across the county fled to nearby Briggsville. When they heard that the governor had sent arms and that Stockton was arresting white vigilantes, the Chinese celebrated, exploding firecrackers and beating gongs. Stockton had indeed saved the lives of hundreds of Chinese miners, but despite the initial jubilation, many soon left the Siskiyou diggings for mines farther north; others abandoned their dream of gold and found work in towns along the coast.[26] Eventually, Sheriff Stockton brought the rioters from the "Shasta wars" to trial before Justice Keene in Shasta. Keene quickly pronounced each culprit "not guilty."

In 1853 three thousand Chinese men mined the riverbeds and creeks in Shasta County. By the end of the decade only 160 remained; slightly more than 100 were still miners, many now under the protection of white employers; 14 were merchants. Nine Chinese women lived in Shasta, calling themselves "seamstresses," although many were in fact runaways from enslaved prostitution in San Francisco, where they had been kept in cages and forced to service twenty to thirty white and Chinese men per day; most died within a few years, of syphilis.[27] On rare occasions some fled to the Christian missions; others ran away to rural towns. When the roundups came, they were often recaptured and returned to San Francisco.

The Chinese era of the gold rush came to a violent end. The Shasta wars had virtually emptied the gold fields of Chinese miners, foretelling the roundups that would spread across California for the next forty years.[28]

DRIVEN OFF THE LAND: NATIVE AMERICANS AND THE FIRST ROUNDUPS

As fantasies of easy wealth disappeared, near at hand was a working model for mass purges—the rout of native people. The invasion of gold miners devastated the Indians of California, and their enforced removals provided law, license, and cover for the roundups of the Chinese.

The Miwoks had discovered and worked the first gold mines in the southern Sierra Nevada. When Indian miners recognized the new value of gold, however, they quit delivering it or trading it for beads, weight for weight. Colonel Richard B. Mason, stationed in California to lead the military campaign to remove the Indians, estimated that half of the first miners were Native Americans—"conscripted" through forced peonage.[29]

The mother lode of gold rested on the traditional lands of the Nisenan, Maidu, and Miwok people. For hundreds of years mountain tribes built their villages beside creeks and rivers—spawning runs for salmon, drinking grounds for wild game, but also rich in gold. Under the terms of Mexico's independence from Spain, half the mission lands in California were to be reserved for Indians, and under the Treaty of Guadalupe Hidalgo, this land was still legally protected. But with the gold rush, few native people were able to remain on their land.

John Charles Frémont, California's first senator, decided that Congress should draft "some particular provision . . . to divest [Indians] of these rights."[30] Both the 1848 Treaty of Guadalupe Hidalgo and the first California constitution outlawed slavery, but in 1850 the legislature passed Chapter 133 under the ironically titled Act for the Government and Protection of Indians—better known as the Indenture Act. (Sequel acts were passed in 1851 and 1855.) The act legalized the kidnap of "loitering and orphaned" Indians—that is, Indians living on land desired by white miners. Indian "vagrants" were arrested and auctioned for domestic or farm labor. If at the end of the terms of their bondage Indians could not support themselves, they could be arrested for vagrancy and sold to work off their bond, again and again.

"As there is no further west, to which they can be removed, the General

Government and the people of California appear to have left but one alternative in relation to these remnants of once numerous and powerful tribes . . . : extermination or domestication," explained three federal Indian commissioners, Dr. Oliver Wozencraft, George W. Barbour, and Redick McKee.[31] In 1851 these three inexperienced men were sent to remote Indian lands by the U.S. government to make treaties with California tribal leaders. Hiring mule drivers as translators, the commissioners set forth in wide buggies and long mule trains, with inaccurate maps, across wild rivers, through redwood forests, over rugged land marked by narrow Indian trails. They spent only a few hours with each tribe, rushing native leaders through documents they couldn't read, and offering beads, cattle, and clothing to encourage them to "sign" what amounted to eighteen different treaties. There were many tribes they never reached. At times they placed warring tribes on the same lands.[32] In return for relinquishing claims to their traditional lands, for acknowledging the jurisdiction of the United States government, and for agreeing to refrain from hostilities against white settlers, Indians were "given" about 7.5 percent of the land of California, to be set apart as reservations.

But even 7.5 percent was too much for white miners to accept. California's congressional representatives complained that these treaties gave the Indians "extensive tracts of valuable mineral and agricultural lands, embracing populous mining towns, large portions of which are already in possession of, and improved by, American citizens."[33] The Senate rejected all eighteen treaties and left native peoples homeless in a hostile land. In March 1852, military and volunteer militias began driving California's native people onto small parcels of government land, about seventy-five thousand acres each. Throughout the gold rush the government continued to claim tribal lands, and in 1853 California Indians were rounded up in their villages or captured in battle and then marched to "reserved lands" under armed guards. Afterward, militias burned their villages.

The purges triggered a decade of militant Indian uprisings and infamous death marches as the U.S. military forced hundreds of Indians from the eastern half of the Sacramento Valley to the Nome Lackee Reservation in Tehama County. In the not-so-distant future, this area would become a site of Chinese expulsion.

The first governor of California, Peter H. Burnett, vowed that this "war of extermination will continue to be waged between the two races until the

Indian race becomes extinct . . . while we cannot anticipate this result with but painful regret, the inevitable destiny of the race is beyond the power and wisdom of man to avert."[34]

In the early 1850s, to open land for white miners and settlers, bands of miners and ranchers organized volunteer militias or joined U.S. military campaigns to exterminate the Modoc and Mariposa tribes. In Stanislaus County, in 1851, the Army began displaying Indian scalps. With the Pacific Ocean blocking movement west, white settlers insisted that Indians move farther inland, to the arid lands east of the Sierra Nevada. Democratic governor John McDougall (1851–52) urged Californians to copy President Andrew Jackson's "Trail of Tears" and move the Indians "to some isolated position distant from all contact with the whites."[35]

In Tehama County, military and local volunteers razed villages and scalped hundreds of "Mill Creek" men, women, and children.[36] Urged on by state senators and assemblymen from gold-rich Trinity, Klamath, Shasta, and Siskiyou Counties, the next governor, John Bigler (1852–56), wrote to General E. Hitchcock, commander of U.S. forces in California, that with the races unable to "live in close proximity in peace . . . an ultimate evacuation of the Northern Counties by the Whites of the Indians will be unavoidable."[37] To implement Bigler's call for Indian removal, the legislature authorized more than one million dollars for men, arms, and forts—monies the federal government willingly reimbursed. Bigler would soon recommend a similar policy for the Chinese.

Sentiment in the gold towns favored Indian genocide. In 1853 the *Yreka Herald* suggested that whites wage "a war of extermination until the last red skin of these tribes has been killed."[38] In 1866 the *Chico Courant* claimed, "It is a mercy to the red devils to exterminate them, and a saving of many white lives. Treaties are played out—there is only one kind of treaty that is effective—cold lead."[39]

Before 1849, between 150,000 and 300,000 Indians lived in California under Spanish and Mexican rule; by 1860 only about 32,000 survived; the others had died from extermination, from the seizure of their lands, from malnutrition, and from the white man's diseases.[40]

Military massacres, casual murders, and retaliatory killings marked the first two decades of California's statehood. Sixty Indians died at Clear Lake, 75 along the Russian River, 150 on the South Fork of the Trinity, 30 to 40 at the upper crossing of the Klamath. In 1860, on an island in Hum-

Chinese immigrants viewed displacing white settlers and Indians

boldt Bay, 150 Wyot women, children, and elders, a tribe "friendly" to whites, were slaughtered during a harvest ritual. In 1906, Chinese cannery workers seized along the Eel River were held in boxcars on this same tiny island as they awaited deportation.

When native people first encountered the Chinese, some, such as the Miwok, viewed them as new invaders who sought to drive them off their traditional lands.[41] Many tribes shared the goal of Chinese removal and were encouraged by white miners and tax collectors to provoke the Chinese, raid their camps, and collect taxes. But others, such as the Karuk, sensed common vulnerability and likely hid the Chinese.[42]

DRIVEN OUT: LATIN AMERICANS

The deadly combination of vigilante violence and repressive law against the Chinese drew not only upon campaigns against the California Indians, but also on the treatment of Latin Americans—Mexicans, Chileans, and Argentineans who had beaten all the other miners to the gold fields. In early July 1849, Ramón Gil Navarro, an Argentinean mining near the town of Sonora in the Sierra foothills, confided in his diary, "Samuel wrote telling me that a great number of Chileans have just arrived in San Francisco after having been expelled by the Americans from the mines of Sacramento. I have been told that the injustices committed these days against the Chileans or anyone else speaking Spanish are horrible." This "atrocious injustice," he continued, "beseeches heaven for revenge on the person who so cruelly abuses his power and strength."[43]

Homesick and suffering from his first winter in the mountains, Navarro described how white miners, backed by the "orders of a judge that only the Americans had chosen," attacked a hundred desperate Chilean miners in their flimsy houses, stealing supplies they had stored to survive the bitter freeze of the Sierra Nevada winter. But the Chileans vowed to stay in California until they died. Tragically, many kept this promise. Wrote Navarro, "The Americans were enraged at this display of defiance and promised to come back tomorrow and finish off those who refuse to leave." Indeed, they returned in a week. On the cold gray morning of December 12, 1849, five invaded the area known as Chili Gulch and "with blood and fire" assaulted the Chileans.[44]

On Friday, December 28, after enduring days of armed assaults, some of the Chileans broke out of the camp and attacked the American diggings with guns, knives, and rocks, forcing their surrender. The local sheriff arrested the Chileans for starting a riot, and sent them to prison in Stockton, where anti-Chilean revolts erupted. Friends and relatives of the prisoners did not know where their countrymen had gone. Then, without arraignment or trial, the surviving prisoners were suddenly released in mid-1850, and they described how they had been tortured and beaten. Their ears had been cut off, and some of the prisoners had been used for "shooting practice." Several had been hanged.

In the southern Sierra Nevada that summer, purges of Mexicans and Californios—Mexicans who had lived in California before it was ceded to the United States—followed. In July, four Mexican men in Sonora were accused of murder. When the judges dismissed the case for lack of evidence, a mob "impaneled" its own lynch jury, sentenced the men to hang, and granted the frightened prisoners a few moments to pray. While the vigilantes tied a noose and tossed the rope over a tree limb, the judges rushed out from the courtroom, threw themselves across the kneeling Mexicans, and dragged them back to the safety of the jail.

That night eighty white miners, armed with rifles and shotguns, marched through Sonora, demanding the return of the prisoners. When hundreds of Mexican miners and ranchers also gathered in the town, the Tuolumne County sheriff deputized a posse, arrested the entire adult male Mexican population, and held them in a horse corral. The judges held a retrial and again declared the Mexicans innocent, and in the town square a race riot erupted and lasted through the summer night.

On Sunday, July 21, at an open meeting in the plaza, the mob demanded that all foreigners hand over their firearms and leave Tuolumne County within fifteen days. The resolution, quickly printed in English and Spanish, was posted on gates and stores throughout the town: "The outcasts of every nation under Heaven have combined to disturb us; and we think that now they have been effectually silenced."[46] Mexicans were assaulted; many fled.

Soon the California legislature passed the Foreign Miners' Tax, a simple code that would compel thousands of miners from Latin America and China to leave the United States. The tax required all miners who were not U.S. citizens to buy a license for the outrageous monthly fee of twenty dollars (about four hundred dollars in today's currency); the tax collector would receive three dollars, and the rest would be split between the county and the state. Irish, English, Canadian, and German miners immediately protested, and the law was quickly rewritten to exempt any "free white person" or any miner who could become an American citizen.[47]

Within days of the law's passage, a vigilante army of three hundred armed white men stormed into the Mexicans' diggings in the town of Columbia to collect the first tax. The miners from Mexico and South America refused to pay. In May 1850, Mexican and Peruvian miners organized an armed rebellion in Sonora, led by two French miners exiled for their role in the revolution of 1848. Placards appeared on gateposts, fences, and barns across Tuolumne County, urging Chileans, Peruvians, Mexicans, and Frenchmen to "go to Sonora next Sunday, there we will try to guaranty security for us all and put a bridle in the mouths of that horde who call themselves citizens of the United States."[48]

On Sunday, May 19, four thousand French, Mexican, and Chilean rebels assembled in a hollow outside Sonora, rode into town, seized the plaza, and poured out into the hilly side streets. Chasing them was a volunteer militia of five hundred tax collectors and Anglo miners from the gold diggings along the Stanislaus and Tuolumne Rivers. Many wore their old uniforms from the Mexican War, a bold and bitter reminder of America's capture of the northern quarter of Mexico.[49]

Suddenly the Anglos raised their rifles and fired on the rebels. Overpowered by the Americans' weapons, the Latino miners retreated.[50] Wrote the *Sonora Herald:* "Alas, as we marched along, what a scene of confusion and terror marked our way! Mexicans, Chileans—men, women and children—were all packed up and moving, bag and baggage. Tents were being pulled down and burros were being hastily packed, while crowds upon crowds were already in full retreat. What could have been the object of our assembly, except as a demonstration of power and determination, I know not; but if intended as an engine of terror, it certainly had its desired effect, for it could be seen painted upon every countenance and impelling every movement of the affrighted population."[51]

At the end of the troubled summer of 1850, vigilantes in Sonora gathered for "the Great Greaser Extermination Meeting." The leaders announced: The "lives and property of American citizens were now in danger, from the hands of lawless marauders of every clime, class and creed under the canopy of heaven."[52] Throughout Tuolumne County, the mob posted five hundred copies of its order: "Peons of Mexico, the renegades of South America, and the convicts of the British Empire . . . leave the limits of said county within fifteen days."

A reign of terror came to Tuolumne. The miner Enos Christman recorded in his diary, "Sunday three Mexicans were tied to the whipping post, and each received twenty-five lashes well laid on. Another Mexican was found with a stolen horse . . . and sentenced to receive 150 lashes, to have one-half of his head shaved, and to leave the country in 48 hours under penalty of being hanged if he ever returned."[53]

At the beginning of 1850, fifteen thousand Mexicans were mining in the southern Sierra Nevada. After the Foreign Miners' Tax was enacted, ten thousand left the gold fields, most to return to Mexico. The town of Columbia shrank from a lively center of ten thousand miners and shopkeepers to an abandoned camp of nine or ten men. Penniless Mexicans, Chileans, and Peruvians fled to San Francisco, where the Chilean consul donated eight hundred tickets so his countrymen could return home. By 1860, four fifths of the Latino population had been driven from the gold country. Only one Latin American male remained in Nevada City. But if the white miners were satisfied with the roundups, merchants sorely missed their Latino customers.[54]

Years later white miners still recalled "the long train of fugitives" leaving the gold diggings and returning home: "Some were going North; some South; the great body was probably bound for home; some by way of the sea; others by Los Angeles and the Great Desert."[55] The Chinese were to follow.

SLAVERY AND THE CHINESE

As the movement to abolish slavery gathered steam in the North and the issue of the expansion of slavery in the territories divided northern states from southern, slogans such as the "dignity of labor" and the "honor of the pick and shovel" took hold in California.

Just months after the discovery of gold, a group of forty-eight men—merchants, lawyers, and artisans—traveled to the fishing village of Monterey and held California's first constitutional convention. At noon on September 1, 1849, with only a few law books and a handful of state constitutions at hand, they began the process of transforming California from a territory into a state. The voice of "free labor" dominated the meetings. Californians wanted no competition from slave labor in the mining districts, for "the labor of the white man brought into competition with the Negro is always degraded." Indeed, any member of this "respectable and intelligent class . . . would leave this country" before he would dig with pick and shovel alongside the African.[56]

By the end of the first week, the California delegates unanimously resolved the issue searing the country: "Neither slavery nor involuntary servitude, unless for punishment of crimes, shall ever be tolerated in this state." But equality of work did not intend equality of rights. Over the objections of the few Mexican American delegates, the convention denied the vote to all women and to "Indians, Africans, and descendants of Africans."[57] It also denied minorities the right to testify against whites in court.

The delegates to the Monterey convention finished the constitution in six weeks and rushed it to the offices of the *Daily Alta California* in San Francisco, which printed 1,000 copies in English and 250 copies in Spanish—a small number for such a large and scattered electorate. On November 13, 1849, out of about 107,000 possible male voters, 12,061 voted for and 811 voted against the constitution. The white men of California were distracted by gold.

Chinese miners arrived in a new state that had just voted to outlaw slavery. But California's admission to the union was part of the Compromise of 1850—a group of laws that included the Fugitive Slave Act, which required the return of runaway slaves. Statehood for California was secured by a federal law that assisted the South in retaining human property.

Although Chinese men who came to the United States were not enslaved, labor contracts, newspaper reports, and shipping logs suggest that some did enter the United States indentured—often to shipping companies or ship's captains. Chinese immigrants were quickly labeled "coolies"—a term for kidnapped, enslaved, or indentured servants that most likely comes from the Chinese characters *ku* and *lí,* translated by some as "rented muscles."

In 1808 the United States had outlawed the importation of new slaves. Now the California constitution promised that Chinese miners were to be free laborers, able to move from job to job; neither their labor nor their debt could be sold between employers. Most Chinese who came to work in the mines, and, later, on the railroad or in the orchards, came voluntarily, but they bore a heavy debt to labor contractors, shipping companies, or the merchants who profited from their passage, the interest on their debts, and, in the end, their labor. These profits helped the class of Chinese elites in San Francisco who quickly formed into six *huiguan,* ruling "companies" based on village and clan affiliations, known as the Chinese Six Companies.[58]

By 1855, nearly forty thousand Chinese immigrants had registered with the Chinese Six Companies, who brokered their passage, found them jobs, provided medicine, organized transportation to the mountains, adjudicated disputes, and demanded discipline. They also tortured immigrants who defied them. One officer, Ah Ti, "inflicted severe corporal punishment upon many of his more humble countrymen . . . cutting off their ears, flogging them or keeping them chained."[59] In a deal with the shipping companies, the Chinese Six Companies issued exit permits that verified that a miner had paid his debts before he could sail back to China. The Six Companies learned how to negotiate with state and town governments on behalf of the overseas Chinese, thus providing them an institutional buffer unavailable to African Americans or Native Americans. By controlling emigration, the Companies maintained transnational links and forged enduring communities.

The Chinese miners who sailed for California were at the front of a global migration of Chinese labor. Although England had emancipated slaves at home in 1772 and had abolished slavery in its colonies in August 1834, by 1850 it needed more cotton to feed its mills and turned to China for cheap labor. Between 1840 and 1900, prompted by English and American bankers and shipping companies, more than two million Chinese laborers—free and enslaved—left their homeland to work on plantations in Indonesia, Malaysia, the Caribbean, South America, Australia, New Zealand, Hong Kong, and Russia.[60]

White miners clung to the myth that all Chinese were coolies, a derelict species of slave. There were, in fact, reasons for this confusion. The United States government did not rigidly enforce the ban on trade in Chinese slaves, particularly women. American brokers in Macao and other southern Chinese ports captured, kidnapped, and indentured thousands of Chinese workers, and they carried more than six thousand "coolie laborers," their bare chests painted with letters marking their destinations, to sugar plantations in Cuba or the deadly guano pits in Peru on ships registered to the United States, ships modeled after the slave ships of the Middle Passage. Other Chinese slaves were transported on American ships to Chile, Ecuador, Panama, and Mexico. A congressional report noticed that the "Coolie Trade . . . seems to have commenced about the time when the [U.S.] laws against the prosecution of the African slave trade were enforced with the greatest stringency."[61]

In 1853 the powerful *Daily Alta California* argued that "most of [the Chinese] in the mines are not free . . . they are coolies, brought here by rich mandarins or merchants to work for little more than a bear [*sic*] subsistence. . . . There is one man in California who has 14,000 coolies at work in our mines—14,000!"[62]

The Chinese, however, insisted that they were free. In 1855, Lai Chun-Chuen, a merchant in San Francisco, published a notice in English on behalf of the Hak-sheung Ui-kun, or Chinese Merchants' Exchange, challenging the rumor that the Chinese Six Companies were importing "slaves of a degraded caste." Lai insisted, "We assure you solemnly that we do not believe that there are any Chinese coolies in this country, who have bound themselves to serve for fixed wages, and who have given their families as pledges to their employers that they would fulfill their contracts. The Chinese in this country are not serfs or slaves of any description, but are working for themselves."[63]

Indeed, there is evidence that some Chinese were transported out of

China as virtual slaves. In the 1850s it is likely that some Chinese immigrants to California had signed misleading contracts and unwittingly locked themselves into forms of bondage lasting up to seven years; some were kidnapped; some were sold by their clans to brokers; and some, desperately poor, sold themselves off in a voluntary form of indentured servitude.

While Chinese maritime revolts, unlike the African mutinies on the *Amistad* or the *Creole,* are virtually unknown, Chinese slave mutinies arose in 10 percent of American voyages. In the mid-1850s, four hundred Chinese in Amoy were enticed aboard the *Robert Browne,* bound for San Francisco. When the emigrants discovered that they were being transported into indentured service, they rebelled and killed the ship's officers. Later they testified in court that they had been promised four dollars a month to work in the United States as freely hired laborers, not as "contract workers."

In March 1860, one thousand Chinese slaves mutinied on the *Norway,* an American ship en route from Macao to Havana. The *Norway* was a copy of a slave ship, with its lower deck fitted into narrow sleeping shelves stacked to the top of the hold. After being locked belowdecks for five days at sea, the Chinese lit fires in the hold and forced open the hatches. The crew hurried to abandon the ship, and the captain threatened to cut the masts, set fire to the ship, and leave with the lifeboats and provisions. Only after the crew killed thirty slaves and wounded ninety others did the Chinese surrender.[64] Describing the mutiny, one Chinese passenger recalled, "Bands of us threw ourselves upon them; Release us or we will burn the ship! We have nothing to lose." Not until 1862, one year into the Civil War, did Congress pass the Prohibition of Coolie Trade Act, which banned any ship that was registered to the United States from transporting enslaved laborers from China into any foreign port.[65]

Yet the vision of "free labor" in California endured for white workers. When southerners campaigned to reintroduce the slave trade, the California Committee on Mines pointed to Chinese immigrants as "an inferior race in our midst, nominally free, and yet, virtually slaves."[66] White miners organized rallies throughout the gold towns to defeat the "coolie bill" introduced in 1852 by Assemblyman George Tingley on behalf of merchants and new corporations. The bill would hold Chinese laborers to indenture contracts they signed in China, even if the contracts were illegal under American law. It would enforce agreements that fixed a number of years of labor,

Chinese slave rebellion on the *Norway*

HARPER'S NEW MONTHLY MAGAZINE, JUNE 1864

and it legalized the "unfree" status of unpaid or underpaid Chinese immigrants. The Tingley Bill marked their difference from American free workers.[67] Although the controversial bill failed, it highlighted the skewed relationship between race and class, and between the rising union movement and Chinese immigrants in the West.[68]

Initially, Anglo miners had no employers. They purchased their own tools at exorbitant prices in San Francisco or Sacramento. Shovels and crowbars sold for ten dollars, boots for sixteen. And few fortunes were made. While white miners occasionally reported "pickings" of five hundred dollars in a day, ten to thirty dollars was unusually high. In 1852, the most prosperous year of the gold rush, a day's "take" of about two dollars (or one dollar profit) was less than the wage in many eastern mills or factories, and by all reports, most Anglo miners came out of the mountains poorer than when they entered.[69] Indeed, the Anglo miner and the Chinese miner were equally self-employed and equally in debt.

Yet still the Chinese came—twenty-five thousand of them—and most white miners viewed them as unwelcome competitors. After the South American miners were forced from the diggings in 1852, 175,000 white miners crowded California's rivers, deltas, and beaches, shoving up against the Chinese, who soon formed one tenth of the state's population.

Many local newspapers claimed the Chinese had overrun California. In July 1852, the *Daily Alta California* wrote that "every gulch and ravine" is now filled with Chinese miners, and "an American emigrant can hardly find room to pitch his tent."[70] The area was tense, poor, and crowded.

"WHERE WILL BE THE END OF IT?"

Facing competition on all sides for increasingly scarce gold, white miners lashed out at the Chinese, forging a political voice and vigilante unity. In 1855–56, the California legislature's powerful Committee on Mines repeatedly declared that the Chinese were "odious and degrading," and the legislature shuffled through a series of bills that sought to expel them: "Mongolian and Asiatic races" were "not white in the constitutional sense of the term"; Chinese miners were threatening the "superior race." By targeting the Chinese as a race, town councils, county supervisors, the state legislature, and the courts built a judicial base for expulsion.

Despite the new constitution, slave codes seeped into California law, city codes, and town ordinances—codes that outlawed intermarriage and denied minorities the vote, the right to sit on a jury, and access to homesteads. At a miners' meeting in 1854, Springfield passed a resolution stating that "no person not an American citizen . . . shall be competent to act on any arbitration, or trial by jury." "An Act for the Protection of Foreigners" required an immigrant to have a license to prosecute an action in a California court, effectively depriving Chinese miners of judicial protection. The state's Committee on Mines resolved that the "importation by foreign capitalists of . . . peons and serfs" had become "a danger to the tranquility of the mining regions."[71] By 1852, in the eyes of the American legal system, the Chinese were becoming black.

Unlike all other immigrants to the United States, a Chinese person could not be naturalized, and in 1855 the state legislature assessed a fifty-dollar fee on each immigrant who was unable to become a "citizen of California." California forced Chinese immigrants to pay medical indemnity bonds and required shipmasters to post five hundred dollars for each Chinese passenger to "relieve the government" of the expenses of sick immigrants.[72] And still the Chinese came.

On October 1, 1858, the legislature announced that it had the constitutional right "to exclude any class of foreigners she may deem obnoxious to her interest, either socially or politically." To protect against "an interchange of population," it also had the right "to expel them entirely from her borders." The legislators hoped that when the ship *Frowning Bird* sailed into San Francisco Bay on September 28, it would be the last to arrive from China. They also hoped that soon the Chinese would return home.[73] But still the Chinese came.

Soon the United States Supreme Court issued the first rulings that would tolerate and, indeed, promote the roundups and expulsion of the Chinese. In 1862, the Act to Protect Free White Labor Against Competition with Chinese Coolie Labor, and to Discourage the Immigration of the Chinese into the State of California required Chinese immigrants to pay a monthly police "capitation" or head tax of $2.50. Because the bill trespassed on federal authority over immigration, the Chinese were able to have the lower court declare the act unconstitutional.[74] But the United States Supreme Court heartily endorsed California's desire to "prevent and remove the evil." Under the doctrine of states' rights, it had upheld Indiana's constitutional ban against a "negro or mulatto" entering or settling in the state. With this precedent, ruled Chief Justice Roger Taney, California could bar Chinese miners because "the people of the States of this Union reserved to themselves the power of expelling from their borders any person, or class of persons, whom it might deem dangerous to its peace, or likely to produce physical or moral evil among its citizens."[75]

California again tried to legislate the Chinese out of the state. In 1862 it levied a "police tax" of $2.50 per month on all Chinese over the age of eighteen who did not mine or produce rice, sugar, tea, or coffee—although rice, sugar, and tea were not grown in California at the time.[76] A Commutation Tax Act required shipowners to pay five hundred dollars for every "alien" on board, but this tax could be "commuted" if each Chinese passenger paid a five-dollar fee. And still the Chinese continued to come.

Of greatest danger was the new Foreign Miners' Tax. The 1850 tax, which had triggered the deportation of thousands of Chileans and Mexicans, had been repealed the following year. The 1852 incarnation, now targeting the Chinese, forced each foreign miner to pay three dollars per month for the right to mine (raised to four dollars in 1853 and six dollars in 1855, with a two-dollar increase each year thereafter). Half the revenue was to go to the county treasury and the rest to the state of California, with a fixed fee set aside for the local collector. In practice the Foreign Miners' Tax was limitless.

Between 1852 and 1870, years in which one billion dollars' worth of *untaxed* gold was mined in California, Chinese miners paid a staggering fifty-eight million dollars to the state, ranging from one fourth to one half of California's revenue.[77] While the Foreign Miners' Tax Law barred "private parties" from ejecting "aliens" who failed to pay, it gave collectors permission to seize and sell a Chinese miner's claim and tools.[78] Fraudulent collectors sprang up all over the mountains; both real and sham collectors visited the same Chinese miners over and over again, assaulting them or threatening deportation if they did not pay up. The *Nevada Journal* observed that the collectors were "a species of semi-legalized robber . . . [who] take advantage of their position to extort the last dollar from the poverty-stricken Chinese. They date licenses back, exact pay in some instances for extra trouble in hunting up the terrified and flying Chinamen, and . . . fatten themselves upon the spoils thus obtained."[79]

In their logs the collectors boasted of harassing and torturing Chinese miners. From 1855: "I was sorry to have to stab the poor fellow; but the law makes it necessary to collect the tax; and that's where I get my profit." And: "He was running away, and I shot to stop him." Another logged: "I took all the dust the rascal had."[80] One miner from Agua Fria recalled: "I had no money to keep Christmas with so sold the Chinks nine dollars worth of bogus receipts."[81]

The tax was a ticket to violent expulsion. One common sport was to tie Chinese miners together by their queues or use their long braids to tie them to trees, as the collectors wantonly looted their bedding, boots, and tools.[82] The editor of the *Placer Herald* reported that he witnessed a tax collector "corral" thirteen Chinese men at a stable in the town of Auburn, in order to "most energetically procure" the sum of four dollars.[83]

The Chinese miners did their best to protect one another from the tax collectors. Some bribed them, some paid them off directly, and some refused to pay at all. Others hid in the woods. Many fought them off. In 1855 a group of Chinese men in Tuolumne and Mariposa Counties attacked the tax collectors and were killed. Reported the *Placer Herald:* "The Chinese try every way in their power to evade the payment of their taxes . . . sheriffs and Collectors cannot . . . go up in the mountains, or on the rivers, to perform their duties as officers, but that the Chinese camps are informed of it by runners. . . . The Celestials immediately scatter."[84]

The tax forced many Chinese miners from their claims. Some found refuge mastering the new technologies of tunneling and quartz mining, working for absentee owners or corporations. But more Chinese kept coming. In one two-week period in 1853, one thousand new Chinese miners entered Shasta County. In Tuolumne County, they bought picked-over claims, diligently worked them until they paid off, and "placered" in the county for four more years.[85]

Not all Californians supported the tax on the Chinese. One white miner argued that the Chinese license fee was "taxation without representation" and could lead to Chinese demands for citizenship.[86] Miners from Shasta predicted that the tax would force twenty thousand Chinese miners into agricultural work down in the valleys and coastal towns, reducing farm wages and local taxes to "so slow a rate that it would be impossible for them to ever raise funds sufficient to take them home; thus fastening upon the State thousands of paupers and introducing a species of slavery more degraded by far, than exists in any of the slave holding States of the Union."

They reminded the state senate that in 1854 the impoverished state and counties gained three hundred thousand dollars from the Foreign Miners' Tax—revenue that would be lost if the Chinese were driven out.[87]

William Perkins, a merchant in Sonora, wrote to the *Stockton Times* that the tax was "illegal, unjust, abortive, and extremely prejudicial to the best interests of the state."[88] The *Times* agreed, reporting that the violence of the tax collectors had "a ruinous effect upon the traders in the southern mines. Business, in many places, is at a complete stand still; confidence is shaken; . . . man is set against man."[89] The *San Joaquin Republican* recalled how the first tax on Latin American miners had "convulsed society" and reported that small towns were losing their Chinese laborers and customers: "Have not this race of men . . . discovered new placers, and been . . . the hewers of wood and drawers of water for *our* citizens? In the cities are they not our attendants in our houses, and in our public rooms? Do they not wash our shirts? The Chinese, in this city [Stockton] alone must expend, and thus throw into circulation, money to the amount of $500 a day."[90]

In July 1850, one month after a violent purge of Latino miners from Sonora, the *Herald* declared: "We want a population each of whom is capable of sitting on a jury, of depositing a ballot, of understanding the drift of a resolution, the prayer of a petition. Such a population the Chinese can't be."[91] The expulsions of early Chinese immigrants stood on the legal and ideological shoulders of a tax that effectively eliminated those rights and defined the Chinese as expendable.

The roundups of Chinese miners began in earnest. Robert Pitkin, a miner panning along the American River, wrote to his parents: "This country is fast getting filled up with Chinamen. They are coming by thousands all the time. The miners in a great many places will not let them work. The miners hear [*sic*] drove off about 200 Chinamen about two weeks ago but they have com [*sic*] back about as thick as ever."[92]

In the spring of 1853, Governor John Bigler issued his dire "Special Message to the State Senate and Assembly on the Chinese Question," granting civic cover for the violent roundups of the Chinese. Bigler predicted that the twenty thousand Chinese immigrants living in California would swell to millions and called for "novel if not extraordinary legislation" to halt Asian immigration. One way would be to prevent the Chinese from exporting their profits from the "precious metals which they dig up from our soil without charge." Another would be to deny any Africans or Asians who displayed any "degrees of mixture" of skin color—whether "copper-colored natives of America" or "yellow or tawny races of the Asiatics"—the legal rights of "white persons." Although he acknowledged that he knew of no Chinese contracts for "involuntary servitude," Bigler insisted that the state had the right to disregard any labor agreements that would be "injurious to the rights, the interest or the convenience" of Californians.[93]

The Chinese's immediate response to Bigler's message was the first widespread demand for Chinese civil rights in the United States. In "Remarks of the Chinese Merchants of San Francisco . . . Upon Governor Bigler's Message" penned by Lai Chun-Chuen, a committee of Chinese leaders defied Bigler's characterization and insisted that the Chinese were honest, thrifty, and lawful. The merchants warned Bigler that if Chinese miners were not "treated with mutual courtesy . . . [and] if the rabbles are to harass us," they would "expose" Americans who lived in China and prospered from the "friendly intercourse" between the two countries. If "our Chinese people in the mines" continue to be subjected to violence and robbery, warned the merchants, "there will be unlimited trouble; and where will be the end of it?"[94]

But the power of the merchants was limited. Standing between deportation and safety was the issue of land. In Montezuma, when Chinese miners, without title to the land, had begun boring into Table Mountain to "secure a portion of its great treasure," white miners confiscated this "expedient" claim and evicted them.[95] How could the Chinese miner keep any claim when towns such as Jacksonville simply decreed, "All American citizens may locate and hold claims"? How could a Chinese miner even survive on a claim limited to twenty square feet, when whites were allowed one hundred square feet, even in China Camp?[96]

The answers devolved to informal associations of white miners—conventions, vigilance committees, and gangs—jealous of Chinese success. White citizens of Grass Valley, citing Bigler's special message, petitioned the state to deny Chinese miners the right to hold any claims in the township because by law they could not enter "the duties and benefits expected of citizens." Grass Valley authorities excluded all Chinese from gold and quartz mines.

In 1852 twenty thousand Chinese miners unwittingly landed in a race war that copied the pattern of the ethnic purges against Latinos in the region. In Yuba County, where many Chinese held lucrative claims along the

Grass Valley Chinatown

rivers, a miners' convention met at Foster and Atchinson's General Store in late April and announced that no Chinese could hold a claim after May 1 and none could remain in the county after May 3, but anti-Chinese riots erupted even before the deadline, forcing the Chinese out of Yuba.

That spring, white miners returned to the gold fields around Columbia to locate Chinese claims that had been abandoned in the routs after the Foreign Miners' Tax. They discovered that a transformation of mining was under way. Surface deposits of gold nuggets, flashing among the gravel in shallow rivers or along sandbars, had become scarce. To get at the gold, miners needed water to wash the ore from the dirt and hillsides. Paradoxically, they needed the Chinese to dig the ditches to carry water from the rivers to the arid diggings. The Tuolumne Water Company eagerly hired Chinese for this project, which cost two hundred thousand dollars.

Chinese laborers reminded white miners of their new dependence on the water companies. While they waited for water, the white miners drank, gambled, and condemned the capitalists, shipowners, and merchants who profited by transporting or hiring Chinese laborers. But closer at hand were the Chinese themselves. On May 8, 1852, the white miners convened the second Columbia Miners Convention to "answer the predisposition on the part of merchants, commercial men, etc. to flood the state with Asiatics

[and] fasten . . . a system of peonage on our social organization."[97] The convention declared that "no Asiatic or South Sea Islander shall be permitted to mine in this district either for himself or for others."[98]

The "lonely miner" knew that he had been replaced by capital-intensive corporations. British and American industrialists had invaded the Sierra and Siskiyou mountains to finance the expensive shafts, driving deep into the mountains to extract gold sealed in hard quartz. To expose the seams of gold, hydraulic pumps drew water from the rivers, and mountainsides collapsed under the force of the high-pressure hoses. The dream of finding a fortune with a pan, some luck, and a couple of dollars for canned beans became even more illusory.

The roundups, the tax codes, the lack of water, the absentee owners, and ultimately the lack of gold signaled the end of the multiracial, multinational gold fever. Frustrated, white miners lashed out at one another and the Chinese. In the first five years of the gold rush, forty-two hundred murders were committed in California; hundreds of the victims were Chinese. California's Committee on Mines announced that the "color, nature, and education" of the Chinese denied them the rights of citizens and the possibility of naturalization; no law would protect them "from the liability of being ousted from any mining claim by citizen miners of this state." Many frightened Chinese miners left the mother lode and trekked to increasingly remote and inaccessible claims. More than four thousand Chinese émigrés returned to China.

Yet the intensity and violence of the first purges belie how few Chinese there were. In 1849, only 325 Chinese immigrants passed through the San Francisco Customs House; 450 were cleared for entry in 1850, and 2,700 in 1851. As word of the violence reached China, the number of new Chinese immigrants temporarily fell, from more than 20,000 in 1852 to 4,270 in 1853. Ethically absolved and legally excused, the roundups of remaining miners continued. In Vallecito, Chinese miners who owned their claims were given ninety days to sell out and go.

In Sonora, harassing the local Chinese had become a "traditional sport." White miners rushed the Chinese camps at midnight, firing pistols to wake the sleeping miners and plundering their tents and cabins. They looted a large Chinese claim along the Yuba River, set fire to the buildings, and declared themselves new owners by right of possession. The legal system didn't blink; a few white friends of the Chinese tried to bring a lawsuit against the vigilantes, but the Chinese were not allowed to testify and it failed.[99]

In Mariposa, near the western entrance to Yosemite Valley, an unsigned placard appeared on a gate in 1856: "Notice is hereby given to all Chinese on the Agua Fria and its tributaries to leave within ten days, from this date, any failing to comply shall be subjected to thirty-nine lashes, and moved by force of arms." Many Chinese obeyed, but others, believing that the unsigned notice carried no weight, remained. On the tenth day the Chinese cabins were torched, driving the miners into an open field, where they were rounded up and beaten. The *Mariposa Gazette* simply remarked that the notice should have been signed so that "John" might know why and by whom he was to be whipped.

Within two weeks of the deadline set by the second Columbia resolution, vigilantes raided a Chinese camp at Deer Creek, near Nevada City, stole more than thirty thousand dollars in cash and hidden gold, and blamed the theft on Mexican "greasers." The Chinese appealed to the sheriff to prosecute members of the mob, but, recalled miner Alfred Jackson, "nobody paid any attention to them. There were over fifty [Chinese] living in the camp and they ought to have been able to protect themselves, but they seem to be great cowards and will not fight under any circumstances."[100]

There was no respite. In 1857, Chinese residents in Columbia were blamed for a fire that destroyed many buildings and again were forced to move outside the limits of the town.[101] In 1858, the mayor of Mariposa declared that no one could rent to the Chinese because they cooked over open fires, lit firecrackers on feast days, and burned incense sticks before their gods.[102] Chinatown itself, he claimed, was a fire hazard that should be demolished.

By the tense summer of 1858, nuggets of placer gold were gone from the Siskiyous and the gold rush was coming to an end. Desperate, white miners made a final night raid at the Chinese claims on Middle Creek in Shasta, ejecting seventy Chinese and throwing their tools into the rushing river.

The close of the decade saw a last outbreak of Chinese roundups in the gold fields. Across the Siskiyous, the Chinese were given deadlines to leave. In January 1859, white miners in Texas Springs voted 122 to 3 to purge the local Chinese. In Shasta County, miners gathered in Columbia for a final convention and voted to "remove" the Chinese before July 1. Since it was now settled that immigration law was a federal issue, the citizens of Columbia took matters into their own hands, launching a series of purges that continued until the lack of gold nuggets drove whites and Chinese alike down from the mountains, and a fragile peace held in the 1860s.

DRIVEN OUT: AFRICAN AMERICANS AND THE CHINESE

In June 1850, in the dry, hot foothills of Calaveras County, Argentinean miner Ramón Gil Navarro recorded in his diary, "The great company of Negro slaves has been replaced by another one just like it of Chinese laborers. All day long I see the stupid faces of these men who are so civilized and refined in the arts and so brutish in their customs and habits."[103]

The call for "free labor" heard across California meant free white labor. Some ranchers conscripted Native Americans and forced them into the gold diggings, and scores of southerners brought their slaves to the mines.

Despite California's "free soil" constitution, by 1852 three hundred African American slaves worked in the gold diggings.[104] Some were runaways and desperate. Others, lured by the news of California's ban on slavery, left enslaved wives and children behind as hostages and headed west with hopes of discovering enough gold to buy their freedom.[105] Black freemen also traveled to the gold fields, seeking enough wealth to purchase their families out of slavery.[106] By 1850, one thousand free African Americans had traveled across the plains and mountains to California to pan for gold or escape slave catchers set loose by the new Fugitive Slave Act. *The Freeman,* Philadelphia's abolitionist paper, celebrated two freemen who returned to the East in 1851 with thirty thousand dollars after just four months in the gold fields. Many blacks pursued this dream and headed west.[107]

Yet once there, they discovered that in fact California tolerated slavery. A slaveholder could safely bring his slaves into the state, force them to return to the South, or sell them if he could not afford the expense of their passage home.[108] In April 1852, California passed its own Fugitive Slave Law, declaring that all slaves who had escaped before California's admission into the Union were runaways who could be reclaimed. In the case of *In re Perkins,* the California Supreme Court ruled that although California was a free state, Carter and Robert Perkins could reclaim three black slaves and compel them to return to the South.[109] In *Ex parte Archy* (1858), the court added that a master could keep his slaves in California if he declared that he was there as a temporary resident.[110]

Purges of African Americans shadowed those of Latinos in the gold fields. When a Georgia-born slave owner died in Placer County in 1852, his black slaves abandoned his mining claim and moved to town, where an "assembly" quickly forced their landlord to evict them. To challenge discrimination, three colored conventions met in San Francisco and Sacramento between 1855 and 1857 and pressed California to mete out justice "to all, without respect to complexion."[111]

CHINESE RESISTANCE

T*he Sonora Union Democrat* wrote: "Poor John; he is kicked and cuffed from one end of the state to the other. Even though he pays his foreign- and poll-tax promptly, he has to pack up and leave should he be so unfortunate as to hit upon a spot that pays him more than a couple of dollars a day, but 'might makes right,' so he dares not murmur."[112] But the Chinese did more than murmur. They purchased arms, created strong organizations to protect their jobs, and often refused to abandon their homes and claims. And despite overwhelming barriers, they turned to the legal system for redress.

Blocking their path, however, was the bizarre case of *People* v. *Hall* (1854). On August 9, 1853, George Hall, a white miner, accompanied by his brother and one other man, assaulted and robbed a Chinese placer miner on the Bear River in Nevada County. Hearing shouts, the miner Ling Sing left his tent to help but was shot and killed by Hall, who, with his companions, was arrested by the sheriff. Based on the testimony of a Chinese witness, the judge sentence Hall to hang.

But twenty-nine-year-old Hugh C. Murray, chief justice of the California Supreme Court, overturned Hall's conviction. Murray ruled that long ago "Asiatics" migrated to the American continent across the Bering Strait and "descended" into Indians. The Indians were therefore Chinese and the Chinese were Indians, and thus unable to testify in court either "in favor of, or against a white man."

Even though Murray acknowledged that discoveries by "eminent archeologists, and the researches of modern geologists" had established that tribal people were really American "aborigines" and not descended from Asians, he maintained that *race* was a "generic" term that excluded "everyone who is not of white blood." Wrote Murray: "Indian as commonly used, refers only to the North American Indians, yet in the days of Columbus all shores washed by Chinese waters were called the Indies, therefore all Asiatics were Indians." The word *white,* he added, "necessarily excludes all other races than Caucasian."

Murray would "decide against admitting the testimony of the Chinese on the grounds of public policy" because "nature placed an impassable difference" between "us" and people "marked as inferior" and "differing in language, opinions, color and physical conformation." This "impassable difference" denied Chinese both "the right to swear away the life of a citizen" and "the privilege of participating with us in administering the affairs of our Government."[113] It was better to release a convicted murderer than to tamper with white supremacy, asserted Murray.

People v. *Hall* stimulated a rash of roundups, for now, with the promise of all-white juries and the absence of any Chinese testimony, conviction of a vigilante became virtually impossible. Not until five years later, in *People* v. *Elyea* (1859), did the California Supreme Court overturn the ban against Chinese testimony, declaring that the color of a man's skin was not a reliable measure of his competence to serve as a witness or to testify in court.[114]

Yet the Chinese persisted in turning to the courts in both criminal and civil cases, and occasionally they prevailed. In *Quam* or *Quang Chew* v. *Sales and Johnson,* a Chinese man in Nevada County proved to an all-white jury that he was a merchant and not a miner, and forced the tax collectors to return his money.[115] Indeed, the Chinese residents of Nevada County were successful in 51 percent of the cases they initiated against whites, particularly when they hired white attorneys.[116]

The violence that hounded the Chinese in gold-rush towns reveals a painful paradox: Chinese emigration was threatening the very institutions it was supposed to protect—the Chinese family, the Chinese village, and the Chinese clan.[117] To preserve a national identity under assault, Chinese miners, skilled in the traditions of rural community, formed kinship organizations, wore Chinese clothes, imported food, refused to cut off their queues, and maintained extensive correspondence with families in China.[118] Another kind of Chinese resistance to the roundups and, indeed, to the

Chinese man with queue

painful rupture of immigration itself was to forge communities in the United States and, at the same time, create international families, with wives and family in China who faced the long or permanent absences of their sons, fathers, and husbands.[119] Funds and letters (sometimes written by scribes) were carried by *shuikes* or "water guests" on visits to China and created a strong chain of intimate communication and financial commitment.

The Chinese miners were a transnational people, facing east and facing west, migrant and immigrant, sojourner and settler. In towns such as Grass Valley, French Corral, North San Juan, Washington, Bloomfield, and Nevada City, Chinese merchants sold goods that tied the miners to their homeland, providing rice, dried fish, mail from home, notices of jobs, and links to the Chinese Six Companies. In segregated Chinatowns near their diggings, they built temples and cemeteries, constructed levees to raise catfish and trap turtles for soup, planted lilies and trees of heaven, and opened brothels, gambling halls, and opium houses.

In the town of Sonora, Chinese stores were built protectively, side by side. Off narrow alleys, merchants, laborers, and boarders shared small shacks and visited Chinese doctors, herbalists, barbers, launderers, vegetable peddlers, and cooks. Jinshanzhuang (Gold Mountain Firms) imported books and magazines, preserved lichees, pineapples, ginger, smoked flower fish, and dried blackfish and eels. By 1867 China had shipped more than eighteen million pounds of rice to the West Coast.[120] In 1855 a Chinese theater opened in Auburn's Chinatown. Many Chinese communities had their own gold buyers and assay offices; one group of miners even constructed a separate fort on Shepley Flat to protect their gold. In many Chinatowns, such as Antioch's, homes and stores were connected by a web of hidden underground tunnels—built for cold storage, for communication, and for escape.

By the winter of 1851, China Camp had become the commercial, social, and religious center for the Chinese in the southern Sierra Nevada and a depot for every item brought into the diggings. Stagecoaches, freight wagons, and mule trains arrived daily, laden with food, clothing, and tools. Fifteen hundred pack animals and five hundred wagons brought Chinese goods into the mountains. Ancient traditions of food preservation made it possible for Chinese miners to have a much more varied diet than white miners, who disdained the unfamiliar salted duck eggs, cabbage, and turnips, the dried fish and mushrooms, and the melons, squashes, and persimmons grown from seeds carried from China.

Christians hoped that mining areas would provide an evangelical stepping-stone to Asia, but eager home missionaries found no converts.[121] China Camp, like Oroville to the north, had three temples to serve Buddhist, Taoist, and Confucian miners. White Americans' contempt for the endurance of Chinese culture emerged in the popular tune "John Chinaman," sung throughout the mining camps:

I thought you'd cut your queue off, John
And don a Yankee coat,
And a collar high you'd raise, John,
Around your dusky throat.[122]

The Foreign Miners' Tax had cut the Chinese population by the thousands, but after a few years new arrivals equaled and quickly doubled the number of those who departed the Sonora foothills. Many of those who returned to China stayed only temporarily.[123] Despite the ice and wind, the blackmail, the brutality, and the tax collectors, thousands of Chinese remained in the mother lode and thousands more continued to find their way. In Placer County, at the end of November 1856, there were 12,540 white men, 1,860 white women, 400 male and female Negroes, and 125 Indians. But there were more than 3,500 Chinese men and women, almost one fifth of the population.

Over the years Chinese refugees also returned to Shasta County. Many stayed until railroad work pulled them toward the Rocky Mountains. Indeed, despite the purges, the persecutions, and the lure of railroad work, during the Civil War over 80 percent of the Chinese population in California was still engaged in mining.[124]

FROM GOLD TOWN TO COMPANY TOWN

By the end of the gold rush, California had become a giant company town, owned by and for white men, almost all of whom were seeking to profit from gold.[125] The state required no land surveys, sought no royalties, and refused to interfere with the transfer of mining claims between Anglo and European miners. It placed no limits on placer or quartz mining on once tribal lands. Miners and mining companies could build or wash away trails or roads, dig up farms and fields, or even tunnel under a town's streets, buildings, and houses.[126] The fluming, sluicing, and diverting of water moved forward unabated, filling the rushing clear rivers with slag, tree stumps, and dirt, killing trout, steelhead, and salmon.

Most of the miners who remained in the mountains were Chinese, "scratching" for gold along the riverbeds, particularly during the dry season, or working for the new corporations—in blasting, digging, construction, and extraction. When industry took over the gold fields, white miners lost not only their income and but also their pride as independent adventurers. Prices collapsed, rents fell, investors and lenders withdrew their capital, and stores and mills shut down. And again the blame fell on Chinese miners, the "indispensable enemy,"[127] who had willingly built the water, timber, and mining companies—because they had been driven from their claims.

Despite its evolution into statehood, California functioned as a colony, a faraway land viewed as empty, awaiting civilization and inviting settlement, a tempting place of vast natural resources. With its Chinese population, it offered a seemingly unlimited source of low-paid workers. The "great, detestable, and damnable object" of Chinese immigration, observed one miner, is the "reduction in the price of labor."[128] A correspondent to the *Alta California* well understood the trade-off: "By allowing innumerable hordes of semi-human Asiatics to come to our shores, the trade with Asia will be increased; there will be an increased demand for shipping; the ship owners will make larger dividends; the trade and profits of many large commercial houses will be increased, and the general interests of commerce will be promoted."[129]

Yet gold also launched a union movement in California that thrived in the 1860s and wove together the cry for free labor with the attacks on growing corporate, shipping, and banking forces. Racial issues and economic pressures together provided a platform for the Chinese roundups. As mining towns grew, white carpenters, bricklayers, stonemasons, sailors, and musicians formed labor organizations that gave shape and ready members to the anti-Chinese clubs that sprang up throughout the mountains and along the rivers. Even after the gold rush collapsed, the image of the enslaved Chinese laborer endured in the demands, the newspapers, and the speeches of white miners living in the mountains. During the roundups of 1853, white laborers struck for a ten-hour day and higher wages—demanding shorter hours and higher pay than the Chinese. These early labor unions may have been temporary, issue-oriented, and unstable, but they held to their racial prerogative.

By 1853 San Francisco and Sacramento were overbuilt, jobs were hard to find, and merchants and miners went bankrupt; hundreds of thousands of dollars' worth of supplies were abandoned or sold at ruinous losses. Then, in early February 1855, the financial foundation of California collapsed. Large banking houses in San Francisco—Adams and Company, Bacon and Company, and Argenti and Company—suspended business. In the gold-mining area, local banks, such as George C. Plume's Bank of Marysville and Hamlet Davis's bank in Nevada City, closed their doors. To add to the desperation, the winters of 1854 and 1855 saw little rain, and placer gold stayed locked in the dirt.

The technological inventions of the mid-1850s added pressure to both the white miner with a pick, pan, and shovel and the Chinese miner with wing dam and sluice. The isolated miner gave way to the company that could hire hundreds of men to tunnel into the hills. Journalist Bayard Taylor, having watched a sixteen-foot nozzle blast a hillside with water at 120 pounds of pressure per square inch, wrote that the mountain washed itself away "like a giant bleeding to death from a single vein."[130] By 1859 small river claims lay buried under the gravel tailings as mountains literally dissolved into rivers and streams. Thousands of miners came down from the Sierras and Siskiyous, drifting into manual work in the new vineyards and orchards or in construction for the railroads. When the Civil War came, many white miners joined the Union Army, supporting the North as a fight for the rights of free labor.

Like most whites, few Chinese discovered significant amounts of gold. Forced from the diggings by the violence and by the Foreign Miners' Tax, many moved to rural towns. As cattlemen and sheepherders moved into the foothills of the mother-lode country, ranchers hired the Chinese to build rock fences that would fortify the land against mountain lions, panthers, and grizzly bears. These rock fences still mark the landscape of the Siskiyous, where once Chinese mined in towns named Montezuma, Celestial Valley, Shanghai Diggings, and Canton. Other Chinese who emigrated for the gold rush now worked in restaurants, laundries, stores, and barbershops; some took jobs just to earn enough money to pay their debts and buy a return ticket home.

The mass exodus of white miners from the gold fields during the late 1850s and early 1860s ended the first wave of Chinese purges. For several years Chinese miners were, more or less, left alone. By the end of the 1860s, as Democrats campaigned "No Negro or Chinese Suffrage," the overall population in the mining regions dropped 70 percent, giving the rest of California an abundant supply of white labor for the first time. But the Chinese had not disappeared. Many Chinese went to work for the Central Pacific Railroad Company. After the Civil War, as the economy in the West settled down, Chinese men and women became the workforce for California's new manufacturing industries and construction projects—road building, irrigation, land reclamation, in canneries, jute mills, and cigar-rolling factories, and large-scale agriculture on the new vineyards and orchards.

The few hundred Chinese who remained in the Siskiyou Mountains purchased "washed-out" claims from white miners, reworking the tailings with picks, shovels, and teaspoons. Some Chinese formed their own mining companies, from small cooperatives to corporations that would employ more than one hundred workers by the 1880s. Some who owned their own claims invested in hydraulic or drift mining, extracting up to fifteen hundred dollars in gold each week—an amount that would have resulted in immediate and violent expulsion in the early 1850s. This period of stability lasted until Charles Crocker drove a golden spike into the railroad tracks on May 10, 1869, in Provo, Utah, linking the transcontinental tracks and ending the monumental construction made possible by Chinese laborers, who were immediately excised from the photographs and fired from the Central Pacific Railroad.

The roundups in the gold fields ended, but the legend of the vigilante lived on in sagas and songs. During the first five years of the gold rush, the Chinese became a favorite target of the mountain outlaw Joaquín Murieta, who declared that he loved to "smell the blood of Chinamen." In one mythic story, Murieta robbed a camp of six Chinese miners at Murphy's Diggings, tied the men together by their queues, drew his long bowie knife, and slowly cut their throats. To protect themselves from the famous bandit, Chinese miners collected three thousand dollars in gold for Murieta's capture, a figure large enough to track him down and kill him.

Long after the gold rush, the story of the roundups was sung in bars and at campfires throughout the mountains in the miners' song "John Chinaman":

John Chinaman, John Chinaman,
But five short years ago,
I welcomed you from Canton, John—
But wish I hadn't though.

2

DEAD BRANCHES

Recently the treatment of blacks has been carried over to yellow people. When cobra is unable to release its poison fully it vents its anger by biting wood and grass. Afterwards, no one who touches the poisoned dead branches will escape death. We the yellow people, have we touched its dead branches.

Lin Shiu (Lin Qinnan) of Min County, composed at Seaview Tower Over the Lake, on Chongyang festival of year Xinchou during the Guangxu reign, in a preface to Harriet Beecher Stowe's *Uncle Tom's Cabin* (1901)

Gazing at the evening sky over Los Angeles on October 18, 1871, a reporter for the *Los Angeles Daily News* observed, "The young moon, in setting, has presented a most peculiar appearance for the last few evenings, strongly resembling a semi-circular Chinese lantern of bloodshot hue, suspended in the air over the Western horizon."[1] This crimson hue was foreboding. The next night, the *Alta California* described a more sinister glare over the Los Angeles sky: "Twelve hours ago . . . fifteen staring corpses hung ghastly in the moonlight, while seven or eight others, mutilated, torn and crushed, lay in our streets, all of them Chinamen."[2]

Actually, seventeen Chinese were lynched and two others were knifed to death on the night of October 24, 1871. Their mangled bodies were found hanging from a wooden awning over a carriage shop, from the sides of two prairie schooners parked around the corner, from a gutter spout, and from a beam across the wide gate of a lumberyard. One of the victims wore no trousers, and a finger had been severed from his left hand.

Calle de los Negros

Earlier that evening a hostile crowd had gathered, yet many Chinese had escaped when a Chinese woman fired her shotgun into the mob. Amid the confusion, they hid in nearby vineyards and orange groves or fled across the Los Angeles River. But in under three hours a mob of five hundred Mexican and Anglo men, nearly 10 percent of the population of Los Angeles, murdered a total of nineteen Chinese men in El Pueblo, the center of old Los Angeles, on a narrow street lined with Chinese shops and residences called Calle de los Negros, also known at the time as Nigger Alley, Negro Alley, or Chinatown.

The outrage had begun two days earlier when brokers for two Chinese companies drew their revolvers over a runaway prostitute, Ya Hit. The *Los Angeles Daily News* reported that Ya Hit had married a Chinese man in a "Melican Marriage Ceremony . . . to evade paying the purchase money." The Nin Yung Company claimed that it owned Ya Hit, but she had been "abducted, held, and secreted" by the rival Hong Chow Company. For years both companies had captured runaway prostitutes by forging bogus warrants for their arrests, bribing police officers to seize the women, and paying off judges to convict them for theft, often the "theft" of themselves. Perhaps Ya Hit saw in the "American marriage" a deliverance from slavery. Or perhaps her groom sought a way to own her himself. Although no one was injured by the shots, both men were charged with attempted murder. When Sam Yuen, the leader of the Nin Yung Company, swore to the court that he had six thousand dollars in gold in his trunk to serve as bond, his "warrior" was released and escorted home.[3]

Los Angeles's six police officers were drinking in a local bar on the night of October 24 when again shots were heard throughout El Pueblo. This time, Sam Yuen himself and the leader of the Hong Chow Company had fired upon each other. When the chief of police finally arrived, he randomly deputized a large group of white men from the crowd and ordered them to shoot any Chinese who might try to leave their houses. Eventually Mayor Cristobal Aguilar, the sheriff, and the six police officers showed up in El Pueblo. They surveyed the tense scene and left. Throughout Los Angeles rumors spread that the Chinese had stores of hidden gold and were "killing whites wholesale."[4]

An angry crowd gathered and the lynching spree began. The first man hanged was Wong Tuck. He was dropped by a rope from a corral gate facing Saint Athanasius Episcopal Church, the only Protestant church in Los Angeles. In Spanish and English, impromptu orators provoked the racially mixed crowd, urging them to climb onto the roofs of Chinese dwellings, chop holes in the adobe tiles, and pour gunfire inside.

Terrified, the Chinese ran into the streets; two were immediately seized, shot, and hanged. At one house a flying axe split a lantern and flames shot into the night air. Robert Thompson, a saloon keeper and rancher, was the first and only white man killed, after he charged into a Chinese home. The emboldened mob roamed through the Chinese quarters, finding dozens of Chinese men and women cowering in their homes. Some were already dead or wounded, and their bodies were thrown into the streets to be trampled by the mob. Others were dragged from their apartments and hanged with clothesline. One of the police officers simply handed several Chinese men over to the crowd with instructions to take them to the jail—and they too were summarily hanged. Among them were a young Chinese doctor, Chien Lee Tong, and a fourteen-year-old boy. Some of the Chinese men and apparently one Chinese woman were hanged after they were murdered.

By eleven o'clock that night, the bodies of sixteen Chinese men and one Chinese woman were cut down and laid in two neat rows in the jail yard at Franklin and Spring Streets. The body of Wong Tuck was dragged to the cemetery behind the old fort on Moore Hill. The terror was hardly over.

Chinese buildings were looted and riddled with bullets; queues from Chinese corpses were cut off as souvenirs. *The New York Times* reported in tit-

Chinese corpses lying in Los Angeles jail yard. "Eighteen Chinamen were buried yesterday. They presented a most ghastly and horrible sight. Their clothing was torn, and in one or two cases the victims were almost nude. Their countenances were besmeared with blood, their heads and bodies pierced with gunshot wounds, and some of them fearfully mutilated. The ropes by which they were hanged were still attached to their necks, and a number of them were shot previous to being hanged. One or two of the victims had their bodies riddled with bullets."

illating detail: "Every nook and corner, every trunk, chest and drawer in every apartment was . . . carefully and expeditiously ransacked. Locks gave way to the pressure brought to bear against them. Every article of value passed into the hands of the pillagers. Even the victims executed were robbed of everything of value in cash and jewelry they possessed previous to being hanged. One of them, the Chinese doctor, had his garments ripped from off his person while hanging; others had their pockets cut out with knives, which entered into and fearfully lacerated the flesh, the wretches having neither time nor patience to rifle them in the usual way."[5] It was estimated that between fourteen and thirty thousand dollars in Chinese cash, gold, clothing, and furniture were stolen. The mob even took a roasted goose.[6]

California historian Hubert Bancroft witnessed white women and children not yet in their teens participate in the massacre: one young boy was balanced atop an awning from which a Chinese man was hanging, calling for more victims and helping the vigilantes haul up ropes for the next Chinese prey.[7]

Some white men tried to intervene. Henry Hazard (who would later become mayor of Los Angeles) as well as a few housewives hid their Chinese cooks and servants.

Over the next two days, crowds of Chinese men and women visited the bleak jail yard looking for missing friends and relatives. On Thursday, October 26, the Chinese buried their dead in rough red wooden boxes, several to a grave, with their names written on small slats of wood nailed to each coffin.

The Los Angeles lynchings occurred the same year Congress passed the Ku Klux Klan Act, which allowed individuals to sue states in federal court for civil rights violations. Unlike the thousands of lynchings of black Americans, these were not provoked by insinuations of rape of white women. The episode had begun, however, with a wedding. The Chinese had used a white romantic ritual—perhaps to note their new national affinity or to define the ownership of a slave girl. As in the South, the mob in Los Angeles targeted minority men who had deliberately challenged an image of white domesticity and sexuality in a town with few white women.[8]

Perhaps most threatening to whites was that the "Melican" wedding contradicted the myth that the Chinese were in the United States as temporary sojourners. If the wedding was consensual, it implied permanence and family and foretold an enduring Chinese presence in the United States and an interracial future for California. Claimed Bancroft, "The denizens of Negro Alley comprised the dregs of the nations. Asiatic, African, and European, Latin and Indian there lived in unholy association."[9]

The newspapers reveled in the visibility of the violence: "Staring corpses . . . helpless, torn and mangled, more dead than alive, have been dragged by an infuriated, senseless crowd, through our peaceable streets, in the very face of the better portion of the community to finish what was left of their agonized existence at the end of a rope, midst the exultant shouts and jeers of the mob."[10]

Pressured by Chinese merchants and unsavory newspaper reports, the corrupt city government, largely funded by licenses for brothels and gambling dens, reluctantly summoned a coroner's jury to investigate the massacre. Hundreds of Chinese laborers from the large ranches in the county came into town for the hearings and trials. The jury first heard from the police officers (known to demand bribes from the Chinese companies), who testified that they had shown the mob where the Chinese were hiding and then spent most of the evening in the taverns. Next it heard from members of the crowd who swore that both Councilman George Fall and *Los Angeles Star* reporter H. M. Mitchell had urged them to hang all the Chinese.

Hovering over the case, much like the crescent moon, was *People* v. *Brady*, the California Supreme Court decision that prevented a Chinese person from testifying against a white defendant.[11] The jury would never hear the Chinese describe what happened on the streets, or in their homes.

The riot began in a poor neighborhood shared by two hundred Chinese immigrants and hundreds of African Americans and Mexicans. Los Angeles in 1871 was a frontier town where fortunes were quickly made and lost in mining, railroads, agriculture, and the seizure of Mexican land. It was a town where saloons represented 110 of its 285 businesses, where the city marshal was also the tax collector, where twenty thousand dollars had just been spent buying votes in a local election.

The massacre of the Chinese, headlined across the country, exposed California's vigilante nature—just as the state was seeking to attract investment and leave its Wild West image behind. Many in the Golden State who had profited from the gold rush and the railroad now hoped to copy the New South's model of an agrarian economy powered by cheap labor and indebted tenant farmers. But here Chinese immigrants rather than former slaves would provide the muscle.

Local and national newspapers rushed to distance Los Angeles's middle class from the massacre. San Francisco's *Daily Alta California* assured its readers that the riot "commenced at an hour when business men, professional men and all the better classes of our community had retired to their homes."[12] San Francisco's *Daily Evening Bulletin* claimed that the "mayhem" occurred in a part of town where the "denizens are almost cosmopolitan . . . the dregs of society, among whom are some of the greatest desperados on the Pacific coast."[13] *The New York Times* directly pointed to the racism arising from immigration and anxious postwar politics:

> It is well known that the chief objection to the Chinese in California comes from the Irish population. It was from this class that the Democratic Party used to draw most of the political capital which it gained by fostering the prejudices against the Negro. Fleeing to this country, as they claimed, to escape British oppression, the Irish immigrant always made haste to join the ranks of the oppressors here.

> They voted, almost to a man, with the Democratic Party during the long years which that party championed the cause of Negro slavery, and now that slavery is abolished, we find them in the front ranks of the haters and persecutors of the Chinese. The Republican Party of California made a great mistake in trying to secure their votes by catering to their un-reasoning and illiberal prejudices.[14]

The coroner's jury found that "the mob consisted of people of all nationalities," insinuating that the vigilantes were immigrants, primarily Irish and Mexican.

But the real cause of the "excited spectacle," announced the *Times,* was simply that fifty Chinese people lived in Los Angeles: "The mob was determined to clean them out of the City."[15] Days before the riot, it reported, rumors were circulating that "lynchers" were ordering every Chinese person to get out of Los Angeles within forty-eight hours.[16]

Even without Chinese testimony, the grand jury indicted many members of the mob—reports range from 30 to 150 men—but the list quickly disappeared. In the end, eleven men were brought to trial. The grand jury also found that the police officers were "deplorably inefficient" and had disgraced the city.[17]

Ultimately eight men were convicted of manslaughter and sent to San Quentin for terms ranging from two to six years. But the prosecuting attorney had apparently been active in the riot, and one of the defendants was represented by the former attorney general of California, a colonel of the Confederacy. Within months, in a bizarre twist of logic, the post-Reconstruction Supreme Court reversed the verdict: the original indictment was "fatally defective" because it had failed to allege that a victim of the lynching, the late Chee Long Tong, had been murdered. Three weeks later the convicted prisoners were released.

Within a week of the massacre, Sam Yuen sued the city of Los Angeles, demanding the restoration of his property. The jury held that by his very presence Sam Yuen had participated in the riot and furthermore had failed to notify the sheriff or mayor that a riot was taking place; thus he lost the case. The Chinese Six Companies in San Francisco also filed suits against Los Angeles for damages and for the murders of their countrymen. Ultimately, the Chinese in Los Angeles were able to reclaim some of their goods but little of the stolen money.

The Chinese also turned for support to American merchants and missionaries working in China who feared that the L.A. "outrages" would lead to retaliation, putting their own lives and their property in China in grave danger. They called for a congressional inquiry into the massacres and demanded that the U.S. government denounce the "terrorism" against the Chinese.[18] Indeed, by late December the United States government had begun to hear rumors that China would "make war" on Americans living on its soil.[19]

The Los Angeles massacre was probably the largest single mass lynching in California, a ritual of terror and intimidation that coincided with the violence committed against black Americans after emancipation and Reconstruction.[20] From the time of the gold rush, lynching had served as a form of "folk pornography" as well as vigilante justice in the West.[21] At least 302 lynchings occurred in California between 1849 and 1902.[22] Of these, about 200 were of Asian people. During those years there were at least 5,000 lynchings in the United States, including the infamous 1880 lynching of a Chinese laundryman in Denver's Hop Alley, when a mob of 3,000 "gutt[ed]" Chinatown "as completely as though a cyclone had come in one door and passed out the rear."[23]

Victims of lynching were poked, prodded, jeered at, beaten, tortured, hanged, shot, and dismembered. Sometimes they were castrated, sometimes decapitated. Yet even as Hubert Bancroft chronicled the massacre in Los Angeles, he celebrated lynching as Americans' "right of revolution," a democratic expression of the majority's "right . . . to suspend the action of the law . . . whenever they deemed it essential to the well being of society to do so," rather than a lack of "due deference" or "disrespect for the law."[24]

Yet neither violence nor economic panic forced the Chinese community to leave Los Angeles.[25] With ranches and industries getting established, jobs were plentiful for whites and Chinese alike. Although in 1876 the Los Angeles Anti-Coolie Club produced twenty-six hundred signatures demanding the end of Chinese immigration, Chinese continued to move to the city.[26] In spite of the Chinese Exclusion Act of 1882, by the mid-1880s there were 655 Chinese residents in Los Angeles.[27]

In 1877 the city council attempted to clean up the town's image by changing the name of Negro Alley to Los Angeles Street. In 1888 the old Mexican adobe buildings in El Pueblo were demolished and fumigated, but at the turn of the century, more than three thousand Chinese people occupied "Old Chinatown," a neighborhood with hundreds of buildings and stores, several restaurants, three temples, a Chinese school, and a Chinese opera house.[28] Chinatown remained until the 1930s, when the city decided to build Union Station over the neighborhood, and its residents were forced to disperse to other Chinese communities scattered throughout the Los Angeles River basin.[29]

The endurance of L.A.'s Chinatown may be due to the small size and disorganization of the anti-Chinese Workingmen's Party that emerged in tandem with the new union movement. Or it may be due to the rather sudden arrival of white women and children, who balanced a skewed demographic and brought with them schools and missionizing churches that publicized violence against Chinese women, even as they fostered stereotypes of Chinese sinfulness and dependence. Another explanation may be the state's dependence on Chinese farmworkers who "mined" the new wealth springing from California soil: grapes, apricots, oranges, peaches.[30] In a state with few laborers of any sort, as early as 1854 *The California Farmer* suggested that Chinese farmworkers could "be to California what the African has been to the South."[31] Stereotyped in the racial imagination as industrious, docile, and skillful, the Chinese would accept seasonal employment under the control of gang contractors. They were willing to work for lower wages than others, and by 1870 they represented one tenth of California's farm laborers.

The failure of the massacre to evict the Chinese from Los Angeles may also be due to their determined resistance. In 1879, for example, the local Workingmen's Party pushed the city council to levy extra taxes on Chinese peddlers and launderers. The Chinese were instructed to pay the city twenty dollars for each vegetable wagon. The Chinese vegetable peddlers and "washmen" quickly assessed themselves two dollars each to hire a lawyer, gave the city two days to rescind the new tax, and then went on strike, refusing to provide households and hotels with fresh food. The vegetable vendors pressed a test case through the courts, and a county judge ruled that the special taxes were "oppressive, partial, unfair and in restraint of trade and therefore void."

White businessmen feared that an exodus of Chinese workers would destroy the city's tax base, and the city council quickly reduced the excessive fees. Emboldened by their success, the vegetable vendors refused to pay even the revised fee of five dollars per month, and in May 1879 they again went on strike. This time white housewives, eager for fresh food, signed a petition demanding an end to "license taxes" on Chinese vegetable peddlers. Soon Chinese washmen initiated a plan to build an enormous cooperative laundry under one roof in order to face only one tax.

The Los Angeles massacre of 1871 hung like smoke over the basin of the river town, perhaps in itself forestalling further violence. The brutality and the roundups of Chinese people in the 1870s exposed the inchoate state of California as a place of multiple and disputed borderlands and clashing cultures. Although justified at the time in terms of economic rivalry, the decade of racial violence was stamped in the popular imagination as a history whose conclusion of white dominance was already written.

TRAILS OF TEARS

The roundups of Chinese people during this brutal decade occurred at the same time that tribal people were being driven from California's riverbeds, forests, and fields.

The great misnomer of the era was that the land the federal government was rapidly giving away was "unoccupied." As state and local ordinances made it impossible for Chinese immigrants or blacks to own or at times even rent land in the West, military officers, local politicians, industrialists, timbermen, and railroad magnates were receiving land grants from the federal government—land equal to the size of Texas, land that included all the mineral rights beneath. Veterans, easterners, and European immigrants also received free acreage under the Homestead Act. By 1872 millions of acres of California land had been placed in corporate coffers and the Central Pacific Railroad was dictating California politics.[32]

Industrial and agricultural expansion onto "vacant" Indian land required the eviction of tribal people—by roundups and forced removals or by death. The Indian Wars and the reservations forced the United States to confront the heterogeneity of its own people even as it sustained its fantasy of Anglo-Saxon purity.[33]

In the 1870s Indians in northern California—the Miwoks and the Karuks, Yakis and Hoopa—stood in the way of industrialists, unemployed veterans, and recent European immigrants. Indian land covered hauntingly beautiful and valuable redwood forests, mountain rivers rushing over deep mineral deposits, and sunny valleys of fertile soil, sliced by rivers for irrigation and transportation. Investors in agriculture, hydraulic mining, and railroads worked closely with the U.S. military and volunteer militias to clear the Indians off.

Portending the destiny of the Chinese, tribal people were driven from the new timber, farming, and ranching communities, county by county. Tehama County petitioned the federal government to send the military to cleanse the county of Indians. Austin Wiley, editor of the *Humboldt Times,* sought to have the last Indians "removed to parts so far remote as to render their return impossible."[34]

James Beith, a Humboldt County supervisor who would become a mastermind of Eureka's purge of the Chinese people, wrote, "I can never tolerate the idea of moving [the Indians] to some reserve close at hand, for such a course is fatal and most disastrous [*sic*] to our interests. . . . Could we give security to the Indian and an asylum, & at the same time prevent his return—we would—from our eligible position become one of the first counties, in this best of all States." Beith, like Wiley, proposed to force "the entire removal of the Indians to some Island on the Pacific." The San Francisco *Daily Evening Bulletin,* quite simply concluded that it came down to a choice between "deportation and extermination."[35]

A second trail of tears marked the mountains, the coastline, and the rivers of the Pacific Northwest. In 1866 the *Chico Courant* wrote, "It is a mercy to the red devils to exterminate them."[36] During the 1870s, armed citizens' committees in Butte County rounded up, drove out, or killed hundreds of members of the Yahi tribe. Along the northwest coast, eastward along the Klamath River, and down through the Central Valley, volunteer militia and vigilante groups delivered hundreds of Indians at a time—Karuks, Yuroks, Yokuts—to the reservations.

In Shasta, Trinity, and Humboldt Counties the brutal Kibbe Guard, a Klan-like organization of white vigilantes, gathered at night, located and surrounded Indian camps, and attacked at dawn. They marched survivors to the nearest reservation, often in Mendocino County, where many Indians starved to death.[37] Hundreds of Indians escaped and found their way back to their homelands; others were forced onto failing "farms" or reserves; thousands died.[38] Genocide succeeded where the reservations failed, and in 1871 Congress declared that no further Indian treaties would be signed in California.

The remaining California natives were pressured to assimilate through "a system of discipline and instruction" modeled on the Spanish missions and administered by U.S. agents. The federal government required Indians to attend white-run boarding schools and speak only English. "Indian Matrons" were sent into the mountains, white women who, by their very presence, were supposed to infuse Victorian domesticity into tribal life.[39]

In the 1870s, newspaper reports of the expulsion of Chinese people were bracketed by stories of the Indian Wars, the forced removal of tribal people.[40] Throughout 1872 war raged between the U.S. government and the Modocs in Klamath and Siskiyou Counties. White mobs raided Modoc villages and the Modocs retaliated, killing whites who tried to settle on their land. Then, in the spring of 1873, the U.S. Army announced a policy of eviction and extermination of the Modoc people from the areas around Tule and Sorass Lakes in Siskiyou County—places soon to become sites of Chinese expulsions.

With the land secured, visions of orchards, vineyards, cotton fields, and cheap labor shaped Indian policies. The new farmers adopted the hacienda system of the early Spaniards who forced Indians to work in the fields of the missions or the vast ranches.[41] In Butte County, John Bidwell turned to the hacienda policy for Rancho Chico, his enormous orchards outside Chico, and Leland Stanford forced Indians to work his grand farms in Vina. Initially about fifty Indians plowed, gathered seed, harvested, and gleaned wheat for John and Annie Bidwell, who paid them in glass beads and cloth, in part because Annie hoped to cover their traditional nudity.[42]

In areas without many white working families, Indian children, some as young as two years old, were targeted for indenture, most for a period of twenty-three years. *The Humboldt Times* hoped that the Bidwell practice of indenture of Mechoopda Indians would reach the coast: "This law works beautifully. . . . What a pity the provisions of this law are not extended to greasers, Kanakas, and Asiatics."[43]

SOUTHERN EXPORTS

During the 1870s, "Radical Reconstruction"—the brief postwar effort to provide land, personal safety, and political access to blacks in the South—was brutally undone. Southern Democrats packed up their tactics, laws, and violence and took them west. Pressures to refinance southern plantations and to unify a sundered and hybrid nation with the mythic dream of a "white republic" had sabotaged Reconstruction and now would give political shape, legislative sanction, and cultural permission for the roundups of the Chinese in the West.

By 1867 Democrats had swept elections across California by opposing black male suffrage and the ratification of the Fifteenth Amendment. As the party took over California—from the governor's mansion to the state legislature to boards of county supervisors—southern traditions of lynching, racial violence, Black Codes, arson, and policies denying land ownership to racial minorities surfaced in California, Oregon, and the Washington Territory. But the Democrats were not alone. Aware that California's congressional delegations could dilute the power of the industrial Northeast and the reconstructed South, the Republican Party tried to extend its influence in the West on the backs of the Chinese. Both parties understood that if Chinese immigrants became naturalized, they could dilute white power at the ballot box.

Initially the Chinese had benefited from the Reconstruction legislation intended to empower former slaves. The Enforcement Acts of 1870 and 1871 and the Ku Klux Klan Act of 1871 extended the Civil Rights Act of 1866 to "all persons within the jurisdiction of the United States, Indians not taxed excepted." These laws allowed the Chinese "to make and enforce contracts, to sue, be parties, give evidence, and to the full and equal benefit of all laws and proceedings for the security of person and property as is enjoyed by white citizens." Republican senator William Stewart of Nevada declared that it was a national duty to protect the Chinese: "Let no one imagine that the people of the United States, after having made treaties guarantying [*sic*] rights to the Chinese, after having constructed the Pacific railroad, and subsidized a line of steamers to China for the purpose of cultivating friendly relations with that ancient civilization will allow a few evil-disposed persons to break the laws and trample upon the rights of these people."[44]

But the lynchings, massacres, and roundups of the Chinese in the West altered the national political landscape. If the eastern states did not share the West's obsession with the Chinese, they surely understood that California, Washington, and Oregon would tip the balance of power between the Democratic and Republican Parties. Some California newspapers warned: "If the authorities of Washington refuse or neglect to take hold of this Chinese question, the inhabitants of California must solve it themselves."[45] As Congress turned its attention to the West and the West turned its attention to Congress, Chinese roundups continued to rage across rural California.

Soon the western branches of the Democratic Party granted vigilantes the political blessing and legal codes that would sanction assaults on the Chinese. By the end of the decade, the Workingmen's Party, an arm of the Democratic Party, codified its plans to call for a second California constitution in 1879 to eliminate the Chinese from the state.

From the time of the gold rush, a racial overlay emerged that treated Indians, African Americans, and Chinese in the West with similar brutality in legislation, in land policy, and in labor practices. Local codes and state laws denied them citizenship and excluded their testimony against whites. Displaced Chinese miners and railroad workers soon fell into a system of sharecropping copied from southern postbellum land and labor policies.[46] Contracts of black tenant farmers in the South and Chinese field-workers in the West were strikingly similar—both groups found themselves in debt to landowners, and both faced the threat of forced evictions. In practice neither blacks nor Chinese could own the land they planted and harvested or the land on which they built their homes.

As small farmers and white laborers began to rebel against the wealthy agricultural monopolies acquiring the land of California, Chinese field-workers also became objects of their wrath. Almost as soon as the Chinese, forced from the gold fields and railroad construction, moved down to the hot farming valleys, they faced eviction again—from Contra Costa, Shasta, Siskiyou, Napa, Mendocino, and Yuba Counties and the Sacramento Valley.

If, unlike African Americans, the Chinese faced the risk of deportation, expulsion also meant that they could return to the safety of their first homeland. In addition, the rising presence of Chinese diplomats and a Chinese merchant class, and the Burlingame Treaty of 1868, conferred on even the poorest Chinese laborers a different civic status from blacks'.

The Burlingame Treaty and the Fourteenth Amendment should have shielded the Chinese by granting the Chinese the rights to bring lawsuits and to enjoy equal protection and due process of law. But local statutes, common violence, and the "Slaughter-house Cases" of 1873 gutted the treaty and the new constitutional protection. By drawing a distinction between national and state citizenship, the Supreme Court allowed states to disobey the Fourteenth Amendment's protections for "persons," narrowing coverage only to citizens. The court made it clear that the Fourteenth Amendment was intended only to protect former slaves.[47] African Americans' and Chinese Americans' common inability to own land, however, left both groups extraordinarily vulnerable.

In 1870, both political parties agreed to allow persons of African birth or descent to become naturalized. The Civil Rights Act and the Page Act of 1875, however, removed the right of Chinese immigrants to ever become citizens and banned the immigration of most Chinese women. These laws immediately exacerbated ethnic tensions in the West. In San Francisco more than one fifth of the population was Chinese, but another fifth was impoverished Irish. Because the Irish were Caucasian, however, they were eligible for naturalization and quickly formed a large bloc of voters. They turned on the Chinese.

The story of the purges of the Chinese in the town of Chico, Butte County, thus begins in the South. Practices of intimidation and segregation had migrated to the Siskiyou Mountains along with Chico's many recent émigrés from the South.[48] These new citizens well knew the Ku Klux Klan's tactics of anonymous letters, violent night raids, and arson. The use of local ordinances against Chinese immigrants derived from the Black Codes of the Reconstruction South, leaving both blacks and Chinese with few defenses against employers who acted both inside and outside the judicial system. Under the Black Codes, for example, an employer could whip an employee, lock him in stocks, or chain him to a treadmill. In 1867 when two thousand Chinese railroad workers who performed the dangerous work of blasting mountain tunnels went on strike, one of their demands was an end to an overseer's right to whip or restrain them from leaving the road to seek other employment.[49]

"IT'S A WAR OF THE RACES HERE": BUTTE COUNTY AND THE ORDER OF CAUCASIANS

By 1870, thousands of Civil War veterans, African Americans, Irish, Chinese, and Anglo miners and laborers had migrated to the Northwest with dreams of easy gold, industrial jobs, high wages, a short workday, and land.[50] They soon discovered that farming was hardly a road to riches—just a few men held title to vast government grants of fertile land, and they refused to sell their new acreage at fair market value, especially to non-Anglos. The "great giveaway" had smoothly turned "Indian land" into giant farms, and most of the jobs were in the fields of others.

John Bidwell and Leland Stanford, two land barons in Butte County—the largest and most prosperous county in the state—needed farmworkers, and they soon replaced contracted or conscripted Indians with Chinese. Skilled in mining, railroad construction, and "intense" or crowded farming, the Chinese would build the infrastructure of a new county, dynamiting roads, clearing fields, digging ditches to supply water to the mines, and constructing hundreds of miles of stone fences. Soon the Chinese represented more than 20 percent of the farm labor in Butte County.[51]

John Bidwell, onetime Prohibitionist candidate for president, founded the town of Chico at the northern end of the hot Sacramento River valley in 1860. By 1870 his fiefdom, Rancho Chico, with its thousands of acres of pear, apricot, and cherry orchards, was the largest employer of Chinese in the state. Suddenly, Bidwell found himself a leading advocate for Chinese workers and thus the target of anti-Chinese violence.[52]

For many bitter Anglo émigrés, the prospect of a large presence of Chinese "plantation laborers"—indeed, of Chinese neighbors—undermined their ideal of a small family farm in the West. News of anti-coolie clubs forming in San Francisco reached Butte County. For the many unemployed white laborers, the Chinese became a hated surrogate for absentee factory owners and distant landlords. Wrote the young New York journalist Henry George, "California is not a country of farms, but . . . of plantations and estates."[53]

The disillusionment and tension among Chico's small farmers and lumber-mill workers focused on the Chinese—if only the nation could prevent them from entering and expel the Chinese already here, California's "feudal estates" and "aristocratic domains" would lack cheap labor. But growers such as Bidwell and Stanford knew that if Congress excluded Chinese immigrants, it would be impossible for large-scale agriculture to reign in the West.[54] Ever since the Civil War, American farms had been competing in a rough international market as Britain sated its appetite for cotton and its thirst for tea in India and Egypt.[55] Coolies, slaves, and low-paid

Orchard field-workers, Rancho Chico, Butte County

workers in Europe's colonies in Africa and India undercut the wages of most farm laborers in the United States.

Meanwhile Chico flowered as a rural center of Chinese life in northeastern California. Segregated Chinese neighborhoods or small Chinatowns were scattered throughout the town, and the Chinese stayed connected through hidden underground tunnels—basements used for cold storage in the blistering heat and for hiding places during emergencies and police raids. Rumors of a "mysterious" underground community spread in the white press.

The wealth of Butte County—from mining and cutting timber to farming its river-valley soil—could be traced to Chinese workers. Soon anti-Chinese codes took hold in Chico. For eight years, for example, local ordinances forced Chinese ditchdiggers to head directly to their cabins after work. In 1867 the *Butte County Free Press* renamed itself the *Chico Caucasian.*

Efforts to purge the Chinese began in the 1870s when, facing dwindling gold, white miners revised the laws of Centerville and Helltown to read: "No Chinaman shall be allowed on the Butte Creek above the head of the Diamondville ditch in the mines, nor shall they be allowed to hold claims by the purchase above such point."[56] Unemployed white laborers marched through downtown Chico in torchlight parades, carrying banners declaring THE YELLOW DEVILS MUST GO.

The depression of the 1870s seeped into the county, bringing down both the frontier gentry and the new mill workers. The market for luxuries, such as gold watches, dried up; shops closed; and the papers mocked unemployed white men as "tramps" and "vagrants." Theft, bankruptcy, sheriffs' sales, and suicide became common headlines. Hopeless white men returned to the unpromising gold fields, and once-prosperous housewives cooked for boarders, sometimes relying on Chinese servants to help. The wary Democratic mayor of Chico did nothing as the situation became more desperate. Everyone knew that a wave of violence was about to hit. Charley Stilson's hardware store on Second Street sold door bolts by the dozen, and the lumber company hired an armed guard to stand night watch.

The dire situation deteriorated further with the panic of 1873. Jay Cooke and Company, the largest banking firm in the nation, declared bankruptcy in September. Across the country, each month the number of bankruptcies doubled; bitter struggles between laborers and the police erupted in New York and Chicago.[57] Yet even as the national economy collapsed, the

Chinese nanny and white child

Chinese in Chico sold vegetables from their wagons, washed and delivered laundry, cooked and cleaned, and worked as low-paid nannies, private launderers, and gardeners for white women who had never had servants before. White working-class women still took their dirty clothes to the Chinese laundries, and wealthier women still turned to Chinese launderers to wash and iron the delicate fabrics, the elaborate bows and ruffles, the ruching and tucking of their Victorian clothes, which the new white-owned steam laundries could not manage.

The barns and sheds at Rancho Chico would soon burn.[58] In 1876, anti-Chinese zealots unsuccessfully demanded that farmers and ranchers of Butte County dismiss their Chinese employees. During that lush and fertile summer, anti-Chinese "visiting committees" failed to persuade the large growers to fire their Chinese field hands. A newly formed society, the Supreme Order of the Caucasians, turned to boycotts, arson, and ultimately murder to further its goals. A secret chapter of the order, which included a town trustee, several lawyers, and many store owners, vowed to "annihilate" any white person who did not join. It then published a hit list of "public enemies."[59]

1. Anyone who removes a white man or woman or black man or woman (native born) and instates an Asiatic in his place.
2. He who retains in his family an Asiatic nurse.
3. He who gives bail or bond to an Asiatic.
4. He who defends an Asiatic against a white in a court of law.
5. All proprietors of saloons, coffee houses, cigar stores, restaurants, etc. who employ Asiatics.
6. He who teaches Asiatics any of the trades or arts of the Caucasian civilization.
7. He who rents property to an Asiatic.
8. Newspapers advocating the presence of Mongolians in America.[60]

Anti-Chinese rage took hold across the county. In August 1876, in Oroville, just down the road from Chico, half of Chinatown was destroyed by fire, and the *Oroville Mercury* reported, "Many of the people appeared to be pleased that part of the town has been burned, for it was the very . . . lowest of the low. Could a few more of the houses have been taken, it would give us much pleasure to chronicle the fact."[61] Butte County's Order of the Caucasians grew to more than two hundred members and included, as the *Chico Enterprise* boasted, "some of our best citizens."

Meanwhile news of growing unemployment across the country spread. Militant strikes by the Molly Maguires in the East headlined West Coast newspapers, and thefts by white tramps terrified the residents of Butte County. The Order blamed the Chinese for the national economic plight and vowed to force timbermen, farmers, and ranchers to replace all Chinese workers with unemployed white men. Here, too, competition for higher-paid work came from recent European immigrants who vied for the scarce jobs.[62]

White women feared that their new leisure, their freedom to travel east to visit friends and family, and their time for church and artistic clubs—all the result of inexpensive Chinese servants—were in jeopardy. The Order of Caucasians warned that Chinese workers posed a threat to white homes and formed a committee to demand that white housewives discharge their Chinese servants and hire whites or African Americans instead. Yet even the intimidating Order of the Caucasians could not bend these women, whose husbands, ironically, were leaders of the anti-Chinese movement, to fire the Chinese.

In the late autumn of 1876, the new Sierra Flume and Lumber Company quietly leased its sash and door mill to a San Francisco firm that brought two hundred Chinese mill workers up to Chico. On December 9, 1876, posters circulated through town demanding that Sierra Flume fire its Chinese workers and replace them with whites.

That Saturday night, hundreds overflowed the town hall, winding onto the balcony, down the stairs, and into the streets. More than seven hundred men signed a petition demanding "white only" employment at the mill. Frustrated with the pace of the movement, a group of sixty men, including the justice of the peace, walked out of the meeting and gathered in a dark and cold forest to form the Laborers' Union, a secret club to drive the Chinese out of Butte.[63] A. M. Ames, the club's first president, recalled that their secret oath was to "drive out the Chinese by killing them or stampeding them."[64] Despite its enticing secret codes ("You" was the password, "Nine!" was the cry of distress, and a raised arm with an open hand was a call for help), there was little secretive about this organization and its membership overlapped with the Order of the Caucasians.[65] In public, the union debated plans to steal explosives from the mines to blow up Chinatown, to burn Sierra Flume, to murder John Bidwell, and to assassinate the white constable who guarded the Chinese quarters. At one meeting, stableman Hank Wright promised his fellows, "If the council order me I will go out and return immediately with Bidwell's scalp."[66]

Sierra Flume rejected the union's call for a "white wage," and the men who advocated violence brazenly held a series of open meetings in the armory, the town hall, and the elaborate chambers of the Bank of Butte County. They reminded the citizens of Chico that the Order's constitution bound "each camp and every individual Caucasian . . . to impede, harass, . . . destroy [or] annihilate" every "merchant, manufacturer, and trader, traveler, mechanic, and laborer" who gave patronage or work to any Chinese person.[67]

The Chinese were just as public in their response. Knowing full well that neither the police nor the mayor would protect them, they flocked to Stilson's Hardware Store and bought every shotgun and six-shooter in stock.[68] Perhaps the anti-Chinese Anglos would falter if they saw the willingness of the Chinese to fight fire with fire. Visible to all who passed, the Chinese began target practice by the railroad tracks.

The Chinese display did little, however, to quell the reign of terror sweeping across Butte County. Arson seemed the weapon of choice in January 1877. On Saturday night, January 27, Hank Wright and Hayden Jones met at the home of Watson Roberts, where they retrieved a hidden vat of coal oil and set fire to Yee Kee's butcher shop; fully prepared, the Chinese had water ready and quenched the flames. A few nights later, one of Bidwell's buildings burned to the ground, and an exuberant white crowd rushed to watch.

Local politics fueled the fires. In early February 1877, anti-Chinese candidates won a majority of seats on Chico's town council and an officer of the Laborers' Union was elected town marshal. Chico had voted for terror. Night fires were lit at barns where Chinese farmworkers slept. In March, the Order tried to burn Old Chinatown itself.[69] With rifles in hand, Chinese men threatened to shoot anyone who assaulted them. As the violence raged, Chico's civic leaders made no move to investigate the fires or press charges against the vigilantes. In frustration, Bidwell launched his own search for the arsonists but found little help. White property and business owners did not want their buildings to suffer the same fate.

Chinese laundry at Chico Creek (burned)

Surprisingly, Chico's white women continued to support the Chinese. When female members of the Congregational church learned that their minister, Reverend Lysander Dickerman, was attending secret anti-Chinese meetings, they boycotted his services and called for his dismissal. Dickerman, they declared, had become "detrimental to the cause of Christ." Dumbfounded, Dickerman expelled the women from the congregation and then transformed the church into the town center for anti-Chinese activities.

In February, Hank Wright and Hayden Jones torched Chinese quarters along Butte Creek and shot at the Chinese as they fled from their homes. Again, no investigation followed. In Chico itself, members of the Supreme Order of the Caucasians set fires at the Flume Street and railroad Chinatowns, and in early March they ignited sacks of straw and coal oil inside a building in the heart of Old Chinatown. That night the Chinese marched through Chico in protest, banging cymbals and playing music. But no white official stood against the mob, and the fires continued. At the Patrick ranch, a white gang opened fire on the Chinese who tried to save their burning barn; the six horses inside died in the fire. In early March, Sierra Flume itself went up in flames, torched by the Laborers' Union.

On March 9, a Chinese camp bordering the railroad tracks was set on fire. The terrified men escaped toward the safety of the larger Chinese communities at Bidwell's Rancho Chico and at Leland Stanford's ranch in nearby Vina. The Order of the Caucasians burned Ah Shu's laundry at the Davis ranch, blaming him for the failure of the white laundry. As Chico burned, the local newspaper warned its readers that merchants from San Francisco and Sacramento would soon refuse to ship goods to Chico, "for if a fire occurred these men know that they would never recover a cent for merchandise sent here."[70]

THE LEMM RANCH MURDERS

Five days later, Chico was a scene of carnage. On the night of March 14, a crew of six Chinese men was clearing brush on the heavily wooded farm of a German immigrant, Christian Lemm, about a mile and a half east of town. Since white men had rejected his offers for this rough work, Lemm ignored letters from the Laborers' Union ordering him to fire the Chinese workers.[71] At nine o'clock, Eugene Roberts, a butcher; John and Charles Slaughter, launderers; Fred Conway, a ranch hand; Hank Wright, the stable owner; and Thomas Stainbrook, a young farmer met at the stables. They hiked east from town, taking cover by the side of the road, intending to drive out the Chinese by burning their crude bunkhouse on Lemm's ranch.[72] They crossed Lemm's newly cleared field, climbed a fence, and snuck up behind the shack. Inside, some of the Chinese men slept, while the others, lying on their bunks, talked by candlelight about their wages that Lemm had withheld.

Roberts, in the lead, was surprised to find the Chinese men still awake. He whispered to his companions that if they did not murder the farmworkers, they would testify about the fire. His comrades agreed. They burst into the cabin, drew their revolvers, and ordered the Chinese men to sit at the foot of their bunks. One of the farmworkers, Wo Ah Lin, later recalled (in translation): "Six men came into the cabin, one of them searched for money while the [illegible] held pistols near us. We were sitting on the bed, and hung down our heads, afraid that the men would fire at us. They got between two and three dollars. They took some of the clothes off the bed, put them into a pile in the center of the room, threw coal oil on the pile, and then fired the shots which killed my companions. Their final deed was to set fire to the oil drenched clothes."[73] The whites then torched the cabin and fled. They took different routes back to town and agreed to swear that they had spent the evening at Wright's stables.[74]

Only two farmworkers survived the night. Each vigilante had placed himself in front of a Chinese man and fired point-blank. Wo Ah Lin threw his hand across his face and the bullet only grazed his arm. He fell back onto his bunk and pretended to be dead. Once the white gang was out of the cabin, he ran for help: "I threw my person on the fire and put it out. Could not tell a German from an American, but know the murderers were white men because I heard them say, 'God Damn.'"[75] Wo rushed to the ranch house, but Lemm, his wife, Mary, her sister, and a neighbor all refused his pleas for help. Badly wounded, Wo staggered into Chico, reaching town around midnight. There, too, no white person would help him.

The cabin "was a horrible sight," an excited ranch hand reported the next morning. "The first Chinaman we saw was lying partly across the door dead with his brains oozing out. We had to step over him to get in. The next two lay on their bunks dead, the fourth had been shot in his head and his brains were oozing out and he lay moaning. He died while the inquest was being held. The fifth Chinaman we found across the slough under a buckeye bush, he was shot in the breast, the bullet ranging downward and lodging in his back. He had a jack knife and had cut seven gashes trying to cut the bullet out. Dr. Watts took the bullet out. I afterwards heard that the Chinese doctor of Chico cured him."[76]

With the anti-Chinese results of the recent election fresh in mind, the town leaders sided with the vigilantes. The next morning, after church, the town council announced that it would not allow Wo Ah Lin to hire a physician or even rent a wagon to bring his wounded and dead friends back to town. They refused to permit him to launch an inquest. The *Oroville Mercury* depicted the scene: "At the late Chico massacre, the victims were allowed to lie weltering in their gore all through that long, terrible night, and no hand was stretched forth to assist them, though facts were known to man and the matter openly talked about on the streets of Chico."[77] The *Marysville Daily Appeal* declared: "It is a war of the races here."[78]

News of the Lemm massacre was telegraphed across the nation. Within days, Chico's leaders scrambled to preserve the town's reputation and, more important, their insurance. The *Record* urged every citizen to "do his utmost to have the wretches arrested. It is the only way to restore our good name."[79] But the town trustees appointed Jethro Swain, the president of the anti-

Chinese Laborers' Union, to the small police force, and the mayor appointed leaders of the anti-Chinese movement to serve as county sheriff, justice of the peace, town marshal, town attorney, and town trustees.

Left to protect themselves, the Chinese bought arms, put together their own fire department, stored water, and organized protest marches. They demanded that the Chinese Six Companies send detectives from San Francisco to track down the Lemm ranch murderers and offer a one-thousand-dollar reward. In the middle of fall harvest, other farmers feared losing their low-paid Chinese field hands; Bidwell donated money for the capture of the vigilantes and led a group of farmers to demand that the mayor pursue the murderers. Four days after the massacre, Bidwell and a few of the town's merchants and hotel keepers, boldly defying the demands of the Order of Caucasians and the laborers' union, announced that they would continue to employ their Chinese laborers.

The Order of the Caucasians refused to back down. Bidwell and those who still employed Chinese workers began to receive anonymous letters warning that their buildings would burn if they refused to fire their Chinese employees or if they pursued the investigations: "Get rid of your Chinese help within fifteen days or suffer the consequences." They were signed "Committee."[80] Threatening placards were nailed onto fences. The *Chico Enterprise* printed a letter addressed to Ben True, the town constable, warning, "You will take a fool's advice and keep your damn infernal mouth shut about that little affair, and not try to find out who done it, or to help anyone else find out, for if you do you will surely share as bad and probably a worse fate than [the Chinese] did."[81]

On the nights following the Lemm ranch murders, fires were set in Old and New Chinatown, but the Chinese maintained a rotating guard and quickly extinguished them. Threats to white employers escalated: a housewife, Mrs. Jones, received this anonymous note: "Madame, Have the kindness to discharge your Chinese help within the next two weeks and save trouble." A note to the Union Hotel read, "Sirs: If you would consult your interest, get rid of your Chinese help—all of them—and save your property from the red glare of night."[82] Late on the night of April 8, a notice addressed "To the Public" was nailed to the shutters of a shop in Chico:

> The devil dreeme on the Chinese question. There are three or four men in this city has been making dam fools of themselves in regard

to the damed Chinese that will get anufe of it before the firt of August. You must remember it seldom rains here after the firt of June, and when everything is dry a match will burn without sacks of straw or karseen either, and we will also give the farmers of this country notice to look out this season for everi grain. Every mans ranch reaped or stacked by the Chinaman is liable to tak fire from the Heat of the sack or the spark from the smoke sack. It looks bad to do such work but if our state oficers done do something in pertection of the poore we will half to carry it out ourselves and it will be in a ruff manner.

Signed T. O. Mugins.[83]

In late April the *Chico Enterprise* warned readers against eating fruit or vegetables picked by Chinese farmworkers, claiming they were contaminated with leprosy and diphtheria from being fertilized with Chinese excrement.[84] That summer an Indian was arrested for the murder of a Chinese man, and his defense was that "white people did not like the Chinese; and that if he was killed nobody would care."[85]

The Chinese in Butte County would not be cowed. They telegraphed San Francisco for ten Winchester rifles. Chinese workers at Rancho Chico borrowed weapons from Bidwell, who stood by his refusal to fire them, even after his carpentry shop burned to the ground. "If I had discharged them it would have been interpreted as fear on my part," he later recalled.[86] He mailed copies of the violent bylaws of the Supreme Order of the Caucasians to newspapers throughout the state, asking them to publish the document "to show what men could do."[87]

The case against the murderers and arsonists finally broke when a postal worker identified the handwriting of the threatening notes and shamed the elected officials of Butte County into making an arrest. After two days in jail, Fred Conway confessed to the Lemm murders and disclosed the names of his comrades. His companions, however, had gone into hiding in the forests. Riding across two hundred miles of rugged land, two constables arrested twenty-nine men for the fires in Butte County and for the murders at Lemm ranch.

By the end of March, Chico's three jail cells were jammed with the vigilantes, including Jethro Swain, the former constable. When the Order of

Caucasians vowed to kill any man who "talked," the jail keeper threw its leaders into isolated cells. One by one the prisoners confessed and implicated others. Eugene Roberts admitted that he had splattered oil into the eyes of one of the Chinese men, remarking, "Hell, he won't know anything about kerosene in ten minutes more," and adding, "Dead men tell no tales."[88] It was Roberts who had ordered each of his companions to shoot point-blank into the faces of the Chinese men at the Lemm ranch. As more arrests followed, the Order quickly denied responsibility for the murders and disassociated itself from the accused men.[89]

The trials were to be held in Oroville, the county seat, and hundreds of Chinese from across the county gathered to see the murderers, heavily chained, thrust into prison. Yet even as the arrests mounted and the trials neared, night riders torched more farms and stables where Chinese were still employed.

In April a grand jury rapidly dismissed the charges against most members of the Order of the Caucasians. In late spring, four men pleaded guilty to the murders at the Lemm ranch, and Fred Conway was tried and found guilty. Conway, declared Judge Warren Sexton, on the bench since the gold rush, "may be of infirm judgment and perhaps rather weak minded and therefore be easily led astray by bad and designing men." Despite the chilling confessions, Sexton remarked, "I must say I have some feeling for them that I would not have in some other cases." Rather than ordering the murderers to hang, he sentenced them to twelve to twenty-five years in San Quentin Prison.

In May, prosecutors won arson verdicts against six more men, but despite multiple identifications, no charges were filed against eight others.[90] The Order of the Caucasians' "Council of Nine," who instigated the fires and murders, were never charged. In 1881, just four years after the Lemm ranch massacre, the Order and the local Democratic Party jointly sent hundreds of petitions to Governor George Perkins demanding pardons for the men imprisoned at San Quentin. Perkins, a former businessman from Butte County, shortened their sentences to time served and released them all.

The convictions did not stop the murders, fires, and threats in Butte but were in fact a prelude to the violent purges that roared through the county and nearby areas over the next few years.[91] In June, Bidwell's soap factory was torched, and in November a large barn on his ranch burned to the ground. The next year, 1878, a county convention voted to exclude all Chinese from Butte County, and in November 1878, when the ten-acre Sierra Lumber Plant refused to dismiss its Chinese workers, it was again set on fire.[92] The flames could be seen as far away as Redding, forty miles across the mountains, where a vicious Chinese roundup would soon follow. In April 1879, white miners on Little Butte Creek murdered two Chinese miners, claiming that the Chinese had drawn pistols on them as they sought to collect six dollars for "water rights."

Still the Chinese would not be forced from Butte County. Twenty miles south of Chico, the Chinese community of Oroville, a fertile farming center, likely had the second-largest Chinese population in the county. Today one remarkable temple still holds separate chambers for Taoist, Buddhist, and Confucian worship. Three years after the massacre and the firestorms, the Chinese still represented nearly 20 percent of the county's population.[93] In 1880 at least sixteen Chinese communities dotted Butte County, with hundreds more Chinese men "living out"—mining in small diggings, working on the Southern Pacific Railroad, and raising vegetables and berries along the floodplains of the Feather River.

When Chico's Old Chinatown burned to the ground in 1880, it was quickly rebuilt, this time in brick. In 1895 New Chinatown sprang up, just a few blocks from where the fires of the 1870s had burned.

URBAN WARFARE

In May 1867 the workingmen of San Francisco held a convention to join the movement for an eight-hour day. In California, this national cry was framed as an attack on the Chinese, who worked long hours in laundries and in shoe and cigar factories. Early unions, such as the Knights of Saint Crispin and the Mechanics' State Council, worked with the Democratic Party to pressure San Francisco to pass anti-Chinese ordinances and make it difficult for the Chinese to earn a living, attend school, or find housing.[94] Hauntingly similar to the Black Codes of the South, ordinances that originated in San Francisco infected fishing, farming, and lumber towns across the Northwest.

The 1870 San Francisco Cubic Air Ordinance required each adult to have at least five hundred cubic feet of living space or pay a fine ranging from ten to five hundred dollars. In effect, the ordinance made it illegal to be poor and Chinese.[95] Under the code, in May 1873 the San Francisco police charged into tenements in Chinatown and made mass arrests, hauling a hundred Chinese men to jail and filling the county prison. Many Chinese refused to pay the fines and announced that they would crowd the jail rather than fill the city's coffers—turning the codes into an ironic form of mass civil disobedience.

To frighten the Chinese, in 1873 San Francisco adopted the Queue Ordinance, which allowed prison wardens to shave the heads or cut off the long braids of Chinese prisoners. Convicted under the Cubic Air Ordinance, Ho Ah Kow had refused to pay a ten-dollar fine and was sentenced to five days in jail. When the warden cut off his queue and shaved his head, Ho sued for damages for trespass to his person. Judges Lorenzo Sawyer and Stephen Field ruled in Ho's favor, stating that the Queue Ordinance was unconstitutional under the Fourteenth Amendment because the board of supervisors had imposed "a degrading and cruel punishment upon a class of persons who are . . . entitled to the equal protection of the Law."[96]

The Sidewalk Ordinance of 1870 banned the Chinese from carrying vegetables and laundry in baskets hanging from shoulder poles.[97] Laundry ordinances outlawed washhouses in wooden buildings—at a time when most dwellings and stores in timber-rich California were made of wood. San Francisco also taxed the Chinese fifteen dollars per month if laundry was delivered by hand rather than on horseback. Under the Cemetery Ordinance of 1873, the Chinese could not disinter a corpse in order to have the bones shipped to China for a traditional burial in their home village.

Following the antimiscegenation laws of the South in 1880, California's Civil Code was amended to prohibit marriage between a white person and a "Negro, Mulatto, or Mongolian."[98]

Influenced by the strategic retreat from Reconstruction, cities, county boards, and town councils segregated schools and cemeteries. The California School Law of 1860 barred "Mongolians and Negroes" from public schools, although in 1871 the state conceded that African American children could attend regular schools if local whites did not object; otherwise, if there were ten or more black children, the state would provide separate schools.[99] In 1871, Chinese parents sought to work with the Negro Educational Convention to seek integrated schools, but black delegates argued that a coalition would defeat their own campaign for public schooling. Not until the groundbreaking lawsuit *Tape* v. *Hurley* of 1885 did the doors of public education open to Chinese children in California, but even this ruling gave towns the option of starting separate schools for Asian students—foretelling the "separate-but-equal" doctrine of 1896's *Plessy* v. *Ferguson.*[100]

The Democratic Party's conquest of California began in 1867 with an anti-black-suffrage plank and secured its power through the militancy of the new unions and labor clubs that arose throughout the country following the bank failures and depression of 1873. In 1874 the New York City police attacked a march of thousands of unemployed workers in the Tompkins Square riot. In late 1877 and 1878, twenty Irish immigrants and union coal miners, "the Molly Maguires," were hanged by the state of Pennsylvania, charged by Pinkerton spies during a strike in the coalfields. Within a month of their executions, a railroad strike began in West Virginia and set off the Great Labor Uprising of 1877, when workers from coast to coast launched a general strike. One hundred strikers were killed by the U.S. military, company spies, and vigilante militias.

The political parties quickly understood the power of the new unions. The Democratic convention in 1876 (the peak year of Chinese immigration) vowed to overturn the Burlingame Treaty because it had "exposed our brethren of the Pacific Coast to the incursions of a race not sprung from the same great parent stock." The Republican convention also adopted a "Mongolian plank" to oppose Chinese immigration, its first explicit discrimination clause, and endorsed a motion from the California delegation that its image as the "party of equality" had become a political liability.[101]

In 1876, a joint congressional committee settled into San Francisco's Palace Hotel for a summer by the bay, to investigate "the character, extent, and effect of Chinese immigration."[102] Police officers, diplomats, clergy, doctors, and anti-Chinese leaders led the witness list for the hearings. Frank Pixley, former California state attorney general and a leader of the Anti-Coolie Union, testified that he longed to stand on Telegraph Hill and watch Chinese hang from the yardarms of burning immigrant ships entering San Francisco Bay.[103]

The final report of the congressional "investigation," *Chinese Immigration: Its Social, Moral, and Political Effect,* found that California's concerns about immorality, prostitution, and unemployment all stemmed from Chinese immigrants. The testimony exposed how middle-class anxieties over rising working-class militancy melded with white workers' rage at the Chinese:

"Is it not possible that free white labor, unable to compete with these foreign serfs, and perceiving its condition becoming slowly but inevitably more hopelessly abject, may unite in all the horrors of riot and insurrection, and defying the civil power, extirpate with fire and sword those who rob them of their bread, yet yield no tribute to the State?" Ten thousand copies of the report were distributed to members of Congress, state governors, and newspapers and foretold how the "fire and sword" would be hurled at the Chinese.[104]

With the official support of the Democratic Party, white mobs began to terrorize San Francisco's black, Indian, and Chinese residents. In February 1877, a crowd of four hundred white laborers attacked Chinese construction workers living in company barracks, wounding a dozen men.[105] On the evening of July 23, the Anti-Coolie Club broke in to a mass meeting of unemployed miners, farmhands, mechanics, and shopkeepers who had gathered in front of city hall to express sympathy for the Great Railroad Strike. Led by a marching band, the club members pushed their way to the front of the rally and demanded that it denounce the Chinese. When the crowd refused, the infuriated anti-coolie men marched to Chinatown and began to set blocks of buildings ablaze.

The next day, six thousand men joined a "merchants' militia" to attack the Chinese. When mob leader William Coleman heard that federal authorities had lent the San Francisco police seventeen hundred rifles from the arsenal at Benicia across the bay, he armed his men with hickory pick handles. On the evening of July 25, the Pick Handle riots began as the mob tried to burn the docks of the Pacific Mail Steamship Company, the largest carrier of Chinese immigrants. In Oakland, Mayor George Pardee armed volunteers to protect the Central Pacific Railroad and the jute mills, which had refused to dismiss their Chinese employees.[106]

Assaults and looting in Chinatown marked the last days of July. By early autumn, thousands of unemployed men had formed a workers' political party to purge the Chinese. Denis Kearney, a young Irish American and a member of the "pick handle brigade," emerged as its leader and began his infamous outdoor "sandlot" meetings on vacant lots across from city hall and outside the Nob Hill mansions of such wealthy landholders as Charles Crocker, Leland Stanford, and Mark Hopkins. Kearney understood how to turn rage about unemployment, the price of food, and the huge land grants to the railroads against the Chinese: "When the Chinese question is settled, we can discuss whether it would be better to hang, shoot, or cut the capitalists to pieces. In six months we will have 50,000 men ready to go out . . . and if 'John' don't leave here, we will drive him and his aborts into the sea. . . . We are ready to do it. . . . If the ballot fails, we are ready to use the bullet."[107] He urged his followers to abandon the two-party system and instead form an armed militia.

Kearney warned railroad owners that they had three months to fire all their Chinese employees or "remember Judge Lynch," and he pressed the Pacific Mail Steamship Company to dismiss all Chinese sailors on its Australian and Panama lines.[108] He ended his speeches with the phrase that became the tag line for the roundup movement: "The Chinese must go."

Within days of the July riot, Chinese merchants sued San Francisco's Board of Supervisors for damages. Among his claims for damages, Wong Gow sued the city for the costs of expensive bedsheets of wealthy San Franciscans that were in his laundry during the fires.[109]

In October, as the representative of the Draymen and Teamsters, Kearney launched the Workingmen's Party of California. Just two years later,

"The Chinese Agitation in San Francisco—A Meeting of the Workingmen's Party on the Sand Lots"

FROM A SKETCH BY H. A. RODGERS, *FRANK LESLIE'S ILLUSTRATED NEWSPAPER*, MARCH 20, 1880 the new party managed to rewrite local anti-Chinese codes into the second California constitution. In twenty-two short articles, the new constitution provided that no state, county, municipality, or corporation could employ Chinese, that the presence of foreigners who were "ineligible to become citizens" was dangerous to the well-being of the state, and that "no native of China, no idiot, no insane person, or person convicted of any infamous crime shall ever exercise the privileges of an elector in this state."[110]

Statewide, the vote for the new constitution tallied 78,959 in favor and 67,134 opposed.[111] Because the Workingmen's Party also sought to exclude blacks from industrial and mechanists' jobs, most African Americans opposed the new constitution.[112] Immediately the Chinese consul initiated a series of lawsuits against its provisions. The bans against municipalities and corporations hiring Chinese workers were quickly ruled unconstitutional in *In re Tiburcio Parrott.*[113] Nonetheless, Chinese residents remained ineligible for U.S. citizenship until 1943, when Congress finally removed the barriers to immigration and naturalization.[114]

AFRICAN AMERICANS AND THE CHINESE

Some African Americans, familiar with the racial brutality facing the Chinese, attacked the anti-Chinese codes. The African American *Trenton Sentinel* declared the codes a "disgrace to free America and a sop thrown to the barbarous, unchristian prejudice of hoodlums."[115] When disagreements about the Chinese erupted at the National Labor Convention of Colored Men held in December 1869 in Washington, D.C., California delegate W. H. Hall called for an end to enslaved "coolie importation." Other delegates began to invite the Chinese into black labor organizations. *The Christian Recorder* warned that whites who persecute those with yellow skin would just as easily attack those with black skin.[116]

Yet despite the recognition that whites oppressed both groups, African Americans in the postbellum era were forging a new relation to American nationhood and could themselves participate in discriminating against the Chinese. The black press frequently reenforced stereotypes of the "yellow peril," at times describing the Chinese as "filthy, immoral and licentious—

according to our notions of such things" and expressing disgust for the "grotesque appearance" of the Chinese, whose shaved heads, remarked one paper, resembled "pig tail tobacco."[117]

When California and Nevada established separate schools for Chinese, black, and Indian children, many African Americans objected to their children being educated alongside the "idolatrous heathens." Only when Chinese children learned English and abandoned their "pagan . . . customs and opinions," wrote black Californian W. H. Stephenson to the San Francisco *Examiner,* would he welcome them as "true Californians."[118]

Philip Bell, editor of the African American *Elevator,* urged his San Francisco readers to avoid Kearney's forces, ambivalently conceding that the "vices" of the Chinese "do not justify the whites in oppressing them." Bell wrote that blacks and Chinese faced similar intimidation and he described the shared pressures facing Chinese washermen and black women who took in laundry. Eventually, although Bell opposed the special taxes on washhouses, he recommended a "burdensome tax" on all foreigners and urged blacks to "instruct our tax collectors to discriminate and collect only from the offensive [Chinese] element."[119]

In an effort to establish their own legitimacy as American citizens, many African Americans juxtaposed their new civic status with the stereotype of the Chinese as short-term residents or sojourners. The "Orientals," claimed one black newspaper, would be "less odious and onerous" if they came "with the intention of remaining."[120] Bell concluded that Chinese "habits, customs, modes of living, manner of worship (faith or religion it cannot be called) are all at variance with our ideas."[121] Unlike the Chinese, he said, African Americans deserved the rights of full citizenship, for the black man was "a native American, loyal to the Government, and a lover of his country and her institutions—American in all his ideas; [and] a Christian by education."[122]

To many African Americans, their new freedom seemed vulnerable. In California, where they were banned from white unions such as the San Francisco Typographical Union, African Americans feared for their jobs. In 1869, turning to the vocabulary of slavery, William Hall, a black leader in the Bay Area, denounced the Chinese for the effect "which coolie labor is exercising against poor white and black men."[123] Bell believed that the presence of the Chinese would further reduce blacks' wages, and he asked readers of *The Elevator* to boycott San Francisco businesses that hired Chinese workers: "Let our citizens agree not to employ the Chinese nor purchase goods from them." He urged African Americans to vote only for public officials who would deal with this "thorn in the flesh . . . which must sooner or later fester."[124]

Thus, through the era's vocabulary of nationhood, patriotism, and Christianity, many African Americans distanced themselves from the Chinese, whom they saw as potential pawns in a plan to re-enslave freedmen. Not until the immigration debates of the 1880s would African American leaders assert that degrading the Chinese would not enhance their own opportunities.[125]

A CHINESE MASSACRE

In 1877 President Hayes withdrew federal troops from the South, removing the last forceful protection for former slaves. That same year, the young union movement, picking up momentum from the Great Railroad Strike, took the "Kearney Riots" across the Bay Area and into rural towns.[126] The Workingmen's Party did the dirty work for the Democrats, who gained control of the statehouse, townships, and county councils. The ideology of race and the violent tactics that had destroyed Reconstruction in the South rolled through northern California.

In many towns a ban on owning land made the Chinese, like blacks, particularly vulnerable to expulsion. In the drought-stricken fall of 1877, for example, the citizens in Isleton, along the Sacramento River, vowed to neither lease land to the Chinese nor hire them on ranches, leaving them with fewer and fewer places to farm.[127] Along the dry riverbeds and delta land, anti-Chinese organizations threatened to firebomb farmers who did not evict the thousands of Chinese vegetable growers.

Here the attorney Frederick Bee first enters the history of Chinese Americans. In 1877, on behalf of every Chinese resident who was driven out, he filed suit against Placer County for the destruction of property as well as for business and personal losses caused by the "enforced exodus." Colonel Fred Bee was a forty-niner and merchant in Placerville, a founder of the Overland Telegraph Line, a road builder, a creator of the Pony Express, and one of the few attorneys willing to represent the Chinese in the San Francisco congressional hearings of 1877. He was later appointed Chi-

Chinese Consul Fred Bee

nese consul at San Francisco, first for a three-year term, starting in 1879, and at least twice thereafter. Bee took bold and prompt action following the Chinese massacres of the 1880s, traveling by train, horse, and riverboat to Chico, Denver, and Rock Springs, Wyoming, demanding punishment of vigilantes and mayors alike and creating unique indemnity claims for the violation of international treaties.[128]

Although the poorest of the poor, the Chinese bore the blame for the era's widespread hunger and homelessness. Hearing the threats that farmers who honored their leases with Chinese tenants could expect "the burning of their property," Bee sent a series of letters to Bay Area newspapers asserting that the eviction of Chinese tenant farmers meant less food for the hungry city. In Napa, Sonoma, San Joaquin, and Merced Counties, vigilantes were burning houses and barns leased to Chinese farmers, forcing them to flee, while San Francisco was turning into a city of starving indigents while tons of unpicked fruit rotted on the trees.

Even in a city surrounded by water, fish was becoming expensive as along the coast and in towns up and down the Sacramento River Delta anti-Chinese clubs pushed through codes that targeted Chinese fishermen.

Italian fishermen, hoping to monopolize the shrimp trade, forced the sheriff of Alameda County to arrest forty Chinese shrimpers for using illegal nets. Newspapers reported that other Italian fishermen were seen cutting the nets of Chinese shrimpers, not only limiting their catch but raising the price of fish.

Racial stereotypes began to reflect the desperate economic realities of the decade. The myth of the docile Chinese coolie, readily enslaved and easily purged, gave way to the myth of the scheming ogre, rather like the shifting stereotype of the African American, who morphed from the compliant, happy-go-lucky slave to soulless "beast" after the Civil War.[129]

The danger of the popular image of the evil and wily Chinaman became evident in the small railroad town of Rocklin in the Sacramento Valley, where a stable if segregated relationship between whites and Chinese came to a dramatic end. On September 15, 1877, the body of a white woman was found at a ranch house at Secret Ravine, two miles from the edge of town. The woman, the wife of the ranch foreman, had been bludgeoned with an axe and felled by two bullets. Outside the house lay the body of her husband, riddled with bullet holes. The ranch owner, H. N. Sargent, was discovered nearby, shot through the back, head, and shoulder. Barely conscious, Sargent accused two or three Chinese men who had, quite publicly, come to the ranch to buy a mining claim. Police officers from Rocklin and nearby Roseville arrived at the murder scene and then followed the "traces of Chinese shoes" through the woods, where they arrested ten Chinese miners at their cabins, about 150 yards from where Sargent lay. The evidence against them was thin: the Chinese men were armed with pistols, as were most miners and ranchers, and had "quite a sum of money," which, it was alleged, came from a broken trunk on the ranch. The police took the terrified Chinese men back to Rocklin and arrested them as an angry crowd gathered outside the jail, threatening to lynch them before dawn. Sargent died later that night.

The next morning, while the police began to collect evidence, the mob notified the Chinese residents of Rocklin that they had until 6 P.M. to leave; "those that remained would be driven out." Most of Rocklin's four hundred Chinese had come to the United States in the late 1860s at the invitation of Charles Crocker to work on the Central Pacific Railroad and for the last eight years had lived in the foothill town, working for the hand laundry or for nearby ranches, or growing vegetables in China Gardens, the flatlands on the edge of town. By four o'clock that afternoon, "burdened by their luggage," all of the Chinese in Rocklin filed out of town on foot.

As soon as the deadline passed, a gang marched into the Chinese quarter and demolished twenty-five houses with axes and awls. A flying timber rekindled the fire in a boardinghouse stove, and within a few minutes Chinatown was an inferno. Every shop and house burned to the ground, although the neighboring railroad property was fortuitously saved by Rocklin's water pump.[130]

Despite the verdict of the mob, the police were stymied by the murders at the Sargent ranch. When they announced that they had no "sure and conclusive" evidence against any of their Chinese prisoners, an angry white crowd gathered outside the prison. Fearing that his prisoners might be lynched, the sheriff loaded them on the eastbound express to Auburn, where he could safely hold them in the Placer County jail. As the Chinese men waited for the train to pull out, the mob voted to lynch them and rushed onto the railroad cars shouting, "Have them out!" and "Hang them!" The conductor and the police officers managed to throw the vigilantes off the train, and it finally left the station. When the coroner's jury announced charges against only two of the prisoners, an irate gang rushed through Rocklin, torching what was left of Chinatown.

Three days after the Rocklin purge, the Chinese announced that they would "seek the reparation that they feel sure of securing through the medium of the Courts."[131] Many Chinese either owned or leased considerable land or mining claims within a ten-mile radius of Rocklin, and most of their loans had been fully paid off. The roundup, they declared, was a plan by whites to regain their former property.

The Chinese sought to vindicate their community by discovering the true murderers. On September 18, Bee wired Governor William Irwin, a Democrat, demanding protection for the Chinese, then sent copies of his message to newspapers throughout the state. "I sincerely regret the necessity of calling your attention to the lawlessness and mob violence, now, and for several days past taking place in the immediate vicinity of the State Capital, in the adjoining county of Placer," he wrote. "I fail to notice that the authorities of that county have as yet made any attempt to suppress the armed bodies of men, engaged in driving out, and burning the property of Chinese residents."[132]

Bee reminded the governor of the Chinese rights to safety under the

Burlingame Treaty, adding, "I have no desire to point out your plain duty. You have abundant precedent . . . whereby the state and national authorities have put down mob violence. The Chinaman who has come here under solemn treaty obligations has a right to demand that his life and his property shall be protected the same as that of citizens of the most favored nation."

The next day, Irwin offered a slim six-hundred-dollar reward for the arrest and conviction of the murderers but complained that Bee's "injudicious" publicity had "exaggerat[ed] in the minds of non spectators the amount of disorder which had been caused by the atrocious murders." Irwin still blamed the ranch murders on the Chinese and chastised Bee for creating "an intense excitement in a community already embittered against the race." Nonetheless, Bee demanded that the Rocklin sheriff arrest twenty-eight rioters who had been clearly identified by the Chinese.

The sheriff made no arrests, and the murderers at Sargent's ranch were never caught. Many in the Chinese community believed that it was Sargent's teamster, who disappeared the day of the murder, who had committed the crime. Others accused Chinese gang members or "highbinders" who had been forced out of San Francisco by Chinese merchants frustrated that the city police refused to protect Chinatown. The Chinese never returned to Rocklin, and by 1879 the town was boasting that "no Chinaman can rent a house or obtain employment in the town."[133] Three years later, Thompson and West's popular guidebook, *The History and Directory of Placer County,* bragged, "Not a Chinaman is to be found at Rocklin."[134]

News of the violent purge and the fire at Rocklin quickly spread through the towns of the Sacramento Valley and along the Sacramento River Delta. The next day, the town of Penryn elected a Committee of Three to order the local Chinese out by six o'clock. That evening Penryn "was cleared." And that same day a citizens committee in Roseville, a railroad town surrounded by farms and ranches, gave the Chinese until ten the next morning to go. The following day ten armed men rode into Chinese camps strung along the main Auburn road and ordered sixty Chinese miners to leave the area before midnight "under penalty of death." Once darkness fell across the Sierra foothills, one hundred armed men rode through the forests searching for other Chinese, but all their woodcutting and mining camps had been abandoned. The villages of Pino and Loomis soon followed suit.

During the early fall of 1877, Chinese purges spread along the mountain passes. In Grass Valley, a town on the stage road between the Bay Area and Nevada, fire bells sounded late on the night of September 20, and the townspeople rushed from their homes to discover that Chinatown was in flames. Within half an hour its thirty Chinese dwellings were destroyed. Yet in the opinion of the white residents, the night had been saved. Local firemen "worked nobly, thereby preventing the destruction of property within a few feet of the edge of Chinatown," and the *San Francisco Chronicle* reported that "fortunately . . . nothing but Chinese tenements were destroyed, which numbered forty or so." More than twenty thousand dollars' worth of Chinese property had been ruined, none covered by insurance.[135] The next month fires destroyed the Chinatowns in Walnut Grove and Dutch Flat, Chinese leases were canceled in the foothill towns of the Sierra mountains, and mine owners at Gold Run fired all their Chinese employees.[136]

Fearing that Bee's publicity of the "illegal proceedings" might delay new legislation banning Chinese immigration, Irwin launched his own campaign. He claimed that "all the mischief" in Placer County was done before the authorities could intervene.[137] James McCormick, the Placer County sheriff, wired the governor that he had "seen no one driving Chinamen out of my county. Have been thus far able to protect them, and think I can do so. The excitement is quieting down." The *San Francisco Daily Examiner* reported that the Chinese were not in fact driven out of Rocklin but had "stampeded from near the scene of the murders."[138]

With immigration law and foreign treaties solely the province of Congress and the president, California's elected officials turned toward Washington, D.C. The Workingmen's Party, the Democrats, and the California governor all understood that the Chinese had found cover in a set of legal protections from Reconstruction. The Burlingame Treaty, the Civil Rights Act of 1870, the Enforcement Acts, the Ku Klux Klan Act, and the Fourteenth Amendment's due-process protections were all raised against the vigilantes and the local towns who tolerated the violence or enacted bizarre codes targeted at Chinese immigrants.

Governor Irwin declared that "the illegal proceedings" (the expulsions and the destruction of Chinatowns) were "deeply to be regretted, as they might tend to prejudice the Eastern people against the state in the settlement of the Chinese immigration question." Editorials suddenly condemned Bee for giving the impression that California officials were "calmly looking on while the Chinamen are being trodden in the dust."[139] The *Examiner* wrote that Bee's public protest to the governor was a dangerous act "of unmitigated impertinence" that might excite ridicule "on this Coast," but "in the East and abroad, where the Chinese problem is not understood, and a false sentimentalism prevails in their behalf to the prejudice of our people, his dispatch will be construed to add weight to the belief that the right is all on the side of the Chinese. . . . In this respect it will work injury to our State."[140]

Meanwhile, hundreds of Chinese refugees fleeing towns across the Sierra foothills and along the Sacramento Delta had converged in a guarded camp at the edge of Folsom. On September 21, 1877, vigilantes rode through the hot and barren refugee camp, fired directly into the tents and shelters, and threatened to drown any Chinese person found leaving the makeshift village.[141]

The Chinese were not allowed to return to Rocklin or Roseville, but they did remain elsewhere in Placer County. The 1880 census listed the population of Placer County as 7,125 white males, 4,923 white females, 1,843 Chinese, 235 colored, and 100 Indians. Thirteen percent of Placer County was still Chinese.

The 1870s began with the lynching of sixteen Chinese men and one Chinese woman in Los Angeles and ended with a sweep of ethnic cleansing across the landscape of the West. Politicians in the growing cities and small towns along the Pacific coast, in the hot and fertile Sacramento Valley, and in the old gold rush towns of the Sierra Nevada, seized upon the era's enthusiasm for racial violence: the Ku Klux Klan assaulted blacks in the South, the military and volunteer militias drove tribal people off their lands, murdering thousands, and the Order of the Caucasians, the Workingmen's Party, and the Democratic Party rounded up and expelled the Chinese in California, burning Chinatowns to the ground. In 1877, U.S. troops surprised a sleeping Nez Percé village on the Big Hole River in Montana, killing eighty Indians, two thirds of whom were women and children. In 1879 in Crio Canyon, Texas, white residents posted warnings for all Mexicans to leave the area within three days or face violent reprisals.[142]

By 1880 southern Democrats controlled the U.S. House of Representatives and the Supreme Court. In California over 80 percent of voters supported the Democratic Party, which promised to finish the purge of the Chinese from the state.[143]

On September 20, 1877, within five days of the murders at Rocklin, the *Daily Alta California* wrote, "Whether by accident or otherwise, the 'China-towns' in our mountain cities appear to be fading away before the flames and John himself is seen in his blue blouse trudging off for still waters and safer quarters."[144]

3

THE WOMAN'S TALE

"IN CASE I SHOULD BE KIDNAPPED"

PURGING THE BODY POLITIC

On Sunday, April 30, 1876, a doctor in Antioch, a small town near the confluence of the Sacramento and San Joaquin Rivers, announced that seven young "sons of respectable citizens" were under his treatment after visiting a Chinese house of prostitution.[1] When parents heard that their boys had syphilis, they quickly gathered a group of about forty town residents, divided into teams of five, and marched to Chinatown, which was built on the edge of town by the docks.

The enraged parents pounded on the doors of each of the brothels—the "Chinese dens" or "green mansions"—and warned the Chinese women to leave town by three o'clock that afternoon "or trouble would ensue." The women tied up their clothing and bedding in scarves or shawls and stuffed whatever they could into baskets. With their few belongings swinging from heavy shoulder poles, they trudged to the pier.

As the mob grew, rather than wait for the next steamer bound for San Francisco, the women climbed into a fishing boat and set sail down the San Joaquin River toward Stockton. Also onboard was the local Chinese contractor, probably the pimp or the owner of several of the women. As the

Chinese girl prostitute locked in San Francisco "crib"

laden boat pulled out, the townspeople of Antioch watched from the dock, grimly pleased.

Despite the town's rage it is likely that many of the Chinese women desperately wanted to remain in Antioch. Like other Chinese prostitutes in western rural towns, many had fled from slavery in San Francisco to the river town, forty miles to the northeast. If they were shipped to San Francisco, they faced a return to sexual slavery.[2]

On that bleak Sunday afternoon, the white parents forced only the Chinese women out of town; the Chinese men, mostly gardeners, fishermen, and launderers, were, for the moment, allowed to remain. The residents decided not to "disturb the serenity of the Sabbath" until church was over. But that night the town congratulated itself on driving out the prostitutes "in a dignified manner."

The next afternoon, word flew through the town that the Chinese women had returned. By eight o'clock that evening, Chinatown was on fire. The new fire department ignored the blaze and refused "to stay the progress of the fire fiend."[3] Although Antioch's Chinatown was a jagged row of wooden shacks, it probably could have been saved, as the segregated quarters had been built along the river at Smith's Landing and were connected to the water through narrow tunnels. But as the town watched, all but two buildings collapsed. Terror-stricken, most of the Chinese men fled into the night.

The next morning, volunteers demolished the last two buildings in Antioch's Chinatown. The remaining Chinese paid twenty-five cents each for a ticket and boarded the side-wheeler *Amador,* the next steamer bound for San Francisco. The local paper cheered, "Antioch is now free from this disreputable class."[4]

The purge of the women and the torching of Chinatown capped years of racial contempt in Antioch. Most of the Chinese had immigrated to Antioch from the Pearl River delta in China, in Guangdong Province. They were river people, skilled in building dirt levees against the floods and in farming marshlands and bottomlands. Passengers and freight to and from the Sacramento delta town traveled mainly by the water, and during the heyday of the paddle-wheel steamboats, Chinese passengers were required to stay below in the hold on the "China Deck"—the most dangerous place onboard. If the ship's boiler blew, a constant threat on riverboats, few Chinese passengers would survive. In October 1865 the boiler exploded on the steamship *Yosemite,* and of the 150 travelers drowned or burned to death, 100 were Chinese.[5]

Antioch expressed its contempt for its Chinese residents with codes geared toward segregation, harassment, and, ultimately, expulsion. To enforce segregation, Ordinance 33 imposed a one-hundred-dollar fine, an amount equal to two months' salary for most white men, on any person caught watching an opium smoker.[6] Chinese people could not own land, and a curfew required that they be off the streets by sunset. If a Chinese man violated the curfew, a town officer could cut off his queue.

Many Chinese men living along the delta fished, farmed, or worked at the factories that turned the heavy river clay into bricks. Within days of the April roundup and fire, vigilantes from Antioch attacked Chinese bricklayers in their cabins. When the sheriff ignored their pleas for help, the bricklayers fled and hired on at the nearby Somersville coal mines; the brick factories brought Navahos up from the Southwest to replace them.

The Antioch purge soon spread south to El Cerrito, where many Chinese men were fired from the Starr Flour Mill and from the Vigorite Powder Works at Point Isabel, where they produced dangerous explosives.[7] As news of the Kearney riots in San Francisco reached north into the delta towns, other Chinese working along the river prepared to flee. By 1877 all the Chinese at the Black Diamond coal mines were let go and forbidden to return, even as "washmen." That year fruit growers on the fertile delta mud islands and along the marsh banks of the Sacramento River met in the little town of Isleton and agreed "not to rent or lease land to Chinamen, nor hire them to perform labor upon our ranches."[8]

The eviction of prostitutes galvanized the movement to drive out rural Chinese by purging the women. In the early spring of 1886, during the Chinese roundups in Humboldt County, Sheriff Eugene Demming arrested Chinese women in the lumber town of Arcata and charged them with prostitution. With their bonds set at the exorbitant sum of five hundred dollars, they remained in prison until the trial.[9] On April 16 the women were shipped out of Arcata under Demming's guard. Newspaper coverage and legal documents end the women's story with their expulsion. But what happened to these enslaved women, whose status was so fragile? What became of the Chinese prostitutes forcibly driven from Truckee later that year?

The notion of impure Chinese bodies infecting the young white manhood of the United States provided a powerful physical metaphor for the "cleansing" that would take place. (The issue of the subsequent contagion to white wives was always patent and always repressed.) The Antioch roundup was also anchored in the assumption that Chinese women were slaves, bodily commodities who could be sold, moved, removed.

"THE IMPORTATION OF FEMALES IN BULK": THE PROSTITUTE TRADE

In the nineteenth century, brothels were often called "convents," "hotels," or "green mansions." In a short poem a Chinese prostitute in California decried her few choices:

> *A green mansion is a place of filth and shame*
> *Of lost chastity and lost virtue*
> *Most repulsive is it to kiss the customers on the lips*
> *And let them fondle every part of my body*
> *I hesitate, I resist;*
> *All the more ashamed, beyond words.*

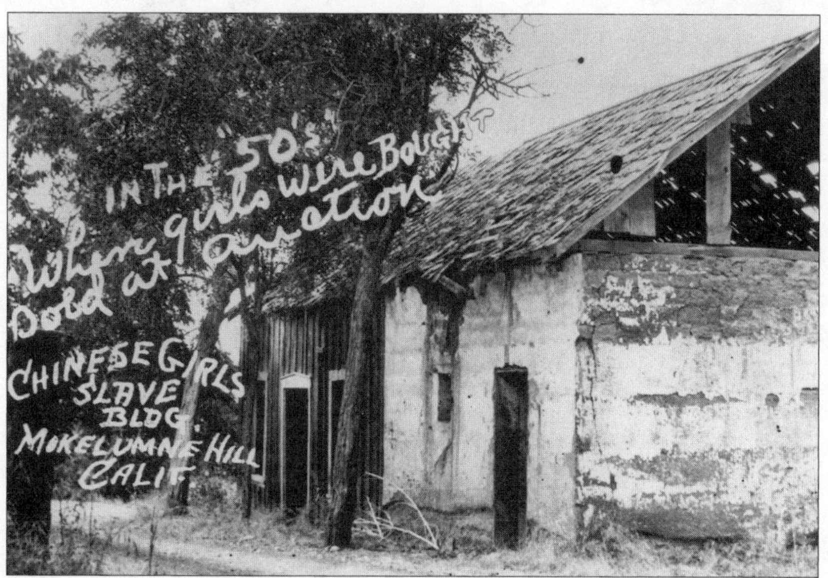

"Chinese Girls Slave Building." House of prostitution in Mokelumne Hill mining town

I must by all means leave this troupe of flowers and rouge;
Find a nice man and follow him as his woman.[10]

Chinese prostitutes shipped back to San Francisco would likely be returned to a street-level "crib," where kidnapped girls were often held, usually by a member of the Chinese Six Companies. Locked in cages or tiny chambers facing busy Jackson or Dupont Street, they were forced to solicit men who passed by; then their owners or madams would open the pen and draw a curtain while the girl serviced her customer, white or Chinese. Soon the city would move the cribs to back alleys, hidden from the view of downtown customers and merchants.

Generally, the top price for sex was seventy-five cents. A "lookee" cost between a dime and a quarter and was pitched to the popular belief that there were anatomical differences between Chinese and Caucasian women, in particular the myth that a Chinese woman's vaginal opening was horizontal rather than vertical.

In 1869 the *San Francisco Chronicle* called the growing trade in Chinese prostitutes "the importation of females in bulk," reporting that "each China steamer now brings consignments of women, destined to be placed in the markets."[11] Some Chinese girls arrived in heavily padded crates, billed as freight, and Chinese brokers bribed customs and immigration officials in San Francisco to let them enter. Others were sent by ship captains and then placed or sold by contractors. Some made their own way to rural towns by trains or wagons; others entered from Canada or disembarked in coastal towns, landing in hidden bays or coves up and down the Pacific coast. Often they followed the routes of Chinese men.[12] In response to demands for prostitutes from Chinese miners and vegetable growers, brokers sent many Chinese women into interior mining and lumber towns under the guard of special agents. There the women were sold to the "trade" or to individual men at rates ranging from two hundred to five hundred dollars "per head."[13]

Most Chinese prostitutes in the American West had been in bondage since a young age, sometimes since infancy. Many were "go-away girls," female babies who were sold, abandoned, or fastened to the wall of the city of Chaozhou, a prefectural city twenty miles from the port of Shantou. There a newborn baby girl could be disposed of—deposited in a basket where anyone wishing to own a female child was at liberty to remove her and do with her as he liked.[14] Most Chinese prostitutes came through San Francisco, imported by criminal societies that by 1860 had taken control of the trade.[15] Brokers in China procured the girls, kidnapping them off the streets or purchasing them from destitute families and selling them at great profit in San Francisco. The enslaved children were brought to the United States by large syndicates that owned as many as eight hundred girls, ranging in age from two to sixteen.

Wealthy Chinese individuals, male and female, paid about eighty dollars to a broker for a girl in China, or between four hundred and a thousand dollars if they bought her in an organized slave sale in San Francisco, often in a designated cellar in Chinatown. After the Exclusion Act of 1882, a one-year-old girl cost a hundred dollars; a girl of fourteen—often termed a "daughter"—cost twelve hundred. The designation of "daughter" usually meant that the girl was part of the *mui tsai* or "little sister" system under which impoverished parents sold a young daughter into domestic service, usually stipulating that she be freed through a marriage when she turned eighteen. During her time as a bond servant, she earned no wages, was not free to leave her "employer," was usually overworked, often suffered physical abuse from her mistress, and was sexually available to her master or his son.

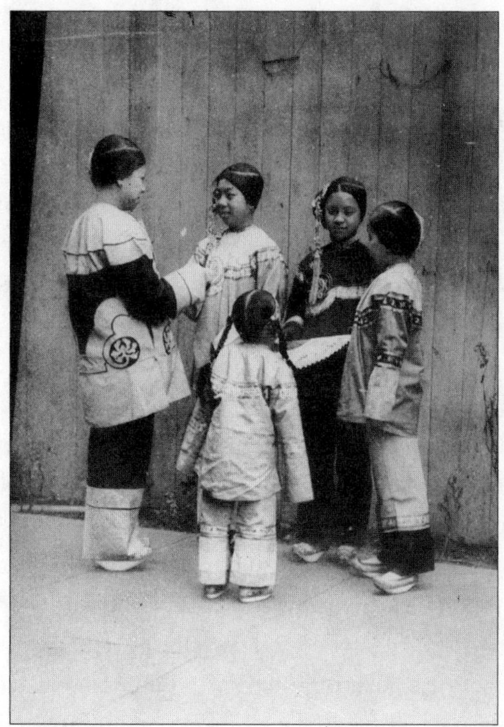

"Rescued Chinese Slave Girls" from San Francisco

To get around the Thirteenth Amendment and laws banning indentured contracts, buyers often paid the purchase money to the girl, who then turned it over to her new owner as she marked or signed a contract indenturing herself. In a typical contract a girl promised to "prostitute my body for the term of _____ years. If, in that time, I am sick one day, two weeks shall be added to my time; and if more than one day, my term of prostitution shall continue an additional month. But if I run away from the custody of my keeper, then I am to be held as a slave for life." Since sickness included periods of menstruation, the length of a prostitute's contract was inevitably extended indefinitely.[16] Despite the abolition of slavery, the sale of humans endured in the West.

In Eureka, 20 of the 220 Chinese residents who were purged from the town in 1885 were women. Their stories lie hidden in census tracts, court records, newspaper accounts, and the spoken memories of their descendants. We know that several women were launderers, three were merchant's wives, and only one was clearly married to a laborer, also a launderer.

"China Mary," a woman with no legal first or last name, resided in the county hospital, marked "with syphilis" in the census. Two Chinese women from Eureka were listed as "daughters," one a fourteen-year-old girl residing with a family from England, another a twenty-three-year-old.[17]

Although two separate laws prohibited Chinese women from disembarking until the California commissioner of immigration was satisfied that they had come "voluntarily" and were of "good character," these laws were easily evaded.[18] Ironically, by allowing the free flow of immigration between China and the United States, the Burlingame Treaty of 1868 increased the sale of Chinese girls and women. Occasionally local police forces boarded the ships before the Chinese women disembarked and sent them to asylums or mission homes that would find them jobs in domestic service. But most often the police turned a blind eye.

Estimates of the number of Chinese prostitutes in San Francisco in 1870 vary from about one thousand to sixteen hundred. The figures are uncertain because they depended on women's willingness to risk self-disclosure, the political goals of local census enumerators, the desire in the public imagination to eroticize the Chinese community, and a widespread intention among whites to downplay the number of Chinese families.

When Chinese women faced roundups, expulsions, and sale, many Chi-

Chinese prostitute from Eureka, California

nese men sought to claim them as wives before their deportation hearings could begin. Some Chinese women managed to run away.

CONTAGION AND IMPURITY

What began when one community purged its Chinese prostitutes quickly became an all-out rout. Chinese women, both desired and despised by whites, were thought to carry within them the power to taint the physical and moral purity of the nation. The infection of the children in Antioch evoked the era's fears of epidemics of diphtheria, tuberculosis, and cholera and raised concerns about the health, safety, and stability of a family.[19]

The belief that perhaps 90 percent of the Chinese prostitutes in San Francisco, for example, were at some time infected with venereal diseases encouraged towns up and down the coast to expel Chinese women or pass antiprostitution ordinances that had little to do with the ethics of trafficking in female slaves. Rather, the codes and the roundups often followed a civic investigation or newspaper account of young white boys, usually aged from ten to twelve, frequenting the "cribs" or brothels in rural Chinatowns. Generally it was the infection of white males, rather than the enslaved status of the Chinese women or the risk of contagion to white women or Chinese men, that prompted civic action.

The dangers of syphilis were indeed real throughout California, and the blame returned again and again to Chinese women. During the California State Senate investigations of Chinese immigration in 1876, a series of doctors testified to the prevalence of the disease among Chinese prostitutes and its impact on white society. The testimony of Dr. Hugh Huger Toland, a member of the San Francisco Board of Health, haunted the national press and the minds of thousands of white parents when he reported cases of a particularly virulent strain of syphilis in white boys as young as five who, he claimed, contracted the disease from Chinese prostitutes.[20]

The anti-Chinese forces had found a new and powerful rationale in medical language and concepts of racial contamination. By the mid-1870s, physicians were making dire claims about the inevitable transmission of syphilis from Chinese prostitutes to white males and, with quiet implication, to white wives, as though contagion flowed in only one direction. The pulpit, press, and medical profession declared that all Chinese women were one of "the most abject and satanic conception[s] of human slavery and the source of contamination and hereditary diseases."[21]

During the era when doctors were increasing their public authority, displacing midwives, homeopaths, and sham "healers," they knew that they could do little to cure contagious and killer diseases. Although it was well-known that syphilis was spread through sexual contact, the 1870s witnessed a quick retreat from medical certification of prostitutes, a Civil War practice intended to preserve the health of soldiers.[22] Many believed that these licenses bestowed state sanction on prostitution and encouraged sex outside of marriage.[23]

Viewed as racially disposed to immorality and "hygienic lassitude," the Chinese female was apparently more diseased than the rest of her community. These medical "diagnoses" increased her vulnerability and that of other local Chinese.[24] By shifting the terms of racial difference from skin color, eye shape, and height to medical pathology, physicians rewrote the science of contagion and thereby the "science" of race.

Without medical care, most prostitutes, white and Chinese, became ill after a short time. In many towns, if a Chinese prostitute was hopelessly diseased, she was cast into the streets or locked in a room with one cup of water and a bowl of rice, to die alone. Most died young.[25]

In the 1870s, syphilis pierced the geographic segregation of California cities and imbued Chinatown with eroticism and a titillating sense of danger. In calling for a racially homogenous America, journalists, clergy, and politicians linked the diseased body of the Chinese woman to the contaminated space of Chinatown, whose crowded streets and alleyways were allegedly more filthy and infected than the crowded streets and alleyways of white slums.

The stage for the Antioch purge had been set by the 1862 smallpox epidemics along the Pacific coast. While there were only sixty Chinese cases of smallpox out of more than sixteen hundred in San Francisco, the Committee to Investigate Chinatown blamed the epidemic on Chinatown itself—a "laboratory of infection—situated in the very heart of our city, distilling its deadly poison by day and by night, and sending it forth to contaminate the atmosphere of the streets and houses of a populous, wealthy and intelligent community." The committee concluded that "the Chinese cancer . . . [must] be cut out of the heart of our city, root and branch."[26]

The press and the pulpit used the smallpox epidemic as vivid evidence of the high levels of interracial contact; the Chinese could not be contained. Despite segregated housing and jobs, white and Chinese men and women interacted closely in rural towns in the West—at popular Chinese restaurants, through the sale of fish and vegetables, in the work of domestic servants, herbalists, seamstresses, shopkeepers, nannies, and launderers, in boardinghouses, at work sites such as lumber mills and railroads, through friendships, and in the sex trade.

MORAL CONTAGION

In an evangelical era, the presence of Chinese prostitutes confirmed the infidelity of married white men and their easy repudiation of Christian morality. Syphilis predicted the fate of the family and the fate of the familyless man in the West. To white women, Chinese prostitutes defiled the Christian ideal of chastity; to white men they represented the frontier promise of freedom from marriage. But syphilis visibly exposed the sexual double standard for men and women even as most medical discussions of the disease excluded its transmission between spouses.[27] Still, the cure was to round up and drive out Chinese women.

From 1854 to 1865 the San Francisco police aggressively drove the "crib prostitutes" from downtown thoroughfares into back alleys and demanded that screens be built to hide the "degradations and vice" from the view of white women and children who rode past on streetcars.[28] In 1865 the police chief urged public-health authorities to "herd" Chinese women to locations just outside of town where they would not "offend public decency." Subsequently, hundreds of Chinese prostitutes fled or were expelled from San Francisco.[29]

But in small rural towns the presence of Chinese prostitutes was harder to hide, as was the sexual promiscuity of white men. Their forced removal served as another model of cleansing an entire community of all Chinese women and men.

The authority that would question the sexual ethics of Victorian America was the medical profession. Following San Francisco's, small towns' ordinances calling for medical inspections of prostitutes forced a dilemma upon physicians: how to provide for safe illicit sex without seeming to validate Chinese prostitution. Radical organizations dedicated to women's rights condemned these police ordinances for singling out prostitutes—white or Chinese—for inspection while ignoring male clients who spread "contamination" as they enjoyed the "vice."

By the mid-1870s it was well-known that syphilis was transmitted sexually, but it was also thought to be hereditary. Physicians did little to lessen the idea that all Chinese bodies carried the disease and that their very presence could infect whites. In 1878, for instance, the *Medico-Literary Journal* warned that if Chinese servants were allowed to raise white children, or cook, clean, and launder in white homes, syphilis would spread from the inevitably afflicted Chinese body into the entire household.[30] Yet even in towns that had purged the Chinese, advertisements in popular newspapers for a "secret formula" for curing syphilis and other venereal diseases testified to how common it was in white prostitutes, who continued working their trade after their Chinese competition was sent away on ship, wagon, or foot, and in white men who had transmitted it to their wives.

By targeting sexual relations between Chinese prostitutes and white men, physicians, journalists, cartoonists, and politicians blamed Chinese women for the new forces challenging the ideal if illusory American home. As women left the farm and family to work outside the home, they initiated public demands for better pay, for a fifty-four-hour workweek, for sanitation, for the vote, and for job safety, exposing the myth of the protective cult of true womanhood. Emigration from Ireland and eastern Europe was bringing thousands of single men and women to industrializing America, as factory work and night shifts pulled both men and women from their homes. Millions of workers lived in tenement housing similar to the "Chinese dens" mocked in editorials and cartoons. The Victorian family was already teetering precariously in the West, where there was a large ratio of white men to white women and an even larger ratio of Chinese men to Chinese women.

The purge of the prostitutes in Antioch also played to fears about the seductive female body, fears intensified in rural California by the low numbers of white women in the Pacific Northwest. Many white women seized on the image of the diseased and enslaved Chinese prostitute to distinguish their own limited status and uphold an image of their own virtue.

Although some physicians included white girls in the circulation of infection, Chinese prostitutes became the counterpart to Chinese male workers—characterized by cheap labor and an immoral lifestyle. Indeed, white prostitution was the result of low wages accepted by Chinese laborers that forced factory girls and servants into unemployment, destitution, and worse.

CONTROLLING WOMEN

The task of vilifying Chinese women fell to ministers, of criminalizing them to town councils, of banishing them to police and to mobs, but the task of controlling their immigration fell to Congress. Between 1870 and 1874 the California legislature tried to criminalize the entry of "lewd and debauched" Asian women by threatening steamship companies with heavy fines for transporting unmarried women.[31] But only Congress, ruled the federal courts, had the authority to exclude the "pestilential immorality," and in 1875, at the urging of California, it passed the Page Act. The Page Act prohibited the immigration of any Chinese woman who was not a merchant's wife and any "Mongolian" woman who entered the country for the purpose of prostitution.[32]

Why target the Chinese women in the West when, in fact, there were so few? In 1855 only 2 percent of the Chinese population in the United States was female; by 1875, it was about 4 percent, or one Chinese woman for every twenty-one Chinese men. These skewed ratios had an overlay of causes, including the U.S. government's policy of keeping the Chinese population both low and temporary by preventing the entry of Chinese women and by assaulting those already here.

But other social and global factors were also at play. News of kidnapped and enslaved Chinese women forced to work as prostitutes on Gold Mountain kept thousands of Chinese women from migrating. Many other Chinese women chose to remain in China, fearful that their husbands might have concubines or other wives in the United States. Further, a Chinese woman was trained to follow the "three obediences"—obey her father at home, her husband after marriage, and her eldest son if she was widowed. Unlike a man, a Chinese woman had no right to divorce or remarry, even if her husband died. A man, however, was permitted to commit adultery, to divorce, to remarry, to practice polygamy, and to discipline his wives as he saw fit. Foreign missionaries in China also discouraged Chinese women's emigration, depicting life in the United States as depraved, promiscuous, and dangerous. Thus Chinese women were reluctant to emigrate, and Chinese men were forced to return to China, albeit temporarily, to have a family.[33]

American consuls in China also made it difficult for Chinese women to emigrate. For example, after the passage of the Page Act, the three American consuls to the port of Hong Kong—David Bailey (1875–77), H. Sheldon Loring (1877–79), and John H. Mosby (1879–82)—extorted extra charges and imposed exorbitant fees on Chinese women seeking passage to California. And travel across the Pacific in steerage class was especially humiliating and hazardous for women, who found themselves surrounded by hundreds of men, sharing crowded bunks stacked from floor to ceiling.

Most of the Chinese women who immigrated to the American West as prostitutes eventually came under the control of the Chinese Six Companies, based in San Francisco. The companies arranged for their procurement, shipping, and sale and controlled the urban brothels. Information about how Chinese women were kidnapped or sold into "sexual slavery" is mostly still hidden to history. But Chinese women made every effort to escape San Francisco, Sacramento, and Seattle, to live in remote towns outside the command of the Six Companies and settle into the familiarity of village life.

This contract between Ah Ho and Yee Kwan, embedded in congressional testimony in 1877, reveals how the American government legalized Chinese women's bondage and anticipated their flight to freedom:

> An agreement to assist the woman Ah Ho, because coming from China to San Francisco she became indebted to her mistress for passage. Ah Ho herself asks Mr. Yee-Kwan to advance for her $630, for which Ah Ho distinctly agrees to give her body to Mr. Yee for service as a prostitute for a term of four years.
>
> There shall be no interest on the money. Ah Ho shall receive no wages. At the expiration of four years Ah Ho shall be her own master. Mr. Yee-Kwan shall not hinder or trouble her. If Ah Ho runs away before her time is out her mistress shall find her and return her, and whatever expense is incurred in finding and returning her Ah Ho shall pay.
>
> On this day of the agreement Ah Ho with her own hands has received from Mr. Yee-Kwan $630.

If Ah Ho shall be sick at any time for more than ten days she shall make up by an extra month of service for ten days' sickness.

Now this agreement has proof. This paper received by Ah Ho is witness.

Twelfth year, ninth month, fourteenth day [1873]. TUNG CHEE.[34]

By the early 1870s, only one third of Chinese women in California lived in San Francisco; by 1880, that fraction rose to about half. The rest found their way to rural towns. Many Chinese female slaves ran away. Many were brutalized. In 1860 when a coroner's jury reported that a young Chinese prostitute had mysteriously died in Shasta City and had been quickly buried at the Chinese cemetery, the girl was disinterred and the coroner discovered that her neck had been violently broken and her body sorely bruised. Which was better, life as a *sausaanggwai*—a "grass widow" in China receiving money from her husband in California—or as a *gamsaanpo*, an abandoned "wife of a Gold Mountain man"? These conflicted drives appeared in Cantonese folk rhymes such as these:

O, just marry all the daughters to men from Gold Mountain:
All those trunks from Gold Mountain
You can demand as many as you want.[35]

If you have a daughter, don't marry her to a Gold Mountain man.
Out of ten years he will not be in bed for one.
The spider will spin webs on top of the bedposts.
While dust fully covers one side of the bed.[36]

Concern over Chinese prostitution was part of a larger American fascination with the sexuality of Chinese women and men. Although half of the Chinese men who immigrated to the United States were married, cartoons in popular magazines and in trade cards alluded to their homosexuality, suggesting that Chinese men disregarded marriage, family, and respectable womanhood. These hostile caricatures may have derived from homophobic fears surrounding crowded all-male mining communities, small-town boardinghouses, and tent camps where men cooked and sewed for themselves.

Before the Chinese Exclusion Act of 1882, 90 percent of Chinese immigrants were single men.[37] In the rural towns that expelled the Chinese, these numbers were even more skewed. Yet the Chinese women who entered, prostitutes included, formed the fabric of Chinatown, and foreshadowed an established, rooted Chinese society in the West.

LEGISLATING THE BODY POLITIC

The Page Act of March 1875—passed in the midst of a depression, a rise in anti-Chinese violence, and the collapse of the myth of domesticity—sought to erase Chinese women from the social cartography of the United States. The act prevented the "landing" of anyone for a fixed "term of service within the United States, for lewd and immoral purposes." Besides Chinese felons, it banned the "importation" of "women for the purposes of prostitution." In fact, the Page Act would have prevented the entry of 90 percent of the Chinese women already living in the United States. Now, by banning admission of all Chinese women except merchants' wives, the U.S. government hoped to force thousands of men to return to China. The Page Act sought to make sure that another ethnic minority would not endure in the West.

Where the Page Act fell short, U.S. consuls stationed in China stepped in, rejecting an untold number of women's applications for visas. Should a Chinese woman manage to receive a permit to sail, she often faced the ordeal of an expensive habeas corpus trial in San Francisco. Hundreds of Chinese women remained in custody, held aboard ships or in prisons, until they could explain their relationships with male émigrés to hostile immigration officers or judges.

Another brutal tactic that prevented Chinese women from emigrating was the seizure of their children, whose parentage was questioned, a case poignantly described in the 1909 story "In the Land of the Free" by Sui Sin Far (Edith Maude Eaton), the first Chinese American fiction writer. This is the tale of a desperate Chinese woman valiantly trying to prove that her son was conceived during a home visit by her husband, a merchant legally entitled to bring his family into the United States. U.S. Customs officers could place the children of Chinese immigrant women in orphanages or foundling homes or even put them up for adoption to white families.

The shadow of the Page Act fell on all Chinese women, for it presumed that their primary work was the sale of sex. Indeed during the 1860s and 1870s, most Chinese women in the United States worked as prostitutes. In San Francisco in 1860, over 90 percent of Chinese women worked and lived in brothels; in 1870, the number dropped to just over 60 percent, perhaps because hundreds of prostitutes had either died or managed to work off the terms of their indenture. It is estimated that by 1880, following the Page Act, between 21 and 50 percent of Chinese women in the United States were prostitutes.[38]

The Page Act in itself acted as a purge. It forced the overall ratio to fall from seventy-eight Chinese females per one thousand Chinese males in 1870 to forty-seven per one thousand in 1880. This number was low enough to risk the future of Chinese America—as the law intended.[39]

A new tactic against Chinese women came with the Chinese Exclusion Act of 1882, which stated that after a visit to China, Chinese laborers (unlike merchants) would no longer be allowed to reenter the United States with their family. When Ah Quan, the wife of a returning laborer, sought to enter the United States, Judge Lorenzo Sawyer of the Ninth Circuit Court ruled against her. According to Sawyer, her own status was irrelevant. After her marriage she automatically acquired her husband's status as a laborer, and she was forced to return to China.[40]

Nonetheless, despite pressures to remain in China with their husbands' families, despite obligations to their own primary families, despite the hardships of traveling with small children, and despite the Page Law, Chinese women did emigrate. Resenting their second-class status in their husbands' families in China, tired of waiting for their husbands' visit or no longer believing their promises of permanent return, many Chinese women traveled, sometimes on foot, sometimes alone, to the port cities and boarded the crowded ships bound for San Francisco or Seattle. Many had entered quickly arranged marriages with Chinese men about to depart for the United States, and these adventurous women barely knew the husbands who awaited them.

Although in the 1870s the U.S. government was still willing to accept Chinese laborers as transient workers, by attempting to prevent the entry of Chinese women and thus the entry of Chinese children, it sundered Chinese family life and community. By 1880 there were more than 75,000 Chinese men in the United States and fewer than 4,000 Chinese women. The Page Act allowed the flow of single Chinese male laborers to continue, a workforce cheaply housed in bunks or tents. It protected rural townships from paying for schools for Chinese children. But as white workers came to realize that without women and children Chinese men would work longer hours and for less money than what might constitute a "family" wage, the Page Act fueled the racial anger of the new labor movement. The Knights of Labor and the Workingmen's Party saw the paradox: single Chinese men accumulated money in California to send home, save, invest, and spend—sometimes on prostitutes.

Under both the Page Act and the Exclusion Law, the wives of Chinese merchants were still allowed into the country. Although these women could not enter as teachers, students, or shopkeepers, they were allowed in as a merchant's household or "body" servant. Their status, ruled federal judge Matthew Deady, "derived" not from the fact that they were married to merchants but from the inherent subservience of a middle-class wife.

Prostitutes and the wives of laborers who had entered the United States before the Page Act now needed to find a way to become merchants' wives, at least in the eyes of the law. Some married laborers managed to qualify as merchants by purchasing a tiny share in a shop or firm, giving themselves and their wives a measure of protection. With this bourgeois cover, laborers' wives entered California, Oregon, and Washington. Some enslaved prostitutes managed to outlive and outlast the terms of their indentures, generally four years, leave the "green mansion," and start a restaurant or small business. Some women were purchased out of prostitution and married to their new owner.

Neither the Page Act nor the Exclusion Act ended Chinese prostitution in the West. Some Chinese women were forced into prostitution to repay a debt for their passage. Some laborers' wives were seized by kidnappers, who sold them into prostitution.[41]

As a group, these were the women who probably formed the first family units of Chinese America. They helped create the early Chinatowns, working as laundrywomen, gold miners, cooks, seamstresses, nannies, madams, and farm laborers.[42] And, by the mid-1870s, they benefited from the shift in Chinese labor from mining and railroad construction to factory work, especially the production of boots and cigars. An enduring class of free and employed Chinese women suddenly seemed possible, thus creating another incentive to drive out the Chinese.

Chinese woman in Humboldt County

DRIVEN OUT ON SMALL FEET

Merchants' wives left fewer marks on history than did their laboring sisters, for they were barred from learning to read or write and apparently left no journals or diaries. Records of their lives come from telegrams, court pleadings, oral histories, some poetry, and family memory, as well as from journalistic and newspaper reports—often sensational, paternalistic, flawed, and obsessed with their bound feet.

We can only infer and imagine the economic, physical, and emotional pain and dislocation of merchants' wives as they were brutally driven out of rural towns. One woman recalled that when a "small foot wife" landed in the United States, she was carried from the ship to her new home in a closely curtained carriage and then "entombed alive."[43] With feet permanently infected and festering, she was not expected to work. She could not comfortably shop or visit friends and was allowed out only after dark.

One merchant's wife reported, probably to a missionary, "In China I was shut up in the house since I was 10 years old and only left my father's house to be shut up in my husband's house in this great country. For seventeen years I have been in this house without leaving it save on two evenings." Life in an impoverished and segregated Chinatown in the raw West was physically difficult for a merchant's wife, who had lost the assistance of servants and extended family in China. Another woman recalled her sense of the advantages that a "natural footed woman" had over "the small foot." The "natural footed woman" could have a room with a window that opened onto the streets, visit other women, shop, travel by streetcars, and "see with her own eyes all the wonders of a foreign country."[44]

Bound feet intensified the pain of being driven out. In the 1885 Eureka roundup, merchants' wives marched to the wharf on feet crushed down to two inches long. When the Chinese from Tacoma were marched out of town in the rain and mud, they had to find wagons not only for their baggage but also for the women who could not hike nine muddy miles on bound feet.

The roundups exacerbated a thousand years of suffering. If a Chinese girl was born into the merchant class, at about four years old her feet were tightly wrapped in cloth strips and her toes forced back toward her heel until the bones slowly broke, to look, some say, like a lotus flower. Her feet were enduringly painful, her body crippled—a torturous gentility that exempted her from labor. Foot binding enforced her chastity and locked her into an invalid's seclusion, where she communicated mainly with servants.

Women with bound feet were entitled to special caretaking, carried through town in curtained sedan chairs, hidden from the life of the street and marketplace, garden and factory. Some suggest that foot binding was seductively and sadistically erotic, with the "small foot" robed and concealed. Certainly, it was a form of child abuse. Performed often with great regret by mothers or nannies, like clitorectomy, it gave an illusive if masochistic image of cultural tradition and mastery over a girl's body.[45]

With its class bias, foot binding assisted the entry of Chinese women into the United States. One immigration official reported, "There has never come to this port, I believe, a bound footed woman who was found to be an immoral character, this condition of affairs being due, it is stated, to

Chinese merchant's wife, Redding, California

Chinese merchant couple

Chinese couple, Nevada City

the fact that such women, and especially those in the interior, are necessarily confined to their homes and seldom frequent the city districts."[46] Yet the merchants' wives were also true pioneers, forging settlements and building communities in new rural towns. With no motive to return to China, these women challenged the stereotype that Chinese immigrants were sojourners who intended to return to their villages or families in China and who sent their earnings home.

The journalistic, evangelical, and political attention to Chinese prostitutes has obscured the everyday lives of other Chinese women who entered the United States, who worked, bore children, built communities during rough times of intimidation, contributed to the family wage, faced harassment, and ultimately endured expulsion. From Mokelumne Hill and Antioch to Eureka, Tacoma, and Truckee, the forced removal of Chinese women devastated the communities they established.

Like antimiscegenation laws directed against African Americans during the postbellum period, the Page Act sought to regulate who would constitute the body politic. Chinese expectations of permanent lives in the United States—expectations tied to naturalization and citizenship—were limited by gender. At the time, the Constitution provided that if a baby was born within the United States, or if a foreign woman married a male citizen of the United States, citizenship followed. Until 1875, a Chinese woman who married a white man could sooner or later become an American citizen.[47] The Page Act both foiled this possibility and banned citizenship for Chinese men who married white female citizens or immigrants (e.g., from Ireland, France, or Germany) who had the right to become citizens.[48]

In 1870 Congress specifically allowed persons of African descent to become naturalized, but not those of Asian descent. The Exclusion Act of 1882 clarified Congress's intent: no state or federal court could naturalize a Chinese person. A Chinese American citizenry was not to be. Granted, citizenship in the late nineteenth century did not guarantee the vote or the right to testify, sit on a jury, or hold property; citizenship did not bestow liberty, autonomy, or civic standing. Nonetheless, it defined identity and belonging. But by limiting the immigration of women, the federal government invoked sexual relations to achieve ethnic cleansing.[49]

In 1907 Congress ended any confusion about whether an American woman would risk her citizenship by marrying a Chinese man, declaring "that any American woman who marries a foreigner shall take the nationality of her husband." This act echoed miscegenation laws passed between 1861 and 1913 in California, Arizona, Idaho, Montana, Nebraska, Nevada, Utah, and Wyoming. These laws criminalized or voided marriages between Chinese—indeed, any people of color—and whites.[50] In short, the American legislative system attempted to stop any chances of a growing Chinese America. Even so, Chinese women kept coming.

Throughout these troubled decades, discrimination against Chinese women was justified by the charge that the Chinese would invade the country and become a permanent and dominant population. In fact, the average number of children per Chinese family in America was remarkably low, statistically less than one child per couple.[51] Perhaps this low birthrate was due to Chinese women's prior history of prostitution and its attendant diseases, perhaps to their average age of thirty or over, or perhaps to the declining number of Chinese female immigrants.

CHINESE WOMEN RESIST

To protect against being sold and sold again into bondage, especially as they were driven from their rural retreats, hundreds of Chinese women and prostitutes fled from slavery. They traveled alone, set up their own businesses peddling vegetables, or hired out as nannies. And against tremendous odds, they turned to the American courts to fight for the freedom of their bodies and their labor.

Racial-purity legislation, the profit in prostitution, and the wider misogyny of the American legal system conspired to heighten the vulnerability of Chinese women. Although organized prostitution was controlled by the powerful Chinese Six Companies, some Chinese communities in the West found ways to defend their women.

The battles over Chinese prostitutes divided Chinatowns, leaving them open to seamy and sarcastic journalism and political diatribe, exacerbating anti-Chinese violence. In September 1872 in Truckee, Chinatown's residents demanded that Ah Too be arrested and charged with kidnapping, drugging, and "spiriting away by force two valuable and beautiful Chinese women" along with $250 in coins. The town constable found Ah Too with the two women on the road, three miles outside of town, and charged him with kidnapping and theft. But within two days, another group of Chinese men, armed with picks and crowbars, tried unsuccessfully to free him from jail. A judge ultimately dismissed the kidnapping charge, claiming he could not figure out how one man could abduct two women while carrying a heavy box of coins.

Three months later, another kidnapping rocked the mountain towns. In December 1872, Ah Quee, from nearby North San Juan, charged that local Chinese men had kidnapped his slave woman, Sin Moy. The local police located Sin Moy and returned her to Ah Quee. Suddenly a group of Chinese men tried to claim her for themselves and shots were fired, seriously wounding Ah Quee. The following January, two organizations went to court over Sin Moy. While the outcome of the long and contentious trial is unclear, the local *Truckee Republican* scoffed at the Chinese for believing that they had "a right to buy women, and had the right to keep them even against their wills." Still, the court had taken the case, and the kidnap, assault, and disputed ownership of Chinese women was regular copy that year in the *Republican.*[52]

Chinese women purged from California towns were often on the run from enslaved prostitution in other towns. A woman who managed to run away from a brothel took a tremendous risk. Fleeing from one rural community to another, she would be tracked along mountain trails by hired gangsters or by Chinese men claiming ownership. In the cities, she might seek refuge at an evangelical mission, where she risked being released to a "husband." Riskier still was a flight to a police station, where she could be simply detained and returned to her owner. Her "husband" could turn to the courts, claiming that she had absconded with clothing, money, or jewelry. Sometimes a gang affiliated with the Chinese Six Companies paid her bail and returned her to their brothel.

In 1877 San Francisco hired a special police force to serve as "peace officers" in Chinatown. These men received no set wages but worked as slave catchers, extorting fees from prostitutes, brothel owners, and men searching for runaway girls. In small towns, placards promised reward money for a runaway Chinese woman.[53] If she was found, the county sheriff, local police officer, or rural lawyer was paid off by her owner.

Although the historical footprints of these runaways have faded, a series of telegrams tells the story of two runaway Chinese prostitutes, Gan Que and Wah How, who escaped from their owners in the spring of 1874. A group of Chinese men desperately tried to track them down, wiring one another with hints about the women's locations or demands for bribes and expenses. They hired police officers and local attorneys, produced false marriage certificates, and finally threatened to turn to the Chinese Six Companies. But Gan Que and Wah How remained on the run, traveling by stage or hiking between towns in the Sierra Nevada foothills—Nevada City, Downieville, Auburn, and Marysville. The men's urgent and cryptic telegrams, often several per day, detail a stirring chase across snowy mountains.

DID THE GIRL WAH HOW NO COME HERE LAST MONTH. I THINK SHE IS KIDNAPED. ANS IF SHE WAS.

Yuk Fong, Virginia City, Nevada, to Luk Chung, March 20, 1874, 1:30 P.M.

SHE HAS NOT COME HERE YET. HAVE NEVER HEARD ANYONE SPEAK OF HER BEFORE. IF I DO I WILL TELEGRAPH.

Luk Chung, Downieville, Calif., to Yuk Fong, Virginia City, March 30, 1874

YOUR WOMAN SHE GO COLUSA. YOU WANT HER GO THERE.

Fong Sing, Tie Yuen, Oroville, to Lem Lun, June 12, 1874, 9:55 A.M.

DON'T YOU LET HER GO. I WILL COME OVER TOMORROW AND SEE HER . . . WHAT TIMES DOES THE TRAIN START. ANSWER QUICK.

Kaw Chung, Downieville, to Fook Sing, Wadsworth, Nevada, July 25, 1874

TELL HER TO WAIT FOR ME TO COME AND IF SHE WANTS TO GO I WILL LET HER. DON'T CARE. ANSWER.

Kaw Chung, Downieville, to Fook Sing, Wadsworth, July 26, 1874

THE WOMAN IS AT VIRGINIA [CITY]. COME TO AUBURN AND I WILL TELL YOU HEAP LOTS.

Ah Tri, Auburn, to Ah Tom, August 2, 1874, 10:10 A.M.

WOMAN WENT TO VIRGINIA TOWN WITH HOW AH SING. YOU BETTER COME HERE AND TALK TO THE COMPANY. KEEP QUIET. I KNOW ALL ABOUT IT. IT IS ALL RIGHT.

Ah Tri, Auburn, to Ah Tom, August 2, 1874, 11:05 A.M.

GUM SING AND WOMAN ARRESTED. HERE TOMORROW. SEND SIXTY DOLLARS.

Tie Yuen Company, Nevada [City, Calif.], to Fook Sing, Downieville, August 3, 1874, 1 P.M.

AH TOM WRITE ME GAN QUE IS AT AUBURN. YOU WANT CATCH HER GO RIGHT AWAY. ANSWER.

Fook Sing, Downieville, to Tie Uen, Wadsworth, August 5, 1874

FOOK SING'S WOMAN HAS GONE TO MARYSVILLE.

Ting Yeu, Auburn, to Ah Tom, Downieville, August 12, 1874, 12:30 P.M.

BRING WOMAN UP RIGHT AWAY WILL PAY THREE HUNDRED DOLLARS. ANSWER.

Sing Lung, Ah Yik to Tie Yuen, Fook Sing, Marysville, August 13, 1874

WATCH WOMAN CLOSE. I COME TOMORROW.

Sing Lung, Ah Yik, Marysville, to Fook Sing, Downieville, August 13, 1874

THE WOMAN IS IN JAIL HERE NOW. SEND ONE HUNDRED DOLLARS TODAY BY TELEGRAPH FOR EXPENSE TO TAKE THE WOMAN UP TO NEVADA [CITY]. YOU NO SEND MONEY SHE NO GO. FOOK SING HE STOP NEVADA. YOU NO GOT MONEY, ANSWER.

Eing Goon to Sing Lung, Marysville, October 5, 1874, 4:20 P.M.

SEND ONE HUNDRED DOLLARS. WE HAVE WOMAN.

Ah Tien, Ah Heing Store, to Fook Sing, Nevada City, October 6, 1874, 8:50 P.M.

KEM SING WITH OFFICER GO DOWNIEVILLE TODAY. HIDE WOMAN.

E. Barry to Ah Wan, Nevada City, October 8, 1874, 10:45 P.M.

WHEN YOU COMING TO PAY. IF NOT IN FEW DAYS WILL SEND OFFICER AFTER YOU.

Tie Yuen to Hong Hi Wien, Nevada City, October 13, 1874, 1:30 P.M.

GIM SING AND GAN QUE IN JAIL. SEND MONEY QUICK.

I Yuen Store to Fook Sing, Nevada City, November 6, 1874, 4:20 P.M.

The telegrams track Gan Que to Sierra Valley, Sierra City, and Downieville, as a series of men demand payment for her capture and return. Yet unfulfilled promises of money, checks, bank deposits, missed stages, and snowstorms stand in their way. Gan Que's flight appears to end with a telegraph to Fook Sing, dated November 25, 1874, from Wadsworth, Nevada:

YOUR WOMAN GO TO SAN FRANCISCO TONIGHT WITH LEE HUNG. SING HOE GO BACK TO CHINA. YOU WANT TO LET HER GO ANSWER QUICK.[54]

Ultimately, Gan Que and Wah How were found, arrested, hidden, and shipped to San Francisco. But for a brief moment in the summer and fall of 1874, they were fugitives with a cause—to save their freedom and their lives. They braved the mountains and the unknown, evading scores of hunters who were frantic to capture and return them to men who claimed them.

Gan Que and Wah How were not alone. Some Chinese prostitutes escaped from their masters; some lived with men as wives or concubines, only to find themselves working for their husbands as prostitutes. Newspaper ads, telegrams, and court cases suggest that a large number of Chinese women in rural towns ran away and a large number of Chinese men fervently sought their return.

In May 1871 in Eureka, for example, Qui Com married Ah Sou, perhaps to escape her owner, Mun Ching, a local merchant, or perhaps out of true love. Either way, Mun procured a warrant for her arrest for grand larceny, claiming that Qui owed him more than three hundred dollars for her passage from China, which he demanded in the form of three years of her "service." But Qui Com had disappeared, and the warrant languished until Mun Ching seized her in the nearby town of Arcata. Qui Com, however, was released under the Thirteenth Amendment, "for she had stolen nothing from him but herself."[55]

Although the Thirteenth Amendment aided Qui Com in her quest for freedom, the experiences of Chinese prostitutes in the West belie the notion that slavery ended with its passage in December 1865. Across the American West, the courts upheld the ownership of Chinese girls. In the *Overland Monthly* of April 1869, the evangelist preacher A. W. Loomis reproduced a placard posted on the streets of San Francisco's Chinatown. Chen Ha was searching for his sister, Ah Shau. Hakka bandits had kidnapped Ah Shau from their village of San in the Shen Ling district of China, taken her to Macao and thence to Hong Kong, where she was shipped to San Francisco. There, according to her brother, she valiantly resisted all efforts to "dishonor" her. Chen Ha finally located his sister, enslaved in San Francisco, and sued for her release. In the trial, Chen Ha swore that he was neither driven by lust for his sister nor seeking to profit from her "use and misuse." Yet his long effort went for naught and the court returned her to the brothel.[56]

The 1885 Alien Contract Law, outlawing the trade in indentured workers and enslaved prostitutes, failed to stop the forced importation of Chinese women held in bondage. In early October 1885, the steamship *Oceanic* docked in San Francisco with the largest number of prostitutes ever brought at one time. Fifty-three adult women and twenty-two female children had been brought over for "immoral purposes." After intense negotiations between the women's procurers and the Chinese Six Companies, who had brokered the deal, the district court granted the women temporary landing rights under habeas corpus laws. The women and children

Mr. and Mrs. Charlie from Tuolumne

were released into the hands of their owners and disappeared into Chinatown.[57] For Chinese prostitutes, the opportunity to turn to American courts for breach of contract, for flagrant abuse, or for their freedom was rare. Indeed, few Chinese prostitutes would outlive the four- to six-year terms of their indentures. The system of enslaved prostitution in itself constituted a form of genocide, or "Driven Out."

RETURN TO ANTIOCH

The history of Chinese women in the West—the forces of Chinese and white men allied against them, their precarious legal status, the presumption that they caused and spread disease, their flights through the mountains—shapes the story of the roundup and expulsion of the prostitutes from Antioch in 1876. After the purge and fire in Antioch's Chinatown, many Chinese men returned. Living on boats moored on the river at the edge of town—fishing, scraping barnacles from the sailing ships from San Francisco, reclaiming marshland, and selling vegetables—they went about their lives. The slavery and prostitution of Chinese women also endured, as did the violence. For a year or two after the purge, only one Chinese woman, the wife of merchant Yee Lee, remained, but soon she was joined by three or four prostitutes. On September 27, 1886, a twenty-eight-year-old Chinese woman, Du Hoo, was murdered in a cigar shop by her former owner; her current pimp had paid only half of the three hundred dollars he owed for her.[58]

Word of the "Antioch outrage" spread to the East Coast, and across the Atlantic to England. On May 4, 1876, the *London Daily News* compared Americans' treatment of Chinese immigrants to Britain's medieval assault on Jews:

> The citizens of Antioch, California, seem anxious to win for themselves a name in the history of persecution. They have cast out the Chinese inhabitants from among them, and have burned the Chinese quarter of Antioch with fire. . . . Our ancestors, had they been bent on annoying the Jews, whose position in England was not so very unlike that of the Chinese in California, would not have expelled the detested people before they burned their quarter. They

> would have seen to it that the Hebrews were carefully fastened up before they collected torches, tar-barrels, faggots, and the other materials of medieval controversy. The people of Antioch have got beyond this truculent way of displaying national and religious hatred. They turned the Chinese out into the open before burning down their miserable hovels . . . a welcome proof that there is such a thing as progress in humanity after all.

The "Chinaman," concluded the British editorial, is in fact a "more awkward customer" than the "irrepressible Negro" because he has far more "natural" intelligence, energy, and "aptitude for a sort of civilization." Similar circumstances, it warned, "used to end up in a massacre of the Jews."[59]

In 1876 Antioch still endured hard economic times and the remaining Chinese faced new risks. Denis Kearney and the Workingmen's Party were stirring up anti-Chinese violence in San Francisco. In the delta towns, blame for unemployment landed on the local Chinese miners and brick makers. In June, the month after the fire, coal miners, mostly Welshmen, were suddenly fired from the nearby Black Diamond Mine. The Ulhorn and Clark brick factory had just laid off its white workers, keeping lower-paid Chinese and recruiting a dozen more from San Francisco. When the new Chinese brick makers arrived at the docks, they were attacked by unemployed white miners and masons and forced back onto the ship. Within a month, another large group of Chinese was expelled from the delta town.[60]

The *Sacramento Daily Record* reported that many whites in San Francisco now were "openly advocating violence" against the Chinese, and there was a "general sense of menace in the tone" of the meetings. One of the anti-Chinese clubs announced that a "stand" of twenty-five hundred new muskets could reach California from New York in ten days. *The New York Times* lamented, "Mob law seems to be the corrective when Californians are disposed to apply it to Chinese evil."[61]

Chinese women quickly became the target of the crusade. As the economic depression worsened, the alleged disease and contagion endemic to Chinese women were posed as the real threat to jobs, culture, and country. Victorian family life was imperiled as white girls left home to work in the mills and as unemployed men moved west. Chinese prostitutes masked the real threats to domesticity: mill girls' twelve-hour workdays, ironworkers' new night shifts, the lost generation of young men killed in the Civil War, and the arrival of thousands of single working girls from Ireland and eastern Europe, who, like the Chinese, were quickly portrayed as hypersexual.

The distinction between Chinese merchants' wives and Chinese prostitutes endured until the Geary Act of 1892 discriminated equally against all Chinese immigrants. American industrialists and bankers trying to forge trade links to China through Chinese merchants in the United States generated the class divide between Chinese women. During the 1870s and 1880s, the treatment of Chinese women in California was part of an expansionist policy, embedded and expressed in the Page Act and the Chinese Exclusion Act, which selectively excluded Chinese immigrants by gender. The two popular images of Chinese womanhood—the diseased prostitute and the "small foot" wife—suggest how the fear of the "yellow peril" was projected onto the body of Chinese womanhood, which must, perforce, be driven out.

4

THE EUREKA METHOD

"WE HAVE NO CHINESE"

The Chinese are coming, Oh dear, Oh dear!
No they are not, they are right here.

—*Northern Independent,* August 12, 1868

Late on the night of February 6, 1885, a gallows was built on Fourth Street between E and F Streets on the edge of Chinatown, in Eureka, a foggy lumber town on California's north coast. Earlier that Friday evening, City Councilman David Kendall had finished his supper and left his home across the road from Chinatown, just one segregated block, to return to his office. At 6:05, as he crossed F Street, he was caught in the crossfire when two Chinese men shot at each other. A friend carried Kendall back to his home, where he soon died. Almost unnoticed in the commotion, Louis Baldschmidt, a twelve-year-old boy who worked in a furniture store, had been shot in the foot.

Within minutes the city was in a "blaze of excitement." A crowd of white loggers, miners, mill workers, sailors, and merchants quickly gathered, chanting "Burn Chinatown!" and "Hang all the Chinamen!" The po-

Eureka's Chinatown

Eureka's Chinatown, Fourth Street and East Street

lice arrested a group of Chinese men before they could be lynched by the growing mob and marched them through the downtown streets as the mob shouted, "Let's go and burn the devils out!" Fearing a riot, the local sheriff called out the Eureka Guard, sending one detachment to protect the county jail and another to guard the armory.

Less than twenty minutes after Kendall was shot, the gaslights at Centennial Hall were lit and more than six hundred white men paraded behind a bell ringer who chanted, "Go to Centennial Hall. Go now!" The angry crowd filled the cold hall, built a decade before to celebrate the hundredth anniversary of the Declaration of Independence. The storehouse for the town's munitions, the hall was only two hundred feet from Chinatown.

Mayor Tom Walsh, who had rushed to the hall from Kendall's deathbed, tried to chair the meeting but was powerless to control the infuriated crowd, bent, as reporters noted, "on summary revenge." The mob shouted out a series of proposals. The first was to massacre every Chinese man in Eureka, but it was "frowned down." The next was to loot Chinatown, tear down the tenements, and drive the Chinese into the redwood forest "unsheltered and unprotected." At this point Charles Huntington, a Congregationalist minister, stepped up to the stage and begged the crowd to listen: everyone deplored Kendall's death, he insisted, but the "Chinaman" had no design on Kendall's life. Kendall's death was a tragic accident, and the people of Chinatown, he said, were as "innocent of his death as I am. They pay their rent, they mind their own business and you have no more right to drive them from their homes than you have to drive me from my home." Besides, Huntington concluded, "If Chinamen have no character, white men ought to have some."

When the sheriff suddenly entered the hall and announced that he could not identify Kendall's murderer, the frustrated crowd endorsed a third motion: a committee of fifteen men should go to Chinatown and order the Chinese to leave Eureka.[1] Two steamships, the *Humboldt* and the *City of Chester,* were in port, and the mob agreed that every Chinese person must be at the docks by three o'clock Saturday afternoon, ready to sail with the next tide. According to Huntington, only the "cool remonstrance" of a few leaders saved Chinatown from becoming a "scene of slaughter and blood" that evening.

That Friday night, the residents of Eureka—Chinese and white—did not sleep. Within two hours of Kendall's death, most Chinese residents were packing what belongings they could, to be ready to leave the next morning. White gangs broke into the stores and looted thousands of dollars' worth of Chinese wares as their owners looked on. Others roughly hauled the Chinese belongings to the warehouse.[2] Long before midnight, many Chinese residents made camp at the dock. By the morning, sacks of their clothing and furniture were piled up on Fourth Street. Even as the Chinese packed, white lumberjacks suggested setting fire to Chinatown. The sheriff, though, warned them off, predicting that the Chinese would later file lawsuits for damages that neither residents nor the city could afford to pay. Instead, he commandeered every dray and express wagon in the city to carry the Chinese belongings down to the wharf.

Throughout the night, the Committee of Fifteen and gangs of roaming men notified the Chinese that they were to be expelled. The committee sent teams of white men into the country in all directions, to force Chinese farmhands, cooks, and timbermen to leave the lumber camps and mills and take only what they could carry from the segregated bunkhouses they called home. The Chinese laborers were forced back to town and "corralled" in the damp warehouse on the wharf. Only one rancher refused to surrender his employee, "Charlie" Moon, whose Chinese name remains lost to history.

Meanwhile, bands of Chinese men fled north along the Arcata road by Humboldt Bay, or south toward the Eel River, under the cover of the redwood forests. Scouting parties searching the woods captured more than sixty Chinese and forced them down to the Eureka docks to sail with the others. A work gang of Chinese men who were building a short-haul rail-

Charles Moon

road that connected the timber tracts to the docks was seized from their outlying cabins near the village of Blue Lake and marched back to Eureka. As the night wore on, twenty more Chinese men were taken to the city jail, accused of shooting Kendall and Baldschmidt. One of the vigilantes, Sam Kelsey, recalled that he and two young boys were delegated to patrol the local trains. They stayed by the tracks most of the night and in the morning boasted that "we . . . got one Chinaman and brought him back."

An effigy of a Chinese man swung from gallows built in the middle of the night on the edge of Chinatown. Nearby a sign nailed to a wooden post warned, ANY CHINESE SEEN ON THE STREET AFTER THREE O'CLOCK TODAY WILL BE HUNG TO THIS GALLOWS.

The Eureka roundup had taken less than forty-eight hours. The local papers reported disingenuously that after Kendall's death there was no further violence in Eureka, and news accounts throughout the state soon proffered the "Eureka method" as a model for a "peaceful" purge of Chinese immigrants. But the pogrom was a night and morning of exuberant violence, detailed painfully in the diary of Charles Huntington, as well as in an oral history of vigilante Sam Kelsey and in reports by the *Daily Times-Telephone,* which hurriedly printed new editions all night long.

On Saturday morning, about three hundred Chinese people followed the buggies and wagons down to the docks. The merchants' wives, with bound feet, hobbled in pain. Several more wagonloads of Chinese men—ranch hands, cooks for lumberjacks and mill workers, laborers contracted to clear brushland—were brought to the docks in the afternoon. Four were merchants who had lived and worked in Eureka for ten to fourteen years. About twenty women—prostitutes, merchants' wives, laborers' wives who had entered before the Page Act of 1875—were forced out of Eureka. The wagons also carried several wounded men and the corpses of two others, victims of recent battles in Chinatown.

At about 2 P.M., a crowd of men and boys chased after a young Chinese man, Charley Way (Wei Lum), who was walking down a white block in the town. Wei Lum had wanted to say good-bye to the minister who had converted him to Christianity. Sam Kelsey recalled, "A couple of kids ran up to me and they said, 'There's a Chinaman going into that house.'" Reverend Huntington's house was built up, about eight feet from the ground, and Kelsey and a friend ran up a plank into the parsonage. As an excited crowd filled Huntington's backyard, Kelsey smashed in the door. He found Mrs.

Huntington and her daughter shielding Wei, who was hiding on his knees behind their vast Victorian skirts. To Kelsey's demand "Where's that Chinaman?" Mrs. Huntington replied, "Charley is here on his way to the wharf; he barely called to say good-bye and ask the prayers of the family in his exile." "We want him now!" cried Kelsey, who, along with a friend, seized Wei Lum by his queue and dragged him through the streets to the gallows.

Huntington and the jeering crowd chased after them. As Huntington described in his journal, the men "put a noose around [Wei Lum's] neck in the presence of hundreds of people without a word of remonstrance from the police or anybody else," but a Methodist colleague climbed onto the scaffold and proclaimed, " 'Boys, take that rope off that boy's neck! If you hang him you'll hang him over my dead body.' " Stunned, the men dropped the noose and dragged Wei to the wharf, where most of the Chinese were now kept under guard. In place of Wei Lum, the crowd hung an effigy of the minister from the balcony of Centennial Hall. Later that afternoon Huntington found Wei in the warehouse at the docks, crying and huddled with his classmates. The minister gave him his Bible, a pair of gloves, and an umbrella, and prayed with him to endure the expulsion as a "bearing of the cross." Then he left.

Confined in the warehouses of the shipping companies, the Chinese were kept under close guard. Hundreds of white townspeople gawked and jeered; others came to say good-bye to their Chinese neighbors, shopkeepers, and employees.

Still others came looking for their laundry. Prompted by a notice in the morning newspaper that "people who have clothes in any of the China wash houses . . . may not be able to find wash house proprietors this afternoon," a crowd of whites raided the laundries, often to be told that the owner had already been seized and taken to the wharf.

It took most of that Saturday to purge the Chinese from Eureka. The Committee of Fifteen and several county officials divided the Chinese into "rival tongs." At the time there was no north-south railroad and Eureka was linked to San Francisco only by narrow Indian trails or by the sea, so the plan was to deport the Chinese on the steamships that usually carried passengers between Eureka and San Francisco. All morning, light skiffs ferried the Chinese to the ships that happened to be in Humboldt Bay. It took twenty-three trips to load 135 men and women onto the *Humboldt* and 175 onto the *City of Chester.* Both steamers were weighted down with tons of the

Chinese's cargo. Bearing his Bible, his new gloves, and his umbrella, Wei Lum, along with 309 other refugees, spent Saturday night on a steamship, likely aware that none of them would ever return to their homes in Eureka.

By the time the laden ships were ready to sail, the tide was out, and dark shoal water barely covered the rocks and the shifting sandbars of the bay. At 6 A.M. on Sunday, February 8, the tide flooded into the bay and Wei finally sailed with his brethren in the cold gray mist, under the charge of the Eureka city marshal. With a strong wind from the north, the ships reached San Francisco early Monday morning. The telegraph wire between Eureka and the Bay Area was down from the heavy February rains, and the Customs House was still closed from the weekend. No one in San Francisco knew what had happened in Eureka. No one met the ships. In haste, the Chinese disembarked and disappeared with their belongings into the safety of Chinatown.[3]

That afternoon, several of the Chinese from Eureka regathered at the Ong Cong Gon So Association's offices in San Francisco's Spofford Alley to describe the purge to the press and to the large Chinese community. There they announced plans to sue the city of Eureka for reparations for their losses and for the fact that the city had let them be routed by a mob.

Back in Eureka, the townpeople also gathered and determined that not only the Chinese but Chinatown itself had to go. They wanted the build-

The *Crescent City*

ings, the traditions, the historical memory and meaning of the Chinese community to be erased. The day before the purge, the *Eureka Daily Times-Telephone* foretold, "If ever an unoffending white is . . . offered up on the altar of paganism, we fear it will be good-bye to Chinatown." The white community immediately fulfilled this prediction. WIPE OUT THE PLAGUE-SPOTS headlined the local paper. "In the very heart of the city of Eureka is a community in which exist slums and festering dens. . . . Our readers will not stop to ask for the location of this leprous quarter. They know it too well. They know it is where . . . under a small heathen horde, acts of riot and assassination are more and more boldly being committed from month to month. They know that it is the pestilential quarter where Chinese gambling dens, opium smoking hell-holes and the lowest brothels abound. They know and acknowledge that this leper's colony is a curse to the city and its future prosperity."[4]

"THE CHINESE ARE COMING, OH DEAR, OH DEAR! NO THEY ARE NOT, THEY ARE RIGHT HERE."

Nestled between the redwood forest and Humboldt Bay, Eureka, with its long inland harbor and narrow split opening to the rough Pacific, was often shrouded in north coast fogs. When white settlers first viewed the bay in 1850, they saw a raw and "uncivilized" Yurok village: "When the sun rose o'er the townsite . . . it was a wilderness, uninhabited by man, and except for the soughing of the wind throughout the timber and the roll of the surf on the beach it was as silent as the dead."[5] To the east the redwood forest spread from the edge of the water up through the mountain ridge, while a low, boggy gulch, "impassable except with an ax to cut your way," slanted toward the south. To the north, where a few small islands dotted the bay, the land was "mercifully" more open, with "only a few scrubby, wind-blown pines . . . and covered with a growth of salal and honeysuckle."[6]

By the winter of 1884–85, Eureka had become a thriving lumber port, and the bay was filled with hundreds of mammoth redwood logs floating in booms, waiting to be shipped out. Along the shore, open spaces now lay between huge stumps where redwood spires, perhaps a thousand years old, hundreds of feet tall, and eight to twelve feet in diameter, had recently touched the sky. The timber that was rolled, handled, moved, and milled came from the giant redwood trees, *Sequoia sempervirens,* that grow along the California coast from Santa Cruz to the Oregon border. The cupola and widow's walk of Eureka's "gargantuan" Vance Hotel, built by timber baron John Vance, topped the town. A few blocks away, Vance's lumber rival, William Carson, was finishing the construction of his equally oversize Victorian mansion.[7]

That winter the rains shut down the mills. But of greater worry than the weather was the serious economic slump pounding the housing, construction, and shipbuilding industries up and down the state, driving unemployed woodsmen into town, to drink, to roam the small port, and to harass the Chinese. White workers who had come west with dreams of opportunity, individualism, rugged endurance, and equality faced instead corruption, radical disparities in political power, and an increasing concentration of wealth that accompanied mechanization in the woods and, soon thereafter, in the canneries. The Chinese roundups arose within the postslavery ideal of free labor and the vision that workers' wages should represent the full value of their labor.[8]

On the night of February 6, the town was filled with disillusioned loggers and sawmill workers, men who had come west from the pinewoods of Maine and the British provinces in Canada. In rainy Humboldt County they worked for only eight months of the year, earning between forty and seventy dollars per month, including room and board and one bath a week. Loggers, clinging to the steep hillsides in spiked boots, worked twelve-hour days, following the sun. In this era of national unemployment, a good part of a logger's wage was sent back to families in towns whose men, like the Chinese, had emigrated in search of work.

In the 1880s, most lumber workers lived in tents in the forest. The first bunkhouse in Humboldt, built in 1884, was ten feet square, with a hole in the roof to vent smoke from the fire in the cabin floor. Most lumber camps did not have indoor plumbing until the 1920s. Generally, white workers had Saturday night through Sunday off and went into town, often to drink, often to visit prostitutes, some of whom were Chinese. The ratio of white men to white women was very high. The white workers who wanted to rid

Eureka of the Chinese were, at the same time, also demanding sanitation, better housing, shorter hours, fixed pay, and the redistribution of the lands granted to the railroads by the federal government.

Two hundred Chinese men and about twenty Chinese women lived in the one square segregated block that was Eureka's Chinatown. Their two-tiered shacks, some built over Chinese stores, were often constructed on stilts out of refuse lumber from the mills. A diagonal slough or gulch cut through Chinatown, but the city had blocked off its drainage when a sidewalk was built on the street, and Chinatown's refuse poured into its interior, a hollow square, raising foul smells and unsanitary fumes. Ducks sailed in the gully and feasted on the garbage. One observer described Eureka's Chinatown as a stagnant swamp where a "pool of water had gathered in the center, and the refuse from kitchens of seventeen houses and outhouses was dumped into this pond. Here green scum formed from the decaying vegetables and filth, gave rise to an odor seasoned by dried fish and opium smell."[9]

Chinatown's land was owned by Casper Ricks who for more than twenty years had leased stores and tenements to the Chinese for six to eight dollars per month. Ricks also owned the Palace Stables up the street. Just before the weekend of the roundups, a story appeared in the local paper that Ricks, apparently chastened by the condition of Chinatown, was "bringing up to grade his Chinese cottages."

Yet as the Reverend Charles Huntington observed, the filth and stench was no more the fault of the Chinese people than of poor white people who also had no "sewerage"; the difference was only "the one were hated while the others were pitied. . . . The blame in both cases rested with the authorities whose duty it was to establish sewers and abate the nuisance."

Another difference was that the Chinese could not own land—a fact that would haunt them for years to come. Eureka's Chinatown was surrounded by white homes, white churches, white stores. Other Chinese residents of Humboldt County lived in remote timber areas, at their employers' houses, in cabins at white-owned ranches and farms, or in houses next to their own vegetable gardens—in community of some sort with whites and native people. Some slept in the cookhouses of the lumber mills. There were few Chinese families, so many of them lived in their employers' homes, as domestic servants, nannies, and cooks.

A crowded and intimate block of hotels, restaurants, shops, boardinghouses, and laundries, Eureka's Chinatown was a community never understood by the town's white residents. Just a few weeks before the purge, one Eureka newspaper mocked, "It is a matter for astonishment to note the large amount of goods which come to the dealers in Chinatown on the arrival of each steamer. We don't care to be familiar with the quality of the shipments, for the fumes which come from the 'hotels' at eating time suggest a bill of fare not entirely made up of rice. Dried fish, pickled eggs of ancient origin, jerked dog and soused rat, are the ingredients used in preparing a genuine Chinese meal."

Despite the ubiquity of disease and violence in frontier towns, Eureka's Chinatown was depicted in the local press as a place particularly rife with sin, crime, and contamination. False rumors of leprosy in the Chinese community emerged across Humboldt County—seizing on fears of the very real epidemics of diphtheria and yellow fever that were endangering everyone in nearby towns such as Red Bluff. Yet here, as elsewhere in the West, hostile editorials appeared alongside announcements of white people enjoying Chinese New Year's, eating delicacies in Chinese restaurants, watching the colorful if unexamined dragon parades, and collecting elegant Chinese porcelains.

Anti-Chinese violence had come quickly to Eureka and the other new fishing and timber towns along the misty north coast—Arcata, Crescent City, Ferndale. In late January 1875, white lumbermen in Eureka had greeted Chinese New Year's with a race riot. Grand-jury documents from 1876 record white children being encouraged to assault Chinese men. Other Chinese were harassed at work—in the mines or while harvesting the wild blackberries, salmonberries, and thimbleberries that grow along the coast.

By the end of the 1870s, on-the-job actions against the Chinese became more organized. At Dungan's Ferry along the winding Eel River, the Cuttings Cannery fired all its Chinese employees. The next year, the Pioneer Hotel in Hydesville announced that Chinese men would no longer work there. March 1882 saw the first large anti-Chinese meeting in Centennial Hall, where, prompted by the Chinese Exclusion Act moving through Congress, the crowd passed a resolution banning the Chinese from California altogether and forming the first standing anti-Chinese committee. Speaker after speaker rose to "review . . . the evils that have grown out of the Chinese population and effect of their presence on the industries of the coast and the curse to the laboring classes."[10]

Yet by January 1884, fifteen hundred Chinese men and fifty women still lived in Humboldt County, "depriving whites" of jobs.[11] In mid-1884, Chinese gangs, called "tongs" or "highbinders" by whites, had drifted up the coast from San Francisco, but Eureka police refused to protect Chinatown. When Chinese gang members or white thugs attacked settled members of the Chinese community, they were released with only reprimands. In the late fall and early winter, shootings in Chinatown increased, but Chinese cries for police protection were ignored, and the county banned only Chinese from owning pistols.[12]

But not all whites in Humboldt County were of one mind regarding their Chinese neighbors. The owner of Fay's Shingle Mill rejected his white employees' demand that they not have to work alongside the Chinese.[13] In the southern Humboldt lumber town of Rohnerville, after a white man refused to pay for his laundry and then shot and killed the Chinese washerman, a local judge sentenced the murderer to six years in San Quentin Prison.

By the 1880s, whites and Chinese in Eureka were expecting a race riot. In the fall of 1884, two Chinese men, Wah Law and Sam Ying, were severely wounded in a shoot-out. Late that winter, professional Chinese gamblers arrived from San Francisco. Fan-tan, mah-jongg, and card games frequently ended in gunshots. On Christmas Eve, bullets fired in Chinatown careened into a white man's bedroom, scattering plaster and lodging in the woodwork over the door. Then, just after New Year's Day 1885, *The Humboldt Times* again reported shots in Chinatown and commented that this "pistol practice . . . thing is happening a little too often of late, and steps should be taken to put a stop to it." On the morning of February 1, a few days before the purge, a brawl broke out in Chinatown in which two Chinese men were killed, three wounded, and eight placed under arrest.

Chinese New Year's would begin on February 15, 1885, and the Chinese worried that gangs from San Francisco would view the holiday as an invitation to a Chinese "tithe-gathering," joined by local whites who would enjoy the violence.[14] Chinatown's residents repeatedly tried to get the police to patrol, and they turned to the local papers to publicize the assaults. But the newspapers reported the murders in Chinatown as signs of inherent Chinese criminality, and the constabulary ignored the brutalities.[15] The editors of the *Daily Times-Telephone* called on the board of health and the city council to purge the Chinese from the town, because "citizens who pay for the privilege are entitled to walk the streets, day or night, without danger of being shot down in such manner."[16]

As Eureka's white citizens quickly coalesced against the Chinese, they took a new interest in federal immigration policy. They were particularly concerned about the recent ruling that gave Chinese consuls the right to issue certificates to Chinese workers to reenter the United States, making the Exclusion Act of 1882 "abortive and ineffectual."[17] Despite the lack of Chinese children in Eureka, hate crimes increased in mid-January following Judge James Maguire's courageous ruling in *Tape* v. *Hurley* that public schools in California must admit Chinese children. In early January, Humboldt County's *Weekly Times-Telephone* called for the destruction of Eureka's Chinatown.[18]

"WHAT WILL THE HARVEST BE?"

On Saturday afternoon, February 7, 1885, as the two ships laden with Chinese and their belongings waited to sail from Humboldt Bay, a large crowd of whites regathered at Centennial Hall to hear the Committee of Fifteen. Victorious from the day's events, the crowd readily accepted the committee's recommendations: all remaining Chinese throughout vast Humboldt County should be expelled, and no Chinese should ever again settle in Eureka. White merchants agreed to sign a pledge "not to give employment to Chinese . . . neither to sell them anything, neither to rent, lease, give or loan them any house . . . nor sell anything to anyone who rents house or houses, tenement or tenements . . . to any Chinaman."

The excited crowd paraded through the streets, voicing their new and expanded demands. That night the Eureka Common Council added another decree: the Chinese quarters were to be declared a nuisance and Chinatown itself should be "removed" to outside the city limits.[19] In only two days the Chinese community in Eureka was gone, and the policy banning its return endured until the 1950s.

Throughout February, Eureka's residents took stock of their actions; an editorial in a local paper pondered, "What Will the Harvest Be?" For most white residents, the financial loss was immediate. Some went into debt to pay higher salaries to new white employees.[20] Landlord Casper Ricks, who had been out of town during the weekend of the expulsion, returned to discover "that he was a loser to the extent of $300 per month by the expulsion of the Chinese, but so far from regretting that event, he was heartily glad of it."[21]

Casper Ricks, owner of Eureka Chinatown

Another urgent concern was dirty clothes. In this damp lumber and fishing town, most residents owned only one or two sets of clothes, and Eureka needed to quickly replace the Chinese laundries. One white woman, Mrs. Fred Vicinus, advertised that she would "convince the people that white women can do washing and ironing better and as cheap as Chinamen did."[22]

White residents tried their hands at growing their own vegetables but complained about their poor results, the lack of variety of food, and the rotting produce that was shipped north from San Francisco. The town suffered from the loss of Chinese laundries, shops, herbalists, and vegetable growers.

The citizens of Eureka now faced what their town would look like without the Chinese: "One thing is certain . . . it will check growing immoralities and keep our money at home, which was being shipped to China with the exception of the little that was expended on rice. Give us white labor by all means. We have no right to crowd out our own people for the sake of encouraging barbarians, who only brought dissension, opium eating, prostitution and leprosy in return."[23] Even the labor-oriented *Humboldt Standard*

Vegetable peddler, Eureka, California

marked the town's hypocrisy: "How do the professions of antagonism appear when we consider the inducements which our citizens have held out to Chinese? Last Friday night men were railing against Chinese and but a few hours before they ate suppers cooked by these same derided people. The men who spoke the loudest wore clothes which had the indisputable marks of the Chinese laundry."[24]

The people of Eureka also had legal worries. When they tried to move into the houses in Chinatown, Ricks first turned them away; Chinese men held valid leases for the premises, he said, and could "come on" him for damages.[25] Nonetheless, within a month a Eureka paper boasted, "the late abode of the filthiest lot of human beings on earth is fast becoming Americanized. Piles of rubbish are being burned daily in front of the houses, signs are being removed, buildings paved and renovated and occupied as cheap residences for men, shops, laundries, etc. The good results flowing from the removal of the Chinese from our city are becoming daily more apparent."[26] Not until 1888, under increasing pressure to "clear away the filthy old shells," did Ricks tear down Chinatown to make room for higher-rent tenants.[27]

The gravest fear was a lawsuit. Even as the "driven-out" Chinese were meeting in San Francisco, the residents of Eureka were predicting that the Chinese would sue either the city or the vigilantes; they were aware that elsewhere, in Antioch and Los Angeles, when "the Chinamen were driven

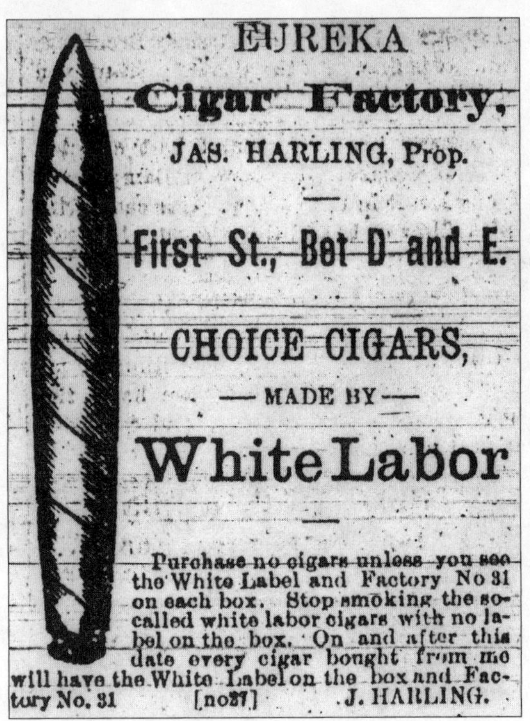
EUREKA
Cigar Factory,
JAS. HARLING, Prop.
First St., Bet D and E.
CHOICE CIGARS,
— MADE BY —
White Labor

Purchase no cigars unless you see the White Label and Factory No 31 on each box. Stop smoking the so-called white labor cigars with no label on the box. On and after this date every cigar bought from me will have the White Label on the box and Factory No. 31 [no27] J. HARLING.

Advertisement for cigars "Made by White Labor"
HUMBOLDT TIMES, FEBRUARY 3, 1886

out . . . the deed was followed by suits in the Federal Courts. . . . That the Chinamen driven off on Saturday suffered pecuniary loss there can be no doubt." With surprising racial myopia, the editorial went on: "Federal Courts are unrelenting in their administration of the laws, and recognize no distinction between white or black, Christian or pagan. To this Court the Chinese will probably appeal for redress."[28] Just outside of town, the fertile Chinese vegetable gardens that provided much of the produce for the city were looted, and the council was warned that it could find itself liable for any lost or destroyed Chinese property.

The flames of the Eureka purge blazed across the state. In the eighteen months that followed, pogroms against Chinese men and women spread from rural town to rural town, forcing hundreds of Chinese to flee. Across Humboldt County, Chinese communities were harassed and then evicted in a story of rage and resistance, defeat and defiance.

What prompted this ferocious ethnic cleansing? Why did communities that had long tolerated Chinese residents, even reluctantly, become so determined to drive them out?

In part the roundups arose from white workers' fears of job competition amid a desperate economic depression.[29] At the time of early union organizing, timber workers and politicians, and closely divided Democrats and Republicans, put aside their rivalries to target Chinese immigrants as threatening the fragile white job market.[30] The Chinese became an "indispensable enemy" who shifted the rage of white workers away from the timber barons. By the 1880s, as the depression and corporate takeovers extinguished their hopes, thousands of jobless men expressed their disillusionment with the "promised land" of the West by blaming the Chinese for their poverty, desperation, and frustrated dreams.[31]

The Humboldt County roundups were also rooted in the common and mundane facts of everyday life—rural work, property, poverty, and isolation.[32] For all of the tirades about lower wages and racial inferiority, whites and Chinese shared small-town life and endured similar conditions. Whites saw in Chinese workers precisely what they hated about their own lives: hard and underpaid work, long hours, poor living conditions, and a dearth of women. Whites lived in crowded bunkhouses; thirty Chinese men slept in a ten-by-ten-foot room in Eureka's new Chinatown.[33] By forcing the Chinese from Eureka, white workers tried to exorcise their own disillusions, their own landless poverty, and their ongoing dependence on the immensely profitable and often corrupt timber industry.

Where anti-Chinese violence occurred, dissatisfaction over housing, sexuality, and work had been percolating. The anti-Chinese actions of white workers and the defiant resistance of Chinese in the Pacific Northwest arose at the moment when Chinese artisan work and lifestyle crossed the new industrial work and factory life of native-born Americans and white immigrants. At this precarious moment of expansive capitalism, whites and Chinese experienced similar pressures.[34] With nothing to sell but his labor, the white man, often greatly in debt, had become a wage slave, trapped in company towns that had settled Chinese communities. Despite white workers' transience and displacement, they nonetheless denounced the Chinese as temporary residents—"sojourners." These are the fears and fantasies that shaped the meaning of race and undermined racial certainty.

The driving out of the Chinese from Eureka was prompted by more than working-class panic during hard times. The leaders of the purge crossed class lines to include merchants and bankers, landowners and tenants, unskilled and skilled workers. Eureka's Committee of Fifteen and the participants in the roundups were mill owners, elected town officers, and small businessmen. The Committee of Fifteen was chaired by H. H. Buhne, Jr., owner of a hardware store and ship chandlery who, in 1886, would go on to become a member of the city council. Others on the committee were Francis P. Thompson, editor of the labor-oriented *Humboldt Standard;* C. G. Taylor, a groceries merchant and agent for the Pacific Coast Steamship Company; Frank McGowan, an attorney; W. S. Riddle, a bookkeeper; Dan Murphy, a city councilman and the owner of the Western Hotel; N. A. Libbey, a bookkeeper and salesman; W. L. Mercer, a city councilman and owner of a harness and saddle store; A. J. Bledsoe, an attorney; W. J. McNamara, owner of a clothing and hat shop. Laborers included W. John Sweasey, James Brown, and James Simpson, a carpenter.[35]

While newspapers blamed the roundups on working people, it was merchants and bankers who chaired the meetings, wrote the editorials, and paid for the Chinese deportees' steamship tickets. Indeed, as the *Humboldt* and *City of Chester* sailed from Humboldt Bay, the Committee of Fifteen's first resolution was "that every man who has no visible means of support and who habituates a house of prostitution or gambling dens to be allowed until Saturday the 14th of February to leave this city."[36]

Local businessmen believed that they too were competing with the Chinese, in this case for steady customers. They also shared laborers' resentment of large-scale entrepreneurs, such as Leland Stanford and Charles Crocker, who employed Chinese contract labor on their railroads and in their vineyards and, worst of all, held large monopolies of vast tracts of timber and mineral-rich land. White merchants, small-scale ranchers and farmers, and the women who ran boardinghouses and food tables perceived the Chinese shopkeepers and servants as rivals. Thus, a coalition crossed class lines to drive out the Chinese.

GREEN GOLD

Rural company towns in California—Eureka, Truckee, Santa Cruz—exposed the illusion of frontier independence, of the enduring autonomy of an agrarian and artisan culture, of the romanticized communalism of small-town life, and of the easy inevitability of a white West.

In Humboldt County financial disparities were glaring: in 1860, before the Civil War, 5 percent of Humboldt residents owned 26 percent of the wealth; the bottom 50 percent owned only 9 percent. The Civil War stimulated a demand for arms, railroad cars, uniforms, and canned goods, launching the industrial revolution in the United States. Yet consumption could not keep up with the new production. Railroad expansion, the growth of heavy industries, and the government's support of monopolies and trusts had inspired the manufacture of goods for which there were no markets. Those who came to America after the Civil War encountered a society struggling to adjust to the rapid displacement of its indigenous population, as well to a vast white and African American migration, from village to city, farm to factory, East to West, South to North, forest to reservation. Throughout the United States, the new American working class, swelled by immigrants from Wales, Ireland, Germany, eastern Europe, and China, was living in squalor, wrenched from native traditions of culture and community.

Thus economics alone cannot explain the roundups. Editorials, labor leaflets, and campaign literature that promoted the roundups in Eureka projected onto the Chinese the needs, dissatisfaction, and disillusion of white workers' own lives. White working- and middle-class racism needs to be understood in terms of the daily life of Chinese immigrants. The explanation for the roundups lies not only in the question of whether race trumps class or class trumps race as the driving force of bigotry.[37] It lies also in common realities—of work, weather, money, roads, and the low numbers of women.

Images and fears of homoeroticism run through the journals, cartoons, and letters of timbermen. The Chinese man was feminized—because he was short, because he wore his hair in a queue, because he had less body hair than Caucasian men did, because he lived among men. These fantasies shaped the era's ideas of race.

The white man's racial rhetoric was, in fact, about himself: the Chinese worked too many hours; the Chinese worker was drugged on opium; the Chinese worker was slovenly; the Chinese debased the town and created the need for civic jobs; the Chinese ate rats; the Chinese were renters; the Chinese lived in overcrowded housing; the Chinese demanded the right to own property; the Chinese were expected to send scarce money back to their homeland. Both the white lumberjack and Chinese cook lived in close proximity to their employers. Employer surveillance was implicit and constant; organizing was difficult and blacklisting was common in one-industry towns and in the small logging community.

Lumberjacks viewed the Chinese as under tight surveillance as well, monitored by the Six Companies. Just as white unionists wanted a hiring hall, the Chinese Six Companies served as employment offices, legal-aid societies, and physical protection groups. During an era of recurrent and severe economic depressions and unemployment, rural white working-class organizations argued that by working without capital-intensive machinery, the Chinese could accept lower pay. They undermined union organizing, thwarting the development of an industrial working class and endangering white earnings by not demanding a "family wage."

The end of the Civil War had spurred a huge demand for wood. In Humboldt County, redwood trees, the tallest on earth, grew in towering green cathedrals and protective tribes or groves.[38] The redwoods tempted the boomtowns of San Francisco and Sacramento with timber—timber easy to plank and resistant to fire. Soon after the discovery of gold, timber lured investors from all over the world into Humboldt County, to cut, mill, and ship redwood for homes, shops, tools, bridges, tracks, and riggings. Hundreds of thousands of feet of California redwood were burned for fuel.

As early as the mid-1850s, nine steam-powered engines—a capital investment of four hundred thousand dollars—milled Humboldt's redwoods. By the 1870s, steam-powered "donkey" engines were moving the mammoth logs by cable to the marshes and millponds along the coast. Another four hundred thousand dollars were spent in logging operations, as primitive railroads with flatbed cars and massive chains, often built by Chinese workers, carried the giant logs to the mills and linked Eureka to the quickly receding forests.[39] Unlike early gold mining, the timber industry was capital-intensive, and by the 1880s, outside investors reaped the profits from trees thousands of years old and seductively tall. As the decades wore on, a few pioneer lumbermen survived, but increasingly, absentee capitalists or timbermen new to Humboldt County opened and managed the industry.[40]

By 1887, lumber production in the county was 120 million feet of virgin redwood per year, and the industry, owned by consortiums from Nevada to Scotland, employed two thousand men in logging, milling, and, at times, manufacturing shingles and shakes. While most investment came from San Francisco or abroad, local money came from leaders of the anti-Chinese movement, such as the timberman John Vance.

Humboldt's ties to a global nexus of imported workers and exported wood, of outside ownership of the mills, and, most particularly, of the land—came from the thousands and thousands of acres of magnificent "timber tracts" bestowed then, as now, by the federal government. The Pacific Lumber Company was principally owned by Nevada entrepreneurs. The California Redwood Company was owned by a Scottish syndicate that had coerced white workers to accept fifty-dollar bribes to obtain and then hand over tracts of acres under the Homestead Act. In timber and agriculture, land itself was an instrument of production, and land ownership—by the syndicates and the railroads—became a major concern of the ten assemblies of the Knights of Labor, the Grangers, the Populist Party, and other workingmen's organizations and unions. Even as white workers demanded jobs in Humboldt, they defeated a series of bond issues, such as those to build connector railroads, as initiatives of the "rapacious maws of an ever devouring monopoly" that paid little in taxes.[41]

And so, within a decade of the discovery of gold, Humboldt County became a major, if isolated, site in the large, global movement of workers, capital, and technology that was transforming the United States and the world. Suddenly the land had become a resource whose first residents—the Tolowa, Hoopa, Yurok, Karuk, Wiyot, and Chilula tribes—stood as barriers to mining, lumber, commerce, and expansion. East Coast entrepreneurs saw the Pacific north coast as unsettled and unoccupied land that invited a harvest of its vast natural resources—timber, salmon, gold, coal, water, and soil. The land and its trees as well as the people were commodities—fungible, profitable, and expendable.

Like early white settlers, the Chinese who came to remote Humboldt County had first been pulled to the Northwest by the discovery of gold along the Trinity and Klamath Rivers flowing from the Siskiyou Mountains. Driven from their mining claims, hundreds of Chinese men saw the possibility of new jobs—in fishing, agriculture, mining, lumber, and transportation—and made the trek. They came through the port of Humboldt Bay almost as soon as the first schooner dropped off white settlers and supplies. Chinese men came to Humboldt County (initially part of Trinity County) in 1850 to mine the gold fields along the Trinity River, which flowed through Karuk (Karok) and Hoopa land. By 1856 there were more than one hundred Chinese miners digging about two to three dollars' worth of gold per day from the gravel banks of the Trinity. At first, whites responded to the arrival of Chinese miners with stolid acceptance, if not outright welcome. *The Humboldt Times* noted that if "Chinamen are satisfied with such pay," then thousands of them will come to the lower Trinity and Klamath, "without any great risk of being soon disturbed by other miners who are not content with such wages."[42]

And indeed, by 1855 the Chinese had begun "pouring in" to Humboldt, coming down from the Siskiyou Mountains and the gold fields at Forks of Salmon, banished from rich claims or driven out by the exorbitant Foreign Miners' Tax. Some hired out to work for other miners and merchants; others bought and registered mines of their own.[43] While white miners could expect to earn sixteen or twenty dollars per day, Chinese miners earned between five and eight dollars, sometimes purchasing, sometimes occupying claims that white miners had abandoned.[44]

In 1868 *The Humboldt Times* wrote: "The Chinese are coming, Oh dear, Oh dear! No they are not, they are right here."[45] After the eastern and western tracks of the transcontinental railroad met in Promontory Summit, Utah, in 1869, Chinese and white miners and merchants again moved west, trekking down from the mountains to settle along the Pacific coast in the growing villages of redwoods. Initially, many Chinese men viewed Humboldt County as a refuge and put down roots in segregated Chinatowns. Other Chinese people found their way to this remote corner of northern California to flee slavery or debts for passage from China.[46]

The Chinese arriving on the north coast were mostly male, often poor, highly skilled in mining, road and railway construction, dynamiting, and farming. Familiar with violence and discrimination, they were eager to finally settle. Humboldt County was traced by tribal trails, divided by six wild rivers that flow from the steep Siskiyou mountain range, twisting down to the Pacific Ocean, and covered with tall and valuable first-growth redwood trees. Without roads and railroads, profitable logging and farming would be impossible.[47] In the 1870s Chinese men built many of Humboldt County's first roads, including the steep and narrow-gauge road along the winding Mattole River between the dairy town of Ferndale and the oil village of Petrolia. They also worked in the lumber mills as fire tenders and swampers, ran laundries, grew and sold vegetables, and labored as domestic servants. Others came to work in the salmon canneries along the Eel River, which two decades later would be the site of the final roundup in the county.

In small towns tucked into coves or estuaries along the rocky coastline, the mutual dependency of white employers and employees belied an enormous gulf in wages, wealth, and living standards. In Humboldt County, wages (the highest in the West) ranged from forty to seventy dollars per month, paid in cash; in the Siskiyous and the Sierra Nevada, wages in timber were about forty dollars per month, paid in scrip, which could only be redeemed at the company stores. Redwood trees, usually twelve to sixteen feet in diameter, spired up to three hundred feet high on steep and slippery fern-covered slopes. Felling them was dangerous. Days were long—twelve to fifteen hours; the ten-hour day in the lumber industry would not be won until 1890. The willingness of hundreds of Chinese workers to endure long hours provoked contempt and insecurity.

The first timbermen—mostly from New Brunswick and Nova Scotia—soon found themselves replaced by new immigrants from southern Europe, and they drifted north into the pine and spruce forests of Oregon and Washington. Meanwhile, timber barons in Humboldt County acquired astounding tracts of redwood forests, seized by the government on their behalf from native people. Few lumber companies in the county owned fewer than 1,500 acres; the Pacific Lumber Company began to fell trees in the mid-1880s after acquiring 12,000 acres of redwood forest, and by the late 1880s, Dolbeer and Carson owned more than 20,000 acres of timberland.[48]

To laborers and timber barons alike, the Chinese were sojourners—because they sent money home, because they were mobile, because they were renters. Racism resided in segregated bunkhouses and leaky tents. It resided in fatigue and in demands for an eight- or ten-hour day to replace the sunup-to-sundown day. It resided in fear of violence from other workers. It resided in all-male communities, quickly thrown together in the woods or along mountain streams, without the sexual, domestic, and religious presence of women and children.[49]

"MAKE THEM LEAVE"

The terms for the roundups were already set before Friday night, February 6, 1885. The anti-Chinese sentiment in Humboldt County had been moving toward its violent climax as the world of the white artisan worker—self-directed, communal, optimistic—was being transformed. Eureka was changing from a mining and lumber port to an industrialized town fueled by steam, run by machinery, and owned by investors who found themselves dependent on immigrants from all over the world. In the remote woods of northern California, the emergence of the night shift (begun in steel mills in the East), the beginnings of scientific management, the fight for the eight-hour day, the growth of a new female workforce, and the arrival of immigrants, such as Germans who brought with them the socialist impulses of the 1848 revolutions, forged a seemingly antagonistic class within an atmosphere of rural town commonality. In 1868, under pressure from the unemployed and the early unions, and as waves of anti-Chinese violence erupted across the state, the California legislature made eight hours a legal day's work, but this was not honored in Humboldt County.

Anti-Chinese feeling arose through the growing labor movement, and in turn it thrust the labor movement into political power in California. While the labor-oriented *Democratic Standard* queried, "What Shall WE Do with Our Chinamen?" the Republican *Daily Times-Telephone* urged the city council to face up to the "disgrace" of having "such a disreputable settlement right in the heart of our city" and remove the Chinese from the middle of town, as local editorials demanded, "Make them leave."[50]

Racial politics cut through the tense conflicts between miners and monopolists, trade unionists and industrialists, Democrats and Republicans, who mutually deployed the Chinese to attract constituencies in the West. Although the Chinese also lived and worked in the South and in the Mountain States, they had been seen as the "California problem"; now several factors converged to turn them into a national "problem." The courts had held that immigration was not a matter for Californians to decide locally but would be determined by Congress and the federal courts. California, however, was a swing state, and members of Congress realized that they could deflect attention away from the collapse of the economy—the destitution and despair across the nation—if they talked about the Chinese.

Two years after President Rutherford B. Hayes withdrew federal troops from the South in return for enough electoral votes to win reelection, California's Democratic platform of 1879 announced:

> [We] were the first in the early establishment of the State Government to proclaim antagonism to Chinese immigration and coolie cheap labor; that it was under a Republican administration that the Burlingame Treaty was made by which Chinese were admitted to the

rights and privileges accorded to emigrants from Europe; that it was a Republican occupant of the Presidential Chair who vetoed the Bill passed by a Democratic Congress to prohibit further immigration of Mongolians, and a Republican minority in Congress which prevented the passage of the Bill over the veto; and that, therefore, it is only to the Democrat Party the people can confidently look to secure legislation that shall abate and abolish the curse and evil of coolie importation, which cripples trade and palsies the arm of white labor.[51]

The contest between enslaved and free labor again emerged as part of white labor's plan to rid California of Chinese workers. This racial pitch was welcomed in Humboldt County, where a third of the voters were southerners still loyal to the Democratic Party.

And so the anti-Chinese movement spread through rural towns, driven by union organizers and eager politicians. Towns adopted the program of "abatement by violence" launched by San Francisco's labor politicians and the core branch of the Workingmen's Party, which was rising to prominence under Denis Kearney, and Bay Area trade unionists who joined the anti-Chinese League of Deliverance, led by Frank Roney.[52] As early as 1870, "sandlot" meetings of unemployed workers rallied under these slogans:

WE WANT NO SLAVES OR ARISTOCRATS

THE COOLIE LABOR SYSTEM LEAVES US NO ALTERNATIVE—STARVATION OR DISGRACE

MARK THE MAN WHO WOULD CRUSH US TO THE LEVEL OF THE MONGOLIAN SLAVE—WE ALL VOTE

WOMEN'S RIGHTS AND NO MORE CHINESE CHAMBERMAIDS

In 1878, by a vote of 2,552 to 258, Humboldt County supported the Workingmen's Party's call for a convention to write a new state constitution. The entire purpose of California's Second Constitutional Convention was to give the Workingmen's Party and the young labor movement the tools to purge the state of Chinese immigrants.[53] The new constitution made it illegal to employ a Chinese laborer in state or local public works. In

May 1879 it passed statewide, with a slim majority of eleven thousand votes, but with a two-to-one margin in Humboldt County.[54] Later that year in Humboldt County, the Workingmen's Party put the question of Chinese immigration itself on the local ballot: 2,308 white men voted against any further Chinese immigration, and 6 voted to allow it to continue.[55]

Labor would remain a powerful force in the county. The young labor movement in Eureka found a unifying voice in Charles Ferdinand Keller. Keller added the interests of small farmers and shopkeepers to the struggle of loggers and sailors, and within a few years became one of the county's leading rebels against mill owners and large cattle ranchers who received free land grants or cheaply bought up hundreds of thousands of acres of fertile farm- and timberland.[56]

"There is an aristocracy exempt from taxation that feed upon the vitals of the nation. . . . They have the money hence they control the labor. . . . This being the case they have the power to declare what a day's or month's labor shall be worth," Keller explained. Laborers, he concluded, "have lost our individuality, and are a nonentity as regards the affairs for the nation."[57] Because Keller believed that the key was land ownership, he began to expose how local lumber companies, in particular the California Redwood Company, were getting around the Timber and Stone Act by finding "dummies"—loggers, sailors, or local merchants—who, for a payoff of fifty dollars, would file for land claims under the Homestead Act and then turn over the land to their employer. He also exposed a syndicate, based in Edinburgh, Scotland, that paid only seven dollars per acre of redwood trees and quickly reaped more than ten million dollars in profits.

Complicit in the fraud, the county's Land Office registrar offered Keller sixty thousand dollars to destroy his notarized accounts, "drop the matter and leave town." But in exposing the swindle of thousands of acres of redwood forests, Keller lost the support of the loggers, who, lacking the capital to harvest or mill redwood, defended the scam of "locating" plots for the lumber companies. The *Standard,* the paper of the working people, sympathized with loggers: this was "the only way a poor man can realize any benefit from his timber right."[58] In fact, its editor, William Ayers, was one of two hundred people who had filed a dummy land claim for a lumber company. Eventually the federal government banned these proxy claims.[59]

When Burnette G. Haskell landed in Humboldt, sometime before 1884, he brought the International Workingmen's Association (IWA) into the county.[60] The IWA recruited sailors in the Eureka local of the Sailors' Union of the Pacific, which was waging a fierce struggle up and down the coast to lift seamen out of virtual serfdom. The IWA sailors adopted the secret cell system of European revolutionary groups and took the name of Karl Marx's First International. But the IWA was local in origin, and it sought to build trade unions and farmers' alliances in Humboldt County. In his labor newspaper, the *Truth,* Haskell urged loggers to destroy the county buildings that kept data on land titles. A week after the roundup of the Chinese, the IWA declared, "If the property owners would have refused to rent property to these heathens, they themselves would have realized more from their property, and not have forced this injury on unoffending citizens."[61] In his cry "War to the palace, peace to the cottage," Haskell was joined by Charles Keller, who signed on to the IWA. The IWA lasted only two years and never implemented its violent threats against the mills or local record offices, but its warnings to pay attention to property rights encouraged the birth of other unions along the rural coast, especially the Lumbermen's Union in 1884, the first union in the Pacific Coast timber industry and soon a leader in the anti-Chinese forces in Humboldt.

The closer white workers got to the Chinese, the more they seemed to despise them. Crowded together with them on long voyages, the sailors in the IWA knew the Chinese well. They witnessed the harsh transport of Chinese immigrants, food, opium, clothing; they saw anxious reunions and reentries, tense encounters with immigration officials, and the sorrowful ritual of returning bones to China for burial. They knew the Chinese were paid less than whites and urged the IWA to continue to link the plight of labor to Chinese wages.

Although Eureka's Workingmen's Party advocated compulsory education for children and the abolition of the electoral college, it was the drive for the eight-hour day that spliced it to the anti-Chinese movement. At virulent meetings in San Francisco's empty sandlots, Denis Kearney made no effort to veil his call for ethnic cleansing: "We have made no secret of our intentions. We make none. Before you and before the world we declare that the Chinese must leave our shores. We declare that white men, and women, and boys, and girls, cannot live as the people of the great republic should and compete with the single Chinese coolie in the labor market. We declare that we cannot hope to drive the Chinaman away or to be working cheaper than he does. None but an enemy would expect it of us; none but an idiot could hope for success; none but a degraded ward and slave would make the effort. To an American, death is preferable to life on par with the Chinaman."[62]

White laborers' perception that they suffered from Chinese competition was pervasive but flawed. Chinese workers mostly took jobs that white workers refused, such as in laundry. When Chinese workers did take logging jobs, white timbermen successfully purged them. John Carr, chairman of the Workingmen's Party of Humboldt County, hypocritically linked fears of Chinese labor to African American bondage: "The nation is yet in mourning for five hundred thousand of her best and bravest sons, who laid down their lives that their posterity might enjoy the blessings of a free country; but no sooner was African slavery abolished at such a dreadful cost of blood and treasure—which will cripple generations yet unborn to make good . . . a far more dangerous and servile race of slaves than those that it cost the nation so much to abolish. Hordes of these Chinese slaves only await the bidding of their masters to invade our land, devour our substance and bring our laboring classes down to their base level."[63]

While the Chinese were despised for working longer hours for lower wages, they were also blamed for the vices of drugs, gambling, and prostitution—indulgences purchased and enjoyed by white customers. In 1868 the Chinese appear in the local press for the first time in reports of robberies, assaults, and attempted murders. These crime reports and police blotters contain the earliest evidence of Chinese men and women in Humboldt. The appearance of the first Chinese in Arcata, a lumber town seven miles north of Eureka on the muddy shores of Humboldt Bay, is marked by a news story of a knife fight in Chinatown.[64]

By the late 1870s, alongside cartoons that pictured slothful and supine Chinese lying by their opium pipes, local newspapers reported that white women were frequently "discovered" in Chinatown, overdosed on opium; some turned out to be prostitutes, and the Chinese were blamed for victimizing innocent and vulnerable girls. The papers failed to note that opium, like its legal and well-advertised liquid sister, laudanum, was a common drug that brought addictive comfort to isolated, homesick, and abused white women living in small rural towns—without their families and without many women friends.

In 1880, Humboldt suffered heavy rains that destroyed its potato crop, a cold winter that killed thousands of sheep, cutting the new wool industry by half, and a plague of grasshoppers that devastated fields and orchards. Farmers, timber workers, and sailors began to see their shared interests. The industrial and agricultural depressions affected everyone in the county. Soon the pressing desire for jobs, for new monetary policies, and for land ownership gave Humboldt County a national perspective. In 1880 the remaining members of the Workingmen's Party dissolved their organization and re-formed as the Humboldt County Greenback Party.

The other organized labor force influencing the purges was the Pacific Coast League of Deliverance. A nonviolent splinter group based in San Francisco and led by Frank Roney, the league had one intention: "to rid the United States of Chinese." Its first rural branch met in Eureka in May 1882. Membership simply required paying dues of ten cents and swearing to the oath "I hereby pledge my honor that I will not employ or patronize Chinese, directly or indirectly, nor will I knowingly patronize any person, directly or indirectly, who does employ Chinese." Its strategy was to sell window cards for one dollar to employers that the League verified did not "deal in Chinese goods." Merchants who still had Chinese goods on hand could display "Conditional Cards" if they vowed "not to purchase any more of the same." The cards, it was hoped, would identify merchants sympathetic to the anti-Chinese cause and would prompt a quiet boycott of shopkeepers, barbers, and restaurants who continued to employ Chinese staff. It would force the Chinese into poverty and drive them out.[65] But in the mid-1880s the Chinese still totaled 20 to 25 percent of California's wage earners.

Labor feared that Chinese immigrants would remain in the United States, become naturalized, and vote. Scared of the edginess of the Workingmen's Party and frustrated by the growing power of corporations and railroads that had "absorbed" public lands in the great congressional giveaway, California laborers turned to the Democratic Party, which quickly delivered the 1882 Chinese Exclusion Act and closed the door on Chinese immigration. The same party that had supported slavery, "the very bane of free labor," now attached workingmen's troubles to the Chinese.[66] The Workingmen's Party had won the county's seats in the state senate and assembly as well as half its local elected positions, defeating a coalition of Republicans and Democrats for the mayor's office and the board of supervisors. But mirroring the national trend, the coalition of workers and small farmers foundered within two years and the local Democratic Party sponged up the insurgent energies and, in particular, the anti-Chinese charge of the Workingmen's Party, the Populist Party, and the Grangers. Racial movements in California were shaped by political struggles contested at the local and state level.[67]

"THE IMPENDING CRISIS HAS ARRIVED"

In May 1880, just months after the town of Garberville expelled all of its Chinese residents, the *Humboldt Standard* warned that lumber mills would soon hire many more Chinese laborers. Framed by exposés about opium dens and prostitution rings in Eureka's Chinatown, the *Standard* declared, "The impending crisis has arrived." By hiring Chinese immigrants, it warned, "some of our mill owners threaten the poor white man who is eking out a miserable existence at a mere pittance."[68]

In March 1882, twenty-one men went on strike after Fay's Shingle Mill in Fairhaven hired twenty-two Chinese workers. Led by the Knights of Labor, timbermen marched to the mill and told Fay they were acting under the "force of public sentiment which is higher than any written law."[69] Fay immediately shipped his Chinese employees out of the county on the next boat. Sensing a rising threat, other mill owners agreed not to employ any more Chinese. Yet backed by the Chinese Six Companies, which insisted that the county honor their contracts, Chinese laborers continued to work on the short-haul railroads between the timber tracts and the docks in the fishing canneries on the Eel River, in agriculture, and on building roads connecting Eureka to small river towns.

In single-industry or lumber towns the anti-Chinese movement fueled an illusion of rural mutuality between worker and employer. The intimate and dependent nature of lumber work made it difficult to build unions and even more difficult to organize strikes. Labor organizing was hard in the redwoods—jobs lasted only eight months of the year, the labor force was transient and dispersed over hundreds of miles, and mills easily found more and more unskilled workers. The first lumber workers' strike in Humboldt County did not occur until 1881.

Meanwhile, typographers sat up all night, sending stories of the roundups along the telegraph wire. The International Typographical Union (ITU) cemented the young white labor movement and stimulated anti-Chinese sentiments across the state. The typographers quickly described, published, and at times created and amplified the news of the roundups, which then spread in small-town and statewide papers alike, such as the *Daily Alta California.* In places in the Pacific Northwest where people and goods still traveled by buggy over widened Indian trails or short-haul railroads—filling in gaps with mule trains and wagons, narrow river steamships, sailing ships, and dugout canoes—typographers connected towns and decided what they would believe. An anti-Chinese drive would be reported in county newspapers throughout the Pacific Northwest within a day or two, at most a week after it occurred. Many small papers even had columns listing the week's anti-Chinese events.

Just at this time in the early 1880s, the Knights of Labor burst onto the national scene and grafted the purges of the Chinese onto the new labor movement. In contrast to craft unions, the Knights promised to build inclusive "vertical" assemblies. Organized in California only one year after the Lumberman's Union, the Knights attracted workers designated by the American Federation of Labor as "unskilled"—loggers and miners—unifying young labor clubs with their demands for a weekly payday, an eight-hour day, and the abolition of child labor. But excluded from the organization that promised to unite as many workers as possible were the Chinese.

Except for gamblers, lawyers, bankers, stockbrokers, and Chinese, all were welcome. The Knights vowed to abolish Chinese contractors and indentured labor and set up its own labor bureau to control job placement. Their Humboldt assembly lasted for five years, the peak years of the Chinese roundups. Led by Millard Fillmore Gardner, the Knights organized assemblies from Crescent City down to the Mendocino County line, and soon Arcata's Assembly 3424 had one hundred members. And the new Knights assemblies in Blue Lake, Bayside, Freshwater, Crescent City, Smith River, Port Kenyon, and Ferndale all promoted the anti-Chinese purges of 1885–86.[70]

Even though jobs filled by Chinese workers in Humboldt County were not jobs early unionists wanted, even after the purges, white workers claimed to still be haunted by the specter of enslaved Chinese labor. The

Knights often reminded Californians that Chinese laborers had been brought in to break a strike at a shoe factory in North Adams, Massachusetts, in 1870.[71]

Humboldt's emerging labor movement—the Knights of Labor, the International Workingmen's Association, the Coast Seamen's Union, the Typographical Union, and the Clerks Union (shop clerks)—was calling for an end to the sunup-to-sundown workday and payment in company scrip. They shared a vision of civic job projects, such as building railroads, sewage systems, roads, and sidewalks. They wanted the federal government to grant public land to workers by extending the Homestead Act. They wanted better food in the company cookhouses and sleeping cots in bunkhouses rather than tents. Living in all-male communities far from the town sheriff, timbermen and clerks wrote in diaries and letters of their fear of other workers who settled disputes with arms.

In these towns along the Pacific coast, whites and Chinese did not have to be forced into consciousness of each other's living and working conditions. Small-town familiarity exposed the myth of "the Mongolian" as a slave or coolie. In Eureka, whites were not urban tourists who came into the Chinese community to shop, inhale, or consume what they disdained in the "exotic" migrant. These towns were "knowable" communities—small in scale, with familiar neighbors and shopkeepers, visible political affiliations recognized by Chinese and white settlers alike. Geographic isolation and local paternalism could mask some racial hierarchies.[72] It is against and through this rural and class commonality—both true and imagined—that real divisions of labor, of social position, of countries of origin, of power, and ultimately of race, were built.

By February 1885, Eureka was being run by its working class. Mayor William Wallace, City Marshal Andrew Hitchings, and Councilmen C. H. Olstead, C. L. Devlin, and W. L. Mercer forged a city government intent on providing jobs in public works—jobs that were specifically denied to the Chinese by the California constitution in 1879, even though this ban had been ruled unconstitutional. The city resurveyed and expanded the town limits, graded and surfaced city streets, built blocks of new sewers, passed an ordinance establishing a "street railroad," widened sidewalks, and replaced the old wooden ones with cement—the project that had blocked the sewage in Chinatown.

"WE MEAN BUSINESS": THE IMPACT OF THE EUREKA ROUNDUP

In the months following the Eureka roundup, the Chinese tried to return to their homes, even as rural communities throughout the county set about expelling their Chinese residents. In 1886 Chinese vegetable peddlers drifted back into town. In January, Charles Mock (or Muk), along with two Chinese friends, tried to purchase property in Eureka. Working through his friend Robert Henry, Mock accidentally let it be known that the lots would be occupied by Chinese people; not surprisingly, all of Henry's bids for blocks of land were rejected. One of the original members of the Committee of Fifteen, A. J. Bledsoe, announced that Mock was "one of the most notorious highbinders on the coast . . . if a fusillade of shots was heard in Chinatown, people knew that Mock was amusing himself." Bledsoe charged that it was "the opinion of many" that Mock had fired the fatal bullet that killed Kendall, and the local papers explained that if Mock became a property owner, he could not be expelled again.

The Committee of Fifteen convened, and two white citizens "advised" Mock to leave town. When he refused to pay for his own deportation, two committee members bought his ticket, and on January 16 he was shipped out of Eureka for a second time.[73] But Mock's visit alerted the city that the Chinese deportees intended to come back.

The Knights of Labor quickly elected several candidates under the "Citizens Ticket" in county races, and swept the Eureka elections in June. The city elected Knights to the offices of mayor, city marshal, and trustee of the Free Library, and to three city council posts.

Then the Committee of Fifteen and the Knights called for the expulsion of all Chinese from the county. "We mean business. . . . Our proceedings so far have been peaceable and orderly, but there is a limit beyond which even Eureka patience may not go." Believing that about sixty Chinese men remained in the county, Bledsoe added, "We do not propose violence. So far we have not harmed a single Chinaman and we do not intend to do so if we can help it. But we do not want them and we don't propose to have them."[74]

Led by Bledsoe, the towns of Arcata, Salmon Creek, Ferndale, Hydesville, and Springville (now Fortuna) followed Eureka's path. During the weekend of the Eureka pogrom, whites in Arcata had initiated an ethnic cleansing of their own. Even before the *Humboldt* and the *City of Chester* sailed out of Humboldt Bay on February 8, George W. B. Yocum had called for a mass anti-Chinese meeting in Arcata. With the bay to the west and the redwoods to the east, Arcata had seen two Chinatowns grow up on its north and south edges, where the Chinese lived in wooden shacks stacked one upon the other. On that fateful weekend an anti-Chinese rally elected a citizens' committee to visit these two Chinese enclaves and tell all residents to leave the town limits "before Wednesday next."

By Thursday morning, February 12, most Chinese residents had been moved into makeshift shelters in the woods and meadows beyond the corporate boundaries of Arcata.[75] The North Fork Mill fired forty Chinese men, who then hid in an empty house in town, afraid to travel the seven miles south to Eureka, where they could catch a boat for San Francisco.[76] The committee led vigilantes on a roundup of Chinese residents, forced them into gravel wagons, and hauled them to the dock, where they were loaded onto fishing boats headed down Humboldt Bay to be shipped from Eureka aboard the *Mary D. Hume.* The steamship companies promised to take all the Chinese men that the law would allow them to carry.[77]

Eureka's "infection [has] caught far and wide," announced James Beith, a Democratic leader of Arcata's Knights of Labor, who noted with some ambivalence that

> this is the very absurdity of Quizotism [*sic*]. Eureka had a partial justification for her action and inspired by that took summary steps. Arcata without a shadow of provocation insists upon measures equally severe. The men of Eureka had a real grievance—those of Arcata none. While in law Eureka could plead strong cause in extenuation—what bar to severe condemnation, could Arcata intervene? This wholesale exodus will bring Eureka in conflict with the Federal courts. There the law will be doled out by the language of the [Burlingame] Treaty; and Col. Bee will insist on damage and restitution according to its phraseology "the privileges conceded to the most favored nations." A few inspired idiots talk of resisting the Federal power and talk of hanging a marshall if he attempts to serve its process![78]

In early 1886, to celebrate the anniversary of the Eureka purge, Arcata expelled all the remaining Chinese. It too formed a Committee of Fifteen, which collected enough money to hire railroad cars and boats, and the Arcata Cornet Band accompanied three hundred men and women to Eureka's festivities. Judge J. P. Haynes told the cheering crowd that "the cry in the past had been 'The Chinese Must Go,' but now it is 'The Chinese Must Never Return.' "

Arcata's Democratic and labor leaders returned from the party determined to take "final action."[79] On February 13, citizens of Arcata called a mass rally to announce that "the time is now ripe . . . for the total expulsion of the Chinese from our midst."[80] Over the last year, reported James Beith, although the Chinese presented a "cordial and cooperative spirit," they refused to leave. Equally deplorable, Beith added, were whites "who hired the obnoxious element" or "harbored them in hovels specially erected to shelter them."[81] On the night of the rally, the working people of Arcata demanded that mill managers and company owners who still hired Chinese workers join the movement to drive them out. Chastened, the owners of the Blue Lake Mill Company and of the Falk, Howley and Company sawmill and dozens of other wealthy merchants, lumber dealers, and manufacturers announced they were ready to vote with the workingmen and endorse "the total expulsion of the Chinese from our midst." Denouncing U.S. treaty obligations with China as an "error of statesmanship," business owners now complained that the Chinese had proved "conclusively that their energies tend to decay not growth, their efforts are demeaning to labor, and a complete undermining of our social structure."[82]

But Arcata was also aware that the Chinese of Eureka had filed a lawsuit for reparations against that city. At a town rally, anti-Chinese leaders called the suit "blackmail" and claimed "the extortionate amount of damage shows that it is not equity they seek but a device of the crafty Mongolians to rob our people by the forms of law." Blustering aside, the city leaders of Arcata feared a suit similar to *Wing Hing* v. *City of Eureka* and resolved to "deprecate all violence or undue force in the expulsion of the Chinese as inviting the interference of the Federal Courts." Rather than copy its neighbor's violent tactics, which they had just celebrated the night before, Arcata's town officials and union leaders agreed to "withhold custom" and to boycott any merchant or individual who bought from Chinese stores, hired Chinese laborers or servants, or contracted with the Chinese for any services. The crowd also charged a Committee of Three to visit every white employer in town and compel him to sign a pledge not to employ any "Coolie, Chinese or Pagan labor" and to "prevent others from doing so by any means."

The exodus from Arcata was slow, sad, and thorough. The Chinese were threatened and intimidated, or, as Beith recalled, "appealed to" by "calling their attention to the too evident danger of their lives and property. The object was to influence their fears so that they might quietly take their departure."[83] The Committee of Supervision, one of the vigilantes' regularly shifting names, terrorized the two Chinatowns, hinting that the Chinese would be assaulted or charged with violating vagrancy codes. It warned Chinese merchants to expect rigid economic boycotts that would sever the "bond which bound the Mongolian to our soil."[84]

The pressure was effective. Over the next two weeks, Chinese woodcutters and laborers began to leave the redwood forests surrounding Arcata and found their way to Eureka to catch a steamship bound for San Francisco.[85] By early April, only twenty Chinese people remained in the town, the A. and M. Rail Road Company was donating cars to ship out the Chinese, and the local steamship companies had reduced the cost for Chinese persons and freight.[86] And so, in small groups of seven or eight, the Chinese of Arcata, some residents for thirty years, passed through the town for the final time. When many refused to pay for their tickets to San Francisco, a white merchant organized a collection for the six-dollar tickets.[87]

On April 24, the *Humboldt Standard* boasted, "Arcata is rid of her Chinese." Two nights later the town threw a party in Excelsior Hall to celebrate. Civic leader Frank McGowan reminded the crowd that when he was a child he had joined anti-Chinese "agitation by the use of a forcible argument in the shape of a brickbat." He recalled that he had been "ably assisted" by many who were now the young businessmen of Arcata and that they had a "marked effect upon the children of Confucius." Nonetheless, concluded McGowan, the "peaceable manner" of the week's purge was in the end more effective. The party ended with the "jolly" auction of the furniture and goods left behind by the Chinese. The town raised fifty dollars.

In the 1887 elections the Knights of Labor took control of the board of supervisors, running candidates on a "People's Party" ticket that included Richard Sweasey and James Beith, who had been leaders in the roundups. A town hall is still named in Sweasey's honor.

Richard Sweasey

"THERE'S NO LAW NORTH OF THE EEL AND NO GOD NORTH OF THE KLAMATH"

The removal of tribal peoples, forced onto the Klamath Reservation in 1855 and Fort Terwer in 1861, opened this land to build a lumber town and a jumping-off spot for miners, mule skinners, and settlers bound for the gold fields and timber forests in Oregon. Here, between the Siskiyou Mountains to the east and the Pacific to the west, the Oregon border to the north and Eureka to the south, gold and copper miners and homesteaders bought supplies for the hundreds of miles of trekking to the north along Oregon's rivers and into the Cascade Mountains, or to the east up the riverbeds into the Siskiyous. Until 1853, men had lived in tents in an arc along the beach, where the redwood forest pushed almost to the ocean's edge. But in less than a year three hundred houses were built in a newly laid-out town called Crescent City. At the raw docks men unloaded from

MASS MEETING.

A Mass Meeting of the citizens of this place and vicinity will be held at Darby's Hall, on Sunday, Jan. 31, at 2 o'clock P. M., to devise some lawful means of ridding Crescent City of Chinese.

R. W. Miller, R. G. Knox, L. F. Coburn and others will address the meeting.

All are invited to attend.

Placard, January 1886

steamers and schooners all the goods needed in the northernmost corner of California and in Oregon. The new town needed roads, and it needed merchants and launderers, domestic servants and mule packers. It needed Chinese men.

Whites and Chinese came through Crescent City, about a hundred miles north of Eureka, seeking whatever gold remained in California. During the 1850s, the Chinese built camps that stretched throughout northern and eastern Humboldt County. They mined in the gold fields along the Trinity and Salmon Rivers. They grew vegetables to supply the fishing village of Trinidad. They trolled for cod, trapped crabs, and dove for abalone along the Pacific and netted salmon along the Klamath River. By the late 1870s, Crescent City had a large and segregated Chinatown with its own stores, washhouses, wooden shacks, shanties, and boardinghouses. The city gave the east end of the cemetery to the Chinese.

The first attempt to purge the Chinese from Crescent City failed. Early in 1856 a group of Chinese bought an abandoned claim. When after working it for eight months the Chinese found gold, the previous owners tried to retake the claim. The claim jumpers opened fire, and one white miner was killed and many others arrested.[88] But the Chinese had legal standing because they owned the property, and the town sheriff and his deputies protected their stake.

Three decades later, on the cold February weekend of the Eureka roundup, Crescent City held its own anti-Chinese parade and made plans to copy the lumber town to the south. Over the next two weeks, with each

Chinese merchant family Tsiau Han Yu, Crescent City

steamship that left port, Crescent City forcibly shipped out several hundred Chinese residents. Most sailed to San Francisco. Finally, only two Chinese women, two children, and two or three men remained. A gang of white loggers came into town, hired a wagon, loaded the Chinese families, hauled them out of town up Howland Hill, and shoved them from the wagon. They were never seen again in Crescent City.[89]

With Crescent City, Eureka, and Arcata at the epicenter of the purges, other Humboldt County towns soon fell into line. In spring 1886, Eureka's Committee of Fifteen bullied the tiny fishing village of Trinidad to expel its one Chinese man, a hotel worker. The remote coastal village of Petrolia also chased out its lone Chinese man.[90]

On the eastern edge of the county, the mountain village of Willow Creek rallied at China Flat, the site of an early Chinese mining claim. Although most of the Chinese miners and woodcutters lived well beyond the little town, on the night of March 17, 1886, the citizens of Willow Creek called for the "total expulsion of Chinese from our midst," acknowledging that they were about to violate America's treaty obligations with China. Willow Creek sat at the border of the Hoopa Reservation, an area of militant Indian resistance to white settlers. Fearing any more violence, the settlers joined with nearby mountain towns to boycott and denounce anyone who sold or leased land to the Chinese and shunned anyone who hired Chinese workers.

In early March Ferndale purged its Chinese residents, and the hamlet of Ellensburg banned Chinese children from the school. Soon the Chinese were expelled from Rohnerville and Springville, Garberville and Hydesville. In the early spring of 1886, Humboldt County took stock of its success. Wrote the *Daily Times-Telephone,*

> Humboldt County will soon be rid of its entire former Chinese population. Eureka has been purged of it for more than a year. Arcata has taken steps which will result in the banishment of fifty or sixty wards of [Chinese consul] Col. Bee. . . . We don't think that what Chinamen are left at Rohnerville and Springville will be there long. Ferndale will be rid of them. Whether or not there is a Chinaman in Hydesville, we are unable to state. Blocksberg never would tolerate the presence of that people, and we are inclined to the belief that there are none in Garberville. As Petrolia has spoken in regard to the matter, it may be taken for granted that her population will not in the future include any of the obnoxious element. Before long citizens who want to know how a Chinaman looks will have to go all the way to the Klamath River to find out.[91]

In May 1885, A. J. Bledsoe, an attorney and one of the leaders of Eureka's Committee of Fifteen, predicted that prosperity would flow from the roundup. The effect of the "exodus," he told a San Francisco reporter, was "most wonderful and gratifying." He boasted that the town's dirty laundry was now all washed by white people, and that "one hundred white men are daily employed at good wages and thousands of dollars have been spent in San Francisco for costly machines for the steam laundries." White men had also replaced Chinese men as cooks and on railroad construction. Bledsoe concluded, "At least 225 white men have obtained employment through the expulsion of the Chinese, and there are many other things which prove the action was timely and beneficial to the prosperity of our country."[92]

In fact, this was not the experience of the white workingman. Hundreds of unemployed whites read of the purges in newspapers throughout California and quickly made their way to Humboldt. The *San Francisco Chronicle* reported: "Never since Humboldt County was first inhabited by white men was so much want known to exist among the laboring class as at the present time. Hundreds of laborers are bereft of the necessaries of life and in a state of semi-starvation. They live on shellfish and sleep in the woods, beneath the cold blast of this northern region. A few are working on the railways at $1 a day, with $1 a week deducted for sleeping accommodations; but most of the workingmen who arrive at Eureka by each steamer are unable to find any work whatever to do. The logging business is unable to keep the old hands employed." The *Chronicle* advised its readers not to "try their luck" in Humboldt: "It is a novel county and some day its great resources will be appreciated. But it seems to be passing through a dark stage in its history, and until that is passed over immigrants had better give it a wide berth."[93]

By 1890 Humboldt was proudly marketing itself as a county free of Chinese people. To recruit white immigrants, the *History and Business Directory of Humboldt County* boasted, "There is not a Chinaman in Humboldt County except in the mines on the Klamath River . . . and they are there only because of the extreme isolation. . . . To those who have experienced the misery of having this degraded and debasing element in their midst, and realize the futility of redress at the hands of the U.S. Courts . . . this simple fact of itself is no small recommendation when seeking a home as far removed from vicious example as possible. Nature's benefactions to Humboldt have been many, but we pride ourselves on having by our own efforts, eradicated a festering putrescent sore from our vitals."[94]

In fact, not all the Chinese had been "eradicated" from the county. Some still lived on Karuk and Hoopa land in the Siskiyou Mountains, a three-day journey from the ocean by dugout canoes up the Klamath or Trinity River or by mules across the steep Bald Hills. Across two mountain ridges from the coast many mined along gravel beds where the Trinity flows out of the Klamath, or where the North and South Forks of the cold green Salmon River meet. Some Chinese miners still worked for themselves; others hired out to new Chinese-owned hydraulic-mining companies. Even in the bitter spring of 1886 the Chinese remained in mountain towns such as Orleans Bar, where they shopped for food—rice, dried fruits, smoked fish, preserved vegetables—especially imported for them at Lord's General Store. They paid with special coins minted for them in China, with Chinese writing on one side and English on the other. They worked, grew food, and settled in the forests and along the narrow river gorges.

The *Humboldt Standard* complained, "We are informed that in one or two mining camps in the vicinity of Orleans Bar, Chinese are employed to do the work. It is needless to say that the miners owe it to themselves and the county to discharge them. Humboldt is making a praiseworthy and earnest effort to cause an exodus of all her Mongolians, and no citizen should retard the good work. Every person employing a Chinaman should at once dismiss him, even at the risk of a little inconvenience. . . . Nearly all have gone now, and a decisive stand on the part of every man in the county is all that is necessary to cause every one to leave."[95]

One resident of Lower Klamath, "L.J.H.," wrote to the *Standard,* "The mining district will have to follow the example of Eureka, for the simple reason that after they are driven out of the cities they will then seek refuge among the miners where some few of their fellow men own mining property, and I dare say in some mining districts they have worked their way in until they own great tracts of valuable mining land. Now, in a case of this kind what is to be done? Give them time to settle up their business before expelling them or call a meeting and appoint appraisers and appraise their property, pay them for it and then make them travel?" In L.J.H.'s opinion, "where they are given time . . . they will undoubtedly do some mischief before they get away. They are something like a rat—the great secret will be to find the hole where they get in." The solution, he insisted, was to make them "get out at the same hole and then [see] that it is sufficiently blockaded."[96] Yet white vigilantes, in their haste, had ignored Native American authority in the eastern mountains of the county.[97]

In the isolated mountain areas of the county some tribal people viewed the Chinese as yet another wave of invaders who were willing to destroy the land in their pursuit of gold, particularly after many Chinese miners became expert at using the hydraulic hoses that washed away the mountains to expose the ore within. Chinese and Native Americans also competed for agricultural work. Describing the potato harvest of 1884, the *Standard* announced that "instead of the Indian who has done that kind of work the abominable 'Heathen Chinese' are swarming in herds to dig the potatoes and take the wages out of the country."[98]

Some Chinese farmers and miners married tribal women and sent their children to the local schools. Folded into the community, they were left undisturbed and indeed, during the violence, given cover. Some were harbored in the Arcata home of William Lord and later absorbed into the Karuk community in the Siskiyous of eastern Humboldt.

Some Native Americans united with the Chinese. In May 1886, for example, when the steamer *Ancon* was about to depart for the north, thirty white waiters walked off the ship after they found three Chinese cooks working in the kitchen. But two Alaskan Inuit sailors refused to join the white men's strike, and when the Steamshipman's Protective Association succeeded in forcing the *Ancon* to fire the Chinese cooks, it also had to fire the Inuit men before white sailors agreed to return.

"CHINESE EXCLUDED": AFTER THE ROUNDUPS

The forced exodus of the Chinese from Eureka failed to improve conditions for anyone. After the 1885 and 1886 roundups, 250 Chinese men remained in the county—20 as cooks, 50 as miners, and the rest as washermen. Their wages were low: twenty-five dollars per month, with board; laundrymen earned twenty-five dollars without board. In all the other occupations in Humboldt County—mining, transportation, timber, and manual labor—the Labor Bureau reported: "Chinese excluded." Wages for whites were only minimally better. After the roundups, a white male cook earned sixty dollars per month and a white laundryman earned forty dollars, both with board. White lumbermen earned sixty per month; bookkeepers and longshoremen averaged seventy dollars; printers earned eighty. To some degree, white women replaced the Chinese domestic workers, and their wages were consistent with the seventy cents on the male dollar that women earn today; seamstresses and laundry workers were paid thirty dollars without board, ten dollars less than men. After the roundups, only 20 percent of workers belonged to the Knights of Labor.[99]

The Chinese could no longer be blamed for the fact that the redwoods were the only lumbering region on the coast without a ten-hour day. A consortium of the ten largest lumber companies and sawmills on the north coast rejected the Knights' demand for a shorter workday, falsely claiming that with the Chinese purged from the county, social conditions and wages had already improved. Even with the Chinese excluded, white wages stayed low.

As the Chinese were being assaulted and deported from Humboldt County, efforts to recruit white immigrants intensified. In the weeks leading up to the February 1885 purge, local papers proudly announced that during just one week in December 1884 the California Immigration Association had imported seven hundred white immigrants from southern Europe. The Humboldt papers hoped that many of these new immigrants might be enticed to settle in the county if they heard that fruit orchards and farming in the sunny part of the county would be "pleasant and profitable." Mill owners subsidized the settlement of Scandinavian immigrants and brought them into Eureka on their own ships to replace workers involved in the Knights. By the turn of the century *The Humboldt Souvenir,* a booklet published by the Chamber of Commerce, invited more whites to settle in "the redwood country" with the promise that they could live in a county free of Chinese!

> One fact makes Humboldt unique among the counties of California, and indeed, on the Pacific Coast—we have no Chinese. Our workmen are not compelled to come into competition with the degraded coolies of the Orient. There was a time when the Chinese had quite a colony here, but in one of the "tong" wars a stray bullet from the pistol of a highbinder struck and killed a prominent citizen of Eureka, who was passing along the street. The community rose as a man and drove every Chinese out of the county. No violence was used they were compelled to go. That was in 1885, and since then Humboldt has had no Chinese. Even in far-off China, the coolies know that they are not permitted to come here, and none ever attempt it.

Still the Chinese tried to return to Humboldt County. In October 1887, fifty Chinese men arrived on the schooner *Golden Fleece* to work in the salmon canneries on the Eel River. Concerned that there were no other skilled cannery workers, the Cutting Packing Company agreed to offer a bond to the county, promising that the Chinese would leave when the salmon season was over.[100]

COMMONALITIES

When unemployment and estrangement replaced the utopian bravado of the western migration, European Americans in the West found comfort and commonality in their whiteness.[101] In the last decades of the nineteenth century, those who controlled the new corporations—the Carnegies and the Rockefellers, the Crockers and the Stanfords, and the Vances and Carsons—sought to limit class struggle, erupting in the Homestead strikes and the Haymarket tragedy, by dividing the new industrial class along racial lines. The physical, cultural, and national differences between Chinese and white—exposed and shaped by advertisements and political campaigns, by cruel cartoons and popular songs—split a global working class residing in California. Chinese Americans challenged a multinational white culture that was struggling to establish itself as inevitable, the norm of the interracial West. Class consciousness became complicit in racism.

These purges exposed commonalities of white and Chinese lives, dreams, and struggles, shaped by a shared rural experience of class. Photographs, editorials, and news accounts of life in Humboldt wrapped images of differences within images of similarities. Rural whites and Chinese experienced common living and working conditions, and it was this that impelled, indeed obsessed, the white working class. Hidden in the speeches, the cartoons, and the ads that provoked the roundups is a reflection, a shadow, of the demands that white workers were making for themselves.

The stereotypes and inaccurate assumptions about Chinese immigrants mirrored the desperate material needs of white timbermen, mill workers,

"A Picture for Employers"

PUCK, AUGUST 21, 1878

and sailors, articulated by their new and very fragile union movement. The ruthless, unthinkable, and previously unread violence of the roundups in Eureka, Crescent City, Tacoma, Truckee, and San Jose conjures a fluid and permeable image in which the white working class saw their own lives reflected in the lives of the Chinese—shared lives of poverty, displacement, backbreaking work, inadequate housing, dirt, lack of women, and communal male living, a vision close at hand to the very new middle class. Rural whites saw in the Chinese their most profound anxieties about their own identity and destiny. It was these commonalities, articulated as racial difference and masked as class antagonism, that shaped the violent roundups.[102] Whites violently expelled the Chinese in part because they looked so familiar. Race, one factor that differentiated them, became the way in which Humboldt looked at the world.[103]

It took barely a century to virtually clear the coast of the redwood forest. Today less than fifty thousand of the two million acres of California coastal redwoods can be found, ancient stands of towering trees now contained in four state parks bordered by highways, barren lumber towns, and scarred hillsides. It took barely a weekend to clear Eureka of the Chinese, who were gone before the wild pink rhododendrons opened and the tiny white trillium bloomed on the forest floor.

5

THE TRUCKEE METHOD

FIRE AND ICE

On May 10, 1869, the golden spike linking the Union Pacific and Central Pacific was pounded into the earth at Promontory Summit, Utah, and eleven thousand Chinese workers immediately lost their jobs. Though not invited to the celebrations of the Transcontinental Railroad, Chinese workers had built the railroad, hauling locomotives over the summit and sleeping by the hundreds in ice caves or tents. They worked a sunup-till-sundown day, slung from cliffs, at times throughout the night, to blast through the mountain with gunpowder and nitroglycerine.

Within weeks about fourteen hundred Chinese railroad workers moved west to Truckee, a rough logging town that lay in a high river valley near the crest of the Sierra Nevada. They arrived as a community—skilled in masonry, tracklaying, ironwork, cooking, and dynamiting. They also arrived with a reputation for demanding their rights from the railroad—striking for better pay or for wages comparable to those of whites, insisting on their own cooks and food. Suddenly, one third of Truckee's population was Chinese—a segregated, low-paid, all-male, and highly organized society.

The history of the Chinese in Truckee begins and ends in fire. Never a site for the gold found along the gravel beds of the American, Bear, Yuba, and Feather Rivers, Truckee was a stop along a high mountain pass, a sunny meadow before the final ascent over the summit of Donner Ridge.

For centuries Native Americans had used the Truckee River route from the mountains above Lake Tahoe to the deserts near Pyramid Lake in Nevada. During the gold rush the little town became a gateway from the East into the California mines, and along the trail, competition for freight and passenger traffic was intense. In 1859 the Truckee Turnpike Company improved the wagon route over Henness Pass, where settlers and miners made the final climb over the Sierra peaks, moving from the Truckee Basin at six thousand feet through passes more than seven thousand feet high, and then down, west, toward the rolling foothills and the gold fields. During the Civil War, small lumber mills, inns, and stagecoach stations sprang up in the river basin. In 1864 the California Stage Company established regular connections between west and east, and Truckee busily serviced the passing stagecoaches, muleteers, and wagons. With the railroads came large lumber mills, and by 1867 the Truckee Lumber Company was supplying wood for trellises, trusses, and fuel.

Finally, in 1868, the Central Pacific conquered Donner Summit and pulled its first locomotive into town. The railroad linked Truckee to the farms and towns of the Central Valley and the Pacific coast, connecting the remote town to the global market of labor and lumber moving between Asia and the East Coast. Suddenly Truckee's lumber mills were busy with orders to supply the Comstock Silver Lode a hundred miles away in Virginia City, Nevada. During winters, the lumber companies sliced into the frozen river and millponds and shipped ice down the mountain, to cool the Comstock mines and to keep California produce fresh on its way to markets in the East. No longer a makeshift rest stop, Truckee was now a full-blown railroad and mill town.

Hundreds, perhaps thousands, of Chinese had died building the railroad. Recruited from teams of disillusioned miners in the West or by Charles Crocker's brokers in China, they had faced relentless perils—from the Sierra winter snows to dynamite explosions to falls from ropes or wicker baskets suspended from the cliffs over the American River canyon as they loaded dynamite into the rocky walls of the gorge.

But most of the Chinese who built the Transcontinental Railroad had survived; many had prospered. Retaining Chinese culture often meant the difference between life and death. While white workers ate beans, potatoes, and occasionally beef, cooks for the Chinese prepared foods imported from China; along the tracks, porters carried barrels of fried oysters, dried bamboo shoots and mushrooms, vegetables, pork, poultry, rice, salted cabbage, dried seaweed, sweet rice crackers, and dried fruit. As white workers drank cold water, often polluted from human-borne parasites, the Chinese drank boiled and purified tea.[1]

As new tracks spidered across the western states during the peak years of railroad building, Truckee became home to the second-largest Chinese population on the Pacific Coast.[2] In 1869, when Republican vice president Schuyler Colfax reached Truckee to catch the train east, he observed to a *New York Tribune* reporter that "Truckee appeared to be a city of John Chinaman, with an appendage of Irish shanties, the inevitable saloons, [and] a very comfortable railroad hotel." Colfax rode past streets of Chinese laundries, barbershops, tea shops, peanut stands, and "non-descript booths, all as like as two peas externally; little wooden barracks feet square, and adorned with big sign boards, persuasive no doubt to the Celestial mind but impenetrable to us."[3]

Truckee's Chinatown, however, was not impenetrable. Between 1869, when the railroad was completed, and 1886, marked by apocalyptic violence, it was burned, invaded, and expropriated over and over again. Over the years, the Chinese community became a target in an ugly drama of race. A series of fires forced the Chinese to leave downtown Truckee and rebuild Chinatown across the river.

In the winter of 1885–86, Truckee's anti-Chinese leaders looked for a new strategy, one that would avoid the risks of arson and the dubious morality and legal pitfalls of the Eureka purge. They sought an approach that would be impervious to criminal and financial challenges in court. It was the editor of Truckee's rural newspaper who would shape Asian American history by launching a plan that would destroy Chinatowns across the state. The "Truckee method" would expel the Chinese by starving them out.

Charles McGlashan of the *Truckee Republican* designed a strict and strangling economic boycott—one that would publicly shame white businessmen who employed Chinese laborers, usher white women into the anti-Chinese movement, and drive out every Chinese man and woman from the mountain town—person by person. Using the rhetoric of nonviolence but inviting all the brutality of the Eureka purge, the Truckee method became one of the principal mechanisms by which Chinese were driven from the West Coast in the mid-1880s.[4]

The Truckee method accomplished its task in ten weeks.

FIRE

After arriving in Truckee, most Chinese worked in the woods, the "green gold of the Sierras," to supply the railroad with fuel, ties, charcoal, and timber. With a large population, Chinatown quickly became a thriving settlement of merchants, vegetable sellers, and woodcutters, rigorously segregated from white neighborhoods. In June 1872 *The Sacramento Daily Union* reported, "Where the railroad comes in the town, there is a rich plot of land where the garden vegetables are cultivated. As you enter the town, you pass it—an eyesore enclosed by sticks and stones, eked out by gunny sacks and waifs, reminding one of a free Negro settlement of the olden times away down south." Just north of this truck garden, in the center of town with access only from an alley on Main Street, the Chinese built their "incongruous row" of "pig's sty order" on land owned by timber and railroad baron Charles Crocker.

For white emigrants moving west, Truckee was a reprieve. It was the first town where they might leave behind the dangers of the Nevada desert and the steep mountain trails of the eastern Sierra mountains. Bound for farming valleys or the lumber towns along the Pacific, here the pioneers found boardinghouses, pure water, feed for their hungry pack animals, and the company of other whites. Although much of the land around Truckee was already owned by the railroads and the town was held in their thrall, many tired settlers decided to stay.

Even as the anti-Chinese movement of the 1870s raged across the West, Truckee's Chinatown was profitable to whites. The Chinese were renters, shoppers, and low-paid laborers, and white agents made money from their legal, real estate, and commercial transactions. Seemingly, this interracial relationship benefited everyone. In July 1875, for instance, Sisson, Wallace and Company advertised that its general store sold mackerel floating in barrels of brine, kegs of English and California pickles, iron, steel, cutlery, tinware, and charcoal. "We also . . . furnish Chinese Labor, at Short Notice, when Orders are properly Guaranteed."[5]

Chinese workers also provided vital laundry services. In a town with few females, Lau Lee, the proprietor of the Truckee Laundry, advertised that he washed all clothes on a washboard, sewed on buttons, and picked up and returned clothes free of charge. Loon Tung Chung advertised in English that he could provide all kinds of "Chinese Clothing and China Goods" and also "furnish all kinds of Chinese Labor."[6]

But the illusion that the Chinese were safely embedded in the Truckee community went up in smoke. The white citizens saw Chinatown as a "lot of dry, closely packed wooden shanties, among which a fire had only to be started to become uncontrollable and insure the almost certain destruction of the town." And on May 29, 1875, fire struck. It devoured Chinatown, then burned several businesses owned by whites, including the town stables, a meat market, a cabinet shop, and a saloon. A "fire train," owned by the railroads, as well as a volunteer hose-and-bucket brigade, quickly saved the rest of Truckee. But the destruction of these white businesses was blamed on the Chinese.

Refusing to move again, the Chinese began to rebuild. Their losses had been high; the Loon Tung Chung Company estimated its damages at thirty thousand dollars. They insisted that a new fire company be based in Chinatown, but the white community purchased a "steamer" fire engine and had it hauled up the mountain from Virginia City, solely for its own use.

Soon after the fire, a vigilante committee formed, calling itself the Caucasian League. The league planned a system of boycotts: all employers in Truckee should terminate their contracts with the Chinese and withhold wages. The plan had its share of opponents. When a major contractor for the Chinese woodcutters refused to cooperate, the League took matters into its own hands, warning the Chinese woodcutters to quit their jobs and leave. The Chinese refused, and throughout early June 1876, gangs invaded Chinatown and attacked the cabins of woodcutters living in the forests, ordering them to get out of Truckee. Again the Chinese refused.

Some League members quickly tired of their "peaceful" methods. Sometime after 1 A.M. on Sunday, June 18, seven men slipped away from a boycott meeting and met up at the home of Dominga Carasco. There they dressed themselves in black clothing, loaded a double-barreled shotgun with wire shot, packed three more pistols and cans of kerosene and coal oil, and quietly left town, following an old trail along Trout Creek for a mile and a half. Soon they came to two cabins where Chinese woodcutters were sleeping.

Two of the vigilantes quietly poured the coal oil onto the roof of one cabin, set it on fire, and took cover in the nearby brush.

Within minutes choking smoke woke the Chinese men. When Ah Ling fled the burning cabin and tried to douse the flames, the vigilantes opened fire, shot him in the abdomen, and wounded several other Chinese men. With the "concealed ruffians" still shooting from behind the brush and trees, the woodcutters realized that they could not put out the fire and also save their lives. They picked up Ah Ling and rushed into the woods, hoping to hide until daybreak. The vigilantes moved on to the other cabin, set it on fire, and again shot Chinese woodcutters as they fled the burning building, trying to protect themselves with blankets.

Under the cover of darkness the woodcutters hauled Ah Ling across Trout Creek and hid in the bushes until dawn. With daylight, the wounded men walked the mile into town, carrying the bleeding man to the house of their boss and landlord, the rancher Joseph Gray. Stumbling through the town, they passed families headed to church, who ignored the desperate group. Gray summoned a doctor, but the next afternoon Ah Ling, forty-five years old, born in the Guangdong Province of China, died in the California railroad town.

Town officials were worried. They knew that a congressional commission was en route to California to inquire into the "Chinese question." They feared that the Chinatown fire and the rout at Trout Creek would "prejudice the minds of the investigators," and they hoped that the commission would believe that only the "ruffian element" objected to the Chinese presence in rural California.[7] The *Truckee Republican* reported that the town was "outraged as if the victims had been Americans." But Truckee's Caucasian League had quickly grown to three hundred members, including the ambitious editor of the newspaper and the doctor who had treated Ah Ling.

"The Trout Creek Outrage" made headlines across the state. On Monday morning, prompted by the unfavorable news coverage, the justice of the peace in Nevada City, the county seat, called for a coroner's jury and hired detectives to track down the murderers. A few Truckee businessmen raised one thousand dollars for a reward, Governor William Irwin added three hundred dollars, and the Chinese community raised another two hundred. Dependent on Chinese woodcutters throughout the mountains, the Central Pacific Railroad sent in its own detective. With this backing, lead investigator Constable Jack Cross ignored threats on his own life, soon identified and arrested all seven men, and jailed them in Nevada City and Sacramento. Isolated from one another and forcefully questioned by Cross, two of the vigilantes, Calvin McCullough and G. W. Getchell, confessed, and the seven co-conspirators were indicted for arson and murder.

On September 25, the first "Trout Creek" trial opened in Nevada City with a test case of William O'Neill, an employee of the Central Pacific Railroad. On the stand, Getchell and McCullough testified that they had planned to shoot each Chinese man as he exited a burning cabin, that Jack Reed had fired the shot that killed Ah Ling, and that the others, including O'Neill, had shot and wounded the other men. Despite *People* v. *Hall*'s ban on Chinese testimony against whites, one of the woodcutters, Ah Fook, took the stand to describe the terrifying night. He explained how the flames had awakened him and how the Chinese men were unable to douse the fire. He told how Ah Ling then grabbed an empty can and rushed from the burning cabin to a nearby creek for water when the defendant and the other members of the raiding party fired on him.

The vigilantes were represented by Truckee's most respected attorney and newspaperman, Charles McGlashan. McGlashan was known for his fine collection of mountain butterflies and his publications on the tragic Donner Party, a group of pioneer families who, trapped in the snow in the high Sierra Nevada, resorted to cannibalism in order to survive the winter of 1846–47. With the Trout Creek murder trial, he would establish his leadership in the anti-Chinese movement and launch his political career. McGlashan orchestrated the selection of an all-white jury avowedly sympathetic to the League. Laughter erupted in the courtroom when one potential jurist stated, "I can hang a Chinaman for killing a white man, but can't hang a white man for killing a Chinaman."

The prosecution laid out the gang's plan to scare the Chinese out of Truckee and the details of the assaults, and the coroner testified that Ah Ling's wound matched the deadly wire shot loaded into Jack Reed's rifle. But the town threw a protective hedge around the accused men. McGlashan placed *fifty* defense witnesses on the stand who provided an assortment of alibis for the implicated men. After nine minutes of deliberation, the jury acquitted William O'Neill of murder and the prosecution entered a *nolle prosequi* (no further charges) against the six other men and abandoned the case in despair.

The white residents of Truckee were delighted. As each defendant was ex-

Charles McGlashan

onerated, the town fired off a cannon. When threats arose against Constable Cross for arresting the seven men, town officials replaced him with gunman Jack Reed. Although the *Truckee Republican* professed to be "greatly incensed over the incident at Trout Creek," it claimed that the murderers were just "some of the idle and dissolute vagabonds who frequent our town," not members of the Caucasian League. As the last defendant of the "outrage" was released, the *Alta California* reported, "Public opinion sanctions the verdict."[8]

Some western journalists, however, were more ambivalent. Sacramento's *Daily Union* wrote that despite the acquittals, "the people of Truckee cannot clear themselves of the responsibility so easily."[9] The *Reno Evening Gazette* declared: "We are forced to think that the whole transaction was a maliciously arranged plot." When the whole history is written, said the *Gazette,* it will reveal a "phase of human depravity and cupidity that would cast a gloom over the dark shades of hell."[10]

Soon economic hard times came to the Truckee Basin. By 1877 the silver bonanza at the Washoe mines had petered out and Truckee's lumber mills were laying off workers. As the decade came to a close, unemployed white laborers became tempted by the menial and poorly paid jobs of Chinese workers, jobs they had once ridiculed.

Then, late one night in May 1878, Truckee's Chinatown was again set on fire. "Lurid, bewildering flames swept over the rickety frames" of the Chinese residences and shops along Front Street. Firemen fought to save the engine house, a nearby store belonging to a white merchant, and the freight depot that housed tons of dynamite. Townsmen rushed through the streets shouting, "The Chinese must go!" The mob hurled stones at the Chinese as they fled their burning homes. After the fire the entire Chinese community crowded into the charred remains. The *Truckee Republican* made the reasons for the fire clear: "The site heretofore occupied by Chinatown is the most desirable in town. If owned by white persons it would soon be covered by delightful residences, and possibly business houses, which would add greatly to the appearance of the town."

Across the Sierra Nevada, vigilantes were rising up against the Chinese. In nearby Reno, Nevada, in 1878, a fire destroyed all fifty Chinese homes, and a Chinese man and woman burned to death as fire engines protected nearby white property. "Chinatown is no more—not a house left to tell the tale . . . [their] houses amounted to nothing," wrote the local paper. But even though the Workingmen's Party gave the Chinese forty-eight hours to leave Reno, the Chinese remained.[11]

Two months after the Reno fire, several homes in Truckee's Chinatown were blown up.[12] In November 1878 the *Republican* warned Truckee's Chinese to "appreciate the fact that as often as they rebuild on the present location, just so often will Chinatown be burned" and vowed, "We are satisfied that Chinatown never be rebuilt on the old site. The Chinese must go." Any white person who tried to help the Chinese rebuild was "imperiling" himself.[13] Businessmen agreed to purchase all lots owned by Chinese, and a Citizens Safety Committee notified the Chinese that they had to leave the city limits within a week. The committee threatened that "if whites or Chinese attempt to disregard the will of the citizens, trouble will ensue." D. H. Haskell, an agent for the railroad, offered to sell enough land for "all Chinatown" across the river.[14]

For weeks the Chinese lived in the burnt ruins, "in the darkness and filth; overcrowded, hungry, and feverish with anxiety regarding the movements of the [white] citizens." Then, "it came like the gentle blast of the Washoe zephyr. . . . The graceful caving in of a roof, or the musical crash of the side of a house, was the occasion of vigorous cheers from the sympathetic populace," reported the *Republican*.[15] But with the Sierra winter approaching, the Chinese resisted the move across the river and began to rebuild Chinatown. The merchant Fong Lee, the interpreter Charlie Sing, and the laborer Ah One made it known that the Chinese community had stockpiled a large supply of Henry rifles, revolvers, and "knives by the hundreds."

Within days, a new club, the 601 (six feet under, zero trial, one bullet), emerged in Truckee. It marked the town with its signature red ribbons and then commanded the Chinese leaders to leave in twenty-four hours "under penalty of death."[16] Backing the 601, the board of supervisors ordered the Chinese to move outside the town limits. The *Truckee Republican* noted there was no "flinching, no talk of yielding, but every man stood ready to execute the will of the citizens" and recalled that the "last conflagration [had] happily consumed every building in Chinatown."[17]

On November 9, 1878, the Caucasian League led more than five hundred residents to Chinatown and tore it down. The rampaging mob destroyed all houses owned by Chinese and warned white landlords to expect to see their own houses "even as the houses of the heathens."[18]

With a petition in hand signed by 160 "legal" (male) voters, the Nevada County supervisors told the Chinese that they must move across the river—outside the corporate limits of Truckee. The demolition of Chinatown "leaves the celestials no excuse for delaying their departure," wrote the *Republican.* The Chinese had one week "to remove," and "yesterday the week expired. Thanks to their unknown advisor, the week has been occupied in rebuilding. It now remains to be seen whether Truckeeites have sufficient mettle to keep their word and make the Chinese go."[19]

By now many Chinese were on the verge of starvation, and the community reluctantly crossed the Truckee River, carrying whatever household goods and furniture survived the inferno. Fong Lee, owner of a brick store, demanded ten thousand dollars from the city for the loss of his property, but Truckee offered only rations of rice. The South Truckee Association, "organized for the purpose of acquiring and owning property, . . . the object especially being to remove the Chinese from Old Chinatown in Truckee to South Truckee, the better to protect the property of white population from fines and to save the Chinese population from violence on the part of disaffected whites," drew up the deeds for New Chinatown.[20]

Forced from the white part of town after five fires, the Chinese of Truckee again began the task of building a new Chinatown. The community grew as the nub of Chinese life for the seven hundred Chinese men and women who then worked in the Truckee River basin. Since the new Chinatown was accessible only by ferry or bridge, Chinese laborers hoped that they might be left in peace.

Truckee was unrepentant. A week after the move, the *Republican* concluded, "Seldom during the history of the Pacific Coast have popular uprisings been conducted with such calmness and deliberation."[21] But while the *Republican* boasted, "There has been no desire to abuse or maltreat the Celestials," nearby newspapers, including Reno's *Record Union,* warned that Truckee was in a state of "complete anarchy."[22] Even as the Chinese began settling into their new homes, the *Nevada Daily Transcript* reported that "excited masses were ready for any riotous act that could have been mentioned. Loud threats of mobbing the Chinese were openly expressed in the streets."

In the early fall of 1878, a Chinese man, Ah Toon, was arrested for the murder of a white man. Three masked white men entered his cell and threatened to hang him unless he confessed. Though Ah Toon desperately insisted on his innocence, the men fastened a rope around his neck and hung him from a rafter. But when their prisoner appeared to be dying, the gang panicked and cut him down, then threw open the jail doors and tossed him out. Soon thereafter, the sheriff announced that in fact he had no evidence linking Ah Toon to any crime.[23]

Little more than a year after the move, fire devoured Chinatown, destroying half of the newly built houses and stores.[24] Fearing that the Chinese might try to come back across the river, in 1880 the town declared that the former main street of Chinatown was now a "public highway," thereby barring any housing. As further insurance, J. F. Moody, owner of the Truckee Hotel and the stage line, homesteaded the street "temporarily." He did it, he said, for the good of the town.[25]

"TO EXECUTE THE WILL OF THE CITIZENS"

By the mid-1880s, about one hundred thousand Chinese workers made their home in the Pacific Northwest. Hundreds were living in Truckee's new Chinatown; hundreds more woodcutters who worked for the railroads lived in cabins scattered across the ridges of the Sierra mountains.

Facing violent roundups from the Sierra Nevada to the Pacific coast, the Chinese developed effective strategies of resistance. Many defended their communities with arms. In some towns they organized strikes and food boycotts, forcing rural towns to realize how dependent they were on their Chinese neighbors for their food, firewood, and cleanliness.

Across the West, the Chinese also found many loopholes in the law. Hundreds of Chinese, in passage from Cuba to China via San Francisco, established that since they were in transit, they were exempt from the Chinese Exclusion Act. Others turned to inconsistent rulings in Chinese port towns where customs supervisors issued emigrating laborers certificates of passage that defined them as "traders," "students," or "teachers." In the United States, Chinese immigrants were flooding the courts with habeas corpus challenges.

In 1884, Congress responded by tightening the 1882 Exclusion Law. This time it banned Chinese immigration from any foreign port for a period of ten years, required more stringent proof of American residency for those who wanted to reenter the United States, and narrowed the definition of *merchant* to exclude peddlers and cannery workers.

ICE

By the winter of 1885–86, chagrined by its reputation for burning Chinatowns and murdering Chinese, disappointed by immigration laws, and excited by the purges elsewhere in the Northwest, Truckee sought a reputable way to expel the Chinese. Led by its newspaper editor, the railroad town replaced arson and assaults with a concerted, organized, and well-focused "freeze out."

Charles McGlashan, editor of the *Truckee Republican,* had closely monitored the Chinese purges along the coast, from Crescent City in the north down to Arcata and Ferndale and the small lumber towns that radiated east from Eureka. He reported the violence spreading north up to Oregon and Washington and east toward the Rockies. In his newspaper he wrote about the September 1885 massacre at Rock Springs, Wyoming, about the white vigilantes in Tacoma who burned two large Chinese neighborhoods and forced their residents onto trains out of the state, and about the threats to burn Chinatowns in Portland, Seattle, and Olympia. As a lawyer and journalist, he was well aware that the Chinese had resisted the purges, and his paper tracked the lawsuits against the rural towns and the claims for indemnity filed by Chinese immigrants and the Chinese government. Suddenly, many rural newspapers were denouncing Truckee for retaining the second-largest Chinese population in California.

One night in November 1885, as he witnessed anti-Chinese feelings swell at a rally, McGlashan realized that the "wealthy classes [were] hardly represented," that the "violent elements [were] present in full force," and that the railroad town might be on the eve of more "bloodshed and incendiarism." What was needed, he thought, was a businessman who would take control of the anti-Chinese movement, and he allowed himself to be "induced" into this role. Although he knew that only a small majority endorsed his view, McGlashan devised a plan to "drive the Chinese from our midst . . . lawfully." He understood that the "incendiary element" ridiculed his vision.

McGlashan also knew that those who wanted the Chinese to remain in the Truckee River basin were beginning to fear another tide of racial hatred. Businessmen who employed Chinese workers, white women with Chinese servants, and railroad and timber barons who held binding contracts with Chinese were reluctant to drive them out. More than seven hundred Chinese men but scarcely a hundred white laborers, he believed, were at work in the wide valley meadows, six thousand feet into the Sierra Nevada. Hundreds of "temperate, industrious white laborers, heads of families," wrote McGlashan, were unemployed and destitute, while "wedfed, well-paid Chinamen" held half the factory jobs, worked in the largest sawmills, or were "encroaching" at the logging camps where more than eighty thousand cords of wood were cut annually to supply the railroad companies. Most of Truckee's teamsters were Chinese. The cooks and cleaners at the hotels and restaurants that supplied this busy crossroads town were Chinese. So were the launderers.

McGlashan's plan was to turn "attention away from the Chinese to their employers" and impose leadership from the "better class of citizens," who would demand that "all individuals, companies, and corporations . . . discharge any and all Chinamen" by January 1, 1886. But these men had long profited from this less expensive labor force. Even though McGlashan arranged that the next meeting be led by mill owners and shopkeepers, it was mostly white laborers who showed up. That night McGlashan won a resolution declaring that a boycott of Chinese workers was in the "interests not only of the laboring men, but of the entire community." But how could he get the town's businessmen to embrace the anti-Chinese movement?

At first, all sides seemed to oppose McGlashan's small team: "They were cursed by the rich employers who were coining money out of Chinese labor, they were cursed by the Chinese, they were cursed by the incendiary element" who believed in more "emphatic" methods. When the Chinese quickly retaliated and launched a boycott against a shopkeeper who had joined McGlashan's committee, the merchants became nervous. Wealthy businessmen who employed or were patronized by the Chinese pulled their ads from his newspaper. For the next seven weeks McGlashan slowly stitched together a cross-class coalition. Diligently, his committee visited every man or woman who employed Chinese workers. When persuasion failed, they threatened the merchants with economic boycotts and public shaming, forging what Chinese consul Colonel Bee called "McGlashan's mob."

On December 5, white residents joined together to demand that all Chinese leave the Truckee River basin by January 1, 1886. At its first anti-Chinese town meeting, Truckee passed a simple resolution that led to the most notorious and organized expulsion of the Chinese since the violent purge from Eureka in February 1885:

> Resolved: That not only the laboring man, but the entire community, demand that all individuals, companies and corporations should discharge any and all Chinamen in their employ by January 1, 1886, and refuse thereafter to give them work of any kind.

At midnight, men thronged the streets, bearing torches and shouting, "The Chinese must go!" The mob "elected" a committee to tell all those who employed Chinese workers that they must obey the resolution by the New Year. Richardson Brothers, a large mill, immediately fired all its Chinese woodcutters and signed a "roll" declaring that the mill would no longer employ any Chinese workers. George Shaffer, a leading timber baron, soon followed. McGlashan's strategy might succeed.

Through the *Truckee Republican,* McGlashan telegraphed events from Truckee across the state and sent copies to the small newspapers that subscribed to the *Republican* as a source for their own stories. He used the paper to advertise for stocks in a steam laundry to replace Chinese hand washers and boasted that he quickly raised seven hundred dollars. Although white women and the landlords of the Chinese laundries opposed this move, McGlashan countered that steam laundries would not only rid the town of Chinese washmen but also make jobs for white women and induce them to move to the masculine frontier.

The Chinese realized that the boycott could make it impossible for them to keep their jobs, sell their wares, or rent property on the mountain. The Labor Bureau Committee was told to make a list of all unemployed white men willing to replace the Chinese and present it to Truckee's business owners. By the end of the second week of the boycott, the committee had obtained promises from most employers in the town that by January 15 they would discharge all their Chinese servants, waiters, and laborers in the mills, lumber yards, and box factories.

In early December, the *Alta California* reported that every employer in the Truckee Basin had pledged to discharge its Chinese laborers prior to January 1. By the middle of that particularly cold month, the Truckee Lumber Company began to fire its Chinese mill workers. The first wave of Chinese mill workers left, and several Chinese women fled to safer towns.[26] By the fourth week of the boycott, more than one hundred Chinese men had been discharged and their positions filled by white workers. Wing Chung Lung, a leading Chinese firm, went out of business, and other firms in Chinatown reached the verge of bankruptcy. White merchants ruthlessly collected their debts from Truckee's departing Chinese residents, and white bankers in San Francisco aided the rout by refusing to offer new loans to Chinese merchants.

The cigar makers soon followed the millworkers and merchants. During the 1870s and 1880s, the Cigar Makers' Union in San Francisco had led many anti-Chinese demonstrations and boycotts. On New Year's night 1886, a train with eight special cars of white cigar makers passed through town en route to the Bay Area. Onboard were four hundred members of the Cigar Makers' International Union from the East Coast, brought out to "displace" Chinese cigar makers in San Francisco. While the train refueled, church bells rang, and a cheering torchlight parade marched up and down the platform led by the local fife-and-drum corps. Women watched from the balcony of the hotel, but many others joined the parade as banners and placards heralded:

GRIT

SUCCESS TO ANTI-COOLIE

NO CHINESE NEED APPLY TRUCKEE STEAM LAUNDRY

That night three new symbols appeared on the banners, portending the violence to come: a cigar box tacked onto a burning torch suggested the destruction of the Chinese workforce and the flames that would burn in Chinatown; a red hatband announced the workers' militancy; and a menacing picture of a rooster crowing "When the Cock crows the Chinaman goes" hinted that by the sunrise, the Chinese would be out.

That night the *Republican* telegraphed other mountain towns that two railcars of muskets and a large box of cartridges had just been delivered to Chinatown. McGlashan announced that "if force is necessary . . . it will be used."

When the news of Truckee's actions reached San Francisco, the Chinese Six Companies, the consulate, and the government of China became alarmed. The Truckee method was spreading. Shingle Springs, Georgetown, Germantown, Ukiah, Sonoma, St. Helena, Orland, San Buenaventura (now Ventura), Marysville, Merced, Aptos, Visalia, Gridley, Pentz, Yreka, Arbuckle, Napa, Petaluma, and Vina had formed anti-Chinese organizations, drafting bylaws and announcing dates to withdraw "patronage" from Chinese residents. Threats against the Chinese of San Francisco, Stockton, and Sacramento endangered these communities. The Chinese minister pressed Secretary of State Thomas Bayard to demand that the U.S. government intervene and stop the violence before "the row has begun."

As purges blazed up and down the West, Bayard forwarded the Chinese's concerns to California's Governor Stoneman, who replied that he had received no notice of anti-Chinese violence from local officers of the peace, nor had any town officials sought his assistance. Instead, Stoneman blamed the Chinese for "crowding the Caucasian race out of many avenues of employment." Although he promised to uphold the law, he refused to intervene in anti-Chinese rallies: "I cannot prevent meetings of citizens." In response to the Chinese minister's demands that the state protect the Chinese, Stoneman noted, "I may say that we are capable of performing that duty without gratuitous suggestions from that quarter." Through widespread publication of this correspondence in local newspapers, Stoneman signaled to Californians that they were free to launch the violent purges.[27]

Indeed, the purge was already under way. With the dawn of 1886 and the pending January 15 deadline, Truckee's anti-Chinese movement began to target each industry in town. On January 2, a Committee of Five visited every cigar dealer to "urge" them to buy only "white" cigars. Other committees threatened the independent Chinese woodcutters; the Committee on Wood Contracts announced that an "uncontrollable current of feeling" in the town "has given rise to apprehension that the masses might join in an uprising that would prove disastrous in its consequences to life and property." Could the "safety and security of the community . . . be maintained . . . while the pitiful cry for bread by the children of white workingmen is continually being mocked by the resounding axes of 500 well-fed well-paid Chinamen?" With "mammoth wood contracts" endangering Truckee's "safety and security," the committee insisted that all the lumber companies rescind their contracts for Chinese labor on or before January 15. The Chinese, they announced, must leave the woods before that date "or seek protection."[28]

But the Chinese community in Truckee had become skillful at organizing its own protection. During the first week in January, Fred Bee and the Chinese Six Companies hired detectives, had a man from outside the Truckee area appointed deputy U.S. marshal, and shipped arms up the mountain to the Chinese. McGlashan realized that the Chinese were preparing to strike back, and the *Republican* telegraphed warnings to rural newspapers. On January 5, under the banner TRUCKEE CHINAMEN ARMED WITH WINCHESTER RIFLES, mountain newspapers reported that two cases of rifles, purchased from white merchants, had been delivered to Tuck Chung. The next day they revealed that a Sacramento arms dealer had shipped a dozen of the finest Colt revolvers to Truckee's Chinese.[29] Bee and the Chinese Six Companies again telegraphed Governor Stoneman and Secretary Bayard asking for troops, and they urged reporters to publicize the dangerous events developing in the Sierra Nevada.

McGlashan was eager to put forward the success of the Truckee method. The *Republican* reported that the citizens of the town were preserving law and order even as they purged the Chinese from their midst: "The Chinese are rapidly driven out of Truckee by peaceful means, and are departing in large numbers." But the January 15 deadline was just a week away, and McGlashan knew that most of Truckee's Chinese had not left.

On January 6 he changed course and declared that after the deadline, the citizens of Truckee "would refuse to be responsible" for the safety of the Chinese.[30] On that day the braid of a local Chinese doctor was cut off and dangled ominously from a sign along Front Street in the former Chinatown.

McGlashan was also coming to see the risks of the purge. As white laundresses, mill workers, and woodcutters arrived "from below" to replace the Chinese, he realized that importing workers from out of town would not solve white unemployment in Truckee, the heart of his righteous attack. Without providing good jobs for unemployed white workers, he would lose the town's support, but such jobs were not to be had.

So McGlashan turned to the *Republican* to shift his argument toward race itself: the boycott, he declared, was "not all race prejudice, as some in the eastern States have affirmed, but a question of industrial economy resolved into this proposition, that white labor is more desirable than Chinese labor." He also insisted that his plan was to "get rid of the Chinese peacefully and within the forms of law" in order to "reverse the premium" that Chinese gained by working for less than whites.[31]

With time running out, the anti-Chinese committee turned to a "very effective mode of warfare"—it arranged for the banks to place liens on Chinese property and attachments on Chinese loans. On January 11, local banks claimed the buildings and called in the loans of two prominent Chinese merchants, Quoin Sin Lung and Tuck Chung, forcing both men to close their stores, declare bankruptcy, and leave town.

In part, the driving out was spread by the rural press. Other rural newspapers quickly echoed the *Republican*'s claims about the progress of the Truckee purge, often cutting copy directly from McGlashan's paper. In every issue, newspapers throughout California reported Truckee's "jubilant" victories and printed a tally of the number of Chinese leaving town; the score rose into the hundreds. (The papers also noted that those Chinese who remained were purchasing more arms.)[32] Less than a week before the deadline for total expulsion, the *Placerville Mountain Democrat* announced that a broker had rescinded his contract with a Chinese crew to cut two thousand cords of wood for the railroad and had hired white laborers in their place, at ten dollars per month, with board.

With just days to go, McGlashan stepped up his campaign. His tactics were incremental and inexorable. He encouraged businesses to circulate trade cards announcing that they "upheld the vision" of the anti-Chinese cause and ask for "Caucasian patronage" in return. When several women who ran boardinghouses refused to fire their longtime Chinese servants, all their lodgers moved out; the women immediately fired their Chinese cleaners and cooks and replaced them with whites. Just one day ahead of the deadline, the Truckee Hotel, the American Hotel, the Sherritt House, and the Pacific Lumber Company buckled. They, too, fired their Chinese staffs.

Toward the end of the last week of the boycott, the constabulary joined the movement and threatened to arrest all Chinese woodsmen for stealing timber from government lands, and many fled from the mountain. Word spread throughout the encampments in the forests, and each day more Chinese abandoned their cabins and made their way to the coast.

Still, McGlashan continued to target the complicit middle class. He knew that many lumber companies had acquired their tracts of thick forests through bribes and fraud, and he threatened to expose mill owners for unlawfully cutting wood on government lands—that is, for wood cut by the Chinese. With the deadline days away, the Anti-Chinese Committee quickly launched investigations of any title on land where Chinese men were still cutting trees, and with McGlashan acting as prosecuting attorney, it initiated legal actions to seize this property.

Warning that the Anti-Chinese Committee would only take legal actions against those who "so bitterly opposed the anti-Chinese movement" or those who used Chinese workers to "perpetrate the lawless devastation of government lands," McGlashan declared, "there will be no compromise, no flag of truce, no cessation of hostilities until the final surrender is made. . . . Such blows will be struck at pocket-books and bank accounts as will prove more telling than violence or incendiarism."[33] With this threat, the committee forced many remaining mills to abandon their contracts with hundreds of Chinese woodcutters who had worked and lived on the mountain since the completion of the Transcontinental Railroad.

The boycott was working slowly. In its first three weeks, approximately one hundred Chinese left Truckee on the westbound train and another hundred were driven out on foot or by wagon, looking for safe towns. By January 15, claimed the *Alta California,* three hundred more Chinese men had lost their jobs but only one hundred had left town. Many went to

Marysville, which celebrated Truckee's racial purges as it undertook its own. Others went up to Nevada City even as the *Nevada Tri-Weekly Herald* hailed Truckee's victory in most of the mills, hotels, and restaurants: "The Heathens Discharged and White Men Given Work."

As the January 15 deadline approached, McGlashan knew that the fate of the purge was uncertain: Would enough Chinese have left Truckee for him to claim victory? Could he hold together a coalition of those who sought to drive out the Chinese "by peaceful law abiding means" with those who would take "recourse to violence"? And what would the purge cost? McGlashan was well aware that elsewhere the "expulsed Chinese" were demanding damages and reparations. The lawsuit *Wing Hing* v. *City of Eureka* and the indemnity demands against the United States for the massacre at Rock Springs and the rout at Tacoma were working their way through Congress and the courts. If *Wing Hing* prevailed, a similar suit would bankrupt Truckee and the dozens of towns following its boycott path.

Hundreds of Chinese men were still in Truckee, and in the last issue of the *Republican* published before the deadline, McGlashan abandoned his "nonviolent" strategy and announced that "Chinese loving wood contractors must look for other protection than was heretofore accorded by the law-abiding citizens of Truckee." Although he "threatened no violence," McGlashan lifted the "responsibility" of a peaceful purge from Truckee's "law-abiding citizens." He acknowledged that violence might cripple the movement, but he vowed that as of Friday, January 15, Truckee would face "a bitter, relentless warfare unto the death." He reminded his readers that this was also a consumer boycott. In a series of articles telegraphed across the state, McGlashan declared that every man who failed to boycott "Chinese lovers" would be boycotted himself. And every man employing Chinese workers "directly or indirectly" would be shamed at a public meeting.

Facing this racial storm, U.S. Marshal Drew, who had been sent to Truckee at the request of the Chinese consul, fled. He announced that he had no fears of any lawlessness on the part of the whites but insisted that "it was and is for the Governor to protect the Chinese in Truckee, not for me."

The Chinese woodcutters now understood that they were facing immediate and violent deportation and decided to negotiate with McGlashan as best they could. They agreed to rescind their contracts if they were paid for wood they had already cut. McGlashan was delighted; the willingness of the

Chinese to abandon their contracts would free the lumber firms who professed to be "heartily in sympathy" with the anti-Chinese movement but who "claimed that their hands were tied by the terms of written contracts."[34]

The most powerful holdout on the mountain was the firm of Sisson and Crocker, which ran one of the largest mills and owned a general store in the center of town. Charles Crocker, whose family built the Central Pacific Railroad, had tried to negotiate with McGlashan and had offered to "bind" the firm to never again employ a Chinese laborer if the committee just let him fulfill contracts, due to expire on June 1. But the confident anti-Chinese faction rejected Crocker's deal. Crocker also announced that the Chinese owed him between six thousand and ten thousand dollars advanced in the form of provisions and supplies, and he could not afford to fire them. White merchants offered six thousand dollars to pay off these debts, but Sisson refused, declaring that his company was now "ready for war."[35] An anti-Chinese mob threatened to tar and feather Sisson's local manager, and the committee sent leaflets to town newspapers across the West, urging citizens to boycott the mills and stores of these absentee owners.

With the end in sight, the anti-Chinese campaign stepped up its activities. It elected McGlashan delegate to the San Jose State Convention of the Anti-Chinese League, and the Committee on Timber Stealing hired a surveyor to investigate Sisson and the other mill holdouts for illegally cutting lumber on government lands. "Bitter and determined men" roamed the streets, and town officers warned Truckee to expect fires in Chinatown.

Desperate, several Chinese merchants took the train to San Francisco to appeal for more help. The timid U.S. marshal refused the pleas of the Chinese consul to return to Truckee because "some accidental drunken row may arise and violence be done the Chinese." He did remind the town that "if any mob should attack the Chinese quarter, it would very likely receive a hot reception, as the Chinese recently received a consignment of guns from San Francisco."[36] Colonel Bee urgently telegraphed the governor, the secretary of state, and Congressman William W. Morrow to send troops to suppress the mob actions. Morrow, who was then seeking to tighten immigration laws, wired McGlashan, "Stop such things as are taking place at Truckee. For God's sake, stop it, or we will be unable to do anything."[37]

McGlashan's plan for a peaceful roundup was dashed. Newspapers from other Sierra towns wrote to the *Truckee Republican* deploring the danger to the Chinese people and to the mountain community as a whole. The *San Francisco Argonaut* warned,

> We see the gathering of a cloud that will burst into a storm of blood across our Sierra. The people of Truckee are acting like madmen, and the community has lost its sense and reason. . . . The fact is probably this: The Criminal and idle part of the population has gained the ascendancy in the town, and is having its own way. . . . Messrs. Sisson, Crocker have the right under the law to refuse to discharge their Chinese laborers; they have existing contracts with them and the Chinese owe them labor. There is no man in Truckee who does not know that it is a cowardly act to come between this firm and their Chinese laborers with threats of violence.[38]

But the boycotters were watching the mills, hotels, and restaurants surrender, and they pressed on, demanding that every California resident sign a boycott petition. Issued by the California Anti-Chinese Non-Partisan Association and titled Circular Number One, it read:

> We, the undersigned, hereby declare that we are in favor of the adoption of all lawful means for the exclusion of the Chinese from the Pacific coast; and we hereby pledge that we will not employ Chinamen, directly or indirectly, nor purchase the produces of Chinese labor.

Instructions were to sign the broadsheet and return it to Charles McGlashan, who swore to publish a list of every Californian who betrayed the boycott. Intensifying the town's anxiety, McGlashan announced that he alone would keep the signatures and from "time to time" expose those who had not yet joined the boycott. Within days of its release, six hundred people from the Truckee area signed their names on the leaflet and returned it in person to the office of the *Republican.* McGlashan then mailed hundreds of copies of the form to towns where Sisson, Crocker and Company had stores, mines, or mills: Sacramento, Los Angeles, and Redding in California, Carlin in Nevada, Yuma and Benson in Arizona, and Camp Rice in New Mexico.

McGlashan also telegraphed blank copies to the leading newspapers of the coast, seeking, in advance of the San Jose and Sacramento conventions, to become the national leader of the anti-Chinese boycott and position himself to run for governor of California. Just as delegates were being selected by county supervisors and packing to leave for the largest racist demonstration in the state capital, McGlashan led a rally in Truckee demanding that Congress withdraw from the Burlingame Treaty and amend the Exclusion Act so that any Chinese person leaving the United States could never enter again. That week he began to publish threats against Crocker himself, and the *Republican* branded the railroad entrepreneur and land baron "a coward because of his action toward the community in which he made his fortune."

On February 11, 1886, Sisson, Crocker, perhaps the largest employer in the Northwest, crumbled. Crocker agreed to cancel his contracts with the Chinese woodcutters, call in his loans, and "attach" the Chinese possessions

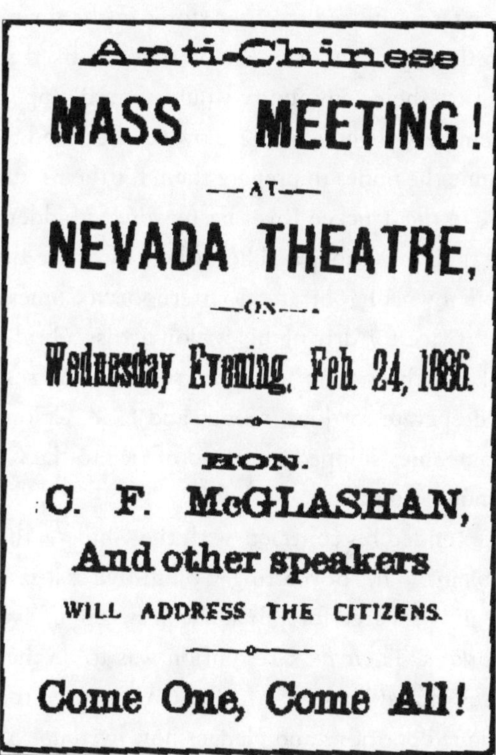

Advertisement and placard for upcoming statewide anti-Chinese convention in Sacramento

TRUCKEE REPUBLICAN, FEBRUARY 1886

at the wood camps. He assured McGlashan and the committees that he would no longer retain even one Chinese worker. In return, the committees lifted their boycott of Crocker's firm. In fact, the Chinese woodcutters had forced Sisson and Crocker to buy out their contracts for several thousand dollars, but as a matter of honor, the townspeople flooded back into Crocker's general store, and McGlashan promised that his business would now increase. Excited by the victory, the Boycotting Committee announced that it was "ready and willing to test their power upon any one who desires their services, but the chances are that no one will apply." Wrote the *Alta California:* "The surrender of Sisson, Crocker and Co. finishes the struggle."[39]

By the end of February, ten weeks after McGlashan first launched the Truckee method, between six hundred and one thousand Chinese people had left the Truckee River basin. Yet a few remained. Yeng Sing refused to leave until he could sell his land. Chung Jan, a shop owner, would not vacate until he fulfilled his wood contracts in Reno and Carson. Because the Chinese were no longer permitted to enter stores in the town, they arranged for butchers to drop packets of meat for them at fixed stops along the tracks. Sensing that their community would soon disappear, the Chinese went to their cemetery, digging in the snow to offer food to the departing spirits and exhume the bones to prepare them for their return to China.[40]

The Chinese in the Truckee River basin were forbidden to use wagons and had to haul their provisions and heavy bags of rice to their camps, four or five miles from town, on foot. In one afternoon, a Chinese man was convicted and fined twice for driving his wagon across a bridge faster than a man could walk.[41] Others were forced to sell their horses cheaply. With their brethren desperate for jobs, rooms, and food, Colonel Bee and the Chinese Six Companies shipped a carload of rice to the Chinese who remained in the mountain valley.

After Crocker ended his contracts with the Chinese, the boycott organizers were jubilant. The Boycotting Committee telegraphed the news across the state and prepared for a final "clean sweep" of Truckee's remaining Chinese workers. Their next resolution was to be their last, for "the back of the curse is about broken." McGlashan promised that if all the citizens who had signed petitions and pledges now lived up to their vows, the remaining Chinese men could not survive in Truckee. "You cannot serve two masters," he warned the readers of the *Republican*:

> Let our mothers, wives and sisters draw their skirts as they pass them on the street. Let them teach the little ones to abhor a Chinaman or his upholder. Let the little fingers be pointed at them, and the first words that fall from their baby lips be "Shame, you China lover." Let the store-keepers show them that their trade is not desirable; let the saloon-keepers refuse to deal out their favorite beverage less than five dollars a drink; let the shoemaker leave their shoes till all the others are done, and then charge double price; let the blacksmith refuse to shoe their horses, repair their wagons, or do their work without receiving China lovers' pay.

Threatening to tar and feather anyone who worked with the Chinese, McGlashan reminded the townspeople that the boycott covered "every Chinese advocate." Those who continued to patronize the Chinese, he threatened, "are known and will be dealt with accordingly." They will be ostracized in the town and "bear the brand of Cain on their foreheads."[42]

As the purge peaked in Truckee, McGlashan traveled the state to promote his "law of boycotting." With the San Jose convention a week away, he declared a statewide boycott of anyone who employed Chinese laborers or purchased Chinese products. He urged all Californians to build on the intense "universal agitation" pressing in on the Chinese; only aristocrats who cared nothing for the people "save to grind money from them" kept the anti-Chinese movement from victory.

At rallies—in nearby Dutch Flat, Grass Valley, Nevada City, across the state line into Carson City, Nevada, then back down through Sacramento to San Francisco—McGlashan carried his strategy of targeting large mill owners and businessmen. He argued against appeals to Congress because he distrusted the eastern states to "frame laws which will relieve us of Chinese oppression." Any act issued from Washington, he declared, was "full of holes through which Chinamen will creep." "Not the law," he argued, "but a universal discharge must effect his removal." McGlashan's incendiary stump speech appealed to Workingmen's Party loyalists: "Northern California is waging a gigantic warfare against the Chinese.... The day is almost won. The Chinese have been routed and are being driven from almost every village, town, and city."

Positioning himself as the statewide leader of Chinese expulsion,

McGlashan telegraphed his recipe, "How to Boycott," to newspapers across California: "Select the strongest, wealthiest firm and the one who is seemingly most impregnable. . . . Search out all his patrons, and boycott his productions, not only at home but abroad." There is not a manufacturer or producer in California, he advised, who could not "be forced to discharge his Chinese" or "be ruined." Then, he counseled, "receive the vanquished firm into the fold as soon as it surrenders. The fox whose tail is clipped will be eager to have the tails of other foxes clipped. The man who is compelled to discharge his Chinese will render valuable assistance in bringing his business rivals to terms."[43] He also urged towns to inform landlords that they could no longer rent houses or rooms to any Chinese person.

To those desperate for cheap labor, particularly farmers and fruit and grape growers, he suggested that they hire from the "thousands and thousands of recently emancipated Negros, who can vote while their children starve." Bring them to California, he advised, where they will work "cheaply and well." Small-town newspapers marveled at the successful expulsion of the Chinese; the Truckee method swept across the state.

On Saturday night, February 13, the San Jose anti-Chinese convention endorsed the Truckee method, and the mountain town celebrated with music, parades, and torchlight processions. McGlashan urged housewives to burn candles in every window and asked ministers to ring all the church bells in town. Truckee could "rejoice" in leading the "efforts of the entire coast" in "getting forever rid of the accursed blot" upon California. The *Truckee Republican* cheered that the Chinese "day is ended in the Sierra. Every burning torch will be a warning that they will not fail to heed, that they must go."[44]

With the surrender of Sisson and Crocker, most of the remaining Chinese decided to leave Truckee. Chinese merchants appealed for funds to transport the unemployed and destitute laborers, but the citizens refused to donate money unless the Chinese leaders guaranteed that in return for transportation out of town and one payout of five hundred dollars, the Chinese people would "depart in a body."[45] Disputes arose within the Chinese community itself when the Chinese Six Companies, labor contractors, and merchants declared that they could no longer fulfill their own contracts with Chinese laborers. Perhaps with the financial investments of the Six Companies in mind, Fred Bee telegraphed Truckee's Chinese not to leave unless they were "compelled."

Soon vigilantes began to abuse and extort any remaining cash and merchandise from the desperate and hungry Chinese who tried to guard their stores and houses. The boycott leaders urged the townfolk to "starve them out," counting on "poverty and destitution" rather than violence to "cleanse" Truckee. Groups of twenty and thirty Chinese left daily, some for towns such as Dutch Flat, where they found a hostile welcome.

The boycott spread. A large landowner in nearby Roseville received an envelope containing one wooden match and an anonymous note, a "hint of what would happen" if he refused to fire his Chinese crew. Rumors floated that the North Pacific Railroad had discharged all its Chinese workmen. The manager of the roundhouse fired its longtime Chinese employees and replaced them with whites. The Central Pacific Railroad, whose tracks were built by the Chinese, canceled its contracts with Chinese woodcutters. The Summit Hotel fired its two Chinese cooks but acceded to their demands for back wages.

Over the weekend of February 16, men from the nearby towns of Boca, Prosser Creek, Cuba, and Clinton, as well as from Carson, Nevada, joined Truckee's night marches. Five bonfires burned in the small town square, and more than four hundred men joined a march several blocks long, appearing, one observer noted, like a "huge serpent of flame." The banner of the Truckee Hose and Engine Company, ORGANIZED TO PROTECT WHITE MEN'S PROPERTY, flew alongside canvas banners bearing the slogan OUR NEXT GOVERNOR, C.F. MCGLASHAN, WHITE LABOR'S CHAMPION. The town's white women stayed in their houses but placed candles and torches in their windows to show their support to the celebrating mob in the streets.

Chinatown was on alert. To defend their homes, the remaining Chinese men formed a long picket and, armed with revolvers, guarded the bridges and river crossings. Many feared another fire. In nearby Carson, Nevada, a Chinese ranch hand committed suicide by firing a pistol through his mouth. The *Republican* laconically commented, "No cause is assigned for the act except a general idea the Chinese have regarding their stay in the country."[46]

Day by day, carloads of Chinese left Truckee, most taking the westbound train that pulled out of town every evening. Some were moving to San Francisco or British Columbia; some decided to return to China. Others accepted a special invitation from Mexico. A few Chinese men who had married women from the Snohomish tribe refused to leave the mountain.[47] Others made secret agreements with their employers to return as soon as the boycott fervor ran its course.

For whites in Truckee, the anti-Chinese movement helped spur the birth of labor organizations. Toward the end of February, the Knights of Labor called its first meeting, organized under the banner NO DESPOTS. NO TYRANTS. NO COOLIES. NO SLAVES. If the now discredited Denis Kearney had found popularity in the cities, McGlashan understood small towns. Prompted by the upcoming convention, dozens of local organizations, such as the Nevada City Anti-Chinese League, formed, elected officers, and chose their delegates. McGlashan had created a statewide infrastructure, using the pages of the *Republican* to sell the Truckee method. Little towns such as Sierraville and Loyalton replicated Truckee's model and asked for McGlashan's support.

Appointed by the state executive committee at the Sacramento Anti-Chinese convention to lead the movement, Charles McGlashan founded the California Boycotting Committee to create boycott clubs in all the counties, cities, and towns in California that would lead the purges of Chinese throughout the state. Even before the Truckee expulsion was complete, he announced that he would remain in the Bay Area at a salary of two hundred dollars per month, a wage he quickly would forgo as he immediately faced criticism that he was using the cause to advance his personal interests. But McGlashan's future looked bright. The *Foothill Weekly Tidings* observed, "That anti-Chinese convention of Sacramento is going to make the next governor of California."[48]

Some of McGlashan's plans failed. The expensive steam laundry, built to replace the Chinese washhouses, closed; the new laundry was simply too large and expensive for the needs of the small railroad town, and the Truckee Laundry Association was sued by its major investors. As the spring of 1886 approached, large-scale farmers, food processors, and cannery owners realized that they would not be able to carry on their businesses without the Chinese. Some firms, such as the J. Lusk Cannery, announced to McGlashan and the Boycott Committee that they would keep their Chinese butchers and canners: "When we tell you that these men have all been with us from ten to fifteen years, and it takes from three to five years to learn the business, you can see that this is the vital point . . . that cannot be interfered with." In fact, although ads for white workers appeared in every journal, cheap white labor did not emerge, and mountain inns and hotels faced a summer season without food, while lumber camps could not staff their cookhouses.

Still running a daily column called "Boycott the Traitors," the *Truckee Republican* listed the names of markets, hotels, and merchants who refused to fire the Chinese. The paper implored the town not only to boycott these firms but to refrain from any social contact with the merchants themselves. Even the peddler who sold coffee at the train depot refused to serve the Chinese who were passing through Truckee on their way west. In late May, to skirt the boycott, John Bidwell, one of the state's largest growers, who relied on Chinese and Indian field-workers, shipped his produce to Penryn, where it was repacked and relabeled and then sent up to Truckee, Reno, Carson, and Virginia City. In towns where white workers were beginning to fill the now open jobs, rumors circulated that the leading employers had formed a consortium to reduce the wages of the white workingmen below the wages paid to Chinese employees.

FIRE

Despite its vision of a "freeze-out," many of Truckee's citizens still dreamed of fire. On June 17, 1886, Truckee's Chinatown again burned to the ground. Just as the fire broke out, two white men from nearby Grass Valley were seen lurking in Chinatown, "enjoying cigars in a spot where they could command a view of the China quarters. It is rumored that as the first whiff of smoke appeared, they gave a boy a bit to run down to the bridge and see if the shanties were on fire." Just after noon, the fire whistle sounded, and, reported the *Republican,* "the greasy shanties" became "one mass of flames."

The Truckee Hose and Engine Company rushed to protect the town bridge, which was thronged with people who wanted to watch Chinatown burn. Although a large fire engine had been specially designed to draw water from the Truckee River, on that day the town leaders decided that the river's steep banks made it impossible to get the engine down to the water. Instead, they hauled the engine alongside a fireplug on the whites' side of town and stationed a locomotive between the river and Chinatown. Watching in horror as the fire raged, a town judge ordered the train moved, but another ordered that it be kept in place to protect the white side of town.

Soon the few remaining Chinese abandoned any hope of saving their homes. They rushed to gather their bedding and blankets and take them down to the river. With only two water tanks and some bits of hose, there was little they could do to save Chinatown. Throughout the afternoon, they used buckets to pour water over the hot debris and cool the ground. Amid the charred embers, they searched for anything that might remain.

The fire took the lives of two Chinese men, Ah Juy, thirty-nine years old, and Tem Ah Yeck, thirty-five. Both natives of China, they suffocated in a cellar, locked behind iron doors, guarding two silver watches, six bars of silver bullion, and some jewelry.

The *Truckee Republican* reported that "it was late in the afternoon when the fire companies withdrew. They had made strenuous and heroic efforts to save the bridge." That afternoon a coroner's jury was impaneled and, after thirty hours of meetings, it deduced that because the key to the iron door was found on one of their bodies, Ah Juy and Tem Ah Yeck had deliberately locked themselves inside a fireproof building. The fire, concluded the jury, "originated from causes and persons which we are unable to determine."[49] McGlashan's newspaper, however, maintained that the fire was either the result of carelessness or the incendiary act of a "Chinaman." Regardless, the paper now cheered that "dirty, filthy Chinatown has been cleansed and purged of its disease breeding nastiness."

That month McGlashan announced the start of a new labor party under his leadership and pledged that by the 1888 elections, he would have an organization in place whose purpose "shall be to bury monopoly, stifle corruption, protect the rights of the American laborer and free our state from the Chinese evil."

All the while, Truckee remained wary of a lawsuit. Even as the boycott was beginning to take hold in late January 1886, the Grass Valley newspaper printed an interview with Colonel Bee, the Chinese consul in San Francisco, who promised, "We propose to do everything lawful in the way of getting redress for these wrongs." He added that it was his duty to bring suits against Santa Cruz, Truckee, and Felton, similar to the *Wing Hing* case against Eureka. But unlike Eureka, Truckee was able to hide behind a legal loophole: because it was not an incorporated town, there was no culpable municipality. There was no entity to hold responsible even if the "Truckee citizens had forced the giving up."[50]

By the end of 1886, only a handful of Chinese remained in Truckee. O. Lonkey, who made wooden fruit crates, withstood the town's threats and continued to hire Chinese woodworkers. Notices appeared in the *Republican* warning him that it was "sheer madness to attempt to check the cyclone of public opinion." The paper declared that unless Lonkey fired his Chinese employees, "every man in the Truckee basin will denounce and despise you as an enemy of white labor, and a man who is unfit for association with white men." The article was signed by William O'Neill, secretary of the Anti-Chinese Boycott Committee, the same William O'Neill who had been arrested and released ten years earlier for the murders at Trout Creek.

"Remember," warned the *Truckee Republican,* "the present struggle is a final one."

6

THE CHINESE REWRITE THE LETTER OF THE LAW

On the morning of January 21, 1886, Deputy U.S. Marshal B. J. Alerman boarded a steamship in San Francisco and sailed three hundred miles up the coast to Eureka. Once there, he walked from the docks to city hall. In the office of the county clerk, Alerman filed a lawsuit, *Wing Hing* v. *City of Eureka.* He then went across the hall to serve papers on Mayor Tom Walsh, who had chaired the fateful meeting in Centennial Hall that launched the purge of Chinese people from Humboldt County. That day the Chinese took historic steps to win reparations.

Just a year before, on Monday afternoon, February 9, many of the Chinese men and women who had been driven out of Eureka over the weekend had quickly regathered at the Ong Cong Gon So offices in San Francisco's Spofford Alley. They described the violent purge to the local Chinese community and the white press. Colonel Fred Bee, the Chinese consul, made it clear that the Chinese held the city of Eureka responsible: "There is a Sheriff and other officers of the law in Eureka, and they ought to have arrested all lawbreakers." The Chinese from Eureka, he added, were peaceable merchants "whose business has been broken up by their expulsion. Somebody will have to pay for the injury done them." They would only "wait quietly till the excitement dies down and then seek redress in the courts."[1]

Bee announced that the Chinese would sue Eureka for their lost property and for being forced from their homes by mob violence. He reminded the angry audience that the Chinese government had readily paid American citizens over seven hundred thousand dollars "in full liquidation" when Christian missions were destroyed in the anti-American riots in Canton. "The Eureka case," he warned, "will establish a precedent, and if America will not indemnify Chinese, China will not indemnify Americans."[2]

Eleven months after the Eureka roundup, just before the statute of limitations ran out, the Chinese refugees, some now living in San Francisco's Chinatown, others dispersed across the West, went on the offensive. On January 21, 1886, Wing Hing, a twenty-five-year-old merchant, filed *Wing Hing* v. *City of Eureka.*[3]

Acting as "assignee" for fifty Chinese men and two Chinese women, *Wing Hing* demanded reparations and monetary compensation for racial violence. They sued Eureka for "carelessness or negligence," claiming the city was liable for a total of $75,245 for lost property "removed, carried away, and destroyed" by the rioters. These claims ranged from $60 to $7,000 per individual. The Chinese also sued for $37,670 in damages—for being the objects of a riot and mob action due to the city's neglect of its legal duty. These individual claims ranged from $200 to $6,000.

The Chinese sued Eureka for debts that they could never collect, for the loss of their future earnings, and for the very experience of being driven out by a mob. They hoped to get back into their homes, back into their jobs and businesses, and recover their losses. They also hoped to punish the city and recover their dignity.

On behalf of the Chinese government, Colonel Bee announced that the Chinese would also sue the cities of Santa Cruz, Felton, and Truckee, among other places that imitated the roundup in Eureka. He hired two well-known San Francisco attorneys, Hall McAllister and Thomas D. Riordan. *Wing Hing* v. *City of Eureka* soon made headlines across the West.

Eureka's town leaders, union officers, and vigilantes knew that a lawsuit would be a test case for other purges.[4] The *Sacramento Bee* predicted that *Wing Hing* would be "the beginning of a long list of suits that will be brought against many towns and cities."[5] Nevada City's *Daily Transcript* cautioned other towns that were about to "start in and drive out the Chinese. . . . Let's wait awhile and see how that suit against Eureka, Humboldt County, turns out."[6] Foreseeing a host of cases if Eureka lost, the *San Francisco Chronicle* concluded that we "must fight the matter to the bitter end." Eureka would need money to win the case—"plenty of it"—so "all the energies of the people of the Coast should be bent toward stopping, with the present suit, this species of litigation."

The Eureka attorney, Indian hater, historian, and member of the Committee of Fifteen A. J. Bledsoe disagreed: "The talk about actions for millions of dollars is the sheerest nonsense. The total damages maintained by the Chinese by being driven out did not exceed $2000." But even he acknowledged, "The people of Eureka are aware that, as a matter of law, they are liable for actual damages inflicted on the Chinese, but if Consul Bee or any one else undertakes to collect more they will have their hands full."[7] The editor of Eureka's *Daily Times-Telephone* smirked at the notion of damages: "The facts of the case are simply that they left for their own protection against hostile demonstrations; that they were assisted to take away their worldly goods, and that not a dollar was due them from the citizens of Eureka."[8]

REPARATIONS AND THE LEGAL STRATEGY OF *WING HING*

The plaintiffs in *Wing Hing* faced profound hurdles. How could the Chinese appropriate the American legal system that was so sorely abusing them? How could refugees, fearful for their immigration status after the Exclusion Act of 1882, take public action? How could they gather evidence when they were not allowed to return to Eureka? How could they safely represent the Chinese women when many had fled to Eureka from enslaved prostitution in the Bay Area, only to find themselves back in San Francisco's Chinatown? How could they place a dollar amount on a mob forcing them to leave their community, with barely time enough to pack a few belongings? And how could they sue a city?

Wing Hing was wrapped around a few smart legal strategies that allowed the Chinese to sue a city, establish its negligence, and claim the right to safety in the United States. Legally framed as a negligence action, *Wing Hing v. City of Eureka* was an early and unique demand for reparations, a term popularized near the end of the Civil War by General Sherman's field order and Thaddeus Stevens's bill to give freed slaves "forty acres and a mule." *Wing Hing* was also a precursor to reparation demands that would follow well into the twentieth century—by African Americans, Hawaiians, Japanese Americans, and Jews. The concept of reparations, "justice that repairs," relies on evidence of continuous stigma and economic harm to a group.[9] Demands for reparations are typically put forth by people of a shared race or national origin who have been similarly harmed—by the loss of land, resources, educational opportunity, or political recognition. Because reparations force the offender to make amends, the claim goes beyond monetary compensation for lost property.[10] A demand for reparations implies that even undoing the harm would not undo the wrong.[11]

The doctrine of reparations as a meaningful remedy for violations of human rights thus implies that some form of redistribution of wealth must be involved in the realization of liberty.[12] Whether for Australian Aborigines, New Zealand Maoris, or Native Americans, reparations speak loudly to the economic implications of racism and break through the fantasy that liberty is priceless.

Wing Hing constructed negligence in an original and highly political way. Quite simply, the Chinese were saying that the city's duty to protect its residents meant all its residents; this duty did not change simply because some residents happened to be Chinese.

Two groups of Chinese immigrants joined forces to sue the city of Eureka: twenty-one were merchants, and the rest were laborers—vegetable peddlers, ranch hands, prostitutes, domestic servants, cooks, fishermen, road builders, and railroad construction workers. Laborer Taw Sang typically claimed that he "was residing with his family" when the mob broke into his "premises," and he listed in detail what was destroyed or what he was forced to leave behind.

Given the dearth of narratives by early Chinese immigrants, and particularly those who were driven out, *Wing Hing v. City of Eureka* provides a unique window into the Chinese view of their work, their role in a rural town, and the horror of being purged.

Sun Sing, the "occupant and proprietor" of a vegetable garden that provided produce to Eureka homes, boardinghouses, ships, and hotels, sued for

$1,920 for items that had not made it onto the steamship. Neither his garden, his trees and plants, nor his wagons and horses sailed on the *Humboldt* or the *City of Chester.* Ye Hop and Chan Dan Mon were both fishermen, forced to leave their boats, nets, and catch behind. Two women were parties in the suit: Ah How sought $1,780 in property and $1,000 in damages, and Tai Kim sought $850 in property and $500 in damages.

Tort law is meant to restore victims to the position they were in before they were injured. If the *Wing Hing* plaintiffs were victorious, the city of Eureka would have to dip into its coffers to pay the Chinese for the grave injustice of being driven out of their homes, fishing boats, farms, and shops.

In order to claim redress for the mob violence perpetrated on them, the Chinese chose to identify themselves racially, as members of a group "similarly situated." They crossed their own class and gender lines—merchant, laborer, wife, prostitute—to overcome the vast economic differences that their claims expose. They sued as a group because the violence perpetrated against them treated them as a group.

The shared national identity of the Chinese plaintiffs pointed to the illegality of the roundup. Although each refugee demanded a different sum of money, all of the Chinese residents of Eureka had been born in China. Chinese merchants and laborers alike built on the fact "that at each and all of the times hereinafter mentioned, the plaintiff was, and still is, an alien, to wit, a native and subject of the Empire of China." This reminder announced that they were entitled to powerful protections under the Burlingame Treaty, which granted Chinese and Americans alike free migration—for trade, for taking up residence, and for "curiosity." Signed in 1868, just three years after the Thirteenth Amendment abolished slavery, this treaty declared that any "migration" of people between the United States and China must be voluntary. Any removal of citizens against their will would constitute a penal offense. *Wing Hing* opened with the signal that Eureka must pay for violating this powerful treaty.

The decision to sue the city, rather than the mayor, the Committee of Fifteen, or individual vigilantes, also shapes *Wing Hing* as a demand for reparations and not merely a call for civil damages. Their case rested on the view that the "proximate cause" or the "initiating event" was the purge. The city should have predicted the harm it caused—indeed, intended to cause. The consequences were "foreseeable." What's more, by boasting of its actions, the town declared its culpability. Financial payment to the Chinese would provide compensation, deterrence, and retribution. It would also mark Eureka's contrition and humility.

In *Wing Hing*, the Chinese stated that on a weekend in February 1885, a riot by "a mob of disorderly and riotous persons . . . acting together and without authority of law, riotously broke into the premises" of twenty-seven Chinese merchants and "carried away . . . and totally destroyed their goods, merchandise, furniture, fixtures, clothing, personal effects, money and provision"; "drove" the owners of the firms, and their clerks and servants, from their stores; "and caused them to be removed beyond the corporate limits thereof." The city had failed to protect them from trespass and assault. The merchants did not own the land of Chinatown, but they certainly owned merchandise, furniture, fishing equipment, and perishable goods.

Moreover, *Wing Hing* declared, the riot was a direct response to an order from the mayor and elected leaders that demanded that all Chinese persons leave their homes and businesses and move outside the corporate limits of the town within twenty-four hours. The city had "due notice of the assembling of the mob and of the riot," and it "failed and neglected to quell" the riot, to disperse the mob, and to protect the property of the Chinese firms and individuals named in the lawsuit. The mayor of Eureka had chaired the meeting at which the roundup was planned, and members of the city council had served on the Committee of Fifteen, which planned and implemented the purge. The city had violated its duty of care, and by its negligence, it forced a mass removal of a people.

The Chinese wanted to get their case into federal court and out of the local court, which was usually biased against them. With Article 1 of the Constitution on their side, they knew that state and local courts had no legal jurisdiction over conflicts between Chinese citizens and American cities or states. Thus the suit declared their "diversity of citizenship." By putting the case together as an early form of class action, the Chinese could make claims totaling more than seventy-five thousand dollars, and thus enter the federal courts.

The Chinese also had a powerful (now defunct) statute on their side. The California Political Code had been passed in 1868, a hopeful moment in Reconstruction. It declared that "every county and municipal corporation is responsible for injury to real or personal property situated within its corporate limits, done or caused by mobs or riots."[13] Without this law in place, Eureka would have been protected under the common-law doctrine of "sovereign immunity." This doctrine originated in the medieval fiction that the "king can do no wrong" and offered cities, mayors, sheriffs, and police forces a shield from liability. The Chinese used a law from an era of mob violence against Mexicans, Indians, and African Americans to sue the city of Eureka as a "remedial right" of a minority people whose property was destroyed by mob violence.[14]

THE JUDGE

The Chinese believed they had an ally on the federal bench in Judge Lorenzo B. Sawyer. For more than two decades, they had looked to him to overturn anti-Chinese ordinances in the vast Ninth Judicial District, which covered much of the West.[15]

Judge Sawyer was known for accepting legal loopholes when the Chinese sought to reenter the United States after the Chinese Exclusion Act of 1882. After *People* v. *Hall* banned Chinese from testifying against whites, Sawyer ruled in *People* v. *Awa* (1865) that a state could not necessarily be construed as a white person, and he often allowed a Chinese person to act as a witness.[16]

Sawyer abhorred the concept of states' rights, which he called "the parent of many heresies."[17] He routinely wrote of his contempt for local codes such as the queue ordinance and the ordinance outlawing laundries in wood-frame buildings as "crudities, not to say the absurdities, into which constitutional conventions and legislative bodies are liable to be betrayed by their anxiety and efforts to accomplish, by indirection and circumlocution, an unconstitutional purpose which they cannot effect by direct means."[18] In 1886, the year of *Wing Hing,* Sawyer complained that "all Chinese [immigration] applications are in fact denied, and those of Caucasians granted."[19]

When deciding cases involving Chinese people, Sawyer often relied on the language of the Fourteenth Amendment, which offered equal protection under the law to "persons" and "inhabitants," not just to "citizens." In fact, Chinese merchants from San Francisco had introduced language into the Civil Rights Act to protect themselves from selective taxes or regulations and to prevent different punitive or penal treatment of aliens and citizens. Sawyer looked to these critical provisions, which probably represent the first impact of Chinese immigrants on the U.S. federal legislative process.[20] After the Supreme Court in *Yick Wo* v. *Hopkins* (1886) invoked the Fourteenth Amendment to stop California from banning Chinese laundries in wooden buildings, the Chinese increasingly used this clause to win significant victories.[21] The judge who would rule on *Wing Hing* had described his judicial stance: "We have, heretofore, found it our duty, however unpleasant, at times, to maintain, fearlessly and steadily, the rights of Chinese laborers."[22]

THE DEFENSE: "THE EXODUS OF THE CHINESE WAS THEREFORE, IN LAW, VOLUNTARY"

Eureka's legal response was a quick and simple strike at the heart of the case: a full and blanket denial that "mob violence" or an "expulsion" ever happened. Judge S. E. Buck, the city attorney, maintained: "History gives no example of any community of our race ever acting with such forbearance. By a few citizens [the Chinese] were told to leave within a specified period. They left, possibly in anticipation of the expulsion they knew they richly deserved, but not at the dictation of a mob, not by any exhibition of force, they called for no protection of police or Sheriff. . . . A large, unarmed, peaceable and unorganized assemblage, without the slightest indication of insult or menace, witnessed their exodus. . . . The exodus of the Chinese was, therefore, in law, voluntary."[23]

The city quickly filed a motion to strike all references to an expulsion.[24] Eureka simply denied that the Chinese were ever driven out: the "city, as a corporation, or through its official head, did not banish the Chinese." No "mob of disorderly or riotous persons assembled," nor did it create a riot or cause the Chinese to "be removed beyond the corporate limits of the city." Indeed, the Committee of Fifteen was only "chosen to keep the mob of excited men from doing any acts of violence."[25]

That argument would leave Eureka with only the claim that it had caused Chinese property to be destroyed, and to that, it responded that the Chinese property was worthless. Ignoring the fact that the Chinese had to leave behind fishing nets, horses, wagons, and furniture, the city moved to strike the language that each Chinese firm or individual was "transacting business in the city," had "valuable quantities" of property, and "sustained great damage by breaking into their premises and the total destruction of their business."[26]

But if any damage or loss of property did occur, claimed Eureka, then "the same was occasioned by the willful acts, negligence and carelessness" of the Chinese.

A major part of Eureka's defense, both in court and in the popular press, was its accusation that the Chinese exaggerated their losses. Even *if* Eureka had a duty to protect the Chinese, and even *if* it did not protect them from a race riot, then it owed them only their back taxes. As soon as the case was filed, the city marshal (who had enforced the purge and accompanied the ships carrying the Chinese to San Francisco) produced the city's tax rolls for the year 1884. He announced that the whole of Chinatown paid taxes on $2,300 worth of property. Indeed, he showed that only eighteen Chinese residents had paid any taxes, with Kow Lung paying the most: $4 on $125 worth of furniture.

Based on these numbers, the minimum amount due the Chinese should have been $2,399—the value of their taxable property. However, Eureka oddly and illogically claimed that it owed the Chinese only $22—the amount of city taxes paid by the Chinese. Eureka surely knew the meaning of its tax documents. Since the passage of the Homestead Act of 1862, public land was available only to immigrants who were eligible for U.S. citizenship, by definition excluding the Chinese. Eureka had allowed the Chinese to hold title to real estate, and $22 was all the Chinese had contributed to the tax rolls in 1884.

Eureka's legal strategy was to set up *Wing Hing* as an ordinary tort case about failing to stop a few white men from moving some worthless Chinese belongings—a simple civil action. Just because the Chinese were run out of town did not mean, said Eureka, that it had violated contracts or leases that gave the Chinese the right to live and conduct business on certain properties in town.[27]

During the lawsuit, Eureka's newspapers recalled the scene early on the

Saturday morning of the purge when wagons commandeered by the sheriff hauled "all the goods and chattels belonging to the aggregated Chinese" to the wharves and reported that nothing belonging to the Chinese remained in the town; not "one dollar's worth" of Chinese property was taken or destroyed. The *Daily Times-Telephone* urged the Chinese consul to amend his complaint before "Eureka laughs herself to death over this farce in one act."[28]

Other papers throughout the state echoed Eureka's stance. The *San Francisco Chronicle* claimed: "Chinese cunning has overreached itself in the case of the suits for damage brought against the city of Eureka for the eviction of the coolies about a year ago. . . . No looting of [Chinese] premises was permitted, and it is on record they carried away on the steamer the next day every scrap and parcel of their personal belongings, as well as of the merchandise."

Eureka then told its own version of the roundup in interviews with the local paper: "The city . . . through its official head, did not banish the Chinese." After the town heard of Kendall's death, there was a "simultaneous rush" by white people: "It was simply a body of excited men goaded to desperation by the atrocities of the heathen in this city." "Acting spontaneously," citizens selected the Committee of Fifteen, to whom was "intrusted the duty" of seeing that the Chinese were "removed from the city in a peaceable manner." Despite reports that the mayor had ordered the town to purge the Chinese in twenty-four hours, the *Daily Times-Telephone* concluded that "the corporate power is no more responsible for what was done than is Humboldt County or the State."[29]

The *Times-Telephone* then defined what came to be known as "the Eureka method": "Shortly after we had said they must go, and they did go, other towns on the coast fell into the line adopted, and in nearly every case where our policy was followed, success in getting rid of the Chinese has resulted. . . . Our course was to send them away without violence, and we did so. No blood was shed, no property destroyed."[30]

Nevertheless, in the winter and early spring of 1886, as the anti-Coolie Leagues, the Order of the Caucasians, the Workingmen's Party, the Knights of Labor, and Democratic Party clubs made plans to expel Chinese laborers and merchants from towns across the West, they kept their eye on the *Wing Hing* lawsuit.

THE OUTCOME

Politically, *Wing Hing*'s strategy worked. Across the West, the filing of the suit was seen as a courageous and bold act of the "expulsed" Chinese taking a collective stand against enforced deportation.

Legally, though, it failed. The Chinese plaintiffs did not know that their former advocate, Judge Sawyer, was changing his legal and racial views. In March 1886, Judge Sawyer rushed through a hearing and agreed to strike all sections of the complaint that held Eureka responsible for the mob action, for the loss of Chinese business, and for driving out the Chinese. Only the claims for property losses due to the city's negligence remained, and they had been undercut by the tax rolls.

The illogic of depending upon the tax rolls to determine the value of the Chinese property might well have been acknowledged by a friendlier judge.

Only four years after *Wing Hing,* Sawyer commented, "I don't think we want any Chinese and I think there is a good deal of people that we don't need—that we can just as well dispense with. I think the time has come when we don't need to hold out any extraordinary inducements to the poorest class of any nation to come here. It would be better if we had come to that conclusion a great while ago."[31] Sawyer explained that his newfound objection to Chinese immigration was rooted "in the distinction of races. It is a great misfortune to this Country that we have the negro in the Country. The Chinese are vastly superior to the negro, but they are a race entirely different from ours and never can assimilate and I don't think it desirable that they should. And for that reason I don't think it desirable that they should come here."

The true danger of the roundups and purges, wrote Sawyer, was to the economy: "You cannot do that without destroying and breaking down our own industries. There is scarcely an industry on this Coast that would not be ruined were we to drive these men out. Our fruit industry would be ruined and many of our manufacturers also.... If they never bring their women here and never multiply ..., their presence would always be an advantage to the State.... When the Chinaman ... don't bring his wife here, sooner or later he dies like a worn out steam engine, he is simply a machine, and don't leave two or three or half a dozen children to fill his place."[32]

Perhaps *Wing Hing* never stood a chance. The secretary of state quickly reminded the Chinese legation that the *Wing Hing* plaintiffs had more rights than American citizens, since they could choose to take their case to federal or state court.[33]

Despite the prominence of the case, its outcome was unclear. Over the next three years, both sides agreed to a series of continuances. In November 1888, Eureka moved to dismiss the slim remaining action, claiming that it could only be tried in Humboldt County and, strangely, that *Wing Hing* should be dismissed for failure to prosecute. And Sawyer obliged. On March 2, 1889, he ruled that the "plaintiff take nothing by this action" and charged the Chinese fifteen dollars in court costs. Lost to history is why Thomas Riordan, an aggressive San Francisco attorney who regularly represented the Chinese and was paid by the Chinese consul and the Chinese Six Companies, failed to take this case to the end. Perhaps the Chinese plaintiffs were dispersed to other parts of the state. Perhaps they believed that a loss was inevitable, or that the possible gains were too small—the city had essentially gutted the case. Or perhaps there was a quiet and discreet settlement.

Wing Hing undermined the view that the Chinese would quietly suffer being driven out and that Chinatowns were just slums. Through their very claims for property the Chinese insisted on the value of their community, their property, and their culture. But Judge Lorenzo Sawyer let twenty-two dollars stand between an illogical legalistic appeal and the brutal loss of a Chinese community.

REPARATIONS FOR THE ROCK SPRINGS MASSACRE

One of the most violent racial episodes in the history of the West occurred in Wyoming, almost at the same time as the Chinese expulsion from Eureka. In the fall of 1885, about 250 miles west of Cheyenne, 331 Chinese men and 150 white men worked in Rock Springs, Wyoming, at a vast coal mine owned by the Union Pacific Railroad. The Chinese had labored in the mines since 1875, when 150 of them had been brought there to break a strike.

That year federal troops had been sent to keep order, and the white miners, realizing their defeat, decided to return to work at a reduced wage.

But the company retained only fifty of its original five hundred miners, adding more Chinese in relation to whites over the next tense decade. By 1883, however, the Knights of Labor, whose national membership had increased dramatically to seven hundred thousand nationwide, organized the white miners at Rock Springs, building on their mantra, "The Chinese must go!" By 1885 the wages of Chinese and whites were apparently identical—as the miners somehow extracted nearly four tons of coal per day for three dollars per day, or seventy-five cents per ton.

In the early autumn of 1885, the Knights of Labor asked the Chinese miners to join in a strike. The Chinese refused and violence began. On September 2, a force of about 150 Irish-born miners marched to Chinatown armed with shotguns. After firing a volley into the air, they ordered the Chinese to leave. The Chinese fled, pursued by the white miners, who now fired directly at them. The Chinese quarters were set ablaze, and thirty-nine houses owned by the company and about fifty owned by the Chinese burned to the ground. Those Chinese miners who remained in their homes that day, perhaps because of illness or injury, perished in the flames.

As the afternoon wore on, white miners visited the various mines in the camp, locating all four hundred Chinese who were still at work and driving

"The Massacre of the Chinese at Rock Springs"

HARPER'S WEEKLY, SEPTEMBER 26, 1885

them out. By late afternoon, none remained. Most were hiding in the nearby hills, and about fifty died of exposure and starvation as they tried to reach the Green River and escape from the mine. It first appeared that seven Chinese were murdered outright and many others wounded by gunfire. Those numbers rose dramatically over the next few days.

The response of the Chinese government was immediate. Cheng Tsao Ju, the Chinese minister in Washington, D.C., again complained to Secretary of State Thomas F. Bayard. China also sent a top-level delegation to Wyoming, consisting of Wong Sic Chen, Chinese consul at New York, and Colonel Fred Bee. Bee reported to the Chinese minister that the murderers were white immigrants who "brutally shot down" the Chinese, surrounded their dwellings, "robbed them of everything valuable," and then set them all afire. "Those who attempted to escape from their burning buildings were shot down or driven back into the flames. Fifteen remains of those burned have been taken out, not one of which could be identified." Bee was convinced that the criminals who murdered the twenty-eight Chinese would never be "brought to punishment."[34]

After thoroughly investigating Rock Springs, Fred Bee also reported that although the Chinese miners had refused to join the strike, they had not been accused of lowering whites' wages, as all were paid alike. But the Chinese had angered the Knights of Labor by serving as scabs in the coalfield strikes.

No one protected the Chinese. The action of the police, said Bee, was a "burlesque," and the justice of the peace, himself a member of the Knights of Labor, had imposed "paltry" sums of bail. The coroner, Bee added, called but one witness, only to confirm that a Chinese man was in fact dead. The coroner acknowledged that even more bodies had probably disappeared and that Chinese miners believed that they "were either completely burnt or eaten by dogs and hogs, or left in the wilderness."[35]

Secretary of State Bayard's response was tepid and reluctant. He told Minister Cheng Tsao Ju that the Chinese were free to "reside in any quarter which they may select" without consulting the "pleasure or prejudice" of native inhabitants. It was their "refusal to join with the other residents in a movement for an increase in wages" that caused them to be "set upon, robbed, and murdered."[36] He expressed his regrets and assigned only two army officers, General A. McCook and Lieutenant Groesbeck, to accompany the Chinese commission.

Rock Springs Chinese Investigation Commission. Left to right: Lieutenant Groesbeck, Tsang Hoy, Fred Bee, Wong Sic Chen, unknown and General McCook.

In late November, Cheng again wrote to Bayard that it was possible to identify the murderers. Not only was the attack at Rock Springs unprovoked, but it had occurred in "broad day-light." Yet no one had been charged. Cheng insisted that Bayard have the murderers "brought to punishment." In the name of the emperor and government of China, Cheng demanded that the Chinese subjects be "fully indemnified" for the losses they suffered, which he estimated at $147,748.74, and that the U.S. government make "pecuniary indemnity" for the injuries and devastation to the Chinese community in the Denver riots of 1880.

Cheng ended his communiqué with a veiled threat, reminding the American secretary of state of the principle of "reciprocal justice and comity." "American citizens in China," he asserted, "have no other and no greater treaty guarantees and rights than Chinese subjects in the United States." The United States, Cheng recalled, had demanded and received "a large sum of money" from the government of China for losses when Chinese mobs burned or destroyed American houses and missions. The United States had also demanded that local authorities in China rebuild the missionaries' houses and indemnify the country for plundering American homes.[37]

The forceful reaction by the Chinese government prompted a quick response from both the secretary of state and the American press. Bayard blamed the "race prejudice on the 'lawlessness of men not citizens of the United States engaged in competition with Chinese laborers' "—that is to say, the Irish. He also suggested that the "privileges and immunities" of Chinese subjects in the United States were greater than those extended to American citizens residing in limited areas of China.[38]

Harper's Weekly declared that the Rock Springs Chinese had a "clear right" to protect their "persons" and their property "by force." It predicted that the commission "will find . . . that the assault on the Chinese was wanton and unprovoked; that they had given no excuse or occasion for it, having been peaceable, law-abiding, industrious, and respectable." The Chinese, *Harper's* reminded its readers, were in fact preparing to obey an arbitrary order to leave Rock Springs within an hour when they were attacked by a mob that was "in the last degree inhuman and worse than brutal." Under the direct authority of the U.S. government, justice had "broken down at the very outset." *Harper's* observed that the Chinese men were murdered in broad daylight in the presence of hundreds of witnesses and that the coroner's jury in Wyoming had quickly determined that they had come to their deaths by being burned and shot by "persons unknown"—a phrase often used to avoid blaming a lynch mob. Similarly, the grand jury failed to indict the ringleaders.

Harper's viewed the massacre at Rock Springs as part of a national epidemic of unrestrained violence against minority groups. Since the facts of the case were undeniable, the United States government "will have to aver that its people in Wyoming are in a state of semi-savagery; that they are liable to outbursts of violent passion springing from race prejudice; that they have been taught to believe that they, though the most ignorant and backward of people, judged by the standard of the Christian religion . . . are the chosen of the heart, to whom all outside barbarians are hateful and inferior." Concluded *Harper's,* a shameful nation will have to acknowledge that it does not have the system of government to "repress or punish the violence of these irresponsible creatures."[39]

These deeds were "not the crimes of natives but of foreigners, whose presence in the country is much less desirable than that of the Chinese themselves." The mob actions at Rock Springs would not have occurred "except for the consciousness of the general although passive support of the community, which was the real support of the Ku-Klux outrages in the Southern States."[40]

Furthermore, Americans living in China "might justly expect the severest retaliation for the barbarous treatment of the Chinese in this country." Both missionaries and businessmen abroad were keeping a close eye on the indemnity bills. Ironically, noted *Harper's,* at the very moment of "these wanton attacks upon the helpless Chinese . . . the chief Chinese officers in the viceroyalty of Canton had just paid their annual subscriptions to the charitable medical relief society for Americans and English" who were residing in Canton. "The contrast in humanity and Christian charity is not favorable to the Irish immigrants accused of abusing the hospitality" of Americans. In the presence of these crimes, "a general massacre of Americans in China might be justly anticipated" and the U.S. government's comments that it can do nothing to stop the violence "puts it before the world in a ridiculously imbecile light." *Harper's* noted that while Congress's resolution in favor of Irish home rule pandered to the Irish vote in this country, "there is no Chinese vote. But the Chinese are human beings, and there is such a thing as American Honor."[41]

In July 1886, the American ambassador to China, Charles Denby, wrote to Secretary Bayard describing two serious "outrages" on American missionaries at Chungking, one at a medical mission hospital and another at a mission station four hundred miles southwest of Canton, where placards appeared on the walls demanding that the "foreign devils" go and their buildings be destroyed. A missionary and her small daughter fled by boat to Canton; an attack on other missionary women "grew, as all of our evils in China do, out of troubles in the United States."[42]

Soon after the Rock Springs massacre, the Chinese demanded financial indemnity and Bayard disclaimed any U.S. liability by insisting that Wyoming was simply a territory, "a rude commencement of a community at the outposts of civilization," and that the United States was not accountable for illegal acts committed by these individuals.[43] But intense pressure hit Congress from the Chinese Foreign Office in Peking and from Ambassador Denby, who insisted that the massacre threatened the safety of American investors as well as missionaries in China.[44] Fearful of the loss of trade with China and its market of four hundred million "heathens," the House of Representatives appropriated $147,748 for reparations for Rock Springs under the "Belmont Act."[45] The Senate approved the measure 30 to 10 and added another $130,000 to cover "all other losses and injuries sustained by Chinese subjects within the United States at the hands of residents thereof."[46] The money was paid directly to the government of China for "losses sustained by Chinese subjects by mob violence." The United States government eventually paid out a total of $424,367 for damages to the Chinese, incurred from incidents in Tacoma, Seattle, Rock Springs, and Redding. It is not clear that any of the money went to the Chinese who had been driven out.

DRIVEN OUT OF THE WASHINGTON TERRITORY

Soon after the massacre at Rock Springs, violence again came to the Pacific Northwest. On September 7, 1885, in the hop fields of Squak Valley (Issaquah) in the Washington Territory, a band of white and Native American farmworkers, angry over the higher wages paid to Chinese hop pickers, fired into their tents and murdered three Chinese men. Another mob burned the barracks of thirty-six Chinese coal miners near Newcastle, Washington. The violence quickly spread to Seattle and Tacoma. A host of groups, from the Knights of Labor to the Turnverein, a national club of German immigrants devoted to gymnastics and intense exercise, joined in the efforts to drive the Chinese out of the Washington Territory.

Jacob Weisbach, the mayor of Tacoma, was the president of Washington's territory-wide Anti-Chinese League. In October, he led a torchlight parade through Seattle, carrying a banner declaring CHINESE MUST GO. Within days, vigilantes murdered three Chinese men, and on the night of October 24, hundreds of white citizens set fire to Seattle's Chinatown. A notice in the local papers announced that all the Chinese must leave the Washington Territory before November 1.

Facing threats, Seattle's sheriff insisted that the ambivalent governor of the territory, Watson Carvosso Squire, request help from the United States military. Squire reluctantly declared martial law, and President Grover Cleveland sent a U.S. infantry regiment to Seattle. Throughout the tense winter, federal troops protected Seattle's Chinese.

But when the soldiers left Seattle in February 1886, a mob of fifteen hundred stormed the Chinese section of town, forcing the more than four hundred Chinese residents to load their belongings onto wagons and head down to the docks. Hundreds of refugees, carrying few belongings, were loaded onto the *Queen of the Pacific* and shipped south to San Francisco.

The anti-Chinese riot at Seattle, Washington Territory
HARPER'S WEEKLY, MARCH 6, 1886

Those who could not fit aboard were marched to the courthouse, where an angry mob murdered one Chinese man and injured four others. None of the vigilantes from Seattle was ever prosecuted or convicted.

Minister Cheng Tsao Ju and Consul Fred Bee had pleaded with local and federal governments to intervene. Cheng viewed the violence in Seattle and Rock Springs as a conspiracy to drive out all of the Chinese and warned, "Since the evil-doers of the Territory have been so violent in their conduct, and now threaten to expel all Chinese persons from the Territory, an outbreak like that at Rock Springs may occur at any moment."[47]

In February, Cheng wrote to Secretary Bayard demanding urgent attention to the "deplorable and defenseless condition of many thousands of my countrymen." He was incensed at Bayard's indifferent responses both to urgent telegrams and daily reports in the press that the Chinese had been "driven by violence out of many places, their dwellings burned, their property robbed, and . . . the people murdered, without any serious attempt being made by the authorities to prevent these acts or afford protection."[48]

"It is said," wrote Cheng, "that it is the intention . . . not only to drive them from their localities, but to secure their expulsion from America, so that driven from one town they have no assurance of protection in fleeing to another." The Chinese people, he reported, "with no place of safety to dwell . . . in wretched condition of poverty and fear," were flocking to San Francisco, and "by robbery or abandonment" losing all that they possessed. Cheng demanded immediate military protection for his people.[49]

Fred Bee telegraphed Governor Squire warning that "evil disposed persons have attacked and murdered several Chinese residents, and that further violence is threatened; that in fact the Chinese are to be expelled from the Territory."[50] But Squire was defensive and deceptive; he replied that "local authorities are vigilant in repressing and guarding against further outbreak."

Although Squire acknowledged that mining, manufacturing, and railroad companies were firing their Chinese laborers and that "many of them, fearful of violence, are leaving the disturbed districts," he disingenuously assured the secretary of the interior that "a strong organization of the better class of citizens at Seattle has arrayed itself, under the law, for the preservation of peace and order." At this point, he said, there was no need to call upon the military.

Then Squire reported that both Seattle and Tacoma had set November 1, 1885, as the deadline for all Chinese to leave.[51]

"TACOMA WILL BE *SANS* CHINESE, *SANS* PIGTAILS, *SANS* MOON-EYE, *SANS* JOSS-HOUSE, *SANS* EVERYTHING MONGOLIAN"

Although the speed and brutality of the Eureka purge daunted some towns, and the threat of a Chinese lawsuit restrained others, Tacoma prepared for an all-out race war. Tacoma was a company town, the terminus of the Northern Pacific Railroad. Here white residents complained that the Chinese had taken the "best blocks" of downtown and, with their "inborn insolence" and "vile habits," had ruined property values.[52] The anti-Chinese movement of Tacoma was led by Mayor Weisbach, the candidate of the Workingmen's Union and the Knights of Labor. These labor guilds had come into Tacoma when, despite high numbers of unemployed whites, the

Tacoma mayor Jacob Weisbach

water company hired Chinese workers to lay pipe.[53] The campaign against the Chinese was also aided by a newspaper war between the *Tacoma Ledger* and *The Tacoma News,* both of which found that anti-Chinese violence stimulated their circulation.[54]

Just two weeks after the Eureka purge, Weisbach called for an anti-Chinese meeting to be held at the Alpha Opera House on Saturday evening, February 21, 1885. That night he told the town that because the Chinese were "nuisances" and were violating local health laws, he had grounds to immediately remove them and condemn their stores and tenements.[55]

Weisbach's plan to starve them out crystallized over the spring and summer. By late September, following a statewide anti-Chinese congress in Seattle, Weisbach had appointed a committee to circulate pledge cards to employers and consumers in Tacoma who promised to boycott Chinese workers and shops. The *Ledger* and the more rabid *News* both promised to publish the names of any white person who refused to sign a card. A committee of fifteen delivered notices to the Chinese ordering them to leave Tacoma within thirty days.

Weisbach's initial strategy was to avoid outright violence. It began with a public warning to leave, followed by the deputizing of more than one hundred deputy sheriffs, a display of weapons, and the threat to expose immigration violations. The popular *Overland Monthly* named this form of rapid expulsion the "Tacoma method"—a "practice of communities as far back as history extends, to expel intruders or exile obnoxious members." It acknowledged that from the Christian standpoint of brotherly love, these tactics seemed "monstrous," but from the standpoint of "the corporate orders of civilization" it offered peace, welfare, and the opportunity for the "majority" to rule.[56]

THE ROUNDUP

By foot, by railroad, and by steamer, the Chinese began their exodus. About 150 of Tacoma's 700 Chinese residents, many of whom had been in the city since the early 1870s, left on the train south to Portland, Oregon, or aboard the steamer *Southern Chief,* northbound for Victoria, Canada, before the deadline. Hoping for a reprieve, Goon Gau, a longtime Tacoma merchant, wired Governor Squire, "I am notified that at three p.m. tomorrow a mob will remove me and destroy my goods. I want protection. Can I have it?" The governor never replied.[57]

On the morning of November 3, 1885, two days past the mayor's final deadline, all hell let loose: "When watches and clocks indicated the hour to be 9:30, the shrieking of shop whistles suddenly rent the air. As if by magic the group of men came together, and from all quarters and from their various occupations men came flocking hurriedly. . . . Soon there were about 500 men in solid array, marching up the avenue, resounding with the tramp, tramp tramp of many feet . . . towards the houses inhabited by the Chinese."[58]

Within minutes the steam whistles at the other foundries and mills blew. All the saloons closed, and fifty police stood by as a crowd of more than five hundred armed men took control of the town. Brandishing clubs and pistols, the mob, led by the Committee of Fifteen, went from house to house, up and down the muddy streets of the Chinese quarter and outside the Chinese tenements built along the wharf by the Northern Pacific Railroad Company. They ordered the Chinese residents to leave by 1:30 P.M. on that rainy day. Merchants were given an extra twenty-four hours to pack their wares.

Suddenly, the mob went wild. Rioters began breaking into buildings and ordering people from their homes. How Lung, a merchant and landlord, recalled them bursting into his store:

> On the 3rd day of November at Tacoma I saw a mob of several hundred men on the street. They came to my store and kicked off the door. They took hold of the Chinese that were in these houses, some of them were Chinese women, including my wife, and pulled them out of doors. . . . Some person in the mob pointed pistols at the Chinese but did not fire any pistols. The Mayor of Tacoma, Mr. Weisbach, was there at the time with the mob. He came to my house and said I must go. This was Monday, afterwards that day he said I might stay until Wednesday. The mob forcibly took some of my goods away on the 3rd of November. I do not know the value of the goods they took from me.[59]

When the mob arrived at the home of Lum May, a prosperous dry-goods merchant, Lum's wife refused to go. Several white men dragged her from the house, and later Lum May, supported by an affidavit from a local physician, reported:

Committee of Fifteen, Tacoma

Where the doors were locked they broke forcibly into the houses, smashing in doors and breaking in windows. Some in the crowd were armed with pistols, some with clubs. They acted in a rude, boisterous, and threatening manner, dragging and kicking the Chinese out of their houses.

My wife refused to go, and some of the white persons dragged her out. . . . She lost her reason and has ever since been hopelessly insane. She threatens to kill people with a hatchet or any other weapon. . . . She was perfectly sane before the riot. . . . I saw my countrymen marched out of Tacoma on November 3rd. They presented a sad spectacle. Some had lost their trunks, some their blankets, some were crying for their things.

Lum knew that Weisbach was watching the spectacle, and when he rushed to him for help, the mayor replied, "You get out . . . you must go, and I mean my word shall be kept good."[60]

As the riot continued, distraught Chinese merchants sent urgent telegrams to Governor Squire in Olympia. "Mob driving Chinamen out of town. Will you not protect us?" wired Ten Sin Yee Lee. From nearby Puyallup, Goon Gau wrote, "People driving Chinamen from Tacoma. Why sheriff no protect. Answer." Squire wired back curtly, "Telegram received. I have telegraphed facts to the Government at Washington."[61]

The violence lasted all day. Some of the vigilantes charged into Chinatown on horseback; some slipped in by boat; the rest of the mob marched from house to house, breaking down doors, smashing windows, and looting the Chinese residences. After each house was attacked, a squad of white men remained to make sure that the Chinese packed and left. Even while the rout was under way, many Chinese quickly stopped by the homes of their white friends to say good-bye and leave farewell presents. Eventually the mob gathered the Chinese, and Weisbach wired L.Q.C. Lamar, the secretary of the interior, that everything was under control and that there was no need for federal troops. By midafternoon, two hundred Chinese residents of Tacoma, with whatever belongings they could carry, were corralled at the wharf. Vigilantes nailed placards to wooden gates and doors, listing the few townsfolk who had tried to protect the Chinese.

At two in the afternoon, in a pelting north coast rain, the Chinese men and women began the march under guard to Lake View Junction, a railroad station on the Portland line of the Northern Pacific Railroad—a railroad that they had helped build. The merchants' wives who, with bound feet, could not manage the nine-mile trek climbed into open buggies and drays. About two thirds of the way, a few of the men "gave out" and were transferred to wagons.[62] The rest of the Chinese slogged through the heavy mud. As soon as they reached Lake View, their belongings were dumped on the wet ground and the buggies returned to town. There was no cover and no food. A few found shelter in abandoned railroad sheds, some in a stable; a few were allowed into the station house. Most spent the wet and cold night outdoors. At about one in the morning, buggies carrying bread, crackers, and cheese arrived from Tacoma, and the food was distributed to the refugees. Governor Squire later acknowledged that "a large number of them had no other cover than that afforded by rough open sheds without flooring. . . . Being wet and cold there is not doubt many of them suffered from exposure." In fact, two men died because of the harsh conditions.[63]

As trains passed through the remote railroad crossing, those refugees who had cash paid their own fares to get away alive; seventy-seven Chinese purchased tickets for the morning train, thirty paid the group rate of $120; the rest spent $6 each for southbound tickets to Portland. The Chinese had to pay for their own expulsion. Others began to walk the 140 miles to Portland and were seen for days after the purge marching southward along the tracks. The rest were loaded into boxcars on the 3 A.M. freight train.

By the evening of November 3, except for a few domestic servants who were allowed to stay behind to pack or to guard their employers' homes, no Chinese residents remained in Tacoma. One resident, John Arthur, boasted in a letter to Governor Squire, "*Fuit Ilium.* The Chinese are no more in Tacoma, and the trouble over them is virtually at an end. Yesterday they were peaceably escorted out of town and put upon the freight and passenger trains this morning." Arthur assured the governor that soon "Tacoma will be *sans* Chinese, *sans* pigtails, *sans* moon-eye, *sans* joss-house, *sans* everything Mongolian. . . . It affords me genuine delight to recall my assurances to you . . . that the Chinese would be got out of Tacoma without any trouble, and [I] point to the denouement in confirmation."[64]

Well aware of *Wing Hing* v. *City of Eureka,* Tacoma awaited a similar lawsuit, and the Committee of Fifteen set out to destroy evidence of the roundup. Accompanied by Health Officer McCoy, the committee visited Chinatown with plans to condemn the buildings. But the mob preceded them, and over the next two days, they burned Chinatown down. The local fire chief claimed that he could not save the Chinese houses because his hoses had been cut during the blaze. Curiously, though, firefighters were able to save the nearby mill as well as the tracks and buildings of the Northern Pacific Railroad. On November 6, the Chinese houses on the wharf that were owned by the railroad company also burned to the ground.

THE CHINESE DEMAND JUSTICE: "PROMPT ACTION MUST BE TAKEN, OR THE SAME OUTRAGE WILL BE ENACTED ALL OVER THE TERRITORY."

The Chinese in Tacoma had anticipated a roundup and had made plans for legal action even before the raids began. Although many sold their goods and property to white friends, others established the financial value of their pending losses.[65]

China's diplomats responded quickly to the terror and devastation in Tacoma. Again, the Chinese immediately invoked the Burlingame Treaty, which both brought Chinese immigrants under the protective umbrella of the Fourteenth Amendment and made it a penal offense to remove Chinese subjects involuntarily.

Rapidly exchanging telegrams, the Chinese legation monitored the purge even as it was taking place. On November 5, as Chinese subjects were trudging in the cold toward Portland, Minister Cheng Tsao Ju in Washington forwarded an urgent telegram to Secretary Bayard from On Yang Ming, the Chinese consul general at San Francisco, demanding the safe return of the Chinese to Tacoma: "Several hundred Chinese driven from Tacoma, Washington Territory yesterday, are now in woods without shelter or food. Merchants given until today to pack their goods and leave. No effort made by the governor or authorities to protect them. Prompt action must be taken, or the same outrage will be enacted all over the Territory."[66]

Within the next few weeks, demands for restitution came from Chinese merchants and laborers now dispersed across the Washington Territory and the West. Although they had quickly scattered to San Francisco, Portland, Seattle, Port Townsend, and Victoria, British Columbia, Chinese merchants and laborers from Tacoma collectively filed seventeen civil claims against the U.S. government for $103,365 in damages. These demands were ultimately granted through congressional action, including the Belmont Act of 1888.

NO GREATER EVIL

On November 6, three days after the brutal exodus, Federal Marshal J. W. George subpoenaed twenty-seven leaders of the purge who were hiding out in Portland and ordered them to appear before a federal grand jury sitting in Vancouver, Washington, 130 miles to the north. He then subpoenaed fifteen white residents of Tacoma to testify on behalf of the Chinese.[67]

The U.S. attorney at Tacoma, W. H. White, had personally heard the Committee of Fifteen threaten to blow up the houses of any Chinese person who did not leave town and was determined to prosecute the mayor and the mob. White wrote to the U.S. attorney general, "Evidence . . . warrants me in saying that no greater outrage was ever committed against the laws and government of these United States."[68]

On November 7, just four days after the purge, the grand jury indicted the mayor, the Committee of Fifteen, and "diverse others." It found that these "evil disposed persons" and three hundred more "did conspire confederate combine and agree . . . to make insurrection against the laws of the United States of America and to incite, set on foot, assist, and engage in insurrection" against the laws of the United States. It decreed that the men "unlawfully, seditiously, riotously" met over a period of forty-eight hours and then, "with force and arms attacked and broke open" the stores, shops, and dwelling houses of more than two hundred subjects of China. They "beat, bruised, wounded, ill treated, banished [and] drove out of and away" the Chinese subjects and "do still intend to hinder" them from returning to Tacoma. The mob prevented the Chinese from enjoying the rights of citizens of a most favored nation under the Burlingame Treaty.

The grand jury charged that Weisbach and his men had deprived the Chinese of "equal protection" under the law "with intimidation, force, and violence, banishing from, and driving out and away from their houses, homes and abiding places." Finally, the mayor, the elected officials, and the other men from Tacoma were charged with "arraying and disposing themselves in an insurrectionary, traitorous rebellion," to prevent Chinese people's right to travel and enjoy residence.[69]

Immediately after the indictments were released, Judge John Hoyt ordered the arrest of the mayor, Councilmen Dolphus B. Hanna and E. G. Bacon, probate court judge James Wickersham, the fire chief, and the president of the YMCA, as well as six carpenters, three blacksmiths, three merchants, three journalists, two butchers, two plumbers, a draftsman, a photographer, a brick mason, a civil engineer, a boatbuilder, a molder, a farmer, and a shoemaker.

Concerned that the arrests might lead to an armed uprising, the Justice Department ordered four companies of the U.S. Army, still garrisoned in Seattle after the anti-Chinese riots, to Tacoma. The troops reached Tacoma at noon, and that afternoon the U.S. marshal arrested twenty-seven alleged conspirators.

The next morning, a stunned crowd watched their elected officials and judges join the other prisoners, form into a column of twos, and, with the mayor at the head, march to the train station. Tacoma's residents quickly raised five thousand dollars for a defense fund. When the marshal remarked to Judge Hoyt, "You've got some of Tacoma's best citizens under arrest," Hoyt soberly replied that the crime was "one of the gravest known to American law."[70] The prisoners pleaded not guilty, and Hoyt fixed bail at five thousand dollars each and released them all. He then set trial for the first Monday in April.

The prisoners returned to Tacoma as heroes. When their train passed through Lake View, where the Chinese had spent the cold night just the week before, the Steilacoom Band played. The fire department (which had watched while Chinatown burned) led a torchlit parade as the train finally pulled into the crowded Tacoma station. Speaking for the white women of Tacoma, Rose Stannous thanked the men for sweeping "away the slaves that had taken the bread from the people's mouths and from their children's mouths." Because of their courage, Stannous added, the women's "eyes no more meet the unclean Chinamen." Within days the citizens of Tacoma were making regular visits to the courthouse to donate to the bail fund.

Quickly the defendants moved to quash the indictments, in part because six of the grand jurors were women and hence "unqualified to serve," but Judge Hoyt denied the motion and ordered the case to trial.[71]

A CRIMINAL TRIAL

To the surprise of the mayor and the other defendants, a group of white ministers, bankers, mill owners, neighbors, and merchants who had all stood by during the purge suddenly came forward to testify on behalf of the Chinese. The Chinese, they said, were their customers and friends, not the "immoral caricatures" despised by the city leaders and the mob. The minister of the First Baptist Church described how he watched the Chinese, reputable converts to his church, pleading with the mayor just for time to pack their stores.[72] The Reverend Barnabus MacLafferty reported that the few Chinese who remained in town could not purchase food to send to the refugees at the station, and that the bakers and storekeepers refused even to sell them bread.

Of great risk to the city, the chief clerk and cashier of the Northern Pacific Railroad Company endorsed the Chinese's claims about the financial effects of the purge, and the superintendent of the Tacoma Mill testified to the wealth, property, and investments of the Chinese merchants. Unlike most Chinese residents in California and Wyoming, the Chinese in the Washington Territory had the right to own land. Only after the purges in Seattle and Tacoma did the Territory prohibit land ownership by immigrants not eligible for citizenship—that is, the Chinese. This ban was not eliminated until 1952.[73]

Again the Chinese turned to the protective language of the Burlingame Treaty, which made it a penal offense to deprive Chinese immigrants in the United States of "the same privileges, immunities, and exemptions in respect to travel or residence, as may there be enjoyed by the citizens or subjects of the most favored nation."[74] In other words, they argued, a purge, an expulsion, a driving out, was an international crime.

The mayor and the Committee of Fifteen, by contrast, turned to two racially marked Supreme Court decisions as precedents—*Dred Scott* v. *Sanford* (1857) and *United States* v. *Harris* (1883).[75] In *Dred Scott* Chief Justice Roger B. Taney ruled that slave owners could seize their runaway slaves in territories as well as states, even in territories where slavery was illegal because African Americans—free or unfree—were not citizens of the United States. Thus, they did not have rights in the eyes of the federal government. Mayor Weisbach claimed that because the Chinese could not become citizens, they were similarly unprotected by the Constitution.

Dred Scott had been completely discredited by the Thirteenth Amendment, which abolished slavery; resurrecting it in order to justify a brutal racial pogrom made no sense. But in 1885, the use of a legal technicality to oppress the just claims of a racial minority was still common.

Just two years earlier, the Supreme Court in *Harris* had overturned the convictions of a mob of white men from Tennessee for killing an African American man and beating several others, holding that the Ku Klux Klan Act had been declared unconstitutional.[76] Furthermore, the court had ruled that the Ku Klux Klan Act was aimed only at "private" conduct. And private conduct was a matter of states' rights. In response to the charges that Weisbach and the leaders of the purge had conspired to deprive the Chinese of equal protection of the law by "purposely with intimidation force and violence banishing from and driving out and away from their houses, homes, and abiding places," the Weisbach defense, relying on *Harris,* argued that territories, like states, had the right to make and enforce any law not inconsistent with the Constitution, in this case criminal statutes for offenses by individuals.

Weisbach also opposed the prosecution's use of the Fourteenth Amendment to protect the Chinese. He reiterated the view of the Supreme Court—a court eager to erase the Civil Rights Act and the Ku Klux Klan Act—that "due process" was only a protection against arbitrary power of the *government,* not of *individuals.* The Chinese, he argued, had not been harmed by the government.

By invoking the precedents of *Dred Scott* and *Harris,* the Tacoma defense managed to exonerate the vigilantes. By arguing that the Chinese, as a racial minority, lacked legal standing, the defendants persuaded the court that the federal government did not have the power to forbid towns to banish the Chinese.

Weisbach also sought to undercut the Chinese use of the Burlingame Treaty. During the purge, the defendants claimed, none of the vigilantes interfered with a police officer who was trying to uphold Burlingame. Besides, they insisted, treaties were binding only on governments, not individuals. Finally, the defense argued that all the Chinese in Tacoma had violated the Chinese Exclusion Act of 1882 and all were in the country illegally.[77]

When the defendants turned to the charge of inciting and engaging in insurrection, they maintained that only citizens could be guilty of insurrection, and the indictments did not specifically allege that the mayor, fire chief, or city councilors were American citizens. In any case, assault, battery, and forcible detention were not acts of insurrection against a government.

With a claim that would bear on future race riots, Weisbach's lawyers maintained that *had* the mayor ordered the mob to disperse and *had* it refused, *had* the U.S. marshal attempted to make arrests and been resisted, *had* the president or the governor issued a lawful proclamation that the people refused to obey, then there would have been an insurrection. But since no legal official tried to stop the violence, there was, quite simply, no insurrection. In other words, the mayor's willful negligence, which enabled the race riot, contaminated the insurrection case against him.

Finally, the defense brought forth a series of witnesses who testified that Mayor Weisbach and other leaders of the roundup were law-abiding citizens who intended no harm and did none. The sheriff of Pierce County, Lewis Byrd, testified that during the "agitation" he had encountered a mob of two to three hundred men, led by the Committee of Fifteen, and with stunning disingenuousness he recalled: "I asked them what they were doing, and they said, nothing; I asked them what it meant, and they said, nothing in particular; I asked what they were going to do; and they replied that they were merely endeavoring to ascertain how many Chinese there were in the city. The crowd appeared orderly and was troubling nobody. I then demanded of the crowd generally that they keep the peace and interfere with nobody and they said everything would be quiet and nobody would be interfered with." Byrd said he saw nothing that would have justified an arrest and, in fact, spent the day in his office.[78]

For his part, the mayor maintained that he relied on the sheriff's observation that the anti-Chinese committee notified the Chinese to leave in a manner "as orderly as a common procession." Nothing required his "interference." In fact, he neither saw arms nor heard abusive language used against the Chinese. He did hear that the Chinese "had gone" to Lake View with the intention of taking the morning train to Portland. Concerned that they might be without food, the mayor had two 140-pound boxes of crackers, 150 loaves of bread, and two rounds of cheese delivered to the encampment from his own store, for which, he said, he was never compensated. He recalled "no remonstrances from the Chinese and I saw none of them crying."[79]

In the end, the Chinese refugees lost every aspect of the case. All the charges against Weisbach and the Committee of Fifteen were dismissed, and the prisoners were released. The Chinese claims for damages evaporated when the county treasurer displayed the tax rolls of all the assessed Chinese property in Pierce County at $10,083.

The Tacoma News observed that these newly "free men have done this city a great service, for which its citizens are duly grateful,"[80] and the Tacoma Turnverein threw a ball in their honor. In the next election the anti-Chinese ticket campaigned in defense of the purge and won every open seat. Weisbach did not seek reelection as mayor, but the candidates who supported the Tacoma method polled 72 percent of the vote.[81]

But these legal defeats did not end the Chinese's drive for reparations and indemnity. While the Chinese won neither the *Wing Hing* suit nor the conviction of Mayor Weisbach and the Tacoma Committee of Fifteen, the United States government did pay reparations. In March 1886, President Cleveland, concerned about Christian missionaries and hoping to protect trade with China, sent a message to Congress urging legislation to indemnify the Chinese who suffered from the riots in the "Pacific States and Territories." On October 19, 1888, Congress authorized more than $270,000 in indemnity compensation to the government of China for the Tacoma massacre and other anti-Chinese violence, such as the roundup at Felton, California.[82] A year later, in August 1889, the United States government paid $8,000 to the Chinese consul to indemnify the Chinese who were compelled to leave Redding by the anti-Chinese "League of Forty."[83]

AN EARLY CASE AGAINST POLICE HARASSMENT: SAN JOSE

On April 24, 1891, Quen Hing Tong, a Chinese merchant, sought an injunction against the city of San Jose to stop police harassment in Chinatown.[84] The Chinese accused the town of hiring a small private force posing as police officers, who entered Chinese shops at eight in the morning and stayed until eleven in the evening, threatening residents and customers, and discouraging whites and Chinese alike from working, shopping, and residing peacefully in Chinatown. The Chinese alleged these officers were personally paid by the mayor of San Jose, S. N. Rucker. They also sued Mayor Rucker, the chief of police, and the three "special police officers" for damages.

Back in 1887, fearing that their new community was again in danger, Chinese merchants in San Jose had built a nine-foot picket fence around the entire Chinese quarter and posted notices not to trespass.

Quen Hing Tong asked the federal court of the Ninth Judicial District to ban Darcy, Byrne, and Brown from entering Chinatown and acting as regular police officers under "color of law." Quen, the major tenant of Chinatown, called for the court to enjoin the three fake officers from injuring and intimidating the merchants and rendering his leases worthless.

The Chinese were asking for injunctive relief from police harassment and for monetary relief in the amount of five thousand dollars. With *Quen Hing Tong* v. *City of San Jose et al.,* the Chinese gave clear notice that they would not be forced out.

TO MAKE "JOHN CHINAMAN . . . TRAVEL"

For a brief time in the mid-nineteenth century, San Jose held the promise of becoming a successfully integrated town.[85] The dependent economy of farming, the large size of its Chinese community, and the power of a few white leaders committed to honorable relations with their Chinese neighbors, tenants, and employees might have created a stable interracial community.

The Chinese had arrived in San Jose early in the 1850s, when thousands walked fifty miles from San Francisco through the sunny Santa Clara Valley on their way to the gold fields in the foothills of the Sierra Nevada. When their dreams of gold died, they returned to the warm and fertile valley, many to cultivate new fields of strawberries, raspberries, blackberries, and gooseberries.[86] Chinese farmers and farmworkers soon controlled the berry fields, and Chinese communities grew in the ranching and farming towns of Mayfield (now Palo Alto and Sunnyvale), Mountain View, Gilroy, Campbell, and Cupertino. Unlike in Eureka and Truckee, which were company towns dominated by timber and railroad barons, here were Chinese farmers who reclaimed marshlands, tilled the fertile soil, designed and built irrigation systems, and planted and harvested the berries and the new fruit orchards.

In 1880 one sixth of California's farm-labor force had been Chinese; by 1890, it was three fourths. In San Jose, unlike most other towns in the West, one quarter of the Chinese population was women. To most whites, Chinese women signaled descendants—generations of Chinese children who might be naturalized.

The diaries of the farmer William A. Z. Edwards reveal both the interracial dependency of rural work and the long exploitation of Chinese farm laborers in the valleys near San Jose. During the 1860s, Edwards moved to the Santa Clara Valley from the gold fields, where he had been a leader in the vigilante movement. At first he grew hay, barley, and wheat. But when he started planting fruit trees and berries, he needed more hands—skilled hands—and turned to the Chinese. Edwards paid the lowest going wage, one dollar per day, to clear fields, grade roads, and dig irrigation ditches.

Excerpts from his diary of 1872 and 1879 describe his relations and reliance on Chinese workers:

> June 6 [1872]. Paid a Chinese $1.50 for 1 and ½ days work hoeing strawberries.
>
> July 24. Adam, Ah Jim and I with the team hauled and stacked loads of barley from the east field.
>
> December 16. I commenced building a house for my Chinese strawberry planters and got the foundation and floor laid.
>
> December 17. Check Kee and Jim helped me to work in the shanty. We got the sides up.
>
> December 23. Check Kee and I built a kitchen at the west end of the shanty. Let Ah Coy 10 acres in my east field for five years. He to plant the same with strawberries and vegetables. I to see the same and divide equally with him after all expenses are paid. I to furnish the house and tools and water and chests and sacks. Ah Coy and I signed our agreement to the above effect and W. S. Braughton witnessed it.
>
> January 17 [1879]. A.M. I plowed ditches for Ah Ji. P.M. I took strawberry plants to the Brokaw Place and plowed roads and ditches. Ah Jim commenced planting strawberries.[87]

Whereas the mines and mills operated according to strict racial hierarchies, on farms whites like Edwards and Chinese like Ah Coy had close working relationships that complicated and shaped the anti-Chinese violence that was emerging in the valley. Over the next two brutal decades, the Chinese found support from white interests—in some cases simply white self-interest, in other cases close and long friendships.

Yet often white farmers were willing to betray their financial interests in exchange for the safe commonality of whiteness. An 1869 pamphlet from the Santa Clara Democratic County Committee asked, "Shall white men rule over this country or shall we be ruled and tyrannized over by Blacks and Chinamen?"[88] As early as 1869 the *San Jose Daily Mercury* declared, "The Chinese as a class have very little more natural fitness for American citizenship than the wild bushmen of South Africa. . . . They are human beings and should be protected, . . . but we do not want *such* citizens, nor do they want to become citizens."

Like many northern counties, San Jose passed mining codes, taxes, and cubic air and laundry ordinances that targeted Chinese immigrants. Chinese supporters were called traitors. In February 1869, 166 Chinese people attended the opening of the First Methodist Episcopal Missionary Sunday School. After Reverend Thomas S. Dunn took the occasion to protest the county's racist ordinances, the church was burned to the ground and the minister received a letter decorated with a skull and crossbones, warning him to leave town or die. Dunn read the letter to his congregation and quickly raised twenty-five thousand dollars to rebuild the church.

One year later, the first of many fires raged through Chinatown, quickly burning the wood-frame homes and stores. Destitute and homeless, more than five hundred Chinese refugees lived for a time in shacks and camps near the Guadalupe River.

By 1872 Chinatown had been reborn. When Ng Fook, a merchant from San Francisco, built the houses in fireproof brick, white citizens immediately passed a resolution excluding this area from San Jose's fire protection.[89] Yet Chinatown thrived again—with barbers, herbalists, astrologers, butchers, bakers, musicians, and several professional writers who transcribed letters to be sent to families and villages in China. Other residents worked outside Chinatown as cigar makers, woodchoppers, and domestic servants. The community grew—there were a dozen grocery stores, a fish market, a temple, and a large traditional opera house. Chinese women worked as milliners, seamstresses, prostitutes, and housewives. Soon Chinatown included several children.[90]

In 1878 and 1879, Denis Kearney visited San Jose, his "sandlot orations" inciting crowds against the Chinese. In June 1878, the local branch of the Workingmen's Party vowed to use the ballot to make "John Chinaman . . . travel."[91]

As anti-Chinese sentiment rose around California's Second Constitutional Convention in 1879, growers sensed that they were trapped. Small farmers in the valley were failing as large growers developed the vast land claims seized from tribal people and from Californios. Yet despite the racial violence throughout the state, the shipping companies and brokers in China continued to send Chinese workers to farming areas. Almost 8 percent of Santa Clara County's population of thirty-five thousand was Chinese.

The new California constitution had passed, and in 1880 the state legislature quickly made it a misdemeanor for a corporation to hire a Chinese person. Ranchers, growers, and cannery owners in the Santa Clara Valley began mass firings. When the president of the local Sulphur Bank and Quicksilver Mining Company forced the state to overturn the ban as a clear violation of the Burlingame Treaty and the Fourteenth Amendment, some in the county turned toward federal immigration law. The ethnic makeup of San Jose could be written in Washington, D.C.

But distrusting federal intentions, San Jose chose fire as its weapon of choice. By the mid-1880s San Jose saw six consecutive Chinatowns, all built on prime lots in the center of town, burned out by arsonists. Yet the Chinese always rebuilt. During these years San Jose also passed ordinances that limited Chinese laundries, prohibited fireworks, outlawed Chinese prostitution, and banned carrying baskets on shoulder poles.[92] Yet the town tolerated vigilante acts against the Chinese. In 1879, when two apparently drunk men shot at and assaulted a Chinese man, they accepted an easy bargain: both pled guilty to battery and were fined ten dollars.[93]

Remarkably, neither the ordinances, nor the fires, nor the Exclusion Act of 1882 could diminish the Chinese presence. By 1890 an all-time high of 2,723 Chinese people lived in the county—likely an underestimate, as the census was taken in the spring and the Chinese population would have been highest during fall harvest.

In 1885 an Anti-Coolie League surfaced in San Jose. Summer programs that hired white students to plant, fertilize, prune, and harvest the fertile land had failed to drive out the skilled Chinese farmers, but the stoning of Chinese children forced the Chinese to stick more closely to Chinatown. In January, San Jose voted to close all the Chinese laundries, and the Anti-Coolie League planned to start a co-operative laundry, with three hundred subscribers donating five dollars each.

After demagogue Charles O'Donnell arrived on an anti-Chinese tour, twelve large fires burned in Chinatown.[94] But when these fires also failed to rid the city of the Chinese, white residents looked to legal means.[95] When San Jose developed plans to build a new city hall just across the street from Chinatown, white merchants complained about the "blight" of Chinatown. Congregants of nearby Saint Joseph's Church objected to the "sins and smells" of Chinatown. By the end of the year, the city passed new anti-laundry laws.[96]

The Chinese struck back. On January 7, 1886, as the news of Truckee's purges reached San Jose, the city arrested nineteen Chinese men for operating laundries in wooden buildings. Immediately, Chinese laundrymen refused to return the shirts, trousers, underwear, and bedding of hundreds of white customers. Across the trades, the Chinese began a "slowdown," but it was their refusal to finish and return the laundry that stunned the Anti-Coolie League. Local papers bannered SAN JOSE IS CAUGHT WITHOUT A CHANGE OF LINEN as the Chinese washhouses remained closed. Within days, white residents petitioned the council and chief of police to exempt the Chinese washhouses from the laundry codes, but the anti-Chinese faction held firm and announced a citywide boycott of all council members who signed the petition.[97] One week later, after nineteen more Chinese washermen were arrested, the Chinese closed all the laundries in San Jose.[98]

By this time San Jose's Chinese could no longer purchase property and were forced to lease buildings or hold "ground leases" on land that they would pay to improve. Some Chinese merchants turned to white "front men," who, for a bribe, would purchase the property and hand it over. As a result some of the buildings in Chinatown were owned by its merchants and residents. As the city council moved to force the Chinese to vacate the downtown site, key to the city's redevelopment plan, the Chinese announced that San Jose would pay dearly for any property seized in a forced expulsion.

The first statewide anti-Chinese convention was to meet in San Jose in February 1886, and the Anti-Coolie League invited all the state and county anti-Chinese clubs.[99] The convention opened on February 4 and quickly elected Charles F. McGlashan, "the Hero from Truckee," as its permanent chairman. McGlashan called for a new organization, the California Non-Partisan Anti-Chinese Association, which would use the boycott to carry the anti-Chinese movement legally through the violent spring of 1886. The convention quickly adopted Kearney's slogan: "The Chinese must go."

With the boycott under way in Truckee, the convention endorsed McGlashan's plan to purge all Chinese people from the state. He demanded a signed pledge from "every man, woman and child" not to patronize or "deal with" any Chinese person, and had fifty thousand copies of the pledge printed. It also appeared in newspapers across the state. The convention agreed that local committees would publish the names of any Californian who refused to sign the pledge:

> The Chinese must go. We the undersigned, hereby declare that we are in favor of the adoption of all lawful means for the exclusion of the Chinese from the Pacific Coast; and we hereby pledge that we will not employ Chinamen, directly or indirectly, nor purchase the products of Chinese labor.[100]

The next month the San Jose delegates reassembled in Sacramento and soon merged with the larger Sacramento convention, whose members were appointed by the boards of supervisors from nearly every county in California. The extremists were in control.

With the news of the *Wing Hing* suit spreading through the papers, the convention boasted that it had mapped out a strategy to protect towns from the legal reprisals of the Eureka method. The county delegates tried to pick a date "after which the people are not to be held responsible for the safety of those who employ or patronize Chinese," and the delegates from the San Jose convention wanted "to oppose any and all temperate methods, and to insist on foolish radicalism that threatens to do much injury to industrial interests in California."[101] The convention ended with the announcements: the town of Arroyo Grande had given the Chinese twenty days to leave and in Redding at one o'clock in the morning all downtown buildings occupied by Chinese had been destroyed by fire, the work of an unknown "incendiary."

The anti-Chinese movement was stunned when the Chinese won a major legal victory in the laundry cases. In 1886, U.S. Circuit Court Judges Lorenzo Sawyer and Stephen Field and District Judge George Sabin voided San Francisco's ordinance requiring special permits for laundries in wood buildings; the ordinance, they wrote, would have forced the washmen to close down or "drive them outside the city and county of San Francisco to the adjoining counties, either of which result would be little short of absolute confiscation of a large amount of property . . . for a long time invested in these occupations." The laundry ordinance deprived the Chinese of their property "without due process of law . . . in contravention" of the Fourteenth Amendment and the Burlingame Treaty.

The federal court not only reversed a California State Supreme Court decision but added that only the U.S. Supreme Court could overturn the decision that protected the interests of "so large a number of Chinese residents, who have been for many years pursuing their peaceful and useful avocation in the laundry business in San Francisco without any serious injury to the city or its citizens but to the great convenience of many."[102] Anti-Chinese organizations were enraged, and in San Jose, the salesman for the Columbia Soap Works and Johnson's Starch sought to sidestep the ruling by offering white laundresses and launderers soaps, starches, and "blueing oil" at wholesale prices for eighty days in an effort to drive "out the Asiatic laundries."

In February 1887, C. W. Breyfogle, the Republican mayor of San Jose, sent a confidential letter to every physician in San Jose asking that they secretly visit Chinatown to determine whether it was a "menace to health." Seeking "full evidence . . . showing that Chinatown be at once condemned and the nuisance abated," he promised "the best legal talent that may be engaged" so that the "Chinese may be ordered to vacate the premises now occupied by them."[103] Breyfogle also zealously collected evidence about Chinatown's fire hazards and sewage problems from the chief engineer, the street commissioner, the city attorney, and the chief of police, and he concluded that the earth "beneath Chinatown is filth laden in its every ore."[104]

To erase the traditional boundaries of Chinatown, the mayor searched old maps and land titles. On March 25, 1887, Breyfogle and the common council declared all of Chinatown a public nuisance. And, seeking to condemn Chinatown, expel the fifteen hundred to two thousand Chinese, and sell bonds to buy back the land for the city, the mayor and the common council voted to remove Chinatown from San Jose. The city then filed suit in Superior Court against several white landholders who leased to the Chinese.[105] Meanwhile, the boot and shoe dealers in San Jose agreed that after April 1 they would no longer purchase goods made by Chinese labor. The anti-Chinese boycott even targeted the café in the Women's Christian Temperance Union building.

Still San Jose's Chinatown grew; it was the economic and social center for three thousand Chinese farmworkers, for domestic servants who lived in their employers' houses, and for local Chinese merchants and laborers.

"HEAT AND DESTRUCTION"

In 1883 Chinatown had organized its own volunteer fire department, equipped with ladders and buckets, and rehearsed its fire brigades. But at three o'clock on the afternoon of March 4, 1887, most of the Chinese had gone to a gambling house to hear the announcement of the lottery winner. No one was there to witness the arson in Ah Toy Alley, which had been set ablaze a few minutes earlier. Chinatown thought it had prepared for danger.

Most of Chinatown was destroyed, although, as the *San Jose Evening News* reported, with "superhuman efforts" the city's Alert Hose Fire Company "saved *the ground on which* Chinatown was located and prevented the spread of the fire to the surrounding buildings" [italics added]. The Chinese buildings burned, it said, because the firemen found "poor hose" and "low water pressure." Even aided by the mayor and some city councilmen, the Chinese fire brigade was unable to check the flames because someone had drained the Chinese water tank. It was not by chance that during the two weeks preceding the blaze prominent white property owners in Chinatown had added heavily to their fire insurance.[106]

The night of the fire, some of the Chinese found shelter with friends, others slept on the floors and tables of a large laundry building, and still others slept outside in its drying yard, as the newspaper put it, "enjoying the cool air after the day of heat and destruction." By the morning of March 5, all that remained of Chinatown was one brick building, a theater, where many Chinese workers had recently watched the opera *The Romance of Three Kingdoms.*

Two months later, the *San Jose Daily Herald* declared, "Chinatown is dead. It is dead forever."[107]

The city council tried to prevent the resurrection of Chinatown in the center of town. It announced that the scorched property that abutted the new city hall would be "more valuable for other purposes," and it hoped that the new police headquarters would frighten off the Chinese. The city began to investigate the land deeds and titles in an effort to establish a claim to all the land that was occupied by Chinatown. In the ashes it found the ruins of the Mexican city center.

SAN-DOY-SAY TONG HUNG FOW

In June, two quite different Chinatowns began to rebuild. Chinese laborers gravitated toward the outskirts of town along the Guadalupe River. Mitchell Phillips, owner of the nearby San Jose Woolen Mills, built "Woolen Mills Chinatown" to keep his Chinese laborers nearby. He leased the property to a broker, Chin Shin, who in turn rented houses and beds to Chinese mill, cannery, and glove-factory workers. Chin Shin also built the Garden City Cannery there and employed hundreds of Chinese himself.

But the Chinese merchants built their Chinatown across the street from city hall. They had defeated an injunction, raised by the Home Protection Association, against their landlord John Heinlen, a sympathetic German refugee and wealthy rancher who had purchased the land in 1867. Nonetheless, the city contained its size by forbidding the use of any traditional Pueblo lands "for the benefit of any Chinese or Mongolians."[108] Only two weeks after the fire, merchant Quen Hing Tong signed a master lease for fifteen hundred dollars per month. Fearful of another fire, Heinlen and the Chinese merchants worked with popular architect Theodore Lenzen, who had designed many of the town's prominent mansions and the new city hall, to plan a protected enclave, surrounded by a high picket fence covered with barbed wire.[109] All of the buildings were to be made of brick and face inward. The merchants would post signs, in English, at each entrance reading NO ADMITTANCE and PRIVATE GROUNDS, and the maze of small, unpaved, but gated streets were to be locked each night.[110]

The city was well aware of the Chinese's defiant stance. During construction the *San Jose Daily Mercury* commented, "The place hasn't been roofed in yet, but there's no telling what may happen if the high fence and barbed wire fail to keep out objectionable visitors."[111] At the cost of sixty

Market Street Chinatown in San Jose before the fire, 1887

White citizens observe the burning of Chinatown

thousand dollars, San-Doy-Say Tong Hung Fow—"San Jose's Chinatown"—sprang up. Both white and Chinese residents called it Heinlentown or Heinlenville. Schools, restaurants, and shops opened, and a new temple, Ng Shing Gung, was decorated with silk hangings and equipped with incense burners and the finest bells outside of Canton. San-Doy-Say Tong Hung Fow again became a spiritual and cultural center for the Chinese throughout the Santa Clara Valley. Historian Connie Young Yu, whose grandparents lived there, recalls that the walls gave Chinese families a great deal of safety: "Children could play in the streets. No ruffians on horseback were liable to ride down the main street and drag Chinese by queues as they once had in the past."[112]

The only way in or out was through barred gates that were closed by a white watchman every night. As soon as fences and signs were torn down by white citizens, they would be "rebuilt and replaced as before," and yet another sign, NO THOROUGHFARE, would be nailed to the posts. Under trespass common law, the Chinese, as legal tenants, could control who came into Chinatown.

Yet the gates and barriers did not stop whites from entering Chinatown with the intent of driving out its residents. During the tense summer of 1891, local papers stirred up stories of gang warfare between the two Chinatowns. The police launched a series of raids and made mass arrests in Heinlenville for holding lottery and fan-tan games.[113] Although there were no witnesses, the Chinese defendants were sentenced to two weeks in jail and fined fifteen dollars each, solely for being present when fan-tan games were played.

Rumors—for example, that Chinese butchers were selling pork affected with hog cholera—damaged Chinese businesses. Outside Chinatown, Chinese pedestrians were jumped and beaten on the streets, and a Chinese farmworker, Sing Lee, was slashed across the face while he was picking fruit. Ah Ling, a longtime ranch hand, was murdered walking into town. But no arrests were made. One landlord raised a Chinese man's rent for one room from $6.50 per month to $250.[114] On a summer night in July, white police officers encouraged Chinese residents to set off fireworks and then immediately arrested them for violating a new city ordinance.[115]

But of particular concern was the mysterious appearance of a small special police force. Heinlen and the Chinese merchants monitored the ubiquitous officers and noted their every movement. Chinese sentries were posted night and day across Chinatown, and on the slightest suspicion of anything "unfavorable," they notified one another with secret signals.

QUEN HING TONG V. CITY OF SAN JOSE

In the early fall of 1891, disgusted that the "police" showed no signs of letting up, the Chinese sued San Jose. In *Quen Hing Tong* v. *City of San Jose,* Quen accused the city, the chief of police, Richard Stewart, and the three "special police officers," James Darcey, Joseph Byrne, and W. H. Brown, of "conspiring together" and "intending to injure" him, to make all his Chinese tenants "uncomfortable" and their property worthless. Without warrant or right, the three "officers" daily entered Chinatown, "terrorizing the tenants and driving away the customers" and "intimidating and overawing customers" by threats and by the constant exhibition of their "stars, or badges of office."

These three special officers, claimed Quen, were also violating city codes that required all patrol officers to wear uniforms.[116] Quen submitted affidavits from ten Chinese men who stated that because of the presence of Darcey, Byrne, and Brown, they were two months behind in the rents and owed two thousand dollars.

With this suit, Quen declared that the loss was greater than a few thousand dollars: Chinatown itself was at risk. Because the mayor had hired this irregular police force, Chinese people were being driven out of San Jose. The injunction would protect the Chinese from huge and incalculable losses—of displaced families and business, of battery and assault, and of forced relocation.

The Chinese were trying to avoid the fate of their brethren from Eureka. They understood the goal of the police intrusion into Chinatown, and they took preemptive legal action to prevent being driven out. They could have demanded large sums of money, but that might have acknowledged the inevitability of expulsion. By seeking injunctive relief, they signified that they wanted to stay. Implicitly, they also spoke for many who had been forced or burned out.

San Jose was taken by surprise and maneuvered to dismiss the case. It even had a Chinese man pose as Quen Hing Tong and move to withdraw the lawsuit. But by February 1892 the case was set for trial.[117]

Who were these officers? Who hired them? What was the effect of their constant surveillance? Why were they sent to Chinatown?

Quen argued that the three men had been sent to intimidate Chinatown and ruin the merchants. They had been illegally appointed by the mayor, who arranged that their salaries be secretly paid by the white owner of Woolen Mills Chinatown. Despite repeated requests from the Chinese, none of the thirteen regular members of the police force had been willing to stop or deter the "special officers." Now Quen's only recourse was to turn to the court.

To justify his claims and receive a permanent injunction, Quen would have to prove irreparable harm. He had signed a seventeen-year lease with Heinlen for $863 per month, $10,359 per year, or $176,113 for the life of the lease. Quen's risk was hundreds of thousands of dollars.

Aware that Chinese witnesses would be challenged, Quen provided a series of depositions from white men who described the police harassment. John Heinlen, the landlord, George Heinlen, his attorney and agent, and W. T. Wheeler, agent for the merchants, swore under oath that they witnessed the three defendants pose as police officers, sit in the doorways of the Chinese shops, and prevent customers and friends from entering. The phony officers claimed "at all times the right so to trespass" and ignored the watchman's orders to leave. Instead, they prevented customers from "passing in and out . . . for hours at a time." Ultimately they "overawed, intimidated, and frightened" the Chinese merchants until through "fear of disturbance and arrest" they gave up their businesses.

The "officers" also encouraged Chinese gang members or "highbinders" to destroy stores, laundries, and restaurants. The violence had reached the point where the tenants had moved away. John Heinlen swore that the three men were paid by the managers of one of the other Chinatowns. He provided a blueprint that made it clear that the only way in or out of Chinatown was through five pairs of bars that he personally had constructed. Darcey was heard to declare that the three officers "intended to and will drive all the Chinamen out of . . . Heinlen's Chinatown" and that "money was no object."

Thus, the Chinese claimed that *tortious interference* terrorized their customers and placed their tenants and themselves in fear of immanent harmful contact with the officers who "wrongfully and unlawfully" claimed police privilege.

No other remedy at law would work. If a merchant tried to eject a special officer, Quen swore, he "would have the whole Police force of the City to contend with, and it would only end with a riot and breach of the peace." In *Quen Hing Tong v. City of San Jose,* the Chinese creatively fashioned a remedy to thwart the police harassment that would drive them out of town.

SAN JOSE'S DEFENSE

San Jose attacked every piece of Quen's case. The chief of police, Richard Stewart, swore that it was he who had "assigned" the three defendants to maintain the peace and enforce the law in Heinlen's Chinatown. He did acknowledge that the Chinese had "partially" closed off the streets, but as chief of police he would often have the gates removed for public travel. Stewart claimed that in fact the Chinese built the gates to prevent the police from raiding gambling games. The police chief never claimed that the three men were real members of the police force. And he never said who paid them. In order to defend entering Chinese property, the city and the police continued to stress the public nature of Chinatown and the illegality of its gambling and fan-tan games.

Finally, Darcey, Browne, and Byrne swore under oath that they were indeed police officers "of" the city of San Jose assigned to patrol Chinatown, and that they "acted" as "police officers." They noted that even if they were "special policemen," the city charter allowed the mayor and the common council to appoint such officers. They all denied a conspiracy with the intent to injure Quen Hing Tong or his business. Finally, they all denied terrorizing the tenants of Chinatown.

THE VERDICTS

Initially, the Chinese were victorious. On August 18, 1891, Judge James H. Beatty of the Ninth Circuit granted Quen's request for preliminary injunctions against the city of San Jose, Police Chief Richard Stewart, and

James Darcey, Joseph Byrne, and W. H. Brown. He banned the three men from entering the Chinese premises except with a warrant, to make an arrest for a crime committed in their presence or for committing a felony. The judge, however, denied all claims for damages. In January 1892 the city moved to set aside the judge's decree, stating that there was no longer any action pending between the parties, implying that they had settled and that the city had backed off. One year later, in February 1893, the case was dismissed for lack of prosecution. Chinatown remained.

Quen Hing Tong v. *City of San Jose* reveals that the Chinese had put down roots in the community of San Jose, developed trustful commercial and personal relations with many white citizens, and sought and accepted the terms of private property. It exposes the difference between what the Chinese thought they were losing and what white officials thought they were losing. Considering the value of the leases, the vacant properties, the loss of business, and the impact of trespass and harassment, the Chinese decision to seek an injunction rather than full monetary compensation for their damages also reflects the difficulty in calculating the costs of being driven out. At its core, *Quen* v. *San Jose* was about the right of the Chinese to live in peace, where they chose, and remain in the community they had built and rebuilt.

Like *Wing Hing* v. *City of Eureka, Quen Hing Tong* v. *City of San Jose* turned to an expansive view of the law to repair racial injustice. It presumed that the law could be color-blind and that the courts should protect and restore the civic rights of the Chinese. The lawsuit hinged on the idea that the court would recognize the brutal facts of anti-Chinese terrorism and believe that after six fires, the Chinese needed to protect themselves with gates, barriers, and fireproof brick buildings.

The years following the *Quen* case were hard ones for the Chinese of San Jose. Throughout the 1890s, San Jose employers reduced or eliminated their Chinese labor force. "Made by WHITE MEN" became a routine advertising slogan for companies in the valley and reflected dwindling jobs for Chinese men.[118]

By 1901 Woolen Mills Chinatown was vanishing. The cannery closed and many Woolen Mills residents had moved to Heinlen's Chinatown. The working-class Chinese community was scattered.[119] Some of the early white employers had passed away, and Chin Shin returned to China. On February 19, 1902, the Santa Clara County Federated Trades Council adopted resolutions that limited employment of Chinese in the manufacturing trades, and many Chinese residents of Woolen Mills turned to farm labor.[120]

Throughout the last decades of the nineteenth century, lower wool prices, the fencing of farmland, and the growth of mills elsewhere in the West decreased the number of sheep in the Santa Clara Valley from fifty thousand to three thousand. After just twelve years, only one of the four commercial blocks of Woolen Mills Chinatown remained. Half the residences were gone. In 1902 Woolen Mills Chinatown burned to the ground, just as the final anti-Chinese immigration law passed Congress and a new anti-Asian movement swept across California.

But San-Doy-Say Tong Hung Fow endured. Many merchants continued to provide services and goods for the Chinese community and the hundreds of Chinese farmworkers and ranchers in the valley. Chinese women and children made a lasting Chinese population possible. By 1900, 10 percent or 33 of Chinatown's 337 full-time residents were female and there were fourteen children under the age of fifteen. The Chinese school on the first floor of the temple grew. Ng Shing Gung, the Taoist temple or *miu,* remained the active center of lunar festivals and religious life.

In the 1906 earthquake that devastated San Francisco's Chinatown, Heinlenville suffered serious damage. The *San Jose Mercury* declared, "Now the time is believed to be ripe to wipe it out for once and for all."[121] But if the Chinese of Heinlenville could withstand eight fires in ten years, they, like the Chinese of San Francisco, could survive the earthquake.[122] Many refugees fled to families in Oakland and Marin County while Chinese merchants remodeled and expanded and the *miu* provided housing as people returned. It was clear that Heinlenville would not be destroyed. By 1912 the barred gates were opened, never to be closed again.[123]

THE CHINESE REWRITE THE LETTER OF THE LAW

Facing laws that were designed to expel them, the Chinese often turned to civil disobedience. When hundreds were arrested in San Francisco for violating the Cubic Air Ordinance, they refused to pay the fines and, instead, crowded the jails, exposing the hypocrisy of the code and frustrating its goal of raising money for the city. To circumvent laws that required an identifying mark on all cigars rolled by Chinese—the origin of the cigar band and the union label—the Chinese adopted Caucasian brand names, such as the Empire or Cosmopolitan Manufacturing Company. In Wheatland, Chinese peddlers sold their vegetables at one fourth the going price in order to drive out the white farmers who were trying to purge them.

The Chinese immigrants turned to American courts to fight roundups, assert their rights to nationhood and community, and demand reparations for being driven out of town. They brought criminal actions against elected officials—mayors, police chiefs, members of boards of supervisors. They forged unprecedented lawsuits for police harassment and intimidation. They created early forms of class actions. They demanded public education for their children. They fought the queue, the shoulder-pole, the laundry, and the cubic-air ordinances. Throughout the 1880s and 1890s, the Chinese in the West used the American judicial system as a site of contact and conflict with white Americans, seeking to establish their rights by putting them within established legal systems of contractual, property, tort, and civil rights. These cases challenge enduring stereotypes of the docile Chinese immigrant.

Still, there were many locks on the doors of the American judicial system. A major obstacle to justice arose from *People* v. *Hall* (1854), in which the Supreme Court of California banned Chinese from testifying against whites. The dangerous myth of the "wily" or "sneaky" Chinese forged another barrier to Chinese testimony. A few towns allowed the Chinese to use oaths from their own legal tradition, such as swearing upon the blood of a freshly decapitated rooster or burning holy papers. But these alternatives had their own problems: in an 1860 murder trial in Tuolumne County, the record notes, "The fact was, the supply of cocks, necessary for the mysteries of the Chinese religion, had become exhausted, and as Charley (the interpreter) stated the oath was binding either way, the Court concluded to waste no further time in the decapitation of roosters."[124]

The legal cases brought by Chinese litigants went well beyond seeking money or even equity. They revealed fundamental beliefs about belonging and citizenship, about identity and identification.

Their demands for reparations establish that the overseas Chinese were what Franklin Ng calls "agents of cultural diffusion"—global people who lived both within and between their first homeland and the United States and made profound impacts on both countries. The Chinese were both tied to their native land and actively involved in integrating into the American West. For them, American law was an image and a symbol for becoming American. The Chinese were not allowed the status of "citizen," and perforce not allowed to turn to the electoral process, but they could go to court—and by appealing to a higher will, they used the legal system to redirect history and to overcome the implied consent of racial violence. Yet the Chinese were always well aware that the law was not above the play of politics, nor was race irrelevant.[125]

Unlike contemporary Japanese, Jews, and African Americans, when the Chinese refugees from Eureka sued for monetary compensation, they were not making demands as descendants of people under assault. They were not seeking to redress the violations or moral debts of their ancestors. Rather, they were claiming justice for themselves. Their cases reflect their belief in the promises of American righteousness. Demands for reparations, as Mari Matsuda reminds us, come from those who have seen and felt the betrayal of the law's promise of neutrality, objectivity, and fairness.[126] By filing these lawsuits, the Chinese were responding to a vision of fairness and neutrality in American law, but they also were responding to their informed awareness as immigrants and members of a racial minority.

The Chinese had the letter of the law on their side but not the system. They knew well how the law worked, they took full advantage of its provisions, and they sought to extend its reach. Using a series of legal options to demand redress, *Wing Hing* v. *City of Eureka, Quen Hing Tong* v. *City of San Jose,* and *United States* v. *Weisbach et al.* went to the core of the violence perpetrated upon the Chinese community. By appropriating key legal terms such as "mob" and "riot," the Chinese identified new legal possibilities for political change. They put their faith, hope, time, and money into a system that could, at times, transcend its own politics through its own language.

By suing for damages as well as for the loss of property, by launching unique police-harassment cases, by bringing criminal actions against a mayor, the Chinese further embedded themselves in the political system of the United States. These legal actions return us to the complex metaphor of "belonging" forged, at once, by racism and by resistance to racism.[127]

The actions of the Chinese in San Jose, Tacoma, Eureka, and Rock Springs also demonstrate legal originality. Across the West Coast, Chinese merchants and laborers initiated thousands of suits to defend and define their rights. And they were often victorious. In San Francisco, the Chinese challenged the city's attempts to impose residential segregation on the basis of race, the first effort of its kind in American history, but in *In re Lee Sing et al.,* Judge Sawyer declared that any ordinance that imposed "race ghettoization" would be a violation of the law.[128]

In the fall of 1885, after masked men in Coal Creek, Washington Territory, kidnapped and choked a Chinese miner to death and burned out the homes of thirty-seven others, the Chinese demanded restitution of more than thirty-nine hundred dollars.

All in all, the Chinese filed more than seven thousand suits in the first decade following the Chinese Exclusion Act, and they won the vast majority of them. Most, however, were immigration appeals. But the Supreme Court surrendered authority when it let Congress hand over immigration decisions to the Bureau of Immigration. In a series of devastating opinions—*Chae Chan Ping* v. *United States* (1889), *Nishimura Ekiu* v. *United States* (1892), *Fong Yue Ting* v. *United States* (1893), *Sing Tuck* v. *United States* (1904), and *Ju Toy* v. *United States* (1905)—the Supreme Court removed the power of federal courts and expanded the power of immigration officials to make final judgments about an immigrant's status—a precedent and procedure hauntingly familiar.[129]

The Chinese brought these suits as part of a strategy of forcing a nation to obey its own laws. Despite the violence and the limits on access to the courts, they acted as if legal judgments could be impartial. The very act of bringing the suits presumed that power could be controlled by the rule of law—that is, that the courts had some autonomy from the racist practices of the time, that the law was a place where the Chinese could hold vigilantes, racist organizations, and even elected government officials accountable. In the law's broadest sense, the Chinese were using it to put forth a model of equality, a vision of how they might coexist in community with whites.

Yet the Chinese ran into local, state, and national legal systems designed to protect white interests—from municipal ordinances that imposed specific taxes on the Chinese, to statewide proscriptions against property ownership, to the Supreme Court's demolition of the civil rights legislation of the Reconstruction era. Following the Civil War, elaborate legal frameworks were erected at the national level to prevent the entry of "undesirable" Chinese immigrants into the United States. With the triumph of states' rights ideology that marked the demise of Reconstruction, federal courts offered little hope to Chinese and African Americans who sought to stop the lynchings and roundups.

Supreme Court justice Stephen Field spoke for many of his colleagues when he wrote to a friend in 1882, "You know I belong to the class who repudiate the doctrine that this country was made for people of all races. On the contrary, I think it is for our race—the Caucasian race."[130] In the "Slaughter-house Cases" the Supreme Court ruled that all persons born in the United States could become citizens, but that the Fourteenth Amendment protected only former slaves from assaults on civil rights.[131] Clearly the Supreme Court had the Chinese in mind. When it held that the Fourteenth Amendment's "due process" clause was enforceable only in cases of violations by or against states but not private citizens, it left both Chinese and blacks vulnerable to vigilante acts and mob violence.[132]

Yet the Chinese wanted to be treated like other recent immigrant groups and use their rights under the protective language of the Fourteenth Amendment, which sought to include previously excluded classes. The legal actions of the Chinese belied the observation in an 1877 Congressional Special Report on Chinese immigration that Chinese immigrants (whose adult population was close to the total number of all the other adult voters in California) did not want to become citizens and did not want to have the right to vote, learn English, or remain in this country. Like civil rights decisions and awards for reparations that would follow, the heroic vision of these suits lay in the injustices they challenged and the use of the law that disadvantaged them.[133]

Just as the Court was insulating white citizens and white immigrants from Chinese Americans' access to constitutional rights, the Chinese persisted in turning to the federal courts to demand civil rights, expose the racial gap between the law as written and as practiced, and reveal the holes in the tapestry of racial control. The legal goals of early Chinese Americans were not only to redress individual wrongs but also to revise policies that tolerated and encouraged the roundups. Even though they were not allowed to play a part in the election of legislators who wrote the laws, and of judges who would apply them, or to serve on juries, have access to translators, or testify against whites, the Chinese turned to courts.

The thousands of legal actions by the Chinese countered the "foreignness" of anti-Chinese legislation. Although the Chinese belief that the American courts would effectively protect their rights under the Burlingame Treaty and the Fourteenth Amendment was misplaced, the efforts themselves realigned the nation's sense of the Chinese community's power. The fear of Chinese lawsuits, their ability to tie up city and county coffers in extended litigation, was profound.

As the decisions kept on coming, it was clear that the Chinese could not count on the courts to change political and economic institutions, to deliver justice, or to provide redress. These cases reveal that the Chinese, like African Americans and Native Americans, were marked as inferior by the law. At the same time, they reveal Chinese Americans' assumptions of access, of due process, of resistance and refusal. The Chinese appropriated public assumptions about American justice even when the law failed to protect their rights. In demanding reparations and redress, they extended the possibilities of the law and provided a warning that the law would be used to examine power.[134]

The Chinese exploited a set of paradoxes, applying clauses of equal protection, which, by definition, acknowledged racial discrimination and violence. They read the American legal system through its loopholes. Paradoxically, these legal challenges solidified both the white community and the Chinese community. But in going to court to resist the roundups and to challenge the power of mayors, police officers, county councilmen, and judges, the Chinese took the law where it was never intended to go.

To combat the roundups, Chinese litigants pushed the boundaries of the postbellum Civil Rights Acts, yet still used their status as subjects of China to demand redress. At times they presumed a common legal status with African Americans; at times they presumed a common legal status with all "persons." These cases undermine both sides of the contradictory stereotypes of the Chinese—the hardworking, obsequious people who allowed the American public to ignore the violence, and the sneaky, rat-eating, and filthy "coolies." Chinese legal resistance broke through both images.

The Chinese contribution to civil rights litigation is generally ignored outside the field of Asian American legal studies. History is still unaware of most of these cases, such as *Yick Wo* v. *Hopkins,* which broadened the interpretation to the Fourteenth Amendment and extended equal protection under the law "to all persons within the territorial jurisdiction, without regard to any differences of race, of color, or of nationality."[135]

From *Wing Hing* v. *City of Eureka* to the prosecution of the mayor of Tacoma to demands that Congress provide indemnity, these cases speak to Chinese immigrants' presumption of an inevitable transfer of identity from outsider to insider. Once "inside," the Chinese discovered that more frontiers remained, and they used the law to cross these borders as well. Of the many barriers—psychological or geopolitical—that the Chinese immigrants had to cross once inside the Pacific Northwest, clearly a tall one was the legal system, a set of spikes constructed in a legislated wall to contain the white dominance of America. The cases were material and symbolic gestures that fought ongoing violence, violence that is better recorded and better remembered than the resistance against it.

7

A LITANY OF HATE

THE 1880s

The Chinese . . . have come to the conclusion that the present movement is different from preceding ones, and that it will prove to be a permanent one. We thought some years ago that all opposition to Chinese came from the Irish, but we have been convinced from subsequent events that the whole people . . . upon the Pacific Coast are earnest in their desire not only to restrict [us] coming into the country, but to expel those already here.

—Ah Hung, quoted in the *Marysville Daily Appeal,* February 12, 1886

In the late fall of 1874, the *Grass Valley Tidings* in the Sierra foothills announced, "We have no feeling of ill will against the Chinese people among us; we would not abuse them nor willingly see them abused; but we cannot help a feeling that we want no more of them; that we want some method found out, if possible, by which those who are already among us may be removed."[1]

By the mid-1880s, Californians had developed two "methods" to purge the Chinese from the Pacific Northwest. As the statewide anti-Chinese conventions in San Jose and Sacramento approached in March 1886, rural towns and counties juggled between the Eureka method (also known as the Tacoma method) of swift pogroms and the equally effective Truckee method of starving the Chinese out. These twin methods lit a firestorm throughout California and much of the West. Everywhere the Chinese defied the violence, but with few exceptions, both the Eureka and Truckee methods worked.

For the most part, small groups of Chinese gradually but inexorably left town, often to find themselves in another town about to launch a similar rout. Many anti-Chinese committees, stunned that the Chinese would not pay for their own deportation, held dances and fund-raisers to purchase train or boat tickets as armed guards marched the Chinese to train depots or docks. Ultimately both methods turned to night raids and torchlight parades in the Chinese quarters. And when the Chinese refused to leave, the pogroms climaxed in apocalyptic violence and fire.

In 1886 the *San Francisco Post* rightly claimed that the intent of the "present movements" was ethnic cleansing: "We are convinced that the whole people, American and others on the Pacific coast are earnest in their desire, not only to restrict the [Chinese] coming to this country, but to expel these already here."[2] The *Sonora Union Democrat* agreed: "If laws cannot be made that will protect from [the Chinese] presence, the people must exert their innate right and with moral sentiment drive him from our shores and relieve the poor workers from degrading competition."[3] The language of class warfare overlaid the language of racial violence; it was "an outrage," asserted the *Red Bluff Weekly People's Cause,* "that the people have to stand quietly by and see the laws trampled upon by a set of villains who are not first to grace the end of a rope, much less a position in the Custom House. But in giving the devil his due, the Chinamen are not altogether to blame. It is the rich man that opens the way. The rich men make the laws and oppress the poor men, and there is no better way of doing it than a steady supply of Chinese coming in from time to time."[4]

The 1880s were a "critical period," the *Weekly Shasta Courier* observed: "This desire to cause an exodus of the little brown man is unanimous. In northern and in southern California, in the Sierras, in the great valleys and in the Coast Range, from Mt. Shasta to Mt. San Bernardino, the people have risen and calmly demanded that the Mongolian shall not stay."[5] By the end of the 1880s, close to two hundred towns in the Pacific Northwest had driven out their Chinese residents.

Following expulsions, mobs or vigilantes seized Chinese fishing boats, nets, vegetable gardens, laundries, stores, and homes; then they burned rural Chinatowns. Visions of a permanent expulsion of Chinese Americans from the United States set the stage for the national deportation efforts of the 1890s.

In searching for a format to describe these acts, I have turned to the writings of Ida B. Wells, the African American leader of the anti-lynching movement, and Maya Ying Lin, who designed the Vietnam Veterans Memorial in Washington, D.C. Both women forcefully and simply listed and named those wronged.

This chapter is a "litany of hate," a topical and chronological register of acts of ethnic cleansing. It also is a record of Chinese resistance. This litany includes virtually all relevant actions that I have been able to locate. I have found the roundups and boycotts boldly recorded in local and regional newspapers, referenced with shame or delight in diaries, journals, autobiographies, historical accounts, and legal documents, disclosed in photographs, scrapbooks, private letters, diplomatic correspondence, immigration papers, and court cases, and decreed in petitions, placards, and minutes of county boards of supervisors.

It is impossible to represent the totality of the rage and brutality, and no words can fully capture the atrocity. But perhaps in the aggregate, in the naming, in the listing, we can witness how widespread and fluid was the movement to purge the Chinese. Given the early condition of the telegraph, often downed by wind and storms, the lack of trains to carry newspapers, the irregular publication and name changes of rural newspapers, and the time lapses between events and reportage in nineteenth-century journalism, there may be small inconsistencies or inaccuracies.

Hundreds of acts of Chinese resistance were suppressed or ignored by the nineteenth-century media. Chinese defiance becomes visible to us now if we approach these documents as "resistant readers" of journals, maps, court transcripts, shop receipts, songs, poems, and letters. Everyday forms of Chinese resistance—keeping cultural traditions, burial rituals, and food habits—maintained communities that were under assault. These are transcendent but not enumerated here. Perhaps the most profound testament to the resilience of the Chinese in the West is that despite the roundups, despite the job and legal discrimination, and despite the murder and the mayhem, the Chinese remained in the Pacific Northwest. During the

1880s, the population of Chinese men, women, and children in California fell by only three thousand, from seventy-five thousand to seventy-two thousand.

I believe this catalogue is still incomplete. There were purges never formally recorded, roundups I never absolutely established, boycotts lost to history, mass murders effaced from public memory. This violent movement for "white purity" was probably far more widespread than we may ever know.[6]

Marriage of Chinese man and Irish woman.
Harper's Weekly, 1869.

1880–1881

ROUNDUPS AND PURGES

In 1880, **Roseville, Rocklin,** and **Garberville** drive out all Chinese residents.

Trustees in **Nevada City** order the Chinese to leave within sixty days.

In October 1881, a fire consumes **Dutch Flat**'s Chinatown. The Chinese are blamed for leaving a lit stove and for being too frightened to use the fire hoses and hydrants. The *Placer Herald* reports that only the four white landlords sustain losses.[7]

The Chinese section in **Auburn,** a small town in the Sierra foothills, burns to the ground.

MURDER AND MAYHEM

On December 31, rioters march through **Denver,** Colorado's, Chinatown, which is "gutted as completely as though a cyclone had come in one door and passed . . . out the rear." One man dies from "compression of the brain."[8]

JOB DISCRIMINATION AND WORK VIOLENCE

In completing construction of Wrights Tunnel connecting **Santa Cruz** to **Los Gatos** and **San Francisco,** the South Pacific Railroad Line discovers volatile pools of oil on the tunnel floor but insists that work continue. Thirty-one Chinese workers die in the construction. During the tunnel's dedication in 1880, no one mentions their sacrifice.[9]

ANTI-CHINESE DEMONSTRATIONS AND RALLIES

California governor George Perkins declares March 4, 1880, a legal holiday for anti-Chinese demonstrations, rallies, and parades.

In 1881 **Eureka** police make mass arrests of Chinese men for "vices" in Chinatown, such as gambling, prostitution, and opium smoking, although whites, particularly white women enjoying these "vices," are rarely imprisoned for them.

GOVERNMENT ACTIONS AND VERDICTS

California wages a legislative war against the Chinese: the "Anti-Miscegenation" Civil Code of 1880 outlaws interracial sexuality or marriage between a white person with a "negro, mulatto, or Mongolian";[10] the Johnson Bill makes it illegal for corporations to hire Chinese workers and permits towns to remove Chinese beyond city limits; a new law decrees that no "alien" can fish. The legislature orders an excessive tax on the Chinese Six Companies, bans the sale of opium, and prohibits business licenses for anyone not eligible to become "an elector," hence, any Chinese person. In 1881 it aids expulsion and deportation by allowing any Chinese person to sail to China without proof from the Chinese Six Companies that he has cleared his debts to the companies.

In the Ninth District Federal Court, Judge Lorenzo Sawyer rules that it is constitutional to charge the Chinese ten dollars to send the bones of the deceased back to China.

At the local level, **Santa Cruz** adopts an ordinance that "no person shall carry baskets or bags attached to poles carried upon back or shoulders on public sidewalks," forcing Chinese vendors to walk in the streets. The Chinese appeal, and this ordinance is later ruled unconstitutional.[11] Prescott, Arizona, orders fines of up to one hundred dollars for being in the presence of a person inhaling fumes of opium—potentially, for just being in Chinatown.[12]

CHINESE RESISTANCE AND ENDURANCE

Ch'en Lan-pin, Chinese minister to the United States, orders Fred Bee, Chinese consul of San Francisco, to investigate the anti-Chinese riot and the murder of a Chinese man in **Denver.** Bee assesses damage at $53,655. Ch'en seeks restitution and protection from the U.S. government, but no Chinese from Denver are paid for their losses. Twenty-four rioters are arrested and released. Four men are tried and acquitted for the murder.

The Chinese Carpenters Mutual Protective Association is formed in San Francisco with branches in Nevada. It establishes a minimum wage at two dollars per day, assists its members when they are ill, and helps them return to China when they can no longer work.[13]

Vigilantes in **Lewiston** are unable to force an expulsion because the Chinese own property.

In response to the anti-Chinese violence, in 1881 the government of China recalls Chinese exchange students from the United States. Yet one Chinese man remains and enrolls in the freshman class at Harvard University. The U.S. Census reveals that more than twenty thousand Chinese reside in San Francisco and almost fifty thousand live in California, suggesting that even in the face of discrimination and violence, many Chinese Americans are determined to stay in the United States.

In a suit brought by the Chinese, the California Supreme Court overturns many of the legislature's discriminatory bills, such as laws banning Chinese fishing or business licenses for individuals not eligible for naturalization. Judge Alfred Rix voids San Francisco's regulation banning laundries in wooden buildings.

Chinese merchant's wife

In *In re Tiburcio Parrott,* initiated by the Chinese, Judges Hoffman and Sawyer of the Ninth District Court rule that the Johnson Act, which forbids states and corporations from hiring Chinese workers, unconstitutional.

1882–1883

ROUNDUPS AND PURGES

Colusa forms an anti-Chinese organization in 1882 to purge the Chinese from the town.

In **Stockton,** in May 1883, the woolen mill fires longtime Chinese employees and replaces them with young white girls.

MURDER AND MAYHEM

In November 1882, arsonists burn **Diamondville**'s Chinatown, and in April 1883, **Dutch Flat**'s segregated Chinatown is torched just before midnight on a Saturday night. The *Placer Herald* notes that "the loss to the Chinamen was not so heavy as to the several white men who owned most of the buildings."[14] In early 1883, rioters storm through **Eureka**'s Chinatown.[15]

Reports of Chinese gang violence in **Eureka**'s Chinatown throughout 1883 are used to spread fear among local whites and encourage the town's plan to drive out Chinese merchants and loggers.

JOB DISCRIMINATION AND WORK VIOLENCE

In **Somersville,** after a celebration of the Chinese Exclusion Act of 1882, white miners strike until all Chinese miners are fired.

In **San Francisco** during the summer of 1882, the League of Deliverance declares a boycott against all stores that hire Chinese or sell Chinese goods. Men wear linen coats or "dusters" painted with the name of the business and the slogan "An enemy to white labor" and ominously parade in front of the targeted stores.

Just after Christmas 1882, Chinese prostitutes are smuggled into the United States via **Vancouver,** Canada, and are sold in the West disguised as Native Americans.

ANTI-CHINESE RALLIES AND DEMONSTRATIONS

In perhaps the largest rally of its kind on the West Coast, more than five thousand whites gather in **San Francisco** in March 1882, demanding "relief on the Chinese plague." **Colusa** starts an anti-Chinese club.

GOVERNMENT ACTIONS AND JUDICIAL VERDICTS

The Chinese make up more than 19 percent of the convicts at **San Quentin,** one of California's two state prisons.

Congress passes the Chinese Exclusion Act in May 1882, halting Chinese immigration to the United States for ten years; President Rutherford B. Hayes declares that the Chinese already in the United States may remain. The United States Supreme Court rules that Chinese from Hong Kong who are British subjects are still covered by the Exclusion Act because of their race, language, and color. The Chinese Exclusion Act is not overturned until December 17, 1943.

CHINESE RESISTANCE AND SUPPORT

The Chinese in **Amador County** form an armed militia of more than fifty members to protect their local community.[16]

In the early summer of 1883, Chinese workers declare a general strike in **Shasta County.**

Chinese miners remain at their jobs in **Dutch Flat,** despite threats, arson, and an influx of unemployed white "tramps."

In **Cincinnati,** Ohio, Lane Seminary, known for its abolitionist tradition, admits Chinese students.

In *Fook Ling* v. *C. S. Preble,* the Supreme Court of Nevada decides that the

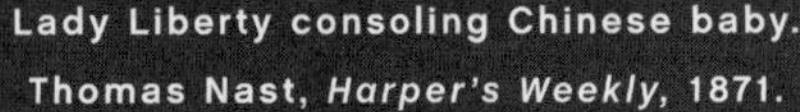

Lady Liberty consoling Chinese baby.
Thomas Nast, *Harper's Weekly*, 1871.

Chinese plaintiff is entitled to purchase government land, overturning the state constitution's ban on resident aliens purchasing, owning, and selling land.[17]

1884–1885

ROUNDUPS AND PURGES

The Chinese are driven out of towns, hamlets, and cities, from **Eureka** and **Arcata** in Humboldt County to **Seattle** and **Tacoma** in the Washington Territory. These purges, violent and well publicized, ignite more than a hundred others in small towns, including **Riverside, Santa Cruz, Stockton, Napa, San Buenaventura, Tulare, Antioch, Wheatland, Bloomfield, Sonora, Sumner,** Washington Territory, and **East Portland,** Oregon.[18]

In February 1885, the Chinese are given twenty-four hours to leave **Eureka.** They are forced onto two steamships and Chinatown is demolished.

Merced announces plans to drive out Chinese "vagrants," prostitutes, and opium dealers by March 2; they are finally routed from the city on Christmas Day.[19] In May 1885, all the Chinese working on the dry dock in **Victoria,** British Columbia, are fired and white men are hired as "substitutes."[20]

Houses rented to Chinese tenants in **Forestville** and other towns in **Sonoma County** are blown up.[21] **Susanville**'s Chinatown is burned out, and the white landlord claims an eight-thousand-dollar loss.

In **Tulare,** where 20 percent of the town is Chinese, fires burn through the Chinese quarter, destroying twenty-five buildings worth thirty-five thousand dollars. More than one hundred Chinese families lose their belongings, and many leave. The citizens push the remaining Chinese to the outskirts of town and burn Chinatown.

Gangs of British and Swedish miners attack Chinese miners at **Rock Springs,** Wyoming, on September 2, instantly killing twenty-eight, wounding fifteen, some of whom later die, and driving hundreds into the desert. The vigilantes torch the homes and bunkhouses of seventy-nine Chinese men; the bodies of the dead and wounded are thrown into the flames.

On October 8, hundreds gather in **Cheyenne,** Wyoming, to celebrate the grand jury's acquittal of sixteen "rioters" for the Rock Springs massacre.[22] One week later, federal troops escort the Chinese, who had refused to join a strike by white miners, back into the mines.

At **Cutting,** along the Eel River in California, sixty-five Chinese cannery workers and fishermen are expelled.

In the hop fields of **Squak Valley (Issaquah),** Washington Territory, on September 7 a band of white and Native American farmworkers, angry at the higher wages of hop pickers, many of whom were Chinese, fire into their tents and murder three Chinese men.

A mob burns the barracks of thirty-six Chinese coal miners near **Newcastle,** Washington Territory.

The Chinese in **Tacoma** are driven from their homes and shops and marched nine miles in the rain to a remote muddy railroad crossing. As townspeople demolish Chinese neighborhoods, the refugees purchase train tickets or hike one hundred miles to **Portland,** Oregon.

Seattle demands that the Chinese leave by sundown on November 6.

Eighteen miles west of **Seattle,** a "mob of Indians, headed by white men" attacks a party of Chinese hop pickers with clubs and stones, killing two and wounding four. The Chinese had replaced Native Americans in the hop fields and had rejected warnings to leave.[23]

Vigilantes give housewives in **Felton** twenty-four hours to fire their Chinese servants. Within days, only one Chinese cook remains.

Vigilantes threaten to "thin" **Santa Cruz**'s Chinatown, and the *Santa Cruz Daily Surf* predicts that its "street gutters will run with gore."[24]

In **Stockton,** property owners, an ex-congressman, and a member of the county board of supervisors raise three thousand dollars to move the Chinese outside the city limits.

Delegations from a secret anti-Chinese club force the Chinese from sawmills, timber camps, ranches, and vineyards at **Lorenzo** and **Boulder** near

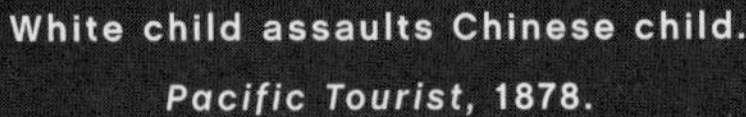

White child assaults Chinese child.
***Pacific Tourist*, 1878.**

"Searching Chinese for Opium."
***Harper's Weekly*, 1882.**

Santa Cruz; in December, white residents celebrate the purge of the Chinese with a dance organized by the Ladies of the Anti-Chinese League.

In November, the **San Jose** mayor and common council meet with the Anti-Coolie League to plan to drive the Chinese out.

Modesto witnesses the third attempt to burn Chinatown to the ground.

Forced from **Florin,** the Chinese flee to **Elk Grove,** where they are not allowed to remain.

In December 1885, **Truckee** starts the boycott movement to starve out the Chinese, launching the infamous Truckee method. In **Wichita,** Kansas, the Knights of Labor begin a boycott of Chinese labor throughout the state.

To escape the pogrom fever, in the winter of 1885–86, many Chinese leave for **New York City** on the overland train.[25] Chinese consul Fred Bee estimates that the Chinese population on the West Coast is declining by more than seven thousand per year.[26]

On December 26, Governor Stoneman reports to the U.S. secretary of state that there is no violence against the Chinese in California.

MURDER AND MAYHEM

Just after January 1, 1885, **Eureka**'s *Weekly Times Standard* urges the destruction of Chinatown.

White mobs in **San Francisco** assault the Chinese as four hundred policemen watch. This launches a violent year in the City by the Bay. Charles O'Donnell and more than five hundred "Sandlotters" celebrate Easter with an anti-Chinese parade, jabbing Chinese in the ribs with their parade canes, pulling them from streetcars, and severely beating them.[27] O'Donnell's "holy day of Easter Sunday" results in injuries to eighteen Chinese. In October, O'Donnell turns his committee into a militia. Led by the Knights of Labor, hundreds of white cigar makers, members of the Seamen's, White Cooks and Waiters, Boilermakers, Iron Molders, Blacksmiths, and Machinists Unions of the Pacific Coast parade in military style. Banners read CHEAP YELLOW LABOR DESTROYED ROME and MUST THE WHITE MAN GO? The next month, twenty-five hundred white laborers carry an effigy of a Chinese man swinging from a scaffold and demand that all Chinese be expelled from San Francisco within sixty days.

In July, the only Chinese man to cast a vote in **Monterey** is shot and hanged by a white mob.

In **Lake Valley,** Texas, Apaches murder Chinese laborers.

Eighteen miles west of **Seattle,** a "mob of Indians, headed by white men" attack a work party of Chinese hop pickers with clubs and stones, killing two and wounding four. The Chinese had replaced the Indians and had ignored all warnings to leave.[28]

In **Red Bluff, Tulare, Forestville,** and **Susanville,** Chinese homes and businesses are blown up. Hundreds of Chinese are left homeless, and ten thousand dollars' worth of property is destroyed.[29]

Near **Red Bluff,** three masked and armed men break into the cabins of Chinese tenant gardeners and vegetable peddlers at the Star ranch. During a midnight raid, the vigilantes seize $255; within twenty minutes the Chinese notify the town officials, but Red Bluff's constables "succeeded in making no arrests."[30]

In **Pasadena,** a baker and several boys set Chinatown ablaze. As residents loot Chinese buildings, the Chinese are given twenty-four hours to vacate the city. Many flee on the train to **Los Angeles.**

Attempts to torch Chinese businesses in **Santa Barbara** fail.

Modesto witnesses three attempts to burn the local Chinatown.

In the fishing village of **Trinidad** in Humboldt County, false rumors of leprosy among the Chinese circulate.

The *Santa Cruz Daily Sentinel* foments an anti-miscegenation campaign to oppose Chinese and white marriage.[31]

Two days before Christmas, the White Labor League of **San Francisco** calls for the expulsion of all Chinese from California.

JOB DISCRIMINATION AND WORK VIOLENCE

On March 25, twenty-one white men strike when Fay's Shingle Mill in **Fairhaven** hires twenty-two Chinese men.

Eureka declares that no Chinese may work on railroad construction along the Eel River.

When Chinese cigar makers strike in **San Francisco,** white cigar makers refuse to hire skilled Chinese workers and send for white replacements from the East Coast.

Spreckles and Company of San Francisco fires all Chinese sailors on its steamships.

Chinese miners at **Coal Creek** in the Washington Territory are run out of camp in September and flee to the **Newcastle** mines, two miles away.

In **Chicago,** on September 11, the Women's Industrial League passes a resolution demanding that Chinese laundries must close.

ANTI-CHINESE RALLIES AND DEMONSTRATIONS

Anti-Chinese associations form, meet, organize boycotts, and parade in **Emigrant Gap, Arcata, Crescent City, San Francisco, San Jose, Lorenzo, St. Helena, Felton, Santa Cruz, San Jose, Boulder Creek, Sacramento, San Buenaventura, Truckee, San Diego, Placerville, Stockton, Oakland,** and **Cheyenne,** Wyoming. Even after the Chinese are driven out, **Lorenzo, Eureka,** and **Boulder Creek** hold rallies to prevent their return.

The African Methodist Episcopal Church in **Chico** protests that its pastor has leased a portion of the church to Chinese merchants.

In December, the ladies of **Lorenzo** hold a supper and dance in honor of the Anti-Chinese League.

In **Sacramento,** fifteen hundred gather to plan a state anti-Chinese convention.

A mass demonstration against Chinese immigrants is held in **Victoria,** British Columbia.

In December 1885, the Anti-Coolie League of Oakland joins with the San Francisco Federated Trades Council to launch an anti-Chinese boycott, set to begin in February 1886.

GOVERNMENT ACTIONS AND VERDICTS

Directly after the Republican Convention platform of 1884 declares, "We denounce the importation of contract labor . . . as an offense against the spirit of American institutions; and we pledge ourselves to sustain the . . . law restricting Chinese immigration, and to provide such further legislation as is necessary to carry out its purposes," the Democratic Convention platform counters with, "We do not sanction the importation of foreign labor, or the admission of servile races, unfitted by habits, training, religion, or kindred, for absorption into the great body of our people, or for the citizenship which our laws confer. American civilization demands that against the immigration or importation of Mongolians to these shores our gates be closed."[32]

Chinese field-workers in Los Angeles, 1870

Congress passes an act to prohibit contract labor. Immigration authorities propose to use thumbprints to identify returning Chinese immigrants. Hoping to bypass Congress, on February 19 the California State Legislature restricts immigration of the Chinese and urges their "departure."

In **Oakland,** all Chinese laundrymen in wood-frame buildings are arrested. The movement to purge Chinese through anti-laundry ordinances soars; in August, the trustees of **Modesto** pass anti-washhouse ordinances and shut down all the Chinese laundries; in September the town trustees of **Watsonville** make it a misdemeanor to open a laundry within the town limits. **St. Helena** taxes "washhouses" $150 per quarter.[33] In November **Napa** uses its "abatement of nuisance" laws under which no person can carry on a business "offensive to the senses or prejudicial to the public comfort or safety," in order to "make a Chinese flight," and twelve Chinese men head to **Calistoga.**[34] **Merced**'s board of supervisors declares Chinese laundries a public nuisance and gives them ninety days to move beyond the town limits. Over the veto of the mayor, the **Stockton** City Council bans all Chinese laundries from the city.

Phoenix, Arizona, reissues a code banning the inhalation of opium fumes.

CHINESE RESISTANCE AND SUPPORT

On January 9, 1885, in one of the most important civil rights decisions in American history, Superior Court judge James Maguire rules in *Tape* v. *Hurley* that Chinese children must receive public education: "To deny a child, born of Chinese parents in this state, entrance to the public schools would be a violation of the law of the state and the Constitution of the United States." In **San Francisco** a segregated Chinese school opens at the corner of Jackson and Powell Streets.

Throughout the West, the Chinese buy and use arms to protect themselves. In **Truckee,** sensing the violence underlying the "peaceable" boycott, on December 31, 1885, they order arms from San Francisco. Following the news of the massacre in the Washington Territory, the Chinese in **Galt,** California, purchase three dozen Smith & Wesson revolvers.

The Chinese riot against police brutality in **Marysville** on March 11, 1885.

On February 9 the Chinese from **Eureka** arrive in **San Francisco** and announce plans to sue for reparations.

The Chinese Six Companies and Chinese Consolidated Benevolent Association demand financial compensation from Congress for injustices against the Chinese in **Rock Springs,** Wyoming, **Tacoma,** Washington Territory, **Felton,** California, and elsewhere. China sends a delegation to **Rock Springs** to investigate the massacre of Chinese miners. In **Tacoma,** authorities arrest the mayor, several judges, and a handful of police officers for the purge.

Consul Fred Bee seeks federal protection for the Chinese in **Seattle** who are being assaulted by a mob, and eventually 125 federal troops arrive.

In **East Portland,** Oregon, the Chinese defy the town's orders to leave.

On October 24, sixty Chinese cigar makers strike in **San Francisco.**

Facing continuous threats in Humboldt County, more than three hundred Chinese miners remain in the Siskiyou Mountains, many on the **Karuk Reservation.** Following a fire in November, Chinese lease land in **Pasadena** from a nearby rancher and build a new community. When their landlord vows to defend them with arms, **Pasadena** resolves to banish all Chinese.

In December, fearing a purge in **Sacramento,** Chinese gardeners refuse to lease any land for the next growing season.

In **Guangdong,** China, in November, riots explode against American missionaries.

In **Los Angeles,** under pressure from Chinese merchants and the Chinese Six Companies, the city council votes 8–2 against a motion to remove Chinatown.

Rejecting the precedent in *Elk* v. *Wilkins* (1884), which prevents Native Americans from being defined as citizens under the Fourteenth Amendment, the Chinese in **El Paso,** Texas, launch a movement to become naturalized citizens. Texas allows state courts to naturalize Chinese people, but they cannot give them the right to vote in any other state, including California. The California Constitution declares that no "native of China" can become a voter, and anti-Chinese organizers argue that Chinese immigrants are not covered

Chinese laborer, Humboldt County

under Fifteenth Amendment protections against denying the vote based on "race, color, or previous condition of servitude."[35]

The African American Methodist Episcopal Church in **Chico** provides a burial ground for the Chinese in its cemetery.

In **Orleans,** Humboldt County, the general store continues to import Chinese food for Chinese miners.

The Chinese fleeing **Seattle,** Wyoming, and California are arriving by train in **New York.** The government of **Mexico** imports twenty thousand Chinese laborers to work in the mines and on plantations.

1886

ROUNDUPS AND PURGES

Augusta, Georgia, revokes Chinese greengrocers' licenses, and the local paper declares that approximately six hundred Chinese "will be waited upon at midnight and marched out of town."[36]

In **Wichita,** Kansas, the Women's Industrial League joins with the Knights of Labor to organize a boycott of the town's thirty Chinese workers. A gang assaults Chinese workers and orders the Chinese laundries to close. The editor of the *Wichita Beacon* urges blacks to ally with whites to drive out the Chinese.[37]

On February 11, **Arroyo Grande** orders the Chinese to leave within five days.[38] Four wagonloads of Chinese refugees flee from **Bloomfield** to **Petaluma.**

At the beginning of March only fifty to sixty Chinese remain in **Arcata;** Chinese prostitutes consent to depart only after they are arrested. **Arcata** holds a fund-raiser to collect the six dollars per ticket to ship the Chinese to **San Francisco.** By the end of the month the last Chinese from Arcata has sailed on the *Humboldt* and **Arcata** declares that it is "rid of her Chinese."[39]

The **Fort Bragg** Redwood Company bows to threats of white timbermen and fires fifteen Chinese lumber workers.[40]

By April, **Crescent City**'s Chinatown is deserted. To celebrate the success of the purge, **Crescent City** blesses its Committee of Twenty-one: "Well done, thou good and faithful servant."

The Chinese are purged from **Carson,** Tuolumne County, and **Petaluma.** Many towns are implementing the resolutions of the Sacramento convention with economic, food, and rent boycotts.

Laundry ordinances, forced sales of Chinatowns, and town decrees drive the Chinese from **Napa, St. Helena, Yankee Jim's, Quincy, San Jose, Santa Cruz, Auburn, Brentwood, Santa Clara, Half-Moon Bay, Daggett, Knights Landing, Red Bluff, Coloma, Shingle Springs, Penryn, Lockeford, Springville,** and **Victoria,** British Columbia.

In April, laborers from nearby **Arroyo Grande** make a night "visit" to ten Chinese working for the Pacific Coast Railway near **Nipomo.** The Chinese are forced aboard handcars, transported twelve miles to **San Luis Obispo,** thrown from the cars, and ordered to walk to San Luis Obispo. They are warned that if they return to work for the railroad, they will be hanged.

Santa Cruz holds a children's parade to promote an anti-Chinese meeting.

Guaymas, Mexico, endures an anti-Chinese riot in March. In **Mazatlán,** rioters attack the Chinese, while Mexicans refuse to let the ship *Sardonyx* land with six hundred Chinese refugees from San Francisco.[41]

Chinese refugees arrive in **Rohnerville** from **Eureka,** but white citizens buy Chinese property and force the remaining Chinese to sail from Eureka on the *City of Chester.*

In **Los Angeles,** ninety hotels discharge their Chinese employees; some respond with a boycott, others leave.

By late spring, thousands of Chinese refugees are moving to the East.

In May, in despair over purges, a Chinese ranch hand commits suicide at the Horton ranch near **Red Bluff.**[42]

By June the intense wave of purges begins to wane. In **Firebaugh,** 325 Chinese sheep shearers are replaced by whites.

In July, twenty Chinese a day leave **Contra Costa County** for **Boston** or **New York.**

In August Chinese miners are driven from **Douglas Island** near **Juneau,** Alaska, and put to sea.

MURDER AND MAYHEM

Placerville's Chinatown burns on the evening of January 3, launching a year of arson and rage.

In **Placer County** and **Marysville,** Chinese men are found murdered.

There are mass assaults on the Chinese in **Chehalis,** Washington Territory.

Foresthill witnesses brutal assaults on Chinese residents.

The entire railroad crew of thirty Chinese men working on the section house in **Lincoln** are "spirited away." Their whereabouts remain unclear.[43]

On January 26, a mob in **Redding** that includes lawyers and judges routs the Chinese and burns Chinatown; nearby buildings owned by whites are saved. The League of Forty goes from house to house to tell the Chinese they must leave by January 31; "gamblers, highbinders, prostitutes, opium fakers, et al." are ordered to leave at once. Chinatown burns. The *Free Press* reports, "Redding is now a white man's town." The United States government will later pay the Chinese consul eight thousand dollars for the damages in Redding.

A rape and murder by a Chinese domestic servant, "the Wickersham outrage," prompts **Cloverdale** to order all its Chinese residents gone within forty-eight hours.[44] The crime is used to launch violent purges of Chinese across northern California.

On February 2, a fire at **Donner Lake** destroys the cabins and tools of Chinese woodcutters.

At **Anderson,** a Chinese man is beaten to death.

Chinese dwellings are raided and Chinese men are assaulted in **Millville.**

In **Olympia,** Washington Territory, a mob attacks Chinese residents and seizes their houses. Led by an employee of the state legislature and a leader of the Knights of Labor, the mob orders Chinese laborers to pack and leave. Chinese residents from across the territory flee to **Vancouver,** British Columbia.

Near **Stockton,** a Chinese fisherman is murdered in his boat and left to drift down the river and out to sea.[45]

In **Alameda,** vulcanite bombs are thrown into Chinese washhouses.[46]

Oakland witnesses attempts to blow up Chinese laundries.

Chinese hop pruners in **Marysville** are mobbed and their houses burned. They are seized and carried to **Wheatland,** where thirty masked men break into a Chinese bunkhouse. There, eleven more Chinese hop pruners are marched to the next ranch, where more Chinese men are rounded up. As an elderly man is pistol-whipped, the mob takes the captives to a third ranch and burns the Chinese cabins. In the mountain cold of February, the mob burns their clothing, pots, pans, work tools, and blankets. The Chinese are turned loose.[47] Chinese shops quickly sell their wares at cost and close.

Chinese laborer with cane, Humboldt County

In **Petaluma,** handbills warning "Discharge your Chinamen; your life is in danger"[48] are nailed to the homes of those who employ Chinese laborers.

Fires destroy two large Chinese buildings in the center of **Portland**'s Chinatown.

In **San Francisco,** hundreds of elderly Chinese refugees arrive by train to return to China. The steamship *Belgic* sails for China with 947 Chinese in steerage, 647 of whom carry return certificates.[49]

In March, arsonists target farms in **Chico** where Chinese are still employed. Large-scale farmer John Bidwell reluctantly agrees to fire his Chinese workers.

The town spring in **Bloomfield** is poisoned and the Chinese are blamed.

Chinese dwellings in the hamlet of **Sawyers Bar** in the Siskiyou Mountains are torched and destroyed. A citizen from Sawyers Bar writes to a Eureka newspaper that he hopes that "we may in time be free from our Chinese brothers, as is your city.[50] White citizens quickly claim all the Chinese land in the burnt-out district.

In **Ellensberg,** California, a Chinese boy is refused admission to school.

Chinese man in western clothing

Sonorans, hearing that Chinese laborers have arrived to build the Buchanan Road and work the Buchanan Mine, demand that the Chinese "vacate" the county and move east.[51] On March 28, 170 armed men leave **Sonora** in stages, buggies, and buckboards to round up the Chinese road workers. At **Somersville** a mob divides into squads of ten and marches eight miles to the mine. Most Chinese flee into the hills, but vigilantes seize twenty-seven Chinese laborers and march them back to **Somersville,** leaving the mine with one cook and two mill hands. The anti-Chinese club in Sonora secretly buys arms and starts to raid Chinese homes.[52] In nearby **Tigre,** the home of a Chinese job contractor is blown up by sticks of dynamite thrown against his house. *The Sonora Union Democrat* writes, "It was a peaceable, orderly, and effective movement . . . showing a determination to keep Chinese labor away from the county. . . . A movement of similar character was never better concluded."[53]

In April, eighty masked men raid the Chinese woodcutters' camps near **Albina,** Oregon, and ship the men to **Portland,** where, facing threats of violence, the Chinese flee.

In **Carson,** Nevada, on May 17, a mob burns the shops of whites who refuse to join an anti-Chinese boycott.

On May 9, **Honolulu**'s Chinatown burns and eight thousand are left homeless.

In the California mountain mining town of **Cherokee,** a local Chinese leader, Ah Tai, is hung in effigy as the citizens parade around the "corpse" accompanied by a marching band.

Seattle prepares for a second massive armed riot against the Chinese.

Women join in attempts to burn Chinatown in **Redding.**

On June 17, **Truckee**'s Chinatown is burned down and two of the few Chinese left in town die, hiding in their basement. The coroner declares that the deaths are "undeterminable" but suggests that both men committed suicide. The few Chinese remaining in the area immediately leave.

In **Dixon** a Chinese man is murdered for opening a laundry.

A deputy fish commissioner in **San Pablo** shoots three Chinese fishermen for using illegal nets. Two are wounded, one dies, and the others are arrested for violating fishing laws.[54]

In July a Chinese cook is arrested in **Colusa** after strychnine is found in local water.

Chico's Chinatown burns.

Modesto's Chinatown burns on July 19.[55]

On July 13 Prudence Kendall, widow of Councilman David Kendall, whose death prompted the **Eureka** purge, commits suicide.

August is marked in **Yreka** by a nighttime fire that destroys two blocks of Chinese stores. As flames spread to white businesses, the Chinese are dragged from their hiding places and "clubbed into work on the engines." Five Chinese children perish in the flames.[56] Chinese refugees sleep on the banks of Yreka Creek, waiting for help from **San Francisco.** Those who remain rebuild on the floodplain across the creek from the town.[57] New Chinatown is flooded out in 1890.[58]

On October 23 **North San Juan**'s Chinatown burns.

In November the fishing village of **Cuffey's Cove** vows to "wage incessant warfare" against the Chinese.[59]

By December, the violence has spread to **San Francisco,** where a strike on the Sutter and Geary streetcar line turns into an anti-Chinese riot, and workers stone Chinese houses.

JOB DISCRIMINATION AND WORK VIOLENCE

In January, almost a year after the Chinese are driven out, a **Eureka** cigar factory advertises that it now employs only white labor and the **Sacramento** Pioneer Mill discharges its Chinese workers.

Tulare pledges one thousand dollars to open a white-owned steam laundry.

Chinese man standing next to chair

In **Oakland,** twenty-four Scottish women and four Scottish weavers arrive to train whites to replace the Chinese in the jute mills.[60]

Although fruit growers object, **Napa** warns against hiring Chinese field-workers. In **Healdsburg** thousands of the "voting sex" demand removal of "Mongolians."

The **Stockton** newspaper agrees to discharge all of its Chinese employees.

In **Albany,** the New York State Workingmen's Convention votes to boycott all Chinese labor and all citizens who "may in any manner assist the Chinese." Trade unions in **New York City** and **Brooklyn** declare a boycott of Chinese laundrymen.

Inspired by **Truckee,** the boycott movement picks up, although in **Lincoln,** white employers refuse to sign the boycott pledge because the petition is distributed on a Sunday. Early in the spring planting season near **Fresno,** vineyard growers, announcing that it is "absolutely impossible" to obtain white labor, reject the boycott. The anti-Chinese club sets up a white-only employment office and four hundred men immediately sign on. **Santa Rosa** and **Arbuckle** residents pledge not to patronize or employ "Chinese coolies or pagans" after March 1.

All Chinese washhouses have been removed from **Cloverdale.**

Chinese cigar makers in **San Francisco** are unable to find customers, and many leave the city to work in orchards.

Coloma boasts that it has completed a local railroad without Chinese labor.[61]

Insurance companies cancel Chinese fire insurance for businesses in **Nevada City.**

African Americans arrive to replace Chinese laborers in **Los Angeles** and **Chico.** An overland train, "loaded with colored people from North Carolina," arrives in **Los Angeles,** and the ten families of men, women, boys, and girls take the jobs of Chinese harvesters in the vineyards and orange groves.[62] **Chico** holds a fund-raiser to import African American workers to replace the Chinese.

To take the place of Chinese workers, **El Paso,** Texas, recruits black and white laborers "regardless of color or previous condition."

Sacramento's Non-Partisan Association recommends that "colored people be substituted for Chinese in California," but the Antioch Club reminds the Sacramento Club of the risks of black voters.

Colusa celebrates the first railroad built in California without Chinese labor.

Blue Lake's lumber mills agree to expel Chinese timbermen.

In **San Francisco** unemployed whites march to the offices of the Mission Woolen Mills and the Selby Smelting Company to demand they fire all Chinese employees.

The chief engineer of the California and Oregon Railroad promises that the nine hundred Chinese grading the road north of the **Sacramento Delta** will be replaced by one thousand whites.[63]

One hundred fifty white cigar makers leave **New York** for California to replace Chinese in the trade.

The boycott movement spreads. **Tehama** and **Orland** agree to boycott both the Chinese and their employers. The Lick Paper Mill of **San Jose,** along with J. P. Pierce's and W. H. Dougherty's large sawmills in **Santa Cruz,** fire all their Chinese employees. **San Jose** begins a boycott of all canneries with Chinese employees.

Marysville's *Daily Appeal* reports that it has replaced its last Chinese employee, a woodcutter, who provided two cords a week for the paper's heating stoves and engine.

By mid-February, the boycott against Chinese workers has spread to **Martinez, Placerville, Stockton, Churn Creek, Wheatland, Sheridan, Healds-**

State Senator Clay Taylor, who sacrificed his political career to represent the Chinese

burg, Fort Bragg, Garberville, Napa, Anderson, Gold Gulch, Santa Clara, Coloma, Auburn, Half Moon Bay, and **Red Bluff.**[64] The Northern Pacific Railroad agrees that it will fire its Chinese workers when it can find enough white replacements. **Rohnerville** forces the Chinese to sell their property. **Rocklin** plans to boycott Chinese and convict labor because both compete with free laborers.

San Jose boot- and shoemakers agree to fire Chinese labor. Skilled cooks, cigar makers, and shoemakers who had "been thrown out of employment by the anti-Chinese agitation" make their way to the mines around **Folsom,** where they take jobs for thirty to fifty cents a day, telling a local reporter that they are "compelled to do something or starve."[65]

In March the restaurant at the Women's Christian Temperance Union in **San Jose** discharges its Chinese staff.

Humboldt County organizers visit mills along the coast in **Mendocino, Gualala,** and **Point Arena,** demanding that they employ only white men. **Point Arena** is pressured not to support any man running for office who employs Chinese help.[66]

Westport's Garcia Mill fires all Chinese workers, and a mob drives them from the town.[67]

Farmers' unions from **Coloma** to **Ukiah** agree to boycott Chinese field-workers if they can find "secure white labor." **Newcastle** fruit growers vow to replace Chinese labor with "desirable whites" but declare that "this cannot be done in a day or a year."

In **Amador City,** the Chinese are fired at coal and clay mines.

The last Chinese worker is discharged from the **Napa** Woolen Mills.[68]

The **Sacramento** anti-Chinese convention demands that Leland Stanford fire his Chinese field-workers.

During April, towns up and down the coast try to starve out Chinese laborers. The Loma Prieta Lumber Company in **Santa Cruz,** one of the largest in California, fires all Chinese employees. **Shingle Springs** boycotts the Planter House Hotel and the only town blacksmith.

More than five hundred whites donate funds to build a steam laundry to replace Chinese washhouses in **Napa.**

In **Victoria,** British Columbia, any company with a parliamentary charter is banned from hiring Chinese workers.

The **San Francisco** Board of Education resolves that neither principals nor teachers in the public schools shall employ, patronize, or aid the Chinese but instead should promote their legal removal.

By May, although boycott fever has begun to wane, the "Strawberry Party" is taking hold: in **Maxwell** the Anti-Chinese League boycotts all berries picked by Chinese. The city of **San Francisco,** white members of the Non-Partisan Association, the Federated Trades, and the Knights of Labor join the berry boycott.

In **Los Angeles,** ninety hotels discharge Chinese workers, and in turn the Chinese boycott all the hotels.

At B'nai B'rith in **San Francisco** the Anti-Chinese League and the Shoemakers' League meet to restrict patronage to white labor.

Thirty white waiters refuse to work with Chinese cooks and strike the steamship *Ancon,* which transports Chinese to and from the United States. Native American cooks and seamen refuse to support the strike.

ANTI-CHINESE RALLIES AND DEMONSTRATIONS

The roundups of Chinese people in California peak in 1886. The movement is local, led by journalists and business, civic, and union leaders. Anti-Coolie clubs, nonpartisan committees, and anti-Chinese associations gather at town halls, church picnics, dances, band concerts, and political party meetings. Anti-Chinese rallies, leaflets, marches, and parades preoccupy the West.

In January the *Sacramento Bee* polls local towns and reports that **Shingle Springs, Georgetown, Germantown, Ukiah, Sonoma, St. Helena, Orland, San**

Chinese men in graveyard

Buenaventura (now **Ventura**), **Marysville, Merced, Aptos, Visalia, Gridley, Pentz, Yreka, Arbuckle, Napa, Petaluma,** and **Vina** have formed anti-Chinese organizations and are holding meetings, drafting bylaws and constitutions, and announcing dates to withdraw "patronage" from Chinese residents. To displace Chinese laundries, many towns form anti-Chinese cooperatives to raise funds or sell stock in steam laundries, most of which fail.

The Ladies National Auxiliary Corps No. 1 of **Oakland** is perhaps the first all-female anti-Chinese society. Wheatland invites women to become honorary members. In **Livermore,** four hundred white women peacefully replace Chinese laborers. **El Dorado**'s Anti-Chinese Association welcomes female members.[69] Facing a petition called "The Declaration of Independence of San Rafael," **San Rafael**'s Anti-Chinese League, with more than 350 members, agrees to let women attend a meeting. The "fair sex" is well represented at **Lakeport**'s anti-Chinese rally at County Court House.[70]

Judges, mayors, and county supervisors lead the anti-Chinese movement. **Petaluma** elects the high school principal to chair the anti-Chinese club. In **Truckee** the leader is the editor of the town paper. With speeches, fund-raising, brass bands, dances, and home-baked pies, anti-Chinese clubs regularly meet in the California towns of **Vallejo, Wheatland, Red Bluff, Placerville, Emigrant**

Gap, Shingle Springs, Yreka, Lincoln, Walnut Creek, Santa Rosa, Santa Cruz, Merced, Pleasanton, Ukiah, Corning, Dutch Flat, Orland, Auburn, Chico, Tehama, Healdsburg, Marysville, Ferndale, Rohnerville, Bloomfield, Mount Pleasant, San Leandro, St. Helena, Hollister, Sacramento, Cloverdale, Tiburon, Yreka, Oakland, Traner, Fresno, Nevada City, Temescal, Colusa, Livermore, San Rafael, Westport, Alameda, Bully Choop, Quincy, Brentwood, Penryn, Crescent City, San Bernardino, Sierraville, Pennington, Magalia, Spanishtown, Pentz, Cherokee, Forest Hill, Grass Valley, Lodi, Arbuckle, San Jose, Duncan Mills, Martinez, Yuba, Todd's Valley, Rocklin, Bald Hill, Michigan Bluff, San Francisco, Rio Dell, and **Stockton. Portland,** Oregon, and **Carson City,** Nevada, hold meetings as well.

Nearly one hundred towns, such as **San Ramon, Sheridan, Aptos, Nevada City, Yankee Jim's, Soquel, Ione, Lockeford,** and **Oroville,** elect delegates to the San Jose and Sacramento statewide anti-Chinese conventions to implement their boycott plans.

Eight thousand people attend a "pledge" meeting in **Santa Rosa. Santa Cruz, Dixon, Auburn, Walnut Creek, Eureka,** and **Tulare** hold spirited anti-Chinese parades and rallies. In **Vina,** secret anti-Chinese meetings are held at Leland Stanford's vineyard.

Across the state, thousands of signatures are gathered for the Knights of Labor petition. After the petition is signed by Governor Stoneman, two former governors, and the chief justice of the California Supreme Court, it is mailed to Congress.

In a typical strategy, **Napa** investigates the "sanitary condition" of Chinatown to "take action deemed best to get rid of them" and forces ordinances to "make the Chinamen live like white people."[71] Absentee owners of Chinatown sell the property for fifteen hundred dollars to new owners, who agree to expel Chinese tenants.[72]

Latrobe "wants to boycott the Chinese but there is not one person of that nationality in that place."[73] Sparsely populated **Markleeville** initiates a boycott against its three Chinese residents.[74]

A children's anti-Chinese club parades through the streets of **Red Bluff** armed with cotton bats and orders the Chinese to leave.[75]

Stockton's local paper urges California to secede from the United States over issues of race and states' rights.[76]

GOVERNMENT ACTIONS AND VERDICTS

Federal immigration law bars Chinese from immigrating, and local ordinances work to expel them.

Trustees of **Sacramento** make it a misdemeanor for any Chinese to reside in the city after the March 1; those who remain face fines of up to five hundred

Sheet music, 1885–86

dollars or six months' imprisonment.[77] **Petaluma** sends a petition to Congress to force the United States to withdraw from the Burlingame Treaty and "rid" the country of Chinese.

Laundry ordinances ban washhouses in wood-frame buildings. **Santa Cruz** outlaws public laundries, punishable with fines of twenty to forty-five dollars. **Stockton**'s police arrest twenty-two Chinese and two whites for operating laundries within city limits; the Chinese prisoners furnish bail, continue work, and prepare to sue. **Oakland** has rolling arrests for laundry-ordinance violations. Sixty-one Chinese washermen are arrested in **Los Angeles** for violating the laundry ordinance and refusing to close by 9:30 P.M. In late November, **Livermore**'s trustees outlaw laundries in the city limits; the Chinese washermen refuse to comply.

It is discovered that California gubernatorial candidate Washington Bartlett, a Democrat running on an anti-Chinese plank, owns a Chinese washhouse in **San Francisco.** Bartlett and Republican candidate John F. Swift both favor Chinese expulsion. Swift endorses a boycott of Chinese workers but only if white men are available for hire.[78] Bartlett barely defeats Swift, 85,001–84,353.

In **Oakland** and **Alameda,** cubic-air ordinances from the 1870s, which in effect make it illegal to live in tenements or boardinghouses, are restored when hundreds of refugees from the roundups arrive in the Bay Area. **Sonora** makes mass arrests for cubic-air violations. The **Santa Cruz** City Council rejects a proposal to remove Chinatown but passes gambling and cubic-air ordinances for the "abatement of nuisances."

Opium raids in Chinatowns increase. Despite the high number of white customers, **Santa Rosa** arrests only the Chinese for opium smoking, with fines of ten to twenty dollars or ten to twenty days in prison.

The city council of **Augusta,** Georgia, purges the Chinese by revoking their greengrocer licenses; the local paper declares that six hundred Chinese "will be waited upon at midnight and marched out of town."[79]

Governor Stoneman of California defends the state's right to charge ten dollars for a permit to disinter Chinese bones so they can be returned to China.[80]

Towns remove hundreds of Chinese by sending them to remote jails. At **San Quentin** Prison, 87 (14 percent) of the 623 prisoners are Chinese; Chinese inmates at **Folsom Prison** number 145, out of 1,200.

In February a petition is filed with Governor Stoneman of California to physically brand all Chinese prisoners and then ship them to China. Apparently Stoneman does not act on this request.[81]

The "Monster petition" from the Knights of Labor, urging abrogation of the Burlingame Treaty, is received by Congress. It is sent via California congressman Charles N. Felton. The petition bears more than three thousand signatures and is 136 feet long.

The U.S. Senate receives a "memorial" from the anti-Chinese convention in Sacramento urging the peaceful deportation of all Chinese residing in the United States.

CHINESE RESISTANCE AND SUPPORT

The *Overland China Mail,* published in **Canton,** reports that anti-Chinese violence in the United States is creating dangerous anti-American threats in China. President Cleveland's initial refusal to pay indemnities for the violent purges in the West provokes riots in China.[82] Charles Denby, American minister to China, blames the roundups in California but is loudly rebuked in American papers.

In **Hong Kong,** protests arise in early March over the anti-Chinese violence in the United States. On May 6 the American Protestant Mission in **Peking** is destroyed and its ministers routed; the missionaries flee to **Canton.** In June, anti-American riots spread across China. In **Chungking,** rioters attack a missionary hospital, destroy the Methodist Episcopal Mission, and injure American missionaries.

Although China had paid more than $700,000 to the United States after anti-American riots at the Christian missions, President Cleveland declares that U.S. indemnity payments and reparations for Chinese are given out of charity. He does endorse reparations for the violence at **Rock Springs.** Congress appropriates $147,700 to China for the massacres. It is unclear if these funds are distributed to Chinese immigrants.

Following the arrests of anti-Chinese vigilantes in **Nicolaus,** federal judge Lorenzo Sawyer extends the Ku Klux Klan Act and rules that forcibly expelling the Chinese is unconstitutional under the Fourteenth Amendment. Awaiting a Supreme Court ruling, the lead vigilante spends a year in jail. Other federal indictments of anti-Chinese vigilantes follow, such as those in **East Portland.**

On February 1, in reaction to **Truckee**'s boycott, Chinese woodcutters at **Donner Lake** burn Anglos' wood camps. Chinese in Truckee and **Plymouth** send to China and San Francisco for Winchester rifles, muskets, and cartridges.

Chinese laundries in **Phoenix,** Arizona, refuse to pay the laundry tax and are sued by the city council.[83]

In *Yick Wo* v. *Hopkins,* the Supreme Court overturns the conviction of a San Francisco laundryman for operating without a permit on the grounds that the city had granted permits to all non-Chinese applicants. This was the first time that a law's application, rather than a law itself, was ruled to be discriminatory under the Fourteenth Amendment. *Yick Wo* becomes precedent for the civil rights cases in the 1960s that seek to strike down statutes that selectively discriminated against African Americans.

Placard for an anti-Chinese meeting called by Mayor Weisbach, Tacoma

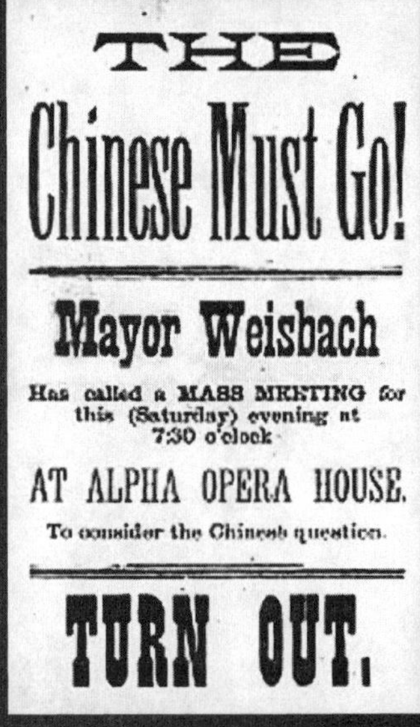

An anti-Chinese riot in Denver, 1880

Chinese laundry workers.
Frank Leslie's Sunday Magazine, March 1881.

The Chinese sue the city of **Tehama** to test its legal right to drive them out.

Although the trustees of **Red Bluff** and the Chinese vice consul advise the Chinese to leave, most remain until they are driven out by force. In February, **Truckee** gives the Chinese one more week to leave, and the Chinese Six Companies ship a railroad car of rice to their starving brethren. Chinese in **Santa Rosa** and **Arcata** refuse to honor the deadline to leave. In **Lincoln** six of fifteen Chinese residents refuse to leave. In April, Chinese in **Shasta** enrage unemployed whites by continuing to take jobs on the railroad.

When three Chinese property owners in **Snohomish,** Washington Territory, refuse to leave, a dynamite cartridge explodes under their house. The men are injured and move upstairs. The next day, shots are fired into the house, but the Chinese "hold fort."[84]

In **Nevada City**, in anticipation of a March roundup, the Chinese fortify their

doors and windows with bars, bolts, and extra "fastenings" and purchase firearms, declaring that they will remain.[85]

Chinese in **Rohnerville** refuse to sell their property.

One year after the purge in **Eureka,** a Chinese merchant, Charles Mock, returns to buy property under the name of a white friend, but he is discovered and deported. Mock refuses to pay for his ship ticket.

Seven Chinese residents remain in **Shasta** because they own their houses and have paid property taxes for many years.[86]

Anticipating a purge from **Santa Cruz,** the Chinese sign leases in the suburb of **Branciforte.**

Throughout California, thousands of Chinese reject the railroads' "incentive" rates and refuse to purchase tickets for the East Coast.

Chinatown, Monterey, California

The Chinese retaliate. In response to nineteen arrests for violating a laundry ordinance in **San Jose,** they close their shops and refuse to return laundry. In **Truckee** they refuse to take domestic-service jobs. In **Wheatland** Chinese launderers, cooks, domestic servants, and vegetable peddlers refuse to exchange their leases on fertile ground for arid truck gardens. Chinese washermen refuse to pay the town's new laundry license fee and stop washing. To undercut white growers, Chinese gardeners offer their vegetables at one fourth the usual price. In February the Chinese residents of **Red Bluff** refuse to sell vegetables to hotels and houses that have discharged Chinese workers or that support the anti-Chinese boycott. Elsewhere they return the laundry folded but unwashed.

The Chinese strike. In March, near **Sacramento,** Chinese hop pickers refuse to work alongside non-Chinese field-workers.[87] On March 15, the Chinese strike in the orange groves surrounding **Los Angeles.**

On May 5 Chinese shoemakers win a strike in **San Francisco.**

On August 12, more than two thousand Chinese hop pickers across the state demonstrate against a wage cut of ninety cents to seventy cents per hundred; the next day in **Vina,** Chinese grape pickers strike for higher wages. Chinese hop pickers in **Santa Rosa** riot to protest their working conditions and ongoing threats of violence.

Many Chinese escape. In **Dixon** the Chinese protect themselves against insidious laundry ordinances by moving outside the city limits. Thousands are in flight. Fifteen hundred unemployed Chinese fleeing the roundups now reside in **Victoria,** British Columbia.

The Chinese Six Companies mail circulars throughout the United States announcing reduced ship fares for any Chinese men who "wish to go back to their own country," from sixty-five to twenty-five dollars. This offer is targeted at the "aged, invalid, and blind." Those over sixty may travel home free.

In **Redding,** state senator Clay Taylor risks his political career by accepting the offer of Ming O. Wang, consul general of the Chinese legation, to serve as legal counsel and prosecute outrages against the Chinese in **Shasta County.** Taylor advises the Chinese not to obey any unlawful command to leave. Ming Wang and consul Fred Bee announce that they will prosecute all parties and municipal governments for any outrages committed against any Chinese residents of **Shasta County.** The Chinese demand financial reparations from **Redding** and publish a list of townspeople who owe them money.

The Chinese file the first lawsuit for reparations: on March 20, *Wing Hing* v. *City of Eureka* is filed in U.S. Ninth Circuit Court in **San Francisco.**

The Chinese turn to the criminal courts. They force the arrests of twenty-one members of the mob who assaulted the Chinese in **Nicolaus** and forced them onto a river barge;[88] they convince the judge to set bail at one thousand dollars, and they seek coverage under the Fourteenth Amendment. In April the Chinese in **Carson City,** Nevada, demand the arrest of anti-Chinese leaders for conspiracy. In June, the Chinese in **Olympia,** Washington Territory, call for arrests and obtain guilty verdicts against anti-Chinese rioters.

Chinese immigrants mobilize the government of China to intervene on their behalf. In February, the Chinese foreign ministers in **San Francisco** file protests with the U.S. government over the roundup in **Seattle.** Cheng Ping, vice consul general, and Cheng Yow, secretary, tour California to assess anti-Chinese actions. The Chinese minister at the legation in **Washington, D.C.,** delivers hundreds of telegrams from California to the U.S. State Department to protest "a concerted movement in progress to drive out the Chinese from all the towns and cities of California except San Francisco." In early March during the **Wheatland** riots, Chinese ministers arrive to investigate the violence and lay the foundation for a claim of monetary indemnity similar to those won from China by American missionaries and businessmen.[89] Some Chinese return to the town. Cheng Ping protests the events in **Nicolaus** to the U.S. government. In December, Fred Bee forces a deputy U.S. marshal to visit the tiny mountain town of **Happy Camp** to stop an anti-Chinese riot.[90]

The Chinese organize support from white farmers. In **Fresno,** fruit growers who employ Chinese field laborers protest the boycotts. Farmers in **Vacaville** protest violence against Chinese field hands. **Duncan Mills** refuses to boycott Chinese labor and announces that it will fire any employee who boycotts Chinese businesses or laborers. Orchardists in **Newcastle** defend their right to hire Chinese workers. **Oroville, Quincy,** and **Grass Valley** refuse to endorse the boycott movement, and hundreds of Chinese refugees move to Grass Valley, where they remain until the turn of the century.[91] Farmers in **Petaluma** reject the boycott and continue to hire Chinese field-workers.

Local authorities in **Sonora** require that a Chinese man be admitted to the county hospital.

On April 30, in **Livermore,** the new steam laundry built to replace the Chinese washhouse fails. In celebration, the local Chinese hoist an American flag over their own laundry.

1887–1890

ROUNDUPS AND PURGES

By the end of this fateful decade, most towns that sought to purge the Chinese have completed their work. Yet a few communities still try to become all-white towns.

Redding resumes the boycott against Chinese labor and commerce.

In March 1887 vigilantes in **Crescent City** compel white farmers to fire the remaining Chinese ranch hands.[92] In June Chinese miners fleeing their small claims on nearby creeks are not allowed to leave through the city; they escape along the **Smith River,** toward Oregon.[93] Several try to return to Crescent City, only to be immediately forced out.[94] In August, **Ferndale** votes to keep the Chinese out of the dairy valley forever. Newspapers report that if any Chinese attempt to reenter **Humboldt County,** the "people would spare no means in their power, even at the loss of life and limb, to force the Chinese out."

In February 1888, the Chinese community in **Watsonville,** swelled by the arrival of sugar-beet workers, agrees to move across the Pajaro River to a more spacious site with better drainage. This is the only recorded voluntary removal of a rural Chinese community.[95]

MURDER AND MAYHEM

In 1887 thirty-one Chinese miners are slaughtered in the "**Snake River** massacre," at **Hell's Canyon** along Oregon's Columbia River; a gang of white farmers and schoolboys rob and murder the miners, mutilate their bodies, and throw them into the river.[96]

After **Colusa** convicts Ho Ah Heung of murder and sentences him to life imprisonment, he is lynched by a mob; the sheriff refuses to arrest any of the vigilantes.

In May, the Chinatown known as Ah Toy Alley in **San Jose** burns to the ground; at the time of the fire, the ten-thousand-gallon water tank is mysteriously empty.

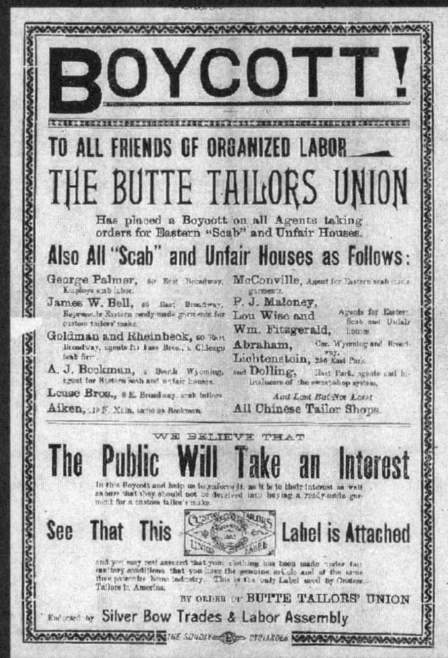

BOYCOTT!

TO ALL FRIENDS OF ORGANIZED LABOR

THE BUTTE TAILORS UNION

Has placed a Boycott on all Agents taking orders for Eastern "Scab" and Unfair Houses.

Also All "Scab" and Unfair Houses as Follows:

George Palmer, 50 East Broadway, Employs scab labor.

James W. Bell, 46 East Broadway, Represents Eastern ready-made garments for custom tailors' make.

Goldman and Rheinbeck, 60 East Broadway, agents for [illegible] Bros., a Chicago scab firm.

A. J. Bockman, [illegible] South Wyoming, agent for Eastern scab and unfair houses.

Lease Bros., 8 E. Broadway, scab tailors

Aiken, [illegible] N. Main, same as Bockman.

McConville, Agent for Eastern scab made garments.

P. J. Maloney, Lou Wise and Wm. Fitzgerald, Agents for Eastern Scab and Unfair houses.

Abraham, Cor. Wyoming and Broadway.

Lichtenstein, 256 East Park

and Dolling, East Park, agents and introducers of the sweatshop system.

And Last But Not Least

All Chinese Tailor Shops.

WE BELIEVE THAT

The Public Will Take an Interest

In this Boycott and help us to enforce it, as it is to their interest as well as ours that they should not be deceived into buying a ready-made garment for a custom tailor's make.

See That This [label: Custom Tailors Union Label] Label is Attached

and you may rest assured that your clothing has been made under fair sanitary conditions, that you have the genuine article and at the same time patronize home industry. This is the only Label used by Custom Tailors in America.

BY ORDER OF BUTTE TAILORS' UNION

Endorsed by Silver Bow Trades & Labor Assembly

THE SUNDAY BYSTANDER

Boycott notice by Butte Tailors Union

In **Yreka,** Chinese camps are assaulted and robbed.

An anti-Chinese riot assails **Temescal.**

In November, a gang dynamites the Chinese washhouses in **Yreka.**

JOB DISCRIMINATION AND WORK VIOLENCE

Facing boycotts, fishermen's "bag net" fees, bans against hiring Chinese to grade roads, physical assaults, high license fees, and expensive certificates to bury their dead, the Chinese population in **Marin County** drops by half, from 1,827 in 1880 (more than 11 percent of the population) to 915 in 1890.

In 1887 all Chinese laundry workers in **San Bernardino** are ordered to quit work after 10 P.M.

Railroads agree to farmers' request for reduced rates to transport Native Americans from **Reno,** Nevada, to break a strike by Chinese hop pickers.[97]

RALLIES AND DEMONSTRATIONS

Celebrations in December 1887 mark the anniversary of the start of the anti-Chinese boycott that led to the purge of **Truckee.**

GOVERNMENT ACTIONS AND JUDICIAL VERDICTS

In February 1887, Congress makes the historic decision to pay reparations for the **Rock Springs** massacre. In August 1889, Congress authorizes indemnity payments for the violent purges in **Redding.**

On October 1, 1888, President Cleveland signs the Scott Act, banning the immigration of Chinese laborers to the United States and prohibiting reentry visas. About twenty-thousand Chinese who had left the United States to visit family in China are refused reentry, including about six hundred who are on ships, en route to America. Mass demonstrations across California celebrate the law, which is quickly upheld by the Supreme Court. The Chinese government never recognizes the validity of the Scott Act.

In 1888, the king and the legislature of **Hawaii** limit Chinese immigration. The Chinese may no longer land in **Hawaii** unless they possess a permit granted by the Hawaiian minister of foreign affairs; these permits are issued only to merchants or professionals.

Codes written to expel the Chinese are extended to the Japanese. In 1888, in order to drive out Japanese fishermen in Mendocino County, **Ukiah**'s board of supervisors levies a fee of one hundred dollars for a three-month license to Japanese fishermen who "bag" abalone in the Pacific Ocean.

A series of court decisions legitimize the expulsion movement. In the case of *In re Thomas Baldwin,* in March 1887, the Supreme Court overturns Judge Lorenzo Sawyer's earlier ruling against the vigilantes from **Nicolaus** and holds that the Fourteenth Amendment does not cover Chinese "aliens."

Child's cap pistol, inscribed THE CHINESE MUST GO, **1884**

In *Chae Chan Ping* v. *United States,* the Supreme Court rules that regardless of prior treaty agreements, the United States may bar an entire race from entering the country if it decides that this race would be difficult to assimilate. *Chae Chan Ping* also upholds the constitutionality of all the exclusion acts.

CHINESE RESISTANCE AND SUPPORT

In August 1887, the Chinese call a general strike in **Sacramento** to protest the efforts of the city to condemn Chinatown.

In the **Sacramento Valley,** Chinese hop pickers strike for higher pay. Growers ask the railroads for reduced fares in order to bring in Native Americans from Reno to break the strike. The Native Americans replace the striking Chinese hop pickers.

Despite the county's claim to ethnic purity, Chinese miners remain in Humboldt County and manage to hold on to their mining claims in **Crescent City.**[98]

Chinese washermen undercut the prices of the new white laundry in **Napa,** forcing it to close in July 1887.

By 1887 Chinese individuals, companies, and cooperatives in **Del Norte County** are working hydraulic mines; the Chinese-owned Del Norte Mine, leased for a percentage of the gold, becomes the most lucrative mine in the county, producing more than $1 million. Chinese miners earn between $1.00 and $1.25 per day.

In 1889 the Chinese return to work at the **Cutting** cannery, during salmon season, defying Humboldt County's ban.

In 1889, the United States government pays the Chinese consul eight thousand dollars in indemnity for the violent purges in **Redding.**

Despite the roundups, the population of Chinese in **Santa Cruz County** rises from 523 in 1880 to 785 in 1890. According to the U.S. Census, the population of Asian and Pacific Islanders in California is 75,218 in 1880 and 73,619 in 1890; in Washington, 3,187 in 1880 and 3,620 in 1890; in Oregon, 9,512 in 1880 and 9,565 in 1890; in Nevada, 5,419 in 1880 and 2,836 in 1890. In New York it was 926 in 1880 and 3,083 in 1890.[99]

8

THE DOG TAG LAW

The Geary Act is an unjust law and no Chinese should obey it. The law degrades the Chinese and if obeyed will put them lower than the meanest of people. It is a cruel law. It is a bad law. Read it and see how cruel the law is to our people. See how mean and contemptible it wants to make the Chinese. We do not want the Chinese to obey it. We do not believe the Chinese will obey it. In making the law the United States has violated the treaties. They have disregarded our rights and paid no attention to their promise, and made a law to suit themselves, no matter how unjust to us. No Chinese can read this law without a feeling of disgust. Many whites say the law is not right. Let us stand together.

—Chinese Six Companies

On September 19, 1892, the presidents of the Chinese Six Companies ordered all 110,000 Chinese immigrants in the United States to commit mass civil disobedience. Red leaflets appeared on the walls and windows of Chinatowns throughout the country commanding Chinese to defy the new Geary Act that required Chinese residents to carry a photo identification card to prove that they were legal immigrants.

Thousands honored the call to disobey the "Dog Tag Law," and they faced immediate deportation. Their refusal to carry an identity card, America's first internal passport, created perhaps the largest organized act of civil disobedience in the United States.

The identification cards had their roots in slavery. Before the Civil War, enslaved blacks had often been forced to carry identifying passes when they left their plantations, and free blacks were required to bear papers proving that they were not slaves. Now, following four decades of forced expulsions in the Pacific Northwest, Chinese immigrants were similarly compelled to carry an "orderly scheme of individual identification and certification" to "protect their right to remain in the country."[1]

In 1892, with a presidential election fast approaching, Democratic congressman Thomas Geary of Sonoma County, California, had seized on anti-Chinese sentiment and wrote an identification bill that easily passed the House of Representatives, 178–43, and the Senate, 30–15. The Geary Act gave a Chinese laborer one year to register for a certificate or face immediate deportation. The identity card was to contain two duplicate photographs that were "securely affixed to the papers by strongly adhesive paste. . . . The photographs shall be sun pictures, such as are usually known as card photographs, of sufficient size and distinctness to plainly and accurately represent the entire face of the applicant, the head to be not less than 1½ inches from base of hair to base of chin."[2]

The Geary Act initiated an intense two-year struggle as the Chinese defied restrictive judicial decisions, repressive congressional acts, and mob violence. As soon as the 1892 act was signed into law by President Harrison, the Six Companies declared, "No other nation in the world treats Chinese like the United States does. . . . We must organize and subscribe money to hire lawyers to defend ourself. We must . . . complain to the ambassadors of our own Government to help us fight against this injustice."[3]

The Geary Act did more than require the Chinese to wear identification cards. It extended the Exclusion Act for ten more years and restated the ban against Chinese immigrants becoming American citizens. Another humiliating provision called for two white witnesses to testify to a Chinese person's immigration status. This was the first time a federal statute included a racial condition on the right to testify. And it was the first time that illegal immigration became a federal crime punishable by a year's imprisonment with hard labor.[4]

Tom Riordan, the San Francisco attorney who had represented the Chinese in earlier civil rights suits, stated: "This Act is clearly unconstitutional . . . if a Chinaman is found in this country without a certificate, the burden of proof in showing that he has a right to remain here is thrown upon him, whereas the Constitution provides that in an action of this kind the man is presumed innocent until he is proved guilty and then the proof of his guilt falls on the Government."[5]

"WE CLAIM A COMMON MANHOOD"

By 1892, thousands of Chinese had escaped from enslaved labor in the Caribbean and from the violence of the roundups in the West. Seeking respite in New England, New York, and the South, Chinese immigrants now lived outside the frontier states. The Geary Act unified Chinese across the country, building a Chinese American identity that crossed generations of immigrants who rallied quickly to put pressure on Washington, organize petition drives, and coordinate diplomatic intervention from New York, Washington, and San Francisco.

In New York and Brooklyn the Chinese Equal Rights League soon enrolled 150 English-speaking Chinese merchants and professionals, most of whom had lived in the United States for more than ten years, some since their childhood. Its leaders pleaded "to the people of this great Republic to deliver their fellow countrymen from this outrageous persecution."[6]

Coming in the early years of the Age of Reform, the Geary Act's assault on Chinese civil liberties prompted white support for the Chinese. On September 22, 1892, more than one thousand U.S. citizens joined with two hundred Chinese merchants and laborers at Cooper Union in Manhattan to protest the Geary Act. The Chinese Equal Rights League declared that by making the Chinese pay the "illegal costs and expenses" of enforcing the law, the bill imposed taxation without representation. Even more un-American, they said, was its provision that a person arrested under the law "shall be adjudged guilty until he shall affirmatively prove his innocence."[7]

The Chinese offensive against the Geary Act drew together strategies of resistance that had been evolving since the gold rush. "As residents of the United States," the league declared, "we claim a common manhood with all other nationalities" that should be recognized according to the principles of American freedom. By claiming a "common manhood" with other American immigrants, the Chinese Equal Rights League sought to dissolve images of difference—in body, religion, dress, food—that saturated American editorials, broadsheets, advertisements, and cartoons and shaped the unequal treatment of the Chinese under immigration law.[8]

The league also attacked the idea that the Chinese were sojourners in the United States. It appealed for an "equal chance in the race of life in this our adopted home. . . . Our interest is here, because our homes, our families and our all are here. America is our home through long residence. Why, then, should we not consider your welfare ours?" The purpose of the Geary Act was to pressure "more than one hundred thousand honest and respectable Chinese residents" to leave the country by forcing them "to wear the badge of disgrace [like] men in your penitentiaries" or to "tag and brand [them] as a whole lot of cattle for the slaughter."[9]

Nonetheless, the league members wanted to distinguish themselves from refugees from the West Coast or enslaved laborers fleeing Cuba, Mexico, and Peru. "We do not want any more Chinese here any more than you do," they asserted. "The scarcer the Chinese here the better would be our conditions among you."[10]

Up and down the Pacific coast, Chinese laborers and merchants demanded help from China and pressured Ts'ui Kuo-yin of the Chinese legation to lobby Congress and the president. Ts'ui complained to Secretary of State James G. Blaine that the Geary Act violated the promise in the 1880 immigration treaty that Chinese immigrants would have the right to "go and come of their own free will and accord." The provision forcing every Chinese resident in the United States to wear an identifying photograph likened the Chinese to convicts and violated "every principle of justice, equity, reason and fair dealing between two friendly powers." He demanded that the secretary of state personally guarantee that Chinese in the United States never again be "abused, beaten, wounded, and murdered."[11]

The Chinese Exclusion Act of 1882 was due to expire. To revive it, many white Americans promoted the toxic myth of a "yellow peril." Popularized by politicians, preachers, and the press, the myth predicted that the Chinese would "swarm" the country and form a dictatorship—of greedy, dirty, dishonest, and fertile yellow men. The House Committee on Immigration and Naturalization reported that after 1892, "there will be no law to prevent the Chinese hordes from invading our country in numbers so vast as soon to outnumber the present population of our flourishing states on the Pacific slope . . . to make this country their temporary home, where in a few years they can accumulate enough to live the balance of their days in China in comparative ease."[12]

Having spent four decades demanding Chinese expulsion, many in California were suddenly threatened by its possibility. In the 1890s, California agriculture was enjoying spectacular growth. Farmers leased small plots of land to hundreds of Chinese tenants for vineyards, orange and lemon groves, and orchards. The cultivation, harvesting, and packing of California's crops depended on Chinese labor. Without the Chinese, the new fruit industry would wither.[13] Farmers also knew that the Chinese were building the long routes and short-haul tracks of the new railroads. Under the land grants, the railroads still controlled hundreds of thousands of acres of arable land, as well as the power of transportation itself—the refrigerated railroad cars, the location of terminals, the grain towers, indeed, the entire nexus on which the sales of the fruit of the land depended. Who else would build and fire this iron web? Some farmers thought that only an "influx" of blacks could replace Chinese labor.[14]

The Geary Act fractured rural political coalitions. While railroad investors, fruit growers, and missionary groups opposed the act, the waning Knights of Labor, the Council of Federated Trades, and workingmen's clubs on the Pacific coast were determined to enforce it. Unionists began to take it upon themselves to turn in unregistered Chinese.

"BLOODSHED AND ANARCHY"

The Geary Act came at a moment of intense labor unrest and industrial violence. In July 1892, President Harrison sent eight thousand militia to assist Pinkerton detectives and break the steelworkers' strike against the Homestead plant, part of Carnegie Steel and Utah Copper, along the Monongahela River, seven miles east of Pittsburgh. The strike ended brutally when Pinkerton guards opened fire on the employees and seven guards and nine steelworkers died. That same month, Harrison sent federal troops to break the strike of silver miners at Coeur d'Alene, Idaho, and thirty miners were killed. Many in the labor movement believed that Chinese immigrants would provide a permanent supply of scabs.

In 1893 a series of business failures and bank closings shook the nation. The Panic of 1893, caused by the completion of the nation's basic steel and railroad requirements, marked the end of an era of easy investment and massive profit and the beginning of six years of crippling unemployment. Millions of Americans were out of work, and those who still had jobs took repeated cuts in already low wages; the Chinese field-workers' wage of one dollar per day was in fact higher than the sixty cents earned by many white textile workers. As growing economic disparities provoked new racial tensions, the national government had to tread lightly on California farmers' demands for cheap labor.

The nation was divided; fifteen states and territories sent to Congress and to President Harrison urging them to deport the Chinese,[15] prompting the *Los Angeles Times* to comment, "If we can keep out the Chinese, there is no reason why we cannot exclude the lower classes of Poles, Hungarians, Italians and some other European nations, which people possess most of the vices of the Chinese and few of their good qualities, besides having a leaning towards bloodshed and anarchy which is peculiarly their own."[16]

The Geary Act embodied the dilemma of the Chinese as a racial problem and a racial solution.[17] By April 1893, Chinese leaders and the Chinese legation had let it be known that they would contest the act. The Chinese vice consul in San Francisco, Qing Ow Yang, begged his government, "Do you know what the Geary bill means to the laboring Chinese in this country? It means, sir, that they are placed on the level with your dogs. If you have a dog, a black and tan, a Llewellyn setter, a pointer, you buy a license tag for it and fasten it to the dog's collar, and the number in the dog's tag is its immunity from arrest by the poundman. Under the Geary bill the laboring Chinese carry their number in their pocket and any man who so desires may stop them and demand to see their 'tag'. . . . We ask that our Government protect its children."[18]

Protests also arose within Congress. Illinois representative Robert R. Hitt had tried to stop the Geary Act's passage and now denounced the act as a return to the days of slavery: "It is proposed to have 100,000 . . . men in our country ticketed, tagged, almost branded—the old slavery days returned. Never before in a free country was there such a system of tagging a man like a dog to be caught by the police and examined, and if his tag or collar is not all right, taken to the pound or drowned or shot. . . . Never before was it applied by a free people to a human being with the exception (which we can never refer to with pride) of the sad days of slavery."[19]

At first most Chinese men found ways to avoid registering for the identity cards. With rising threats of racial violence, many Chinese purchased revolvers, ammunition, and knives. When the California Jute Mill threatened to fire any Chinese employee who refused to obtain a certificate and helped the Bureau of Internal Revenue set up secret offices, the Six Companies ordered the jute workers to strike. Chinese laborers let it be known that if they were seized and deported, they would join mounting efforts to drive American missionaries and businessmen out of China.

The Six Companies foiled other Bureau of Internal Revenue plans for secret registration. Registrars, paid one dollar per certificate, offered to visit homes so domestic servants could sign in private. Many Chinese residents, fearing that the identity cards exposed their homes, refused to register at any site. Some declared that only the "Christianized Chinese" registered. Those who believed that the only way to remain in the United States was to register rightly feared retaliation from their brethren.

Congressman Geary was stunned by the Chinese resistance and sought indictments against Thomas Riordan and the leaders of the Chinese Six Companies on charges of conspiracy for advising the Chinese to disobey the Geary Act. As evidence, Geary cited one circular, widely distributed in Oakland and San Francisco and published in War Kee's *Oriental Chinese Newspaper:*

> This new registration law is not right. All the authorities we have consulted agree to this.
>
> We have employed five attorneys to go to Washington to the United States Supreme Court to fight this unjust law. Wait until the 5th of May until you do anything in this matter. Wait and we will help you.
>
> The Chinese ministers have gone to the head men of the United States Government to get decisions and we soon hope to get them in order that our people may not be arrested and sent to jail.
>
> You will not have to be arrested and sent to jail if these decisions are favorable, as we think they will be.
>
> You ought to do what is right and not take money for registration and thus lose your respectability.
>
> Jung Wah Woy Quoon, or Six Companies[20]

Facing conspiracy charges, the Six Companies showed more caution but continued to urge each Chinese immigrant to uphold the boycott against the certificates and to contribute one dollar toward the legal case. They made a deal with the Pacific Mail Steamship Company to carry only passengers who presented tickets marked with their permission.[21]

In March 1893, with the final date for registration only two months off and few Chinese registered, John Quinn, collector of internal revenue in San Francisco, announced, "On May 5, all Chinese in this district who do not possess a registration certificate will be arrested. . . . As fast as the Chinese are arrested they will be lodged in the county jails, and when these are filled arrangements can easily be made for accommodating more of them at Angel Island, or any other place that the Government may designate."

Overwhelmed by the Chinese resistance, Quinn also requested permission from Washington, D.C., to station a cordon of guards around Chinatown, seize all Chinese immigrants who refused to register, and confine them on Mare Island in San Francisco Bay until they could be deported. Quinn wanted to hire 180 men who would work in three eight-hour shifts, guard all exits to Chinatown, and commence a systematic house-by-house search, "picking up" unregistered Chinese. Two months before the deadline

San Francisco Police Department Raiders Squad

for registration, he sent a squad of six men to raid Chinatown and arrest residents who could not produce certificates.

But the Chinese's mass refusal to sign up for cards was effective. In April, impressed by the Chinese organization and daunted by the difficulty of implementing the Geary Act, the government seemed to back down. John Mason, the federal commissioner of internal revenue, temporarily dispensed with the requirement for photographs and reduced the requirement for "credible" (that is, white) witnesses from two to one.

On April 9, the *San Francisco Morning Call* bemoaned, THE GEARY RESTRICTION LAW EMASCULATED. Even though all Chinese basically looked alike, asserted the *Call,* "it would be next to impossible to deceive an expert with an official seal across the photograph pasted on the certificate and a duplicate photograph on an official register."[22]

Even without the photograph requirement, most Chinese still refused to register. Chinese farmworkers in Watsonville explained to the registrar that they had decided simply to "refrain" from completing the forms. The U.S. government did not know what to do next. As the country awaited a court decision, only 3,169 of the estimated 110,000 Chinese in the country had registered.

By March, 303 Chinese people had been sent back to China, but deportation from New York via San Francisco to China cost $1,000. The May deadline had not yet arrived, and from the initial $100,000 appropriated for imprisonment, "conveyance of Chinese persons to the frontier or seaboard for deportation," registration costs, forms, salaries (from three to six dollars per day), traveling expenses, and two dollars' per diem for agents, and for deportation itself, only $16,866 remained. The appropriation for the next two fiscal years amounted to a paltry $50,000, a sum that was also supposed to pay for border inspectors.[23] Many Democrats on the Pacific coast were concerned that President Cleveland would back down. There were not enough courthouses, jail cells, or judges for such an endeavor, let alone revenue to pay for it. In a time of desperate financial depression, deporting a hundred thousand people was just not good economics. Where were the resources going to come from?

The Geary Act also put American expansionism at risk. Leland Stanford—senator, farmer, and railroad tycoon—observed: "There are four hundred millions of people over in China and, by all ordinary rights we ought to be cultivating a trade with them that is eventually to grow to immense proportions." Stanford argued that the new refrigerated railroads and steamships could transport goods from the East, through California, to China, but, he insisted, "we need the Chinese here to work in our fields, vineyards and orchards and gather our fruit and do the common labor of the country. I do not know what we would do without them."[24]

With the deadline just days off, Secretary of the Treasury J. G. Carlisle ordered state district attorneys and Bureau of Internal Revenue collectors to stop making arrests until arrangements for the "imprisonment and deportation" could be perfected.[25] The government was also trapped in a legal paradox: imprisonment required conviction by jury, but deportation did not.

As the tense spring wore on, Chinese immigrants developed new ways to resist the Dog Tag Law, and the government invented new ways to expel them. The Six Companies launched strict boycotts against any Chinese merchant who had registered or who had provided translators to the government, denouncing them as collaborators. They also filed complaints for health violations against any restaurant owner or butcher who had registered. On most days, fewer than ten or twelve Chinese residents in San Francisco sought certification. In rural towns, Internal Revenue posted the dates when they would arrive for registration, but agents soon realized that many Chinese showed up with flawed papers containing identical technical errors. By omitting information or providing irregular photographs, the Chinese successfully frustrated the revenue officials; compliance seemed impossible.

With the deadline only days away, it appeared that the Chinese had won. Only 1,000 of the 15,000 Chinese in Oregon and Washington had obeyed the Geary Act; in California fewer than 900 of the close to 100,000 had complied.[26] No Chinese residents registered in the Oregon towns of Albany, Salem, McMinnville, or Corvallis. But taking no chances, on May 1, the Six Companies "placarded" all of the Chinatowns in Oregon, forbidding the Chinese to obey the law:

> FROM THE SIX COMPANIES TO OUR CHINESE BRETHREN IN ASTORIA—YOU ARE FORBIDDEN TO REGISTER WITH THE WHITE OFFICIALS OR TO HAVE ANYTHING TO DO WITH THEM. OUR IMPERIAL GOVERNMENT IS WATCHING THIS MATTER AND PROTECTING OUR PEOPLE. WE HAVE ENGAGED MR. RIOR-

DAN, THE SAN FRANCISCO LAWYER, AND ANOTHER IN SAN FRANCISCO, ONE IN WASHINGTON, THE UNITED STATES CAPITAL, AND ONE IN NEW YORK. ON THE 5TH OF MAY FOUR PROMINENT CHINESE BROTHERS IN NEW YORK ARE TO BE ARRESTED BY THE GOVERNMENT FOR NOT REGISTERING AND THEIR CASE WILL BE TRIED BY ONE OF THE HIGH COURTS OF THE COUNTRY ON THE 12TH OF MAY. OUR MINISTER HAS ASKED THE PRESIDENT OF THE UNITED STATES NOT TO ARREST ANY OTHER CHINAMEN IN THIS COUNTRY BECAUSE THEY DID NOT REGISTER UNTIL THIS CASE IS TRIED. THE AMERICAN PRESIDENT HAS GRACIOUSLY SAID, 'LET THIS BE SO.' YOU WILL THEREFORE NOT REGISTER, UNDER HEAVIEST PENALTIES IF YOU DISOBEY.

By Order of the Six Companies.[27] [translation]

Still, the Chinese were afraid that the government would find a way to initiate mass arrests and deportations. Wong Chin Foo and Tom Yuen of the Chinese Equal Rights League in San Francisco wired President Cleveland: "We fear the State of Oregon as fugitive slaves feared South Carolina, and we will look upon Cleveland and his party for protection as the Negroes looked upon Lincoln."[28]

Two days before the end of legal certification, telegrams flew from the desk of Secretary of State Walter Gresham warning of danger to the Chinese. At the direction of President Cleveland, Gresham put the governors, in particular Henry Markham of California, on notice to protect the Chinese.[29] The Chinese minister urged Cleveland to provide military protection for the Chinese and stop arrests until the Supreme Court ruled on the law. But Gresham announced that the Department of State would not intervene if an anti-Chinese riot occurred. If local safeguards were inadequate, he said, the duty to defend the Chinese would fall to the Department of War. Yet during the violence that was indeed to come, the Department of War stayed away.

At four in the afternoon on Friday, May 5, the books closed on registration, and the Bureau of Internal Revenue claimed that more than 2,000 of the 28,000 Chinese living in San Francisco had registered. But in fact, the posters, meetings, and warnings of the Six Companies had paid off. In San

Diego, only 15 Chinese had registered; in Los Angeles County, the number was 103 out of 5,000. In Sacramento a "handful" registered; in Chicago 945 of 2,500 registered. The results were clear: the Chinese in the United States would not comply.

As the deadline for registration drew closer, the leaders of the Six Companies urged their members to rush to San Francisco to fortify Chinatown in case Geary was ruled unconstitutional. Wrote *The New York Times,* if it did not occur to Californians that the Geary Act "represented a persecution of a proud and spirited race,"[30] the danger was clear to the Chinese. Ow Yang King, secretary to the Chinese consul general, warned that even in areas with few Chinese residents, such as small mining towns in Montana, the "rough element" was threatening to take the law into their own hands if the Geary Act did not survive. The Six Companies proclaimed they and their countrymen would never let themselves be "tagged like dogs."[31]

THE TEST

May 5, 1893, the deadline for registration, came and went. The next morning on Mott Street in New York's Chinatown, two Chinese laborers, Wong Quan and Fong Yue Ting, and laundryman Lee Joe, chosen in advance by the Six Companies, stepped out of a crowd of concerned Chinese and were arrested by U.S. Marshal John Jacobus for the crime of being Chinese laborers without certificates of residence. Wong Quan and Fong Yue Ting were also charged with failing to apply for residential permits, and Lee, who had tried to register, was charged with presenting himself for certification with Chinese witnesses rather than "one credible white witness." The arrest was monitored by the attaché from the Chinese legation, the Chinese vice consul, and a crowd of reporters and well-known constitutional lawyers.

The lawsuit *Fong Yue Ting* v. *United States et al.* was initiated by the Chinese in an attempt to defeat the Geary Act in court. Judge Addison Brown of the United States District Court in New York immediately ordered the three men deported, set their bail at five hundred dollars, and remanded them to the U.S. Marshals Service. Fong Yue Ting and Wong Quan declared that their arrests were unconstitutional and that they had been in the country for thirteen years and had always planned to make their home in the United

States. They immediately sought habeas corpus petitions. Two days later, San Francisco attorney Tom Riordan appealed their deportation order to the Supreme Court.

Fong Yue Ting raised questions critical to Chinese Americans and to all other immigrants. Its implications were prescient. Did Congress have unfettered power over aliens within the borders of the United States? Did Congress have the right to expel foreigners regardless of treaty obligations? Were Chinese immigrants, by virtue of their long residence, "denizens"—midway between citizens and transient aliens? Did the Geary Act violate the Fourteenth Amendment's prohibition against the taking of property or liberty without due process? Could an immigrant be denied the right to challenge the ruling of a customs officer in court? Did the Geary Act violate Fifth and Sixth Amendment protections when it permitted imprisonment with hard labor without a prior indictment or jury trial? Under the Geary Act, who was a merchant and who was a laborer? Was a launderer a laborer? Finally, did deportation itself, "transportation for life," constitute cruel and unusual punishment and violate the Eighth Amendment?

The Supreme Court took only five days to rule on the case. Before a stunned crowd the Court announced a 5–3 decision to sustain the Geary Act.

The Court ruled that if, as a sovereign nation, the United States had the power to exclude any person or any race it wished, it must also have the power to deport any person or any race it wished. The court concluded that in passing the Geary Act, Congress was simply enjoying its unrestricted power to deal with resident aliens. In the majority opinion, Justice Horace Gray outlined a new and draconian vision for how the American government could treat Chinese residents: "No formal proceedings are required and none is necessary."

The full burden of proof now fell to the Chinese. Testimony, said Gray, would be based on race: to prove he has "resided in the country, he must produce one credible white witness." Under naturalization laws, he added, Congress had the power to determine what witnesses could be subpoenaed. If a law was inconsistent with a treaty, the "law-making power" prevailed.

The Court thus declared that China could do nothing to save the Chinese. Local police or immigration officers could now proceed toward deportation "without trial of any sort." Because the purpose of the arrests was for deportation rather than imprisonment, a Chinese immigrant had no constitutional right to a trial by jury or to protection against unfair and un-

THE QUESTION OF THE HOUR: *Uncle Sam:*—Gosh! I've got this critter lassoed right enough but how in thunder am I going to git him over thar to China?

THE WASP, 1893

usual punishment. "It is not banishment, in the sense [of] the expulsion of a citizen from his country by way of punishment," explained Gray. Deportation was simply a means of forcing an alien who did not comply with the conditions of immigration to return to his own country: "He has not, therefore, been deprived of life, liberty, or property, without due process of law." Constitutional protections, wrote Gray, "have no application."

Particularly troubling was the power the Supreme Court gave Congress to decide who was a "person," undermining the Fourteenth Amendment's protections for "all persons."[32] Because the Chinese were no longer "persons," they lost any "absolute right to remain."[33] The ruling could not have been more devastating for the Chinese.

Justice Stephen J. Field and his nephew and fellow justice, David J. Brewer, dissented, stating that "brutality, inhumanity, and cruelty cannot be made elements in any procedure for the enforcement of the laws of the United States." If Gray had his way, they said, "Congress might have ordered the executive officers to take the Chinese laborers to the ocean and put them in a boat and set them adrift."

Field was prophetic about what would happen if the Court abandoned the rights of immigrants of any nationality, and hence, of any race. Wrote Field, "It will surprise most people to learn that any such dangerous and despotic power lies in our Government which will authorize it to expel at pleasure in times of peace whole bodies of friendly foreigners of any country" who are here by our own permission. The *Fong Yue Ting* decision, said Field, makes it possible for Congress, "at its pleasure [to] expel at any time the Irish, German, French and English people."[34]

Justice Brewer also condemned the majority for trampling on the Constitution: "It is not possible that any law can be put into effect that shall take property from the people within our border for which compensation is not given." In Brewer's view, deportation "is a deprivation of liberty and a removal from home, family, business and property. This can be considered nothing less than punishment of the severest nature."

In California, many towns celebrated the surprising victory. Los Angeles, Santa Rosa, San Rafael, and Santa Cruz held parades and fired antique cannons. But federal officials were daunted by the economic and logistical implications of *Fong Yue Ting.* Democratic attorney general Richard Olney reported that it would cost $6 million to deport unregistered Chinese, and he had only $16,806 left in his fund.[35] About one third of the Chinese in the United States had entered illegally, and they would face immediate deportation if they tried to register. Unless thousands of Chinese either voluntarily registered or left for countries such as Cuba or Brazil, which wanted their labor, the ruling would bankrupt the government.[36]

How to now purge the hundred thousand Chinese laborers living in the United States? Even though a federal judge in southern California ordered the mass evictions to proceed, Congress appropriated no money to enforce the law. It simply extended the registration deadline for another six months and then recessed for the summer.

The Chinese government was stunned. Toward the end of May, China informed the U.S. State Department that if any actions were taken under the Geary Act, all relations with China—diplomatic and commercial—would terminate. All Americans in China would be forced to leave, and trade would end. Rumors flew through Shanghai and Canton that American missionaries were about to be deported.

The situation for President Cleveland was perplexing and embarrassing. He was well aware of the economic implications of China's warning. During 1892, a year of desperate unemployment and economic collapse,

U.S. exports to China had totaled more than $15 million, while imports from China were just $4 million, of which $879,000 was for opium.

Cleveland, too, was surprised by the Court's decision. Suddenly his reputation with China was seriously undermined. He certainly did not expect the overseas Chinese to leave voluntarily. Many Americans held to the notion that each Chinese person was still entitled to a jury trial, and Cleveland knew that enforcing the Geary Act would clog the courts for five to six years. The Chinese had also made it absolutely clear that they would not pay for their own deportation. Neither would the Chinese Six Companies or the Chinese consulate. And Cleveland faced intense pressure from missionizing churches not to arrest or prosecute unregistered Chinese.

Fong Yue Ting launched a summer of political instability and legal confusion. Within two weeks the Chinese consuls and the Six Companies initiated a second test case in the New York Circuit Court. This court allowed the Chinese to be deported for failure to register or carry identity cards if "proper provision" for payment was available. Without funds, the Geary Act was, for the present, moot. Local Internal Revenue agents were instructed not to make arrests unless Congress funded the act.[37]

Meanwhile, because the Six Companies had confidently predicted that the Supreme Court would overturn the Geary Act, they lost a great deal of authority within the Chinese community. The Court's ruling unleashed tensions among the companies, and internecine riots broke out in Chinatowns throughout the United States.

CHINESE WOMEN UNDER THE GEARY ACT

To provide some measure of legal cover for themselves and their children, Chinese women had a strong incentive to register under the Geary Act. Forty runaway prostitutes and their five children signed for identity certificates at the Chinese Christian Mission in San Francisco, where they were examined, measured, questioned, and photographed.[38] And to protect an "asset" worth anywhere from five hundred to five thousand dollars, owners of enslaved prostitutes also wanted to make sure that the women remained in the United States. These merchants invited Internal Revenue officers to register women at the brothels.[39] Having the prostitutes sign up for identity cards in their "domiciles" stopped them from using the outing as a chance to flee.

The implementation of the Geary Act reveals how the American legal system endorsed the prostitution of Chinese women. When some Chinese men complained that the registration process was "promiscuous" because it forced men and women into one public space, the Bureau of Internal Revenue agreed to register Chinese women privately, at a photographer's shop or even at their homes. But the private registration of prostitutes upheld the deliberate confusion between legitimate and sham marriages that funneled enslaved babies, girls, and women into the United States.

The U.S. government estimated that in the 1890s, nearly half of the two thousand women in San Francisco's Chinatown were "in bondage." Some, called *muey chay,* had been "leased" or indentured by impoverished parents to work as servants and nannies for Chinese merchants until they reached marriageable age. But the majority were enslaved prostitutes, sold by their fathers, kidnapped or decoyed by procurers, shipped to Hong Kong or Macao, and from there exported to the United States, which they entered, often with bribes to customs officials, as merchants' wives or daughters.

The identity cards, mailed by the hundreds to China, facilitated these bogus "marriages" by providing legal immigration papers. Women and young girls were dragged off boats and taken, often under a prearranged writ of habeas corpus, to an American judge, who signed a new certificate with a current photograph. Sometimes an immigrant girl was carried to a rural town, with her registration certificate handed from vendor to vendor.[40] In one case, a husband sent a certificate to a woman in China, based on a contract for their engagement signed when they were infants. Although the court noted that "there was . . . danger of imposition" to the woman, she was allowed to enter the country as the man's wife.[41]

THE SUMMER OF 1893: VIGILANTES, VIOLENCE, AND VIOLATIONS

With the enforcement of the Geary Act in limbo, "implementation" fell to vigilantes. Judge E. R. Ross of the U.S. District Court proved their powerful ally, as time and again he legalized the roundups. The Federated Trades of Los Angeles filed the first affidavit to deport unregistered Chinese cooks and cigar rollers when it compelled the Internal Revenue commissioner to issue a warrant for Wong Dep Ken, a cigar maker. Aware that Congress had provided no money to enforce the act, the U.S. district attorney tried to stall. On August 11, 1893, Judge Ross held that imprisoning Wong Dep Ken and forcing him to perform "hard labor at San Quentin" was unconstitutional, but deporting him was legal. An armed U.S. marshal escorted him from Los Angeles to the Port of San Francisco and put him onboard the steamship *Río de Janeiro* bound for Hong Kong.[42] Wong Dep Ken became the first deportee under the Geary Act.[43]

During August and September, buoyed by the Supreme Court's verdict, fierce roundups struck the hot and fertile Central Valley, as unemployed white men from the West and Midwest sought work in the vineyards, orchards, canneries, packing sheds, box factories, and fruit dryers. With white labor now available, many local farmers, fearing for their own safety, fired their Chinese employees and expelled their Chinese tenants.

In farming communities and agricultural towns from the South to the West, members of the Populist Party and the Federated Trades resolved to purge the Chinese who, by the thousands, were now planting, pruning, and harvesting California's crops. Within two months of the *Fong Yue Ting* ruling, a riot broke out in Atlanta, Georgia's Chinatown after several Chinese registered and deposited their photographs at the federal courthouse, indicating their intention to remain in the United States.[44]

Mass violence came to the remote mountain town of Como, Colorado, where Chinese miners were searching for placer gold in the high meadows. On August 1, 1893, hearing of threats, they barricaded themselves in their cabins, but at midnight a white mob lit the fire. Surprised that the local fire department doused the flames, the enraged gang used logs to batter in the doors and again set fire to the light-frame buildings. This time the cabins quickly burned to the ground. The mob robbed two Chinese laundrymen who were known to serve as bankers for their community as they fled their homes. With their Chinatown scorched, many miners left Como.[45]

In San Francisco and Sacramento, local labor unions demanded that U.S. marshals begin mass arrests of all unregistered Chinese. With funding uncertain, the marshals, for a time, refused.

On the same day as the Colorado fire, an outbreak of fires charred the town of Fresno, leveling several mills and packinghouses, not all of which employed Chinese workers.[46] The chief of police received anonymous letters warning that if he wanted to protect the rest of the town, he had better drive out all the Chinese. Two weeks later, on the dry, hot morning of August 14, a spontaneous anti-Chinese rally erupted downtown. Many in the crowd were unemployed miners who had drifted west from Idaho, Montana, and Nevada. To clear the streets of five hundred angry, hungry, and destitute men, a businessman started an anti-Chinese rally in Kutner Hall. Farmers flocked in to assure the crowd that they would hire white laborers as soon as the Chinese field-workers were gone.

The rally broke up to canvas the town's shops and demand that the merchants make the same promise. Afraid of the mob that was overtaking the town, several owners of packinghouses and vineyards quickly agreed to fire their Chinese staffs. That night many Chinese field-workers took refuge in Fresno's Chinatown. By the next evening, demands for a Chinese roundup had spread to Bakersfield.

On the night of August 15, rioters invaded the vineyards near Fresno. Yet another white mob raided the Fracher Creek Nursery, captured the Chinese workers, stole their money and belongings, and killed a Chinese man with a blow to his head. Under guard, the nursery workers were marched toward Fresno in the valley heat when the sheriff came upon the hostages and released them. That week Chinese packers at the nearby Earl Fruit Company were forced onto the train to Fresno, where they were given five days to leave the county.[47] Gangs forced Chinese men out of the local vineyards and destroyed their tent camps; hundreds of unemployed white workers and vagrants milled around Fresno's streets and watched the Chinese depart.

The vigilantes realized that local authorities would do little stop them. In Madera the county sheriff urged ranchers and farmers in the "raisin district" to fire all the Chinese harvesters. By August 17 hundreds of Chinese had left the orchards and vineyards, trying to hide in Chinatown but often assaulted as they fled the fields. The anarchy in the Central Valley continued.

On August 30, three bombs exploded, killing one man at the house of Sam Lee, a leading Chinese merchant. The owner of a large vineyard quickly fired three hundred Chinese farmworkers and replaced them with young white boys brought in from San Francisco to work for fifty cents a day. The children assaulted any Chinese who tried to remain.

The roundups did not solve the crisis of massive unemployment. Even after the purges, there were few jobs for whites. Hunger exacerbated the riots. Toward the end of August, Fresno's Presbyterian church was nightly providing eight hundred meals to white men, some of whom had not eaten for days. The city council's plan to give meal tickets to "idle men" for cleaning alleys failed when it ran out of money. The supervisors moved some of the "tramps and ruffians" out of town by forming them into chain gangs to clear roads or do field work.[48]

In a change from the roundups of the 1880s, however, local farmers and businessmen united to protect their harvest, their machinery, and their field-workers. More than one hundred ranchers and farmers set up a system of telephone scouts to spread the word about vigilante actions, and they demanded that the sheriff protect their Chinese employees.

But soon farmers had little money to hire harvesters of any race; whatever work was available went to whites. With the harvest under way, the packinghouses also gave preference to new white workers over experienced Chinese, whose complaints were met with threats of deportation. Businesses failed. The mines at Copperopolis, which employed three hundred men, closed abruptly. White miners who for over a decade had lived in the town owned by the Union Pacific Railroad were suddenly homeless, on the road with their wives and children, trudging fifteen miles toward the nearest railroad, in Millville.

That summer pogroms erupted throughout the Central Valley. On September 1, in the small farming town of Selma, a posse of forty men drove out all the Chinese residents. That night the Chinese returned. The next day a vigilante rang Selma's fire bell and, as the police watched, a mob marched to Chinatown, broke down doors, and pulled the Chinese from their homes. As dozens of whites marched the Chinese toward Fresno, others plundered their houses and businesses. Finally the police opened fire with Winchester rifles and captured some of the rioters. The Chinese slowly hiked back to Selma, where they found the mob still pillaging their homes and most of their belongings destroyed or stolen.

Cries for deportation spread to the cities. In Sacramento, Antone Menke fired all his Chinese hop pickers and replaced them with two hundred white men, women, and children. In Tulare, Paige's Orchards dismissed all the Chinese and Japanese workers and hired whites in their places. After a mass demonstration in Stockton, farmers ordered Chinese workers off the fields.

In Bakersfield, a desperate and hungry army of unemployed rallied and declared: "Be it resolved by the citizens of Bakersfield and Kern County, in mass meeting assembled, that we are strongly in favor of all legal measure looking to the deportation in accordance with the Geary Act of such Chinese as may be in our midst."[49] Some hundred destitute men a day drifted into town seeking food and work, and an army of unemployed men milled about in the streets.

Local leaders and business owners tried to alleviate the hunger. The Kern County Board of Supervisors offered a meal ticket to any man who spent two hours cleaning the streets. Local raisin growers secretly agreed to give hiring preference to white men, offering wages of 75 cents a day with board or $1.15 without, undercutting the Chinese, who refused to work for less than $1.40. The police force added twenty-five men, but the sheriff feared that he would never be able to control the anti-Chinese forces. Governor Markham agreed to call out the state guard.[50] Sensing the danger facing Chinese field-workers, the Six Companies urged the Chinese leaders in Bakersfield to come at once to San Francisco, where the companies would begin legal efforts to claim damages and demand reparations.[51]

By late summer 1893, anti-Chinese violence had broken out from Ontario, Huron, Tulare, and Vacaville up to Calistoga in the Napa Valley. In Saratoga farmers canvassed cheap hotels, where they found destitute white men living on one meal a day. Now these men were willing to take the field and cannery jobs of three hundred Chinese and Japanese men.[52] Hundreds of unemployed white workers in Vacaville rallied and demanded that all employers replace their Chinese workers with whites.

During the last week of August, Chinese field-workers on ranches near Redlands in southern California received night visits at their cabins. Many whites—both strangers and friends—warned them to leave the valley, as mass violence seemed imminent. On the night of August 31, under the watch of the city marshal, two hundred white men marched to Chinatown and told the Chinese to leave within forty-eight hours. But the Chinese had purchased guns and ammunition at the local hardware stores and were prepared to take their stand at two brick buildings in town. Expecting a race war, the sheriffs in Bakersfield and Redlands implored the governor to mobilize the National Guard, but he only alerted local units of possible trouble. Rather than defend the Chinese from assault, a U.S. marshal ordered the arrests of all Chinese men not yet registered under the Geary Act.[53]

In the Napa Valley, on August 17, a mob beat up Chinese laborers as they fled the plum and prune orchards. On September 2, surrounded by the National Guard, the Chinese faced an armed gang in San Bernardino. Unsure whose side the guard would take, they barricaded themselves in their houses all night, ultimately defending themselves with guns and knives. In nearby Mentone, when the Chinese laundrymen refused a gang's order to abandon their washhouses, twenty-five men brutally forced the men to march two miles outside the town limits. The mob stole their belongings and warned them never to return.

Attorney Thomas Riordan telegraphed county sheriff J. P. Booth to demand protection for the Mentone Chinese, but the sheriff wired back, "There has been no violence offered the Chinese at Redlands or Mentone yet . . . the few who were driven off the farms left quietly and peacefully."[54]

In early autumn, riots again spilled into Redlands. On September 1, following a week of anti-Chinese rallies, night raiders broke into Chinese camps in the orange groves. The next day, Governor Markham summoned the National Guard and two hundred deputies patrolled Redlands. Chinatown's electricity was cut as the town was put under martial law, which would last for several days. Unconcerned about the presence of the guard, anti-Chinese leaders announced that a mob would attack Chinatown at eight o'clock.[55]

Redland's elected officials decided they could avoid mob violence by expelling the Chinese. Businessmen submitted the names of all the Chinese who worked or lived in Redlands, and the U.S. district court judge immediately issued warrants for all Chinese still harvesting and packing lemons and oranges.[56] On September 3, the city announced that it would issue warrants for the arrest of all 170 Chinese residents by the next day.[57] But the vigilantes could not wait to raid Chinatown, and that night they set fire to several buildings and looted the shops and the tills. Although the police arrested eleven rioters, none was convicted. The *Pacific Rural Press,* the newspaper for the Grange movement, blamed the attacks on men's "beastly taste for violence and plunder."[58] Anti-Chinese violence spread in the farming areas of Riverside, Selma, Fresno, Vacaville, Madera, Stockton, Bakersfield, Compton, and San Bernardino.

Race violence struck Oregon as well. In Butteville, where hundreds of Chinese were picking hops, two Chinese cabins were blown up, and on September 4, seventy-five white men forced the Chinese from the hop ranches, dragged them to the river, and shoved them onto a boat bound for Portland.

The federal government would neither stop the race war in the West nor pay to deport thousands of Chinese. U.S. attorney general Richard Olney advised the courts that as there were no funds to enforce the Geary

Act, all Chinese being held in local jails should be released; further trials and deportations must await a congressional appropriation. At the same time, Judge Ross announced that he would not tolerate further delays or continuances and would try all deportation cases immediately.

Demands for warrants for the 170 unregistered Chinese men from Redlands were sent to Judge Ross; the district attorney selected twelve for test cases. Members of the Cahuenga Farmers Association announced that if Ross dismissed these cases for lack of funds, they would pay for the deportations themselves, which they estimated at about thirty dollars per person. As the farmers protested that white "anarchists" were taking over the courts, California senator Stephen M. White vowed to push a large enough appropriation through Congress to pay for the deportation of the Chinese.[59]

The purge of the Chinese from California's fields, citrus groves, and orchards made the overall economic situation even more desperate. Fresno's labor bureau had the names of more than six hundred men looking for work, but farmers and nurserymen knew their crops would perish if unskilled laborers replaced the Chinese in skilled jobs, such as "budders" of fruit trees. Banks closed and local stores went out of business.

By early autumn, a meeting of seven hundred armed men in Redlands demanded that farmers immediately fire the Chinese pickers and packers who were arriving for the harvest. A gang of two hundred marched to the Chinese tent camp and warned the men that they had forty-eight hours to get out. In the Cahuenga Valley, small farmers hoping to seize a share of the winter vegetable market from Chinese tenant farmers insisted that the sheriff arrest and deport their Chinese competitors. The sheriff complied, arresting five Chinese vegetable growers and holding them in the county jail. Alarmed by the recent warrants from Judge Ross and fearing expulsion, hundreds of Chinese farmers and field-workers fled the valley.[60] In Santa Monica, it took only one day for the Los Angeles constable and a "gang of frolickers" to clear the beach community of its Chinese residents.

THE CITIZEN'S ARREST

On August 30, 1893, in Los Angeles, Judge Ross "set the Geary Law in motion" when he "regretfully" ruled in favor of a white farmer who made a citizen's arrest of Ah Wong, a field-worker who had not obtained an identity certificate. The effect of Ross's decision was far-reaching: any private citizen could now swear out a complaint against an unregistered Chinese person, and the court would issue a warrant for arrest and deportation.

Ross acknowledged the lack of money to enforce his decision, and he also expressed a fear that sentencing a man to a penitentiary at hard labor for failure to register constituted unreasonable detention, but nonetheless, he demanded enforcement.[61] A congressional appropriation of just fifty thousand dollars, he argued, could launch the deportation process if "common folk" were encouraged to take the law into their own hands.

Immediately after Ross read his decision, the office of Los Angeles County district attorney George Denis was flooded with warrants for the arrests of Chinese men from Redlands and San Bernardino. Denis hoped that the forced deportation of just a few Chinese immigrants would prompt a voluntary "hegira of Chinamen." In Los Angeles, Chinese cooks targeted by the Labor Trades Cooks Union immediately quit both the Natick House hotel and the Cosmopolitan Restaurant and hid in Chinatown. Chinese laborers fled the Cahuenga Valley toward less hostile counties in the north. Within two days of the Ross decision, twenty-six citizen's warrants were issued in Los Angeles County, and the district attorney estimated that the courts could handle six Chinese cases a day. The *Los Angeles Evening Express* headlined triumphantly, EXODUS BEGINS.[62]

Ross's extraordinary decision legalized grassroots racial violence. Selma endured days of attacks on Chinese field-workers; all of the houses in Chinatown were looted, and three thousand dollars in Chinese savings disappeared. Arsonists tried to burn Chinatown by torching an empty freight car on a nearby track. Within days, most of Selma's Chinese fled, many for Riverside, only to be met by members of trade unions bearing citizen's warrants against them. Ranch by ranch, small groups of Chinese fled from Redlands and San Bernardino, seeking refuge in Riverside's Chinatown. A citizens committee from Redlands secured a large number of blank warrants from the court, and the Cahuenga Farmers Association quickly served them on Chinese tenant farmers.[63]

The Los Angeles County jail soon was filled to capacity. A local attorney said he could easily "clean" the city of Chinese if the courts would only try the cases as fast as the Chinese men were arrested.[64] The surge of citizen's arrests lasted through the early fall of 1893. Across the state, hundreds of unregistered Chinese waited in county jails for processing, while the Chinese Six Companies and the Chinese consul general scrambled to delay deportations. As large growers, such as hop ranchers in Oregon, pleaded with their Chinese employees to stay, white vigilantes pressed on, tracking down Chinese men and making more citizen's arrests.[65]

Convolutions and contradictions in the law made deportations difficult. Ross ruled that the Chinese could only be imprisoned if they committed a crime. Unregistered Chinese, he inconsistently observed, were not criminals and could not be imprisoned—only deported. But to hold them for deportation, they first had to be arrested. When they were arrested and imprisoned, Ross refused to issue bail. He also declared that if for any reason, such as a lack of jail space or a lack of funds, a U.S. marshal released a Chinese person following a citizen's arrest, the marshal would be guilty of contempt of court. But, if the marshal did not release the Chinese prisoner, he was liable for damages.

Judge Ross created mass confusion. Chinese prisoners, waiting in crowded jails with neither trials nor deportation hearings in the offing, were suing town marshals for false imprisonment and appealing their habeas corpus status to the Supreme Court. Meanwhile, deportations remained at a standstill even as more counties and townships, such as Santa Barbara, announced that the Chinese must go.

On September 26, U.S. Marshal Gard announced that there were no more funds to enforce deportations. The banks refused to lend him money. The railroad companies would no longer transport Chinese prisoners without pay up front. The Pacific Mail Steamship Company demanded full steerage rates. Gard had personally "caused" the deportation of at least 120 Chinese men, and with hundreds more waiting in county jails, he had no funds to proceed.[66] But Judge Ross's "deportation mill" continued and the treasury found a paltry sixty-three thousand dollars for him to carry on, for the moment.

Ross's decision to allow citizen's arrests was read by the major papers as legal permission for roundups. The anti-Chinese *San Francisco Examiner* announced with glee, "The attempt of the administration to nullify the Geary law has come to a sudden end in this State." The *San Francisco Morning Call* declared Ross's decision a "stimulus to arrest unregistered Mongolians . . . in spite of influences sedulously exerted in Washington." The *Riverside Enterprise* cheered, "Altogether yesterday was a great day in Federal Court at Los Angeles for the friends of labor. It is to be hoped that the good work will now go forward without any new legal hitch. And, by the way, why should not Riverside take a hand at this deporting business?"[67]

The Six Companies warned the Chinese to beware: the Geary Act would now be enforced in the streets. Anti-coolie clubs in the Bay Area and the Sacramento delta received hundreds of blank warrants from federal judges. Chinese immigrants near Fresno and Redlands fled to the hills and were captured on trails, fighting to hold on to their coins and gold. In Los Angeles, District Attorney George Denis promised to issue warrants as fast as the district court could dispose of the cases.[68]

Even as California faced the constitutional, financial, and practical issues of the citizen's arrests, Attorney General Olney ordered that deportations continue, but Governor Markham warned that "an outbreak may occur at any moment unless assurances are given [in] Washington that the laws of the United States . . . are carried into effect within reasonable time."[69]

Markham's prediction soon came true. Violence followed each of Ross's decisions. In Fresno, while making citizen's arrests, a mob killed two Chinese vineyard workers. Vigilantes terrorized ranches, firing into Chinese bunkhouses, assaulting farmworkers with clubs and knives, and "arresting" as many as they could.

Legal, economic, and social chaos reigned along the West Coast. In Tulare, four masked men beat up Chinese vegetable peddlers and stole their savings, even after they produced registration certificates. In Los Angeles, Judge Ross continued to rush through deportation orders, hearing as many as eight cases an hour. And applications for citizen's warrants, particularly from Redlands and the Cahuenga Valley, poured into offices of the United States attorneys.

AMERICANS IN CHINA

American missionaries and merchants in China, fearing retaliation, telegraphed United States officials to stop targeting the overseas Chinese. The Reverend Dr. J. S. Baldwin, who served on the board of a Methodist church that had vast "moneyed interests" in China, wrote that

Chinese viceroys had told him that they would defend their nation's "honor and dignity" by treating Americans residing in China just as America treated Chinese residing in the United States.[70]

In the spring of 1893, more than three hundred American missionaries lived in Peking, Chofoo, Shanghai, Canton, and Hainan, supported by Methodist, Presbyterian, Baptist, Episcopalian, Congregationalist, and the Reformed churches, all of whom hoped to increase their numbers dramatically.[71] Reports that hundreds of Chinese immigrants had been "wantonly massacred" in the United States under the Geary Act led the U.S. Board of Missions to warn overseas missionaries that "exaggerated reports will get out in China" and that the Chinese "populace will do injury" to them before the government can step in and prevent it.

The race war in the Pacific Northwest was causing a diplomatic crisis. A dispatch from Shanghai reported that Viceroy Li Hung-chang had just petitioned the emperor for the right to "exterminate" all foreigners in China. The Reverend C. A. Daniels of the Congregational Board of Foreign Missions well understood the parallel: "The exclusion of Americans from China would affect us seriously," he declared. "We own a large amount of property and have many missions in the field. We fear retaliation greatly. Our missionaries in China have been outspoken against the Geary Act, and I hope the Chinese will realize this if trouble comes."[72]

Yet the government of China also knew that American churches spent close to one million dollars a year in China. The missions sent a series of delegations to Congress and to President Cleveland begging for the repeal of the "Geary Chinese Exclusion Law"[73] and set aside special days of prayer to protect their interests in China.[74] What's more, they declared, the Geary Act did not live up to biblical teachings about the treatment of strangers.[75]

CLEVELAND, CONGRESS, AND CHINA

The Chinese government sent urgent telegraphs and communiqués to Secretary of State Walter Gresham, demanding protection for the Chinese in Fresno, Kern, and Tulare Counties. The Chinese consulate warned the United States to expect violent retribution against American missionaries and reiterated that American Christian missions were most unwelcome. The General Electric Company, seeking a foothold in China, also put pressure on Gresham to not enforce the Geary Act.[76]

But the Geary Act had become a test of the Democrats' commitment to white labor. President Cleveland knew that he owed his reelection to California, but he had backed away from a virulent anti-Chinese stance. He had rejected the Bureau of Internal Revenue's plan to round up the Chinese, hold them in "inclosures," and photograph them, because, he declared, he could not stomach the idea of "herding human beings like sheep and branding them like cattle." Reflecting the national divide, *The New York Times* suggested that if California's Democratic Party was willing to subvert the Constitution with a bill that took away "at a blow, without notice, the rights of persons who put to sea . . . trusting in the seal of the United States," it would receive very little support in the East.[77]

Cleveland believed that the Geary Act was unenforceable, but he was afraid to call for its repeal. He met daily with Chinese representatives, trying to persuade them to accept a deal by which the overseas Chinese could register without retribution. Soon he would submit his annual budget to Congress, and the nation wondered: would the president request funds to implement the Geary Act?[78] Unexpected help came from Congress in the form of the Foreign Affairs and Appropriations Committees, which opposed the Geary Act and would take the political fall for Cleveland's ambivalence.[79]

By September 1893, only $17,000 remained in the account to deport 110,000 Chinese residents, roughly 15 cents for each individual deportation. But no one could agree on the costs. The Treasury Department estimated that $75 was needed to move one Chinese resident to San Francisco, $35 to transport him to China, and 40 cents to feed him—and it argued that it would take $1 million to expel all the Chinese from the United States. Others set the total at $6 million. Whatever the cost, President Cleveland found no agreement on who the Geary Act meant to deport. Who was a merchant, laborer, or gambler? Should photographs be required? And should the government spend so much money in the midst of an economic depression? How could Cleveland protect missionaries in China? Would white laborers and mechanics really take jobs as farmworkers?

Congress scrambled to buy time. Pressured and confused, President Cleveland finally decided that trade with China was more important than the strict enforcement of the Geary Act. He announced a sudden halt to the arrests until Congress decided whether to repeal, amend, or fund the Geary Act at $6 million.[80]

At the same time, China became tepid about the plight of refugees and deportees in the United States. By late October 1893, China had failed to ask the United States to extend the time for registration,[81] which freed Congress to appropriate funds, in small amounts, to enforce the deportation act.[82] Under pressure from missionary organizations, as well as from the railroads that owned much of the fertile land in California, Congress decided to take a gamble.

Representative James McCreary from Kentucky introduced an amendment to the Geary Act that would, in the end, confine and limit the Chinese experience in the United States. Congress had voted to extend the registration deadline, hoping that without China's opposition, the Chinese would comply. But McCreary predicted that three judges would still need twelve to fifteen years to adjudicate the cases. His amendment undid cherished civil liberties: it reaffirmed that a Chinese person was now guilty until proven innocent; it denied the right to bail and the right of habeas corpus; it discontinued all legal appeals under the Geary Act; it required all classes of skilled and unskilled manual laborers to register; it revived the photograph requirement.[83] McCreary hoped that most Chinese would either register or flee to Cuba, Canada, or Mexico.[84] But of most significance to Cleveland, the McCreary amendment granted Chinese immigrants six more months, until May 1894, to register. On November 3, 1893, Cleveland signed it into law.[85]

Quietly, China stood behind the McCreary amendment. The Chinese minister mildly complained to Secretary Gresham that McCreary's solution of a simple extension was a "great disappointment." Then he urged the secretary of state to draft a new treaty that would allow identity cards, ban Chinese immigration, and open trade, all in order to "protect against the antagonism and deplorable disorder."[86]

Having passed the amendment, Congress never came through with enough money to do the job. Over the next few years it appropriated several hundred thousand dollars to cover the costs of registration, arrests, and imprisonment. But estimates for the total deportation of the Chinese in America remained at $6 to $7 million.[87]

"RACE WAR IMMINENT"

By late spring 1894, the extension period was coming to an end. Voluntary registration would expire on May 3.[88] What would happen after the deadline? And what would stop the race war in the West? The shadows of mob violence in the South fell on California. Throughout 1892 and 1893, California newspapers excitedly reported the numbers of blacks who were hanged, dismembered, castrated, or lynched in the South.[89] RACE WAR IMMINENT headlined the *San Francisco Chronicle* when, after a mass lynching in New Orleans, black men asked the governor to provide troops to protect them against a "reign of terror." Headlines in California papers—RACE WAR IN ALABAMA and RACE WAR IN VIRGINIA—likely encouraged brutal raids against the Chinese.[90]

As courts in the West succumbed to mob rule, the model of southern justice was precarious. On September 11, 1893, Judge Joseph McKenna of the United States Circuit Court in San Francisco turned to old fugitive slave laws to reaffirm that judges had the right to issue warrants for arrest and deportation based solely on a citizen's complaint. But McKenna added that a registration case had to be dropped immediately if there was not enough money to deport the Chinese prisoner.

The numbers of those ordered to be deported kept rising, and the status of Chinese immigrants was perilous. Contradictory memos flew from the desk of the attorney general: if a warrant was issued by a U.S. court, a Chinese immigrant must be apprehended; any deportation must await a habeas corpus appeal; Chinese immigrants arrested under the Geary Act must remain in custody. In practice, each locale had a different set of laws. Portland, Oregon, refused to give out blank warrants, but San Bernardino and Riverside continued to distribute them to anyone who wanted to make a citizen's arrest.

During the first three weeks of September 1893, U.S. Marshal Gard shuttled between Riverside or Los Angeles and San Francisco, issuing warrants and delivering Chinese prisoners to the jails in Alameda and San Francisco Counties.[91]

The Chinese remained trapped in legal purgatory, somewhere between deportation and endangered residence, imprisoned in all eleven counties covered by Judge Ross's southern U.S. District Court. Hundreds of Chinese cases were "heard" but not tried, hundreds of Chinese were found guilty of failure to register, and hundreds were deported. The hearings were a mockery: THREE CHINAMEN TRIED IN ONLY EIGHT MINUTES headlined the September 15 *San Francisco Chronicle*, as Ross continued to issue warrants for Chinese in Riverside, San Bernardino, Fresno, Sacramento, and Phoenix.

In the late summer and early fall of 1893, the fruit packinghouses became easier targets for roundups than the fields, as the Chinese were closely gathered, in sweltering sheds and tent camps. During the August harvest, men from the port towns near Los Angeles descended upon Compton. Chinese crews began to sleep in the packinghouses.[92]

Near Riverside, labor agitators threatened to hang twenty Chinese vineyard workers "as an example," if their employer refused to fire all his Chinese employees. The Chinese barricaded themselves in the packing sheds while hoodlums searched the fields and beat up any Chinese who remained. By the final week of September, the streets of Riverside's Chinatown were nearly deserted.

In September white and Japanese pickers went on strike in the hop fields near Sacramento, insisting that they could not live on the wages previously paid to Chinese workers. Decaying vegetables and garbage piled up in the streets. Fruit rotted in the storage sheds and on the trees. Three hundred white, Japanese, Mexican, and Mission Indians arrived and took some of the Chinese's jobs.[93]

Meanwhile, hundreds of Chinese languished in the county jails. Marshal Gard realized that he could pay for their inland transportation, incarceration, and food from monies intended for the maintenance of federal prisoners rather than from the paltry funds under the Geary Act.[94] Vigilante groups moved fast. By early October delegates from the National Trades Unions and the Mechanics State Council began making citizen's arrests in the ranching town of Tustin, where the peanut and walnut harvest had just begun.

California sanctified the violence of 1893. In Norwalk, near Los Angeles, an armed Anti-Chinese League of sixty men informed the owner of a large vineyard that he must discharge all his Chinese employees or see them lynched. Powerless against the mob, he complied.

In La Grange, at midnight on September 26, a local rancher and a saloon keeper led a gang of two hundred white men to the Chinese quarter, looted the houses, pushed the residents to the city limits, and ordered them out. Thirty Chinese men hid at the home of their pastor, the Reverend Mr. Trumble, a missionary whose wife and daughter were alone in the house when the mob arrived and demanded that they surrender the Chinese. Mrs. Trumble stood on her porch, aimed at the crowd with her rifle, and declared that she would shoot the first man to enter her house. The mob dispersed.[95]

By late September, hundreds of Chinese were fleeing for East Coast cities where they hoped the Geary Act would not be enforced. Others boarded ships for Hawaii, and five thousand Chinese soon went to work on sugar plantations.[96] Some found safety in northern California, where hundreds of Chinese showed up for the grape harvest in Sonoma.

Rumors circulated that eastern cities were paying railroad companies to move unemployed men west by promising them the jobs of the displaced Chinese workers.[97] But the L.A. Chamber of Commerce announced that the city still faced an "influx of great numbers of unemployed men in starving condition, for whom no work can possibly be found."

In the spring of 1894, hostilities turned against newly arrived Japanese workers. In March, a white mob in the town of Winters set its sights on both recent Japanese immigrants and Chinese farmworkers who accepted lower wages than whites. In April a crowd seized a Japanese man at random, brutally beat him, and threw him from a bridge. The next day white citizens from Winters notified ranchers that they must discharge their Chinese and Japanese workers. But ranchers, desperate for cheap field labor, refused. In June 1894, the United States Circuit Court denied citizenship to Japanese immigrant Sheblato Saito on the grounds that naturalization was available only to "aliens being free white persons, and to aliens of African nativity . . . and descent."[98] A Japanese person, "like the Chinese, belong[s] to the Mongolian race" and did not constitute a "white person."[99]

Yet Chinese people continued to enter the United States. In 1894, having lost jobs on railroads and coffee plantations in Mexico, hundreds of Chinese walked or swam across the border.[100] Some posed as Mexicans; in the South, some traded their clothes, cut their hair, and painted themselves "black" to look like members of steamship crews. By immigrating to the United States, the Chinese were willing to lose, for a moment, their racial identity.[101]

"THE UNITED STATES WILL BE SORRY FOR THIS SOME DAY"

On the morning of September 8, 1893, many Chinese vegetable peddlers and laundrymen across southern California failed to show up for work. They knocked on the doors of the houses and hotels of their white customers, demanded payment of their bills, and disappeared. Hundreds made their way to San Francisco.

That night Governor Markham wired Secretary of State Gresham, "I am pleased to inform you that open hostilities have ceased and . . . good order has been restored."

On September 10, a day still unmarked in American history, the Chinese consul launched a general strike in California. He ordered all the Chinese in San Bernardino to quit work and buy train tickets to Los Angeles or San Francisco. Emissaries from the Six Companies also arrived in Los Angeles with funds for the quick and wide general strike. Across southern California, Chinese laundries closed, and hotels and restaurants lost their cooks and cleaners. In Los Angeles, even as the court issued three hundred new warrants, the strike by Chinese laundrymen, vegetable dealers, and cooks went into effect.[102]

The next day, with the fall harvest in chaos and citizen's arrests sweeping across southern California, with the jails bursting and the courts jammed with habeas corpus delays, with the Chinese vegetable peddlers, laundrymen, and cooks on strike in Riverside and San Bernardino, Attorney General Olney ordered the U.S. marshals to cease enforcing the Geary Act. There were no funds left, he said, to back up enforcement.[103]

From the moment of the Supreme Court's fateful release of the *Fong Yue Ting* decision, the Chinese well understood the violence they were about to face. The editor of the San Francisco *Oriental Chinese Newspaper,* War Kee, warned Americans that his countrymen "will resent such an indignity as you would if your country proposed to tag you as they tag dogs. Chinese are human beings, not cattle, and they object to having tags placed around their necks. They will plead in your courts for justice until they find that justice is an unknown quantity, and then they will depart from the shores of America. . . . The United States will be sorry for this some day." Warned War Kee, "When your crops remain unharvested in the fields and your factories are closed down because the labor to operate them cannot be obtained there will be such a clamor arise for the return of the Chinese that it cannot be resisted. Then it will be the turn of the Chinese to laugh. Perhaps you will not find it easy to bring them back."[104]

As the issue of deportation was tossed back and forth between the Treasury, the U.S. Marshal's Service, the district court, the Supreme Court, the county jails, and the State Department, and as the date of implementation grew murkier, thousands of Chinese remained on strike. Hotels and restaurants closed because they no longer had cooks, waiters, or even fresh food.

The atmosphere in vineyard and orchard towns throughout Los Angeles County was tense. When a cannery in Colton gave notice that it was cutting wages, the Chinese workers went on strike, while the white laborers remained on the job. On September 11, all the Chinese people working in Tulare and the surrounding countryside quit work and took trains for Los Angeles or San Francisco.

The Chinese also sought to undo some of the more egregious aspects of the *Fong Yue Ting* decision by initiating test cases wherever they could. They lost them all. And, as the verdicts came in against them, they found themselves facing even greater risks. *In re Tsu Tse Mee* granted a Bureau of Internal Revenue commissioner the authority to order expulsion and deportation. With this stroke the federal court, without judge or jury, eliminated the costs and delays of jury trials.[105] Further, now Chinese people who illegally entered the country from Canada could be deported to China rather than returned to Canada, even if they could prove that they were subjects of British Columbia.

With the general strike, the Chinese Six Companies sought to recoup the authority they lost after the defeat in *Fong Yue Ting.* They also faced serious financial losses. As the Chinese were shipped out, hundreds of thousands of dollars that the Six Companies had advanced them instantly disappeared. In the spring of 1893, when the Six Companies sought one dollar from every Chinese resident to fight the Geary Act, Chinese laborers and merchants across the West donated sixty thousand dollars. But with thousands of Chinese refugees now in jail, in hiding, or in flight, the companies needed five dollars per person for their legal efforts, and the funds were not available. In the eyes of Chinese and Anglos, the Six Companies were losing their status as political advocates and legal shields for Chinese immigrants.

Even with class distinctions between merchant and laborer written into the Geary Act, the Chinese community refused to be divided against itself, and many Chinese merchants offered to turn laborers into partners, sometimes by selling a tiny share of a business so that field, cannery, and factory workers could qualify for residency.

Just as African Americans in the East sought refuge in the West, the Six Companies encouraged their countrymen to move. Some Chinese laborers went to northern California, some went to Canada or Mexico, some went to the South or the Northeast; some returned to China. A move away from the Pacific Coast would protect miners and farmworkers as well as make roundups and deportation more expensive for the U.S. government.

Another strategy for self-protection was for Chinese residents to apply for blank birth certificates, which were easy to obtain in this era of home births. Some Chinese simply inserted the name of an adult Chinese person, marked the place of birth as San Francisco, and wrote in a birth date that fit the age of the applicant. With an American birth certificate in hand, a Chinese person could then demand a certified copy from the Hall of Records, a document that legalized him as a "native son" and exempted him from the Geary Act.[106]

Anti-American violence, especially directed at Christian missionaries, again swept through China. During the most dramatic and widespread moment, known today as the Boxer Rebellion of 1900, legions of Chinese peasants rose against westerners and attacked the foreign embassies in Peking. At the end of a fifty-five-day siege, scores of American, British, German, and French missionaries lay dead.

The fate of Chinese converts to Christianity was worse. Targeted by the Boxers and unprotected by the missionaries, they were slaughtered, reportedly by the thousands. By 1904, in Sichuan Province alone, more than one hundred violent attacks had been launched against the Chinese Christians.[107]

In May 1905, merchants, students, women, children, doctors, boatmen, and even beggars in more than twenty cities and small towns in China boycotted American products and imports. Initiated by the Chinese living in the United States, the boycott spread across China via speeches, posters, and even kites. Actors in Shanghai staged anti-American plays. Chinese immigrants living in Southeast Asia, Australia, and Latin America sent tens of thousands of dollars toward the protest. The boycott, one of the earliest and largest popular movements in modern China, lasted only a year but exposed the global knowledge and rage at the roundups in the United States and revealed the transnational community that had evolved among Chinese living and working around the world.[108]

CHINA ABANDONS THE OVERSEAS CHINESE

In 1894, despite its impassioned rhetoric, the government of China again showed its ambivalence about the overseas Chinese and began to cast about for a compromise so that trade with the United States would grow. The Chinese Six Companies saw that they were losing their most powerful ally in the struggle against the Dog Tag Law.

Initially the Chinese legation indicated—in the language of diplomatic courtesy—that it was incensed by the Geary Act. On the day that President Harrison signed the act, Ts'ui Kuo-yin, envoy extraordinary and minister plenipotentiary in Washington, D.C., lodged a protest with Secretary of State Blaine. He declared that the denial of the right of habeas corpus to Chinese laborers was "inconsistent with one of the fundamental principles of justice that exists in China, America, and everywhere God reigns." The Geary Act, declared Ts'ui, was capricious, gave unlimited power to American revenue collectors, and violated treaties between the two countries.[109]

In March 1893, Charles Denby, the U.S. ambassador stationed in Peking, had notified Secretary Gresham that the Chinese had begun to tally all the Americans living in China. American missionaries "greatly feared . . . that the purpose of these investigations is to enable the Chinese Government to formulate some plan of retaliation." Both the Chinese government and American missionaries had sent petitions through his office to repeal the Geary Act, and Denby added his own warnings that the United States should expect "unpleasant recriminations against Americans."[110] He also warned Gresham that the Chinese were prepared to bar American missionaries and businessmen from leaving the port cities to work in the interior.

For many years relations with the United States had been of little interest to China, but now Chinese newspapers printed in the United States had found their way to China and spread the news of the violence, repression, and deportations in California.[111] Warned Denby, "Should any considerable number of Chinese laborers be deported to Kuangsi and Kuangtung, from which provinces they emigrated, it is greatly to be apprehended that anti-foreign riots will ensue."[112] As the spring of 1893 wore on, mail and telegraphs from the American legations in China to the U.S. State Department became more urgent and described the rise of anti-American feeling among the "reading portion" of the Chinese population.

China was also closely monitoring the legal decisions covering the Dog Tag Law. After the Supreme Court upheld the Geary Act, the Chinese ministers asked the United States to delay its implementation until their new ambassador, Yang Yu, arrived in Washington, D.C.[113] But the United States disregarded China's request and continued with the arrests, trials, imprisonments, and deportations. Judge Ross's decision to permit citizen's arrests further enraged the Chinese legation. Ts'ui Kuo-yin called Americans hypocrites for leaving Chinese immigrants vulnerable to violence and abuse while demanding that China protect American merchants and missionaries: "The statute of 1892 is a violation of every principle of justice, equality, reason and fair-dealing between friendly powers."[114] The United States ignored Ts'ui's threats of retaliation and sent evasive replies.

In August 1893, Yang Yu finally arrived in the United States, landing with a deliberately impressive delegation of eighty-five aides, assistant ministers, clerks, wives, and servants. Yang had received his appointment after intervening in the anti-American riots of 1891 in Chinkiang and persuading the Chinese government to pay restitution for foreign losses. Thus he came with a reputation as a powerful friend of the United States.

Before boarding the train for the East Coast, Yang spent a week in California investigating the anti-Chinese violence; once in Washington, D.C., he reported China's concern about the attacks. But the American government rightly guessed that China "may not like Americans, and may object to them being in China, but he does not dislike a balance of trade which is nearly five to one in favor of China, and which any difficulty with the United States would reduce in almost no time, if not destroy altogether."[115]

On August 23, the United States government received China's confidential response to the Geary Act. Word quickly leaked to the press that the Chinese had given an ultimatum: Americans in China would be expelled unless Congress repealed the Geary Act and protected the Chinese in California. Yang Yu threatened to withdraw the delegation and return to China, and the United States War Department ordered the gunboats *Con-*

cord and *Petrel* to join the naval fleet in the China Sea.[118] It seemed possible that a trans-Pacific war might begin.

But the showdown never happened. China made a deal. It ceased urging Chinese immigrants to defy the Geary Act and abandoned its defense of its immigrants living in America; they would now have to fend for themselves.

During these violent months, the Chinese government had been negotiating a new trade treaty with the United States, and many in Congress and in the Cleveland administration quietly counted on the Chinese government to actively help enforce the Geary Act. American industrialists saw the possibility of four hundred million Chinese consumers and wanted nothing more than to build new railroads and warships and the machinery for China's new woolen, silk, and cotton mills. They also jealously eyed Mexico's growing financial leverage in China, and its sales of millions of dollars in silver with which China would finance its modernization, which came through Mexico's welcome attitude toward Chinese immigrants. But American businessmen also knew that they faced a serious disadvantage: the 1894 trade treaty between China and Mexico included the right of Chinese immigrants to be naturalized and hold real property in Mexico.

To forge a trade agreement, the United States abandoned the Constitution and China abandoned its countrymen overseas. China acknowledged that "in view of the antagonism and much depreciated and serious disorders to which the presence of Chinese laborers has given rise in certain parts of the United States," it would no longer object to the registration of Chinese laborers, skilled and unskilled. The Chinese who were currently in the United States could keep "for the protection of their persons and property all rights that are given by the laws of the United States to citizens of the most favored nation, *excepting the right to become naturalized citizens.*"[117] In 1894, Congress ratified a treaty that would fully exclude all Chinese laborers for the next ten years.[118]

With this treaty, China explicitly recognized the right of the United States to require that Chinese laborers register with the government and bear identity cards. Chinese imports quickly increased from 150,000 taels in 1875 to 17 million in 1899. Its exports during those same years rose from 240,000 taels to 9 million.[119]

In 1895 Congress appropriated fifty thousand dollars for the enforcement of the new exclusion act and gave customs officers and BIR commissioners full power to decide immigration issues. No longer could the

Chinese appeal to American courts. Thousands of Chinese were in jail for failing to register; salaries of immigration attorneys and interpreters steadily rose; and the cost of deportation swelled.

"WE ADVISE ALL LABORERS TO COMPLY WITH THE LAW"

For Chinese who were *legal* immigrants, the last chance to register was April 3, 1894. Thousands waited for direction from the Chinese Six Companies—whether to register and carry the photo identity card or defy the new law. Finally, on January 20, a placard appeared on the walls of Chinatowns, although this one lacked the familiar official seal and signature of the Six Companies.[120] The notice decreed that all Chinese must now register under the Geary Act and carry a certificate of residence. A Chinese laborer must also be able to prove that he had entered the United States before the Exclusion Act of 1882. It concluded, in defeat, "We advise all laborers to comply with the law."[121]

Three years after the Geary Act had passed, an internal passport system was in place. The Bureau of Internal Revenue posted a circular in Chinatowns and published it in the Chinese newspapers ordering anyone who had previously registered to do so again, to assure that the immigrant was legally photographed.[122] The new treaty halted immigration from China for the next fifty years.

With great reluctance, thousands of Chinese from San Diego to Seattle began to register. Throughout the spring of 1894, Ambassador Yang Yu and the Chinese Six Companies continued to post circulars in Chinatowns ordering laborers to register. Yang had convinced the companies not to let the legal status of Chinese laborers undermine the trade treaty, which could be quite lucrative to Chinese merchants in the United States.[123]

To everyone's surprise, the fifty thousand dollars appropriated for registration—if not for trials and deportation—was adequate. The government proudly announced that there had been "general compliance" with the Geary Act and McCreary amendment. But between 1896 and 1905, of the 110,000 Chinese living in the United States, 9,571 were arrested for illegal residence and 4,000 were deported.[124]

Between the roundups, the exclusionary laws, the violence, the deportations, and the voluntary if disheartened departures for China, the population of Chinese in the West fell dramatically. The 1880s saw a loss of 37 percent of California's Chinese American population.[125] From 1890 to 1900, the total number of Chinese people in the United States dropped from about 107,000 to 90,000, a loss of about 16 percent.[126] In California, the drop was even more precipitous. In 1890, California had 72,000 Chinese residents; by 1900 that number had dropped by more than half, to 31,000.[127] In Fresno County, the site of citizen's arrests and violence in the fields, the number of Chinese fell from 2,700 in 1890 to 655 in 1900.[128] And with low numbers of women, the Chinese population in the United States would continue to decline.

But these were estimates at best. Many newspapers suggested that the census had always underreported the total number of Chinese residents. After the Exclusion Act in 1882, thousands of Chinese had been smuggled into the country—at small coastal towns, at the Mexican and Canadian border, and in San Francisco. Many were transported by the Merchants Steamship Company to carry Chinese immigrants across the Canadian border.

The American border, then as now, was a sieve. Immigration officials were notoriously corrupt. In one highly reported case, a notary public sold five hundred blank identity certificates, embossed with his seal. In Portland, Oregon, a payoff of twelve hundred dollars per month was made to the special agent of the Treasury Department for "non-interference" with Chinese immigrants seeking to enter the United States, and fifty dollars was paid to the local Internal Revenue for each Chinese person who landed "undisturbed."[129]

Although the federal government announced that 100,000 Chinese registered after the McCreary amendment, the numbers simply do not add up. For one thing, despite claims of voluntary registrations, the appropriation for the enforcement of the Geary Act rose to $125,000 for the year 1896 and to $100,000 for 1897, with extra money to be sent to Port Townsend, Washington. These funds suggest that there were still thousands of unregistered Chinese, and money was needed to "return to China all Chinese persons found to be unlawfully in the United States including the cost of imprisonment . . . and conveyance of Chinese persons to the frontier or seaboard for deportation" under the Geary Act.[130] By 1901, the appropriation had increased to $200,000.

The tallies of certificates also call into question the government's boastful claims of success. The commissioner of Internal Revenue announced that by 1893, the first year of the Geary Act, 13,243 certificates were issued—5,000 in California and Nevada and 1,000 in Oregon and Washington. In 1894, he made the unlikely claim that 106,811 certificates were issued, including 68,800 in California and Nevada and 11,000 in Oregon and Washington. In the district that included Los Angeles and the Cahuenga Valley, only 3,000 of 12,000 Chinese residents registered for identity cards. Meanwhile, many Chinese were fleeing the West Coast—more than 6,000 Chinese men and women registered in New York in 1894, compared with 548 the year before.[131]

In June 1895, after the extension to register legally had passed, nationwide only 52 Chinese signed up for certificates. In 1901, five Chinese men registered for identity cards. According to Department of the Treasury reports, by the turn of the century, 1,540 had registered in Chicago, but 1,000 had not. In California, where sixty-eight deputies had been at work, about 45,000 out of 50,000 legal Chinese immigrants registered in the San Francisco Bay Area, a number well below the estimates and claims of Chinese residency.[132] Some newspaper reports of the time suggested that fewer than 5 percent of the Chinese in California complied with the Geary Act.[133]

California newspapers also reported corrupt registrars. The *San Francisco Chronicle* headlined, MORE COOLIES THOUGHT TO HAVE REGISTERED THAN ARE IN THE COUNTRY. There was no penalty for registering more than once or for registering in several counties or states.[134] With the complicated translation of Chinese names into the English alphabet, many Chinese could register several times in slightly different ways, then sell their extra copies to brokers in Havana, who were reported to pay $100 to $150 for each certificate, or carry hundreds of valid certificates back to China to sell or give away.

In 1894, the Bureau of Internal Revenue arrested dozens of Chinese bearing hundreds of duplicate, fraudulent, or blank certificates. When the immigration agency compared certificates with the census, it became clear that thousands of duplicate certificates had been issued throughout the United States. And when the BIR allowed an English-speaking Chinese person to testify on behalf of an immigrant, it opened a veritable business in witnessing as well as translating.

The state of photography at the time also played a role in confusion and

No. 5379 UNITED STATES OF AMERICA, TERRITORY OF HAWAII. ORIGINAL.

U.S. INT. REV.—Form No. 478.

J B Hopkins

CERTIFICATE OF RESIDENCE.

Issued to Chinese LABORER, *under the Provisions of the Act of April 30, 1900.*

THIS IS TO CERTIFY THAT Fui Kui, a Chinese LABORER, now residing at Volcano Rd. Hilo, has made application No. 16591 to me for a Certificate of Residence under the provisions of the Act of Congress approved May 5, 1892, as amended by the Act approved November 3, 1893, and extended by the Act of April 30, 1900, and I certify that it appears from the affidavit of witness submitted with said application that said Fui Kui Female was within the limits of the Hawaiian Islands, on the 14th day of June, 1900, and was then residing at Volcano Rd. Hilo, and that he was at that time lawfully entitled to remain in the said Islands, and that the following is a descriptive list of said Chinese LABORER, viz:

NAME: Fui Kui AGE: 6 yrs.
LOCAL RESIDENCE: Volcano Rd. Hilo. Hawaii T.H.
OCCUPATION: Female child HEIGHT: 3 ft 3½ in COLOR OF EYES: Dk Brown
COMPLEXION: Dk Brown PHYSICAL MARKS OR PECULIARITIES FOR IDENTIFICATION: Two small scars on back of neck

Fui Kui

And as a further means of identification, I have affixed hereto a photographic likeness of said Fui Kui.

GIVEN UNDER MY HAND AND SEAL this 23rd day of April, 190_ at Honolulu, Territory of Hawaii.

[SEAL]

Roy H. Chamberlain
Collector of Internal Revenue, District of Hawaii.

NOTE.—No Chinese laborer, whether he shall hold this Certificate or not, shall be allowed to enter any State, Territory, or District of the United States from the Hawaiian Islands.

United States Certificate of Residence for Fui Kui, Hawaii

No. 137355 ORIGINAL.

UNITED STATES OF AMERICA. Certificate of Residence.

Issued to Chinese LABORER, *under the Provisions of the Act of May 5, 1892, as amended by the Act approved November 3, 1893.*

This is to Certify THAT Oo Dock, a Chinese LABORER, now residing at Ferry Or, has made application No. 11155 to me for a Certificate of Residence, under the provisions of the Act of Congress approved May 5, 1892, as amended by the Act approved November 3, 1893, and I certify that it appears from the affidavit of witness submitted with said application that said Oo Dock was within the limits of the United States at the time of the passage of said Act, and was then residing at Ferry Or, and that he was at that time lawfully entitled to remain in the United States, and that the following is a descriptive list of said Chinese LABORER, viz:

NAME: Oo Dock AGE: 51 Years
LOCAL RESIDENCE: Ferry Or
OCCUPATION: Cook HEIGHT: 5 ft 3½ in COLOR OF EYES: BROWN
COMPLEXION: Dark PHYSICAL MARKS OR PECULIARITIES FOR IDENTIFICATION: No Marks

And as a further means of identification, I have affixed hereto a photographic likeness of said Oo Dock.

GIVEN UNDER MY HAND AND SEAL this 3rd day of May, 1894, at Portland, State of Oregon.

[SEAL]

Henry Blackman
Collector of Internal Revenue, District of Oregon.

United States Certificate of Residence for Oo Dock, Portland

No. 19437 UNITED STATES OF AMERICA, ORIGINAL.

TERRITORY OF HAWAII. U.S. Int. Rev.—Form No. 478.

D. L. Baldwin

CERTIFICATE OF RESIDENCE.

Issued to Chinese LABORER, *under the Provisions of the Act of April 30, 1900.*

This is to Certify That Yuen [illegible] A. Conchu a Chinese LABORER, now residing at KAPAA, ISLAND OF KAUAI has made application No. 16296 to me for a Certificate of Residence under the provisions of the Act of Congress approved May 5, 1892, as amended by the Act approved November 3, 1893, and extended by the Act of April 30, 1900, and I certify that it appears from the affidavit of witness submitted with said application that said Yuen [illegible] A. Conchu female was within the limits of the Hawaiian Islands, on the 14th day of June, 1900, and was then residing at KAPAA, ISLAND OF KAUAI and that she was at that time lawfully entitled to remain in the said Islands, and that the following is a descriptive list of said Chinese LABORER, viz:

Name: Yuen [illegible] A. Conchu Age: 30 yr

Local Residence: KAPAA, ISLAND OF KAUAI

Occupation: Housewife Height: 5' Color of Eyes: Dk Brown

Complexion: Dk Brown Physical Marks or Peculiarities for Identification: Scar on right eye

And as a further means of identification, I have affixed hereto a photographic likeness of said Yuen [illegible] A. Conchu

Given under my hand and seal this MAY 28 1901 day of , 190 , at Honolulu, Territory of Hawaii.

[Seal.] Roy H Chamberlain

Collector of Internal Revenue, District of Hawaii.

NOTE.—No Chinese laborer, whether he shall hold this Certificate or not, shall be allowed to enter any State, Territory, or District of the United States from the Hawaiian Islands.

United States Certificate of Residence for Yuen Conchu, Hawaii

fraud.[135] Many rural counties, such as Mono and Inyo in California, where several hundred Chinese resided, had no photographer, which made legal registration impossible. Also, at this time many photographic chemicals degraded quickly; registrars reported having photographs in hand that faded before their eyes.

At some point during the 1950s, the National Archives destroyed its copies of all the certificates. Why was the evidence of Chinese expulsions erased? The numbers are now impossible to verify. In the course of researching this book, I found only five identity cards.[136]

Chinese immigrants who had endured brutal violence in America now viewed deportation as a free ticket home.[137] On March 27, 1894, the *Port Orford Tribune* in Oregon invoked a series of common racial stereotypes to acknowledge that some Chinese welcomed deportation: "Chinamen look a great deal alike to western eyes, and the wily celestials are able to dispose of their superfluous [*sic*] registration certificates at good prices. . . . These certificates are also sold to Chinamen who want to make a visit home. They put the certificates into their pockets, and then refuse to register. That gives them a free passage to China . . . and the certificate admits them again when they want to come back."[138]

At the close of registration, the Chinese Six Companies demanded to know what would happen to those who did not register. Where were the Chinese to be "corralled," fed, and cared for while awaiting deportation? The Six Companies had raised and spent more than one hundred thousand dollars in legal and publicity fees to fight the Geary Act; all they had gained was a six-month extension and the replacement of Minister Ts'ui with Yang Yu, whose goal was to gain a trade treaty rather than to protect the overseas Chinese. Despite the profits in trade, the companies continued to hire their own agents to monitor registrations. They also tested the McCreary amendment in the Supreme Court, focusing on the status of the Chinese as citizens of a most favored nation under the Burlingame Treaty, which was still in effect.

And roundups of Chinese residents continued, blessed by judicial and congressional actions. In May 1894, the Del Rio Rey Vineyard in Fresno replaced its white employees with Chinese workers, and within days, dynamite bombs were found under the bunkhouses; the new Chinese workers fled. No arrests were made. That same week, 150 miles to the north, a mob of more than one hundred members of the Industrial Army (a name borrowed from Edward Bellamy's bestselling novel, *Looking Backward,* about a socialist and all-white utopia) raided orchards in Pleasanton and in the Vaca Valley, demanding that farmers deport all Chinese and Japanese employees. The mob looted cabins, beat the Asian workers, and seized many as prisoners. Vigilantes pillaged an apricot orchard recently purchased by a Chinese company in San Francisco. Marching down valley roads and picking up new members along the way, the mob randomly shot at Chinese and Japanese field-workers.

In the Vaca Valley, Japanese and Chinese farmworkers began to sleep in undisclosed places. At one ranch, five masked men discovered the Asians' hidden cabins and tents and assaulted the field hands. Eventually it was the growers, whose property was now worth more than four million dollars, who forced the sheriff to arrest members of the mobs. Their "sentiment," wrote the *Chronicle,* "is united in the purpose to protect the great property interests at stake." As in Vina and Butte, California agriculture became a buffer between Asian Americans and vigilante rule.[139]

The forces for driving out the Chinese had spread—through arms, through the laws, through the courts. More and more, the Chinese entered the United States across the Mexican or Canadian borders, at Key West via Havana, or along the unguarded Pacific shoreline.[140] Many Chinese sailors jumped ship in small coastal towns where there was no customs office. Identity cards became an established part of life for Chinese in the United States.[141] In 1898, Congress voted to exclude Filipinos, and in 1902, Hawaiians.

When the Chinese Exclusion Act was renewed in 1902, the legal gate on Chinese immigration slammed shut for another forty years. By 1904, 20 percent of the Chinese who arrived with certificates of identification were not allowed to land.[142] The legal immigration of Chinese people was over.

CONCLUSION

"NO PLACE FOR A CHINAMAN"

Sec. 190. No Chinese shall ever be employed, either directly or indirectly, on any work of the city, or in the performance of any contract or sub-contract of the city, except in punishment for a crime. Nor shall any provisions, supplies, materials, or articles of Chinese manufacturers or production ever be used or purchased by or furnished to the city.

—City of Eureka, 1941 Charter and Revised Ordinances

At one o'clock on September 30, 1906, twenty-three Chinese men climbed into the light from the hold of the steamer *Roanoke* as it docked in Eureka. They had been smuggled onboard at Astoria, Oregon, by a Chinese contractor for the Starbuck, Tallant and Grant Company, to work in a salmon cannery at Port Kenyon at the mouth of the Eel River. Also onboard the *Roanoke* were ten other cannery workers—four Japanese men and six Russian women.

Port Kenyon was just twenty miles south of Eureka, the town that still lived by the "unwritten law of this county: to exclude Chinese."[1] Anticipating a race riot at the Eureka wharf, Jack Simpson, the local agent for the NNPS Steamship Company, had begged the Santa Fe Railroad to run a special boxcar down to the wharf and secretly transport the Chinese men to Port Kenyon. But the railroad company had refused.

When the Chinese and Japanese cannery workers disembarked, they were surrounded by a hostile gang chanting anti-Chinese slogans, and they quickly returned to the steamer. The crowd at the wharf grew, taunting and threatening the Asian men. Shortly before four o'clock, the afternoon train bound for Port Kenyon pulled up. A Santa Fe engine backed a boxcar onto the side track along the wharf, and the cannery workers were quickly able to board. The conductor hooked the boxcar onto the regular passenger coaches and pulled out for the Eel River valley.[2]

Within hours *The Daily Humboldt Times* ran the headline: CHINESE AGAIN IN HUMBOLDT! TWENTY-SEVEN CELESTIALS BROUGHT TO EUREKA ON ROANOKE FOR CANNERY AT PORT KENYON. The next day the newspaper declared, THE CHINESE MUST GO. It had been twenty years since the violent roundups that drove the Chinese from Eureka, Arcata, Crescent City, and Ferndale. Humboldt County still seethed with racist excitement.

Over the next two days, labor unions held mass meetings at Excelsior Hall in Fortuna and at the Labor Hall in Eureka. With every seat taken, crowds stood in the aisles, crammed the back of the halls, and leaned against the walls. They chanted demands for the Starbuck, Tallant and Grant cannery to fire the Asian men it had brought to work the fall salmon season in Humboldt County. H. L. Ricks, son of the landlord of Chinatown during the 1880s, said the cannery owners did not understand Humboldt's "unwritten law." Vigilante E. M. Frost reminded the crowd, "I was one of the many who herded the Chinese and sent them away in 1885 on February 7th and 8th, and they threatened to bring out the National Guard. But what was the National Guard? The sentiment of the people was that the Chinamen must go, peaceably if they would, but go at all hazards and they did go."[3]

Eureka's Building Trades Council, Fortuna's Board of Trade, and Humboldt County's Longshoremen's Union announced that if the Chinese cannery workers were not ejected at once, hundreds of lumberjacks would ride down to the Eel and close the river. The Bam Boozlers Bunch, a men's drinking club in Eureka, vowed that they would come to the river and "exterminate" the Chinese.[4]

But in 1906, towns along the Eel River depended on the salmon run. The Eel, still a wild river today, begins high in the pine forests of the Salmon Mountains, flowing through steep granite canyons and along towering groves of coastal redwoods, and empties into the Pacific Ocean in valleys marked with redwood trees a thousand years old. Halfway to the coast it meets the Van Duzen River. Around the turn of the century, temporary canneries were built each year to catch and process the salmon on their fierce swim upstream to spawn.

The town of Ferndale, like many others, depended on the Starbuck, Tallant and Grant cannery for 90 percent of its economy—jobs for fishermen, ship suppliers, cooks, and merchants. Many Scandinavian dairymen and ranchers, whose cows grazed nearby in the misty valleys along the Mattole and Mad Rivers, owned shares in the cannery.

Racial violence again threatened remote Humboldt County. Ferndale's Chamber of Commerce met at once to ask the governor either to send up the state militia or to order Eureka's naval militia down to the Eel to protect the cannery workers. Tallant met with Eureka's town officers, pleading with them to let the Chinese stay. Just the year before, Tallant had invested in a cold-storage plant along the river. This year he was to build a permanent cannery, and businessmen and farmers from Ferndale had bought shares in his company worth one hundred dollars each. Thousands of dollars of local money were already invested in developing the factory. The Chinese, argued Tallant, were the only skilled labor available.

Besides, he explained, these Chinese men were not of the "cheap variety" but would earn from two to three dollars per day catching, killing, slicing, boiling, and canning fish—work that whites would not accept. Tallant added that it was really "the Japs . . . who worked for small pay" and it was the six Russian "girls" who had taken the cheapest jobs. Tallant promised that if Humboldt County would just let him keep the Chinese workers for two months, he would guarantee that they would leave the area at the end of the fall salmon run.

A committee of three formed. The men quickly spread the news that Chinese cannery workers had arrived to all the labor camps in Humboldt County. Lumberjacks came out of the redwood forests and timbermen left the sawmills near Loleta and Eureka to gather in the company town of Fortuna. There they resolved that the cannery had "contaminated the air of the county with the filthy Chinese whom the fathers of the present generation were forced to resort to strenuous means to eject."

The lumberjacks warned the chandlers, shipbuilders, and investors in Ferndale and Port Kenyon to fire and deport the Chinese immediately. Otherwise, they threatened, a thousand woodsmen would arrive to "do the job for them."[5]

Top: Advertisement for "The Iron Chink." Bottom: Chinese salmon cannery workers, Fairham, Washington, 1905.

Yet despite threats of lumbermen from Blue Lake to Fortuna, the Chinese refused to quit. The Chinese contractor Lei Eeso declared that a contract with Tallant guaranteed the Chinese men the work of producing twelve thousand cases of salmon at forty-five cents per case, whether or not there were fish. The Chinese, he argued, were skilled workers who could butcher the salmon, prepare the fish for packing, make the cans, and then seal them after they were packed by the white women—women whose virtue was quickly brought into question for working alongside Chinese men.

Lei announced that all of the Chinese men had given up lucrative jobs to come from Oregon down to the Eel River, and they would not leave until they were fully paid for their contract, worth thousands of dollars. The men, he added, were brave and ready to defend themselves to the last.

Tallant and Starbuck were well aware of Humboldt County's pride in the roundups of 1885 and 1886. They believed the lumberjacks' threats and reluctantly decided to abandon the season. The Chinese cannery workers, however, refused to leave the Eel River without their wages for a full season's work. Turning to the citizens of Ferndale for help, the cannery owners began to raise the money to pay off the contract and ship the Chinese out.

Just four days after they arrived in Humboldt County, the twenty-three Chinese men were loaded back onto a boxcar and transported to the Eureka wharf. Hundreds surrounded the train. Finally, at nightfall, when the crowd dwindled, the Chinese were boarded onto fishing boats and skiffs that carried them over to Indian Island in Humboldt Bay, where they were held under guard while they awaited the return of the *Roanoke.*

Within a year canneries along the coast would replace many Chinese with *The Iron Chink.* "Don't fool around with the Question any longer," ran the ads.

ON BELONGING: ROUNDUPS AND RESISTANCE

The Driven Out challenges the stereotype of the Chinese immigrants as sojourners who lived most of their lives clinging to their status and community in China. Only in white culture were the Chinese viewed as temporary residents, draining American resources by sending salaries home, disinvested and disengaged from the United States. A leading Shanghai newspaper, *Shen Pao,* observed, "It is not easy for Chinese to leave America. Those who loved their homes would never have left to go elsewhere. But those in America are those who had fixed their hearts on going abroad in spite of all difficulties. Originally they had no stake in their own home, and were obliged to leave to relieve their own wretchedness.... now . . . as it were, they have burnt their homes; where they live they are not wanted, and they have no longer any desire to return to their native home."[6]

Yet the sojourner myth had prompted laws, codes, and policies that presumed that the Chinese would not assimilate. It blamed the roundups on Chinese immigrants' own urge to return to China. Indeed, it implied that whites were doing them a favor by driving them out. President Cleveland actually blamed the roundups, murders, and mob actions in the West on the "race prejudice" caused by the image of the temporary alien, an image, he said, that "exists in a large part of our domain."[7]

But the Chinese demands for full payment for their work, the lawsuits for reparations, the fight for public education for their children, the building of Chinatowns, the strikes, the purchase of weapons to defend themselves and their communities, the acts of mass civil disobedience, defied Cleveland's logic. They point to a transnational people claiming their rightful status in the United States. Even as they sent hundreds of thousands of dollars back to China, made frequent visits home, at times maintained families on both continents, wrote and spoke in Chinese, honored Taoist, Confucian, and Buddhist beliefs, and, if they could, returned to China to die or sent bones to the family village for burial, the Chinese simultaneously fought at every turn for their rights to property and permanence in the new communities of the West.

The Chinese who vowed to remain on the Eel River until the salmon season ended, who refused to leave Truckee, who married and bore children in the Pacific West, were transnational migrants who developed relationships that spanned borders—legal, familial, economic, religious, and political borders. They remained involved in China and the United States. Instead of viewing the fights against expulsions by the overseas Chinese as evidence of assimilation or as evidence of desperate outsiders knocking at the courthouse door, we should read Chinese resistance to the roundups as a bond in the migration of Chinese people, money, goods, and information.

During the years of the violent roundups, China eased emigration and abandoned its view that émigrés to the United States were traitors. The Qing came to understand the financial and emotional markers that bound the overseas Chinese to their native place—despite dispersion, despite violence, despite prosperity. The Chinese in the American West maintained their traditions of food, dress, work, and national loyalty even as they turned to American courts to defy frontier violence, racism, ethnic-purity movements, and American immigration law.[8]

The roundups and the lawsuits, the letters and petitions against the Driven Out, are paradoxically also a place where the silenced voices of nineteenth-century Chinese immigrants can be heard. Along with scraps of few remaining Chinese newspapers (most of which burned in the fires from the 1906 earthquake in San Francisco), the court cases, the broadsheets, the placards and diplomatic letters hold the scarce public articulations of early Chinese immigrants' perspective and provide the few sources of their self-disclosure.[9]

The Chinese were prepared to meet violence with violence. When organizations such as the Workingmen's Party and the 601 grew as offshoots of white unions, the Chinese in Truckee and other mountain towns purchased revolvers to protect themselves. In Truckee, when white lenders called in business loans and mortgages, the Chinese burned their laundries and lumber camps before they left town. In Red Bluff, when a foreman assaulted a Chinese cannery worker, all the other Chinese rioted and then quit, en masse.

In many towns the Chinese flatly refused to leave. Caught, like whites, in the creation of a new industrial working class, Chinese workers copied the tactics of the white labor movement. Chinese carpenters and cigar makers formed their own unions. In the early 1880s, Chinese launderers won a wage hike to five dollars per day, at a time when the average Chinese daily pay was sixty cents. When a lumber company in Shasta rejected the Chinese demand that they be allowed to order their food and supplies from San Francisco's Chinatown rather than buy at the company store, they declared a general strike. Throughout the vineyards and orchards, the Chinese struck for higher wages, usually in the middle of harvest time. In Red Bluff, Chinese farmers agreed not to sell fruit and vegetables to any hotel owner who was involved in anti-Chinese activities, depriving the innkeepers of fresh food. In Redding the Chinese published the names and enforced a boycott of white citizens who refused to pay their bills.

The legal actions brought by the Chinese during the 1880s and 1890s sought to sever the powerful American fusion of "foreign" and "race"—expressed in the law, in civic ordinances, in ads, cartoons, and fiction, and in the roundups.

At the same time, by insisting on Chinese "foreignness"—in appearance, food, hairstyle, and clothing, and in their all-male communities—anti-Chinese legislators and activists claimed that the Chinese were not immigrants like the Irish, the Italians, the Germans, and the Russians, but were sojourners who were uninterested in remaining in the United States and becoming both American citizens and "American."

INDIAN ISLAND

Fifty-six years of Chinese roundups in the Pacific Northwest came to an end on Indian Island, the same place where the U.S. military and some hired renegades had massacred the Wiyot tribe.

On February 25, 1860, Wiyot women were celebrating the last night of a women's religious festival on what was then known as Gunthers Island. Most of the men had left the island in canoes, to fish and hunt; more than sixty women and children remained behind.

But that night, a local militia, the Hydesville Volunteers, had just lost a commission from the military and were angry. The Volunteers' forays against Indians were not officially sanctioned by the state but were usually funded by thousands of dollars in local and federal donations. After dark, the Volunteers rowed over to the island and tracked down the Wiyot women and children, now hiding in the brush. Then they axed them all, through their skulls.

The massacre was one of four Indian massacres that night; the others occurred along the Elk River, the Mad River, and Humboldt Bay.

When the brutal massacres were discovered, the military forced 450 Indians living along Humboldt Bay on a long march north, to Fort Terwer on the Klamath Reservation, launching three years of the Northwest Indian Wars. "It is a hardship that the natives of the country should be forced to sell their lands," wrote *The Humboldt Times* in December 1861. "It is hard that California Indians are forced from their homes without even the form of a sale to which they are a party. But the settlers upon public lands are not responsible for the wrong. Government has put the land into market and offered inducements to her citizens to purchase and settle thereon. The subject has been soberly discussed by the statesmen of the land, and gravely decided in the United States Senate, that the red men of California have no title to lands in California."[10]

After the Wiyot massacre, the California and national press named Eureka "Murderville." The *New York Century* observed:

> History has no parallel to the recent atrocities perpetrated in California. . . . Humboldt County, in the northern section of the state, has been the scene of a great portion of these outrages. The Perpetrators seem to have acted with a deliberate design to exterminate the Indian race. Their butchery was confined to women and children, the men being absent at the time. They were of the Digger tribes, known as friendly Indians, the most degraded and defenseless of the race, entirely destitute of the bold and murderous spirit which characterizes other tribes of red men. . . . We have spoken of the authors of the butchery as men—white men. So they were. We can invent no logic that will segregate them from our own species.[11]

Chinese cannery workers in boxcars on Indian Island, Humboldt Bay

Chinese cannery workers being deported at Humboldt Bay, California

During the last decades of the nineteenth century, thousands more members of the Yurok, Wiyot, and Chilula tribes were rounded up and held at Fort Humboldt in Eureka, most in a small "circular corral," of which Colonel Lippitt, the commander, calmly noted, "The crowded conditions in this corral were not favorable to the Indians' comfort or health and a high mortality rate resulted."[12] The U.S. military sold many Indian children into slavery, often to work as domestic servants in Eureka or Arcata or on the dairy farms near Ferndale. Years of rape, fraudulent treaties, and the forced removal of Indian people set a stage for Humboldt County's roundups of the Chinese in 1885 and 1886.

DRIVEN OUT

On Indian Island, the Chinese cannery workers were held in an abandoned mill and in empty boxcars until two steamers arrived. On October 8, 1906, a week after they first arrived, the *Roanoke* sailed for Portland, Oregon, with eighteen Chinese men. Two days later the *Corona* sailed for San Francisco with the last five Chinese men. But this time, as the *Roanoke* and *Corona* set sail in the cold October sea, the Chinese, driven from the county in just one week, took with them thousands of dollars in wages for a full season's work.

On December 17, 1943, President Franklin Delano Roosevelt signed Public Law 199, repealing sixty-one years of legal exclusion. Public Law 199 allowed Chinese to enter the United States under a rigid quota system that worked out to 105 Chinese per year.[13]

For thirty-seven years the prediction of the Eureka newspaper held true. As the Chinese again sailed from Humboldt Bay, the *Humboldt Times Standard* boasted, "They will shake the Humboldt dust from their sandals, satisfied the County is a fine place, but no place for a Chinaman."

ACKNOWLEDGMENTS

Many have listened and read, queried and critiqued, hunted and gathered, and made it possible for me to tell this difficult tale.

The community of Chinese American and Asian American historians urged me to tell this story now. I am grateful to Him Mark Lai, the father of Chinese American history, who, in long conversations, shared his perspectives on my documents and photographs; Him Mark Lai encouraged my focus on the forcefulness of early Chinese Americans and the global implications of the roundups. L. Ling-chi Wang, chair of Ethnic Studies at the University of California, Berkeley, helped me to view the resistance to the roundups in the context of Chinese Americans' long pursuit of civil rights, and he graciously created spaces for me to share my work.

The scholars and archivists at the Smithsonian Asian Pacific American Program—Franklin Odo, director, and Terry Hong, media arts consultant—encouraged this quest from the start. Franklin Odo welcomed me into the Smithsonian's Re-Writing Asian American History Collective. Terry Hong's knowledge of Asian American culture and history crosses national boundaries; she extends the field for us all and then puts us in touch with one another. Douglas A. Mudd, manager of the Smithsonian's National Numismatic Collection, identified the Chinese coin found on the Karuk Reservation in northern California. Fath Ruffins, Catherine M. Keen, and Reuben Jackson of the Archives Center at the Smithsonian Museum of American History are knowledgeable about the ethnic-studies resources at the Smithsonian and located rare cartoons, advertisements, and trade cards that helped me understand the popular reception and depiction of early Chinese America.

Gilbert Hom of the Southern California Chinese Historical Society has, over four years, provided documents and data to extend the geographical boundaries of this history. Jeannie Woo of the Chinese Historical Society of America, Wei Chi Poon of the Asian American Studies Collection at the University of California, Berkeley, and the learned archivists at the Bancroft Library helped me locate files upon files of communiqués, letters, biographies, diaries, and photographs, many hitherto unread. Historians Sue Fawn Chung and Erika Lee graciously responded to inquiries as I sought to place local actions in the global movements of people. Historian Mae Ngai's conversations about Chinese labor brokers helped me understand the indebted yet autonomous position of Chinese laborers. My colleague Peter X. Feng at the University of Delaware encouraged me to pursue this story, asked hard questions, and answered many.

My understanding of the Chinese attempts to win legal redress was generously aided by the attorney Davis Yee, who helped me retrieve the Chinese lawsuits and the early California codes upon which these cases relied and understand their legal strategies. Anita Allen, Henry R. Silverman Professor of Law and professor of philosophy at the University of Pennsylvania, explained the political implications of basic tort and trespass cases and shared her perspective on the historic demands implied by Chinese suits for damages and redress. The writings of Charles McClain, Jr., professor at Boalt School of Law, University of California, on early Chinese Americans' use of the American legal system extended my analysis of the cases I uncovered; he graciously discussed our shared frustrations at finding those nineteenth-century attorneys who bravely and creatively represented Chinese Americans. Hon. Peter Panuthos and Kathy Kriege, Esq., helped ground my historical argument through their analysis of legal procedures.

It was a privilege to work with Ron Schoenherr, executive director of PBS/KEET, and Seth Frankel, director of production at PBS/KEET, on the documentary *The Chinese in Humboldt County.*

This book took me on a very real journey that covered thousands of miles across the Pacific Northwest. It began in Humboldt County, California. I am honored that the late Peter Palmquist of Arcata, California, shared his private collection of photographs of early Chinese Americans of the Pacific Northwest and the 1906 purge from Humboldt County. With a mutual desire to have this history told accurately, the librarians and archivists at the Humboldt Historical Society—Matina Kilkenny, Denise Giltzow, Jerry Rohde, Wendy Lestina, and Merry Schellinger—and the librarians at California State University, Humboldt—Ray Wang, director, Chinese Language and Culture, and Edith Butler and Joan Berman of the Humboldt Room—launched my archival work. Wally Hagaman, instrumental in preserving the history of the Chinese in Nevada City and Truckee, California, gave of his time and materials to build my understanding of the purge in Truckee. Historian Connie Yu discussed her own work on the Chinese in San Jose and influenced my sense of the long scope of this history.

I am grateful to Phil Sanders, Sue Sanders, and Laura Sanders, who met with me at their ranch on the Karuk Reservation in Orleans, California, and offered their knowledge of the history of the Chinese in the Siskiyou Mountains and of the enduring Chinese presence on Karuk land. The Sanderses lent me Chinese coins found on their ranch and showed me the collection of financial logs of the Lord General Store, records and artifacts that establish that purges of the Chinese from Humboldt County were never completed.

Librarians and archivists of university rare-book collections, county historical societies, and libraries located and shared hundreds of documents upon which this book is based: Jane Borg, Pajora Valley Historical Society; Richard Caminere and Carlo de Ferera of the Tuolumne County Historical Society; Carolyn Kozo Cole, curator of photographs, Los Angeles Public Library; Joyce M. Cox, Nevada State Library and Archives; Dean Gorby of the Tehama County Museum Foundation; Claude Hopkins, National Archives Pacific Center, San Bruno, California; David Hays of the Archives, University of Colorado at Boulder; Bill Jones, Chico State University Library Rare Books Collection; Paula Jabloner and Elizabeth Stewart of the San Jose Historical Society and the talented staff of the Chinese Historical and Cultural Project in San Jose; Jackie Kerska, Curry County Historical Society, Oregon; Kris Kinsey, University of Washington Libraries Special Collections; Linda Lake of the Lower Lake Museum, Lake County, California; Rachel McKay at the Museum of Art and History, Santa Cruz; George Miles, librarian and photography curator at Beineke Library, Yale University; Jocelyn Moss of the Marin County Historical Society; Patricia Perry, finance director for the City of Sonora, California; Catherine Powell at the Labor Archives and Research Center, San Francisco State University; Joan Rutty, Tuolumne County Library; Chelsea Stanford of the Truckee Donner History Society; William John Shepherd, archivist for the papers of the Knights of Labor and Terrence Powderly at the Catholic University of America; Larry R. Steuben, Columbia College; Stanley Stevens of the University of California, Santa Cruz Library; Gail S. Yu, the Chinese Reconciliation Project Foundation, Tacoma, Washington; Winnie Yeung of the Department of Parks and Recreation, Sacramento, who offered wisdom, enthusiasm, and confirmation.

Archaeologist Andrew Gottsfield guided me through the Sanborn Insurance Maps that helped me retrace the rise and fall of many Chinatowns in California. Daniel Lane of Norwich University located materials on the rebellion aboard the Chinese slave ship *Norway.* Chris Harms of House of Toys graciously located the toy gun and photographed it for this book.

Documents and photographs for this book were found during visits to the California State Archives Golden State Museum; Judah Magnes Collection of Western Judaica; the Del Norte County Historical Society; Shasta Historical Society; the Sutter County Historical Society; the Shasta County Library, Redding, California; the Shasta-Tehama-Trinity Joint Community College District Library; the Contra Costa County Historical Society History Center; New York University; the Wells Fargo History Museum; the City University of New York; the Searls Library of the Nevada County Historical Society; the California State Archives; the California State Library; the California Historical Society; the San Francisco Public Library; Bellevue Community College, Washington; the photography collection at the University of Washington, Seattle; Oakland City Library; Placer County Historical Society; the National Archives, San Bruno, Washington, D.C., and College Park, Md.; and the Library of Congress. I am particularly grateful to the librarians in the Newspaper Collection, the Rare Books Room, and the Map Room of the Library of Congress.

Mary Lee of San Francisco and Connie Young Yu of Los Altos Hills shared their families' history of migration.

My understanding of the photographs collected for this book was enriched by discussions with Laura Wexler, Robin Bernstein, Mary Ting Yi Lui, and other members of the Historical Memory Project at American Studies program at Yale University.

My research assistants, Supaporn Yimwilai, Sara Champa, Therese Rizzo, and Jennifer Dodenhoff, were persevering, curious, intelligent, and informed. Zi-fu Zhao's translations were literate and lucid. The members of my writers group—Carla Peterson, Thorell Tsomondo, and Carolyn Karcher, and my colleague in many journeys through the nineteenth century, Linda Morris—continue to monitor my writing with astute observations and graceful persistence. I am grateful to Tony Platt for discussions on race and eugenics in California.

Joellen Lippett traveled with me to almost all these rural towns. She brought along her experience in photography and material artifacts gained over twenty years at the Oakland Museum, her knowledge of California geography and landscape, her expectation that local archivists would willingly share documents no matter what they might expose about their beloved and hauntingly beautiful hometowns, and her optimism that we could find this history.

I am grateful indeed to the Library of Congress, the Center for Public Broadcasting Stations (CPBS) National Center for Outreach, the Tracy Memorial Trust Fund, the Humboldt Foundation, WNET (New York) PBS Documentary Production, and the University of Delaware for funding for this project.

I am deeply grateful to my agent, Sandra Dijkstra, who brought this untold story of ethnic cleansing to Random House. My editors at Random House, Will Murphy and Jonathan Jao, astutely shaped this vast narrative.

My husband, Peter Panuthos, and my daughters, Johanna Pfaelzer and Sophia Panuthos, accompanied me on this journey, from Big Lagoon in Humboldt County, California, to Xi'an International Studies University, China. I cherish their wit, love, and patience.

I am very grateful for the help, friendship, and guidance I have received.

NOTES

INTRODUCTION

1. In translation. Affidavit and attachment of Lum May, June 3, 1886, *Miscellaneous Letters of the Department of State, 1789–1906,* NARA, M-179, roll 707. Spelling and punctuation are as in original.

   On June 2, 1886, in Seattle, the physician Thomas Merion certified that he carefully "examined the wife of Lum, who was driven out of Tacoma, and from a careful examination and all other evidence I have been able to obtain I am satisfied that her present insanity is due to the experiences then had by her—when driven out of Tacoma. Most of the delusions now entertained by her relate to that experience."
2. Ira B. Cross, *A History of the Labor Movement in California* (Berkeley: University of California Press, 1935), 12, 142. At the start of 1849, there were six Chinese people in California.
3. *Annals of the City of San Francisco,* April 19, 1854.
4. Carey McWilliams, *California: The Great Exception* (New York: Current Books, 1949), 98.
5. Madeline Yuan-yin Hsu, *Dreaming of Gold, Dreaming of Home: Transnationalism and Migration Between the United States and South China, 1882–1943* (Stanford, Calif.: Stanford University Press, 2000), 24.
6. See H. W. Brands, *The Age of Gold: The California Gold Rush and the New American Dream* (New York: Doubleday, 2002), 62.
7. In translation. Affidavit of Tuck Nun (or Tak Nan), June 15, 1886, *Miscellaneous Letters of the Department of State, 1789–1906,* NARA, M-179, roll 707.
8. Affidavit of Yoke Leen, February 21, 1910, Tuolumne County Museum and History Center, Sonora, California.
9. Jacquelyn Dowd Hall, "'You Must Remember This': Autobiography as Social Critique," *Journal of American History* 85, no. 2 (September 1998), 439.
10. China is just beginning to collect records and dedicate museums to imprint the lives of the overseas Chinese. Private discussion, Him Mark Lai.
11. Patrick Hutton, "Recent Scholarship on Memory and History," *History Teacher* 33, no. 4 (August 2000), 539. This discussion of historical memory is also indebted to Alon Confino, "Collective Memory and Cultural History: Problems of Method," *American Historical Review* (December 1997).

CHAPTER 1. GOLD!

1. *Californian,* March 15, 1848.
2. According to Albert L. Hurtado, "when Hispanic settlement began, in 1769, 300,000 native people lived within the current boundaries of California. At the end of Spanish sovereignty in 1821, perhaps 200,000 remained. During the 1850s, after California became a state, the native population fell by 80 percent, to about 30,000." *Indian Survival on the California Frontier* (New Haven, Conn.: Yale University Press, 1988), 1. See also James J. Rawls, *Indians of California: The Changing Image* (Norman: University of Oklahoma Press, 1984), 171.

3. Ira B. Cross, *A History of the Labor Movement in California* (Berkeley: University of California Press, 1935), 10.
4. Alexander McLeod, *Pigtails and Gold Dust: A Panorama of Chinese Life in Early California* (Caldwell, Idaho: Caxton Printers, 1947), 23.
5. Rinn-Sup Shinn and Robert L. Worden, *A Country Study: China,* available online at the Federal Research Division of the Library of Congress, http://lcweb2.loc.gov/frd/cs/crtoc.html.
6. Carolyn Karcher, *The First Woman in the Republic: A Cultural Biography of Lydia Maria Child* (Durham, N.C.: Duke University Press, 1994), 387.
7. This quotation, as well as those in the following paragraphs regarding expansion following the Mexican War, come from Howard Zinn, *A People's History of the United States, 1492–Present* (New York: HarperPerennial, 1995), 146–57.
8. Robert F. Heizer and Alan F. Almquist, *The Other Californians: Prejudice and Discrimination Under Spain, Mexico, and the United States to 1920* (Berkeley: University of California Press, 1971), 156, 188.
9. Pauline Minke, "Chinese in the Motherlode, 1850–70," unpublished manuscript, 1960.
10. Ping Chiu, *Chinese Labor in California: An Economic Study, 1850–1880* (Madison: State Historical Society of Wisconsin, 1963), 12.
11. J. S. Holliday, *Rush for Riches: Gold Fever and the Making of California* (Oakland: Oakland Museum of California, and Berkeley: University of California Press, 1999), 164.
12. Carey McWilliams, *California: The Great Exception* (New York: Current Books, 1949), 81.
13. McLeod, *Pigtails,* 47.
14. Robert Glass Cleland, *A History of California: The American Period* (New York: Macmillan, 1922), 282.
15. Minke, "Chinese in the Motherlode"; Charles Caldwell Dobie, *San Francisco's Chinatown* (New York: Appleton-Century, 1936), 51.
16. Henry Huntley, *California: Its Gold and Inhabitants* (London: Thomas Cautley Newby, 1856), 250.
17. Republished in *CHISPA, Quarterly of the Tuolumne County Historical Society* 13, no. 4 (April–June 1974), 460; transcribed in Huntley, *California,* 250–55.
18. Edna Buckbee, *The Saga of Old Tuolumne* (New York: Press of the Pioneers, 1935), 75.
19. *San Francisco Daily Alta California,* May 15, 1852.
20. Alfred Jackson, *Diary of a Forty-Niner and Guide,* ed. Chauncey de Leon Canfield (Berkeley, Calif.: Clifton Press, 1947), 222–23.
21. "Miners' Meeting," *Placer Herald,* January 1, 1854.
22. *San Francisco Daily Alta California,* February 3, 1855.
23. Shasta Miners Convention Resolutions, February 5, 1859, quoted in Rosena Giles, *Shasta County California: A History* (Oakland, Calif.: Biobooks, 1949), 152.
24. See Mildred Hoover, H. E. Rensch, and E. G. Rensch, "Shasta County," in *Historic Spots in California* (Stanford, Calif.: Stanford University Press, 1948), 161.
25. Stockton also wired the governor three days later, on March 2, 1859.
26. *Placer Herald,* March 3, 5, 1859. Many early references from the *Placer Herald* can be found in Russell Towle, *The Dutch Flat Chronicles, 1849–1906* (Dutch Flat, Calif.: Giant Gap Press, 1994).
27. May Southern's Scrapbook, housed at the Shasta Courthouse Museum.
28. *Placer Herald,* March 3, 5, 1859; Towle, *Dutch Flat Chronicles,* 70.
29. H. W. Brands, *The Age of Gold: The California Gold Rush and the New American Dream* (New York: Doubleday, 2002), 41–42. See also Heizer and Almquist, *Other Californians,* 219–41.
30. Senator John Frémont, "Report to the President of the United States," September 16, 1850. See also Hurtado, *Indian Survival,* 258.
31. Quoted in *San Francisco Daily Alta California,* January 14, 1851. See also Rawls, *Indians of California,* 141.
32. Ray Raphael, *Little White Father: Redick McKee on the California Frontier* (Eureka, Calif.: Humboldt County Historical Society, 1993).
33. California Legislature, *Journal of the Senate,* 3d sess. (Sacramento, 1852), 44–45, 600–601. See also Rawls, *Indians of California,* 144.
34. Quoted in Heizer and Almquist, *Other Californians,* 26.

35. Rawls, *Indians of California,* 142–44.
36. Judith Ann Newton and Michael Newton, *Racial and Religious Violence in America: A Chronology* (New York: Garland Press, 1991), 127, 184, 224.
37. United States Naval Academy, *Records of the War Department,* 1852, RG 98, Pacific Division, box 4, vol. 2, doc. C 10/12, cited in Heizer and Almquist, *Other Californians,* 207–9.
38. The Oregon History Project. See www.ohs.org/education/oregonhistory/historical_records.
39. Episodes in Extermination, available online at www.californiahistory.net/goldFrame-diversity.htm.
40. Bibliography for the discussion of California tribal people includes Jack Norton, *Genocide in Northwestern California: When Our Worlds Cried* (San Francisco: Indian Historian Press, 1979); Rawls, *Indians of California;* Heizer and Almquist, *Other Californians;* the outstanding collection of primary documents in Robert Heizer, *The Destruction of California Indians* (Santa Barbara, Calif.: Peregrine Smith, 1984); and Hurtado, *Indian Survival.*
41. In 1855, for example, when members of the Nisenan tribe in Nevada County refused to move onto the Nomlaki Reservation, Thomas Henley, the local superintendent for Indian Affairs, ordered his troops to force 150 Nisenan into the forts by accusing the Indians of "robbing and killing Chinese, and stealing from the cabins of miners." Hurtado, *Indian Survival,* 144–47.
42. Phil Sanders and Laura Sanders, "The Quiet Rebellion: Chinese Miners Accepted in Orleans Despite 1885 Expulsion," *Humboldt Historian,* summer 1998.
43. Maria del Carmen Ferreyra and David Reher, eds. and trans., *The Gold Rush Diary of Ramón Gil Navarro* (Lincoln: University of Nebraska Press, 2000), 33.
44. Ibid., 68–69.
45. The accused men were: Pablo Martinez, Dionisio Ochoa, Gabina Jesus, and Ruiz Molina.
46. Herbert O. Lang and B. F. Alley, *A History of Tuolumne County California* (San Francisco: B. F. Alley, 1882).
47. Turning to a 1790 federal law that held that only "free white persons" could be naturalized, the tax was soon changed to apply only to those never to be eligible for citizenship, i.e., Latinos and Chinese. Californios, specifically Mexicans, who remained in the new U.S. territory for a year would automatically become American citizens, although the Gwin Act of 1852 would strip them of much of their land.
48. Holliday, *Rush for Riches,* 173.
49. Ibid., 172.
50. Lang and Alley, *History of Tuolumne County,* 30–34.
51. Kevin Starr, *Americans and the California Dream, 1850–1945* (New York: Oxford University Press, 1973), 48–72.
52. The derogatory term "greaser" for Mexican Americans dates apparently back to 1836, and may derive from oil in Mexican cooking.
53. Quoted in Susan Johnson, *Roaring Camp: The Social World of the California Gold Rush* (New York: W. W. Norton, 2000), 218.
54. See Thomas Robertson Stoddart, *Annals of Tuolumne County* and *History of Tuolumne County as It Appeared in 1861 from a Series of Newspaper Articles,* annotated by Carlo De Ferrari (Sonora, Calif.: Motherlode Pass, 1963), 34, 44–45. See also Walton Bean, *California: An Interpretive History* (New York: McGraw-Hill, 1968), and Johnson, *Roaring Camp,* 247–49.
55. Johnson, *Roaring Camp,* 215.
56. McWilliams, *California: The Great Exception,* 48–49.
57. Jack Forbes, "The Early African Heritage of California," in Lawrence B. de Graaf, *Seeking El Dorado: African Americans in California* (Seattle: University of Washington Press, 2001), 88. Note also that, hoping to attract white women to California, and in particular women with property, the convention protected the right of married women to keep their separate property.
58. Him Mark Lai, *Becoming Chinese American: A History of Communities and Institutions* (New York: Alta Mira Press, 2004), 46–74.
59. Ibid., 46–47.
60. Madeline Yuan-yin Hsu, *Dreaming of Gold, Dreaming of Home: Transnationalism and Migration Be-*

tween the United States and South China, 1882–1943 (Stanford, Calif.: Stanford University Press, 200), 10.

61. House Committee on Commerce, *Coolie Trade: Report of the Committee on Commerce to Accompany Bill No. 657,* 36th Cong., 1st sess., 1860, H.R. Res. 443, 4–30. See also Cross, *Labor Movement;* McLeod, *Pigtails,* ch. 5; and Ping, *Chinese Labor,* 9.

    Many Chinese laborers borrowed money from British firms, which agreed to advance $125 for passage, to be repaid from wages. The contract, 1849, printed in English and Chinese, omits and avoids any intermediary contractors. In correspondence, an American consul in Canton reported similar arrangements in South China.

62. *San Francisco Daily Alta California,* July 29, 1853.

63. Lai Chun-Chuen, "Remarks of the Chinese Merchants . . . upon Governor Bigler's Message," 1855, available online at www.huntington.org/Education/GoldRush/Lessons/upper.lesson.5.pdf.

64. "NORWAY American Schooner (192 tons) collided with schooner Fanny Dutard off Neah Bay January 11, 1894; she had to be abandoned by her crew and the wreck drifted ashore and broke up." House Committee, *Coolie Trade.*

65. The coolie trade bill was signed into law on February 19, 1862. It barred "coolies" on any ship registered to the United States from China to any foreign port, but the law did not apply to any "free and voluntary emigration of any Chinese subject." Thus, a free emigration was open to the Chinese. Hyung-chan Kim, *A Legal History of Asian Americans 1790–1990* (Westport, Conn.: Greenwood Press, 1994), 50. Free immigration to the United States from China now was legal and open, a policy made explicit in the Burlingame Treaty of 1868, which, in the years just after the Civil War, underscored the nation's commitment to free labor.

66. California Legislature, *Report of Committee on Mines and Mining Interests* (Sacramento, 1856).

67. See Najia Aarim-Heriot, *Chinese Immigrants, African Americans, and Racial Anxiety in the United States, 1848–82* (Urbana: University of Illinois Press, 2003), 32–42, fn. 30, 31, for a discussion of how the legislative events of May 1852 prompted the "negroization" of Chinese laborers.

68. Bean, *California,* 127; *California Senate Journal* 1852, 67–68, 192, 217, 306–7, 669–75.

69. Cross, *Labor Movement,* 12–13; and Papers of Ira Cross, Bancroft Library, University of California, Berkeley, VI 424.

70. *San Francisco Daily Alta California,* July 7, 1852 or 1853.

71. Heizer and Almquist, *Other Californians,* 155.

72. Zoeth Skinner Eldredge, *History of California,* vol. 4 (New York: Century Company, 1915), 316.

73. California Legislature, Select Committee on Resolutions of Miners' Convention of Shasta County, *Report of Mr. Flint, of the Select Committee to Whom Was Referred the Resolutions of Miners' Convention at Shasta County,* March 28, 1855 (Sacramento, 1856), VA MSS 8-788. A dissenting report, signed only by one assemblyman, Wilson Flint, pointed out that as there were about 50,000 Chinese people working in California, with a profit to the state of 25 cents each, or $12,500 per day, or, $3.75 million per year, their "withdrawal" would cause "serious embarrassments in every department of industrial life." Flint estimated that in addition to their contribution in building the infrastructure of the new state, the Chinese spent an average of $14 million per year. He recommended sending the Chinese to the mosquito-infested tule lands in the Sacramento Valley, to drain the rich swamps for sugar, cotton, and rice.

74. *Lin Sing* v. *Washburn,* 20 Cal. 534, 554–55, 575 (1862). See also Aarim-Heriot, *Chinese Immigrants,* 72.

75. *Smith* v. *Turner,* 48 U.S. (7 How.) 283 (1849); Chief Justice Taney, 7 How., 533; *Holmes* v. *Jennison,* 39 U.S. (14 Pet.) 540 (1840); and elsewhere. Taney also authored *Dred Scott* v. *Sandford,* 60 U.S. 393 (19 How.) (1857), which declared that a slave had no right to sue in federal court because he was nothing more than property and, as such, could never enjoy the rights of a citizen.

76. Hubert Howe Bancroft, *The History of California,* vol. 7 (San Francisco: History Company, 1890), 337–41.

77. During these years, Nevada County, California, alone collected $103,250, almost all from the Chinese. See "The Nevada City, California Chinese Quarter" available online at www.historichwy49.com/ethnic/Chinese.html.
78. Theodore H. Hittell, *History of California,* vol. 2 (San Francisco: N. J. Stone, 1897), 179.
79. In April 1853, the California Legislature had the Foreign Miners' Tax Law translated into Chinese, lithographed, and posted throughout the mining district. A translated copy is available at California State Archives.
80. Dobie, *Chinatown,* 50.
81. Quoted in *Mariposa Gazette,* 1856.
82. Dobie, *Chinatown,* 49; and William Speer, *The Oldest at the Newest Empire: China and the United States* (Hartford, Conn.: S. S. Scranton, 1870), 575.
83. From *Placer Herald,* September 24, 1853, cited in Towle, *Dutch Flat Chronicles,* 8–9.
84. Ibid.
85. Chiu, *Chinese Labor,* 27–28.
86. "Letter from an Old Miner," Mariposa, January 22, 1856, Collection of Western Americana, Beineke Library, Yale University, OL2 S 779.
87. California Legislature, *Select Committee on Resolutions of Miners' Convention of Shasta County, Minority Report,* March 17, 1855, Doc. 16, *Journal of the Senate,* 6th sess. (San Francisco: Redding State Printer, 1855).
88. William Perkins, signed "Leo," *Stockton Times,* from Johnson, *Roaring Camp,* 211.
89. Johnson, *Roaring Camp,* 214.
90. Ibid., 248.
91. *Sonora Herald,* July 14, 1850.
92. Robert W. Pitkin to his parents, from Jones Bar, California, August 16, 1852; Bancroft Library, University of California, Berkeley.
93. John Bigler, governor of California, *Special Message to the State Senate and Assembly on the Chinese Question* (Sacramento, 1853).
94. "Remarks of the Chinese Merchants . . . Upon Governor Bigler's Message, and Some Common Questions; with Some Explanations of the Character of the Chinese Companies, and the Laboring Class in California" (San Francisco: Whitton, Towne, 1855).
95. Cited in *Miners and Businessmen's Directory,* article 16, 81.
96. Ibid., 86.
97. *San Francisco Daily Alta California,* May 15, 1852; and Bancroft Scraps, Bancroft Library, University of California, Berkeley, 253.
98. *San Francisco Daily Alta California,* May 15, 1852.
99. McLeod, *Pigtails,* 60. See also Buckbee, *Old Tuolumne,* 77.
100. Jackson, *Diary,* 222.
101. *San Francisco Daily Evening Bulletin,* September 1, 1857.
102. Dobie, *Chinatown,* 52.
103. Navarro, *Gold Rush Diary,* 126.
104. See de Graaf, *Seeking El Dorado.* At this time African Americans were usually listed in the census without last names, under their employers' addresses.
105. Brands, *The Age of Gold,* 278.
106. Rudolph Lapp, *Blacks in the California Gold Rush* (New Haven, Conn.: Yale University Press, 1977), 21.
107. Ibid., 22, and *Freeman,* March 25, 1852. According to Lapp, this was reported by Frederick Douglass in *The North Star.* Angered by some white abolitionists who condemned the materialism of the black migration to California, Douglass argued that American Negroes should seize any economic opportunity; besides, he noted, financially secure white abolitionists were themselves leaving the antislavery battleground for the gold fields but carrying the antislavery banner to the Pacific Coast. See 14–17. See also Delilah Beasley, *The Negro Trail Blazers of California* (Los Angeles: 1919), 104.
108. See Aarim-Heriot, *Chinese Immigrants,* 39.
109. *In re Perkins,* 2 Cal. 424 (1852).

110. *Ex parte Archy* 9 Cal. 147 (1858). See also Lucile Eaves, *A History of California Labor Legislation* (Berkeley: University of California Press, 1910), ch. 2, "Slave or Free Labor in California."
111. De Graaf, *Seeking El Dorado,* 11.
112. Buckbee, *Old Tuolumne,* 77.
113. *People* v. *Hall,* 4 Cal. 399 (1854).
114. *People* v. *Elyea,* 14 Cal. 144 (1859); cited in Heizer, *Destruction,* 144. The restriction was also repealed, by omission, when the California Code of Civil Procedure became law during Reconstruction in 1872. See also Heizer and Almquist, *Other Californians,* 128–29. But the right of a Chinese person to testify against a white person was only secured through the first Civil Rights Act, later embedded in the Fourteenth Amendment, which gave former slaves and all free men "full and equal benefit of all laws." Using this language, the Chinese in Idaho apparently became the first to formally win the right to testify in court. Charles McClain, "The Chinese Struggle for Civil Rights in Nineteenth Century America: The First Phase, 1850–1870," *California Law Review* 72 (July 1984), 529, 548–50.
115. David Beesley, "More Than *People* v. *Hall:* Chinese Immigrants and American Law in a Sierra Nevada County, 1850–1920," *Locus* 3, no. 2 (spring 1991), 132; and *Quam or Quang Chew* v. *Sales and Johnson,* Criminal Files, Searls Library, Nevada City, California Cab. 6-160.
116. Beesley, "More Than *People,*" 134.
117. Hsu, *Dreaming of Gold,* 13.
118. Ibid., 12.
119. Ibid., 10.
120. Ibid., 34.
121. In 1852 the Rev. A. D. Smith sent five missionaries to California with the charge to think about "where this work is to be done. The fabric to be reared on the Pacific Coast will overlook Asia." More than 40,000 "natives of the Celestial empire," said Smith, have come to California to "see how you build," and many, he predicted, would become "living stones in the spiritual temple." Quoted in Laurie F. Maffly-Kipp, *Religion and Society in Frontier California* (New Haven, Conn.: Yale University Press, 1994), 48.
122. Anonymous, "John Chinaman," in *California Songster,* ed. D. E. Appleton (San Francisco: Noisy Carriers Books and Stationery, 1855), 44–45; cited in Krystan Moon, *Yellow Face: Creating the Chinese in American Popular Music and Performance, 1850–1920s* (New Brunswick, N.J.: Rutgers University Press, 2005), 36–37.
123. Ping, *Chinese Labor,* 142; and Mary Roberts Coolidge, *Chinese Immigration* (New York: Henry Holt, 1909), 498.
124. As late as 1870 the Chinese accounted for over half of the total California mining population. By 1866, the *Shasta Courier* completed a series on the successful mining endeavors of the Chinese in Briggsville. The June 2, 1866, issue announced that "Briggsville . . . now belongs entirely to the Chinese, and the ground heretofore used as a town site is being more profitably used for mining purposes." On October 19, 1867, the *Courier* reported that a Chinese company had paid $1,100 for the site, cleared away the buildings and trees, and within months had taken out an estimated $11,000 in gold. During the 1860s the Chinese also remained in Horsetown, leaving the area only at the end of the decade to work on the railroads. See Priscilla Wegars, ed., *Hidden Heritage: Historical Archaeology of the Overseas Chinese* (Amityville, N.Y.: Baywood, 1993). See also Judith Tordoff and Dana Seldner, "History of Department's Archaeology (1950–1999)," Dept. of Anthropology, California State University, Sacramento, 1987:28 www.csus.edu/ANTH/newanth/anth_dept_arch_history.htm.
125. Holliday, *Rush,* 173.
126. Ibid.
127. Alexander Saxton, *The Indispensable Enemy: Labor and the Anti-Chinese Movement in California* (Berkeley: University of California Press, 1971). This is the classic and foundational study of the role of white labor in the anti-Chinese movement.
128. The first white miners who reached the rich bars of the American, Yuba, Feather, Stanislaus, and Trinity Rivers in 1849 had indeed made from $500 to $5,000 a day, for weeks at a time during '48 and '49. By 1850, however, their income had shrunk to $20 a day, and by the

end of the decade, it was $3 a day—comparable to that of Chinese miners. John S. Hittell, *Mining in the Pacific States of North America* (San Francisco: H. H. Bancroft, 1861), 21.

129. *San Francisco Daily Alta California,* July 29, 1853.
130. Bayard Taylor, *New Pictures from California* 1862, reprint (Oakland, Calif.: Biobooks, 1941), quoted in David Wyatt, *Five Fires: Race, Catastrophe, and the Shaping of California* (New York: Addison-Wesley, 1997), 52.

CHAPTER 2. DEAD BRANCHES

1. With thanks to Paul M. De Falla, "Lantern in the Western Sky," *Historical Society of Southern California Quarterly* 15, no. 1, part 1 (March 1960), for locating this prescient quote, and for his incredibly detailed narrative of the events surrounding the lynching and murders of nineteen Chinese men and women in Los Angeles in 1871. See also Raymond Lou, "The Chinese American Community of Los Angeles 1870–1900: A Case of Resistance, Organization, and Participation" (Ph.D. diss., University of California, Irvine, 1982); and *Sacramento Daily Union, Los Angeles Daily News, Los Angeles Star* from October to December 1871.
2. *San Francisco Daily Alta California,* October 19 and 20, 1871.
3. It is likely that these companies are two of the original Chinese Six Companies. If this is the case, "Hong Chow," as reported in the newspapers, would be a misspelling of "Kong Chow." In the early 1850s the Ning Yung broke away from the Kong Chow in several violent confrontations. The Los Angeles 1871 episode may be part of this split. Private correspondence with Gilbert Hom, Chinese Historical Society of Southern California.
4. Newspaper sources for the Los Angeles massacre include the *Daily Alta California, The New York Times,* the *Los Angeles Star,* the *Los Angeles Weekly News,* the *Los Angeles Evening Express,* the *Sacramento Bee,* and the *Sacramento Daily Union.* Full copy of testimony to the coroner's jury is in the *Los Angeles Star,* October 27–30, 1871.
5. *New York Times,* November 10, 1871.
6. *New York Times,* October 28, 1871.
7. Hubert Howe Bancroft, *California Inter Pocula: A Review of Some Classical Abnormalities* (San Francisco: History Company, 1888), 566–67.
8. Leon Litwack, "Hellhounds," in *Without Sanctuary: Lynching Photography in America,* eds. James Allen et al. (Santa Fe, N.M.: Twin Palms, 2000), 25.
9. Bancroft, *California Inter Pocula,* 562–63.
10. *New York Times,* November 5 and December 15, 1871.
11. *California* v. *Brady,* 40 Cal. 198 (1870).
12. *San Francisco Daily Alta California,* October 25, 1871.
13. San Francisco *Daily Evening Bulletin,* October 26, 1871, republished in *New York Times,* November 10, 1871.
14. Quoted from: *San Francisco Daily Alta California,* October 19, 20, 1871.
15. "War of Races," *New York Times,* October 26, 1871.
16. Ibid.
17. *New York Times,* November 7, 1871.
18. Ibid., November 5 and December 15, 1871; *Los Angeles Star,* December 9, 1871.
19. *Los Angeles Star,* December 23, 1871.
20. None of the major histories of lynching discusses its Chinese casualties. For example, see Arthur F. Raper, *The Tragedy of Lynching* (New York: Dover, 1933); Ralph Ginzburg, *100 Years of Lynchings* (1962; Baltimore: Black Classic Press, 1988); Philip Dray, *At the Hands of Persons Unknown: The Lynching of Black America* (New York: Modern Library, 2003). The exception is the interracial chronology of violence, Michael Newton and Judy Ann Newton, *Racial and Religious Violence in America: A Chronology* (New York: Garland, 1991), which has several geographical inaccuracies, however—for example, placing the anti-Chinese riot in Eureka in the Washington Territory rather than in California.
21. Leon Litwack, *Trouble in Mind: Black Southerners in the Age of Jim Crow* (New York: Alfred A. Knopf, 1998), 304. See also Litwack, "Hellhounds." The work of David Palumbo-Liu,

Asian/American: Historical Crossings of a Racial Frontier (Stanford, Calif.: Stanford University Press, 1999), and Edward Blum, *Reforging the White Republic: Race, Religion, and American Nationalism 1865–1898* (Baton Rouge: Louisiana State University Press, 2005), helped me profoundly in understanding the "racial overlay" I construct in this chapter.

22. Within a few days of the massacre in Los Angeles, *Harper's Weekly* noted that a member of the U.S. Senate estimated that 5,000 people had been murdered by the Ku Klux Klan since the end of the Civil War (*Harper's Weekly,* November 4, 1871). Between 1889 and 1930, 3,724 people were lynched in the United States; more than four fifths of these were African Americans; fewer than one sixth were accused of rape. The nation's famous antilynching leader, Ida B. Wells, estimated in the 1890s that as many as 10,000 black Americans had been murdered in the South since the Civil War [Dray, xi], but the silence and lack of reporting by newspapers, politicians, and police officers make accurate numbers impossible. That number reasonably estimates the number of African Americans who died at the hands of lynch mobs between the end of Reconstruction and the birth of the civil rights movement. Of the tens of thousands of lynchers and onlookers, history records that only forty-nine were indicted and only four were sentenced. This obviously does not include the parties to the L.A. massacre. See Raper, *Tragedy,* 1; and Dray, *At the Hands,* xi.
23. "A Lynching in Denver's Chinatown, 1880," available online at www.americanlynching.com/infamous-old.html#1880.
24. Hubert Howe Bancroft, "Popular Tribunals," *San Francisco History* 1, no. 45 (1887), cited in David A. Johnson, "Vigilance and the Law: The Moral Authority of Popular Justice in the Far West," *American Quarterly* 33, no. 5 (winter 1981), 566.
25. Johnson, "Vigilance."
26. Just two weeks before the lynchings, the *Los Angeles Star* wrote, "There are fewer idlers and men out of employment in Los Angeles than in any other city of its size on the Pacific Coast." Cited in William R. Locklear, "The Celestials and the Angels: A Study of the Anti-Chinese Movement in Los Angeles to 1882," *Historical Society of Southern California Quarterly* 42, no. 3 (September 1960), 245.
27. Bureau of the Census, *Report on the Social Statistics of Cities, part 2: The Southern and Western States, 1887* (Washington, D.C., 1887).
28. Locklear, "Celestials," 97–104.
29. Jon Regardie, "The L.A. Dynasty: Chinese Museum Planned for 1890 Building," Chinese American Museum, www.camla.org/resource/dynasty.htm.
30. See Carey McWilliams, *California: The Great Exception* (Santa Barbara, Calif.: Peregrine Smith, 1976), 152; and Peter Camejo, *Racism, Revolution, Reaction, 1861–1877* (New York: Monad Press, 1976), 218–19.
31. *California Farmer,* May 25, 1854.
32. Mark Wahlgren Summers, *The Era of Good Stealings* (New York: Oxford University Press, 1993), 118.
33. David Leiwei Li, *Imagining the Nation: Asian American Literature and Cultural Consent* (Stanford, Calif.: Stanford University Press, 1998), 1–5.
34. Austen Wiley had served as superintendent of Indian Affairs for California and in June 1864 had made a popular if fruitless recommendation that "hostile" Indians from the northern counties be shipped to the San Pedro or the Santa Catalina Islands off the southern coast.
35. Quoted in James J. Rawls, *Indians of California: The Changing Image* (Norman: University of Oklahoma Press, 1984), 168–70.
36. *Chico Courant,* July 18, 1866. Cited in ibid., 183.
37. Rawls, *Indians,* 161.
38. Ibid., 161–70; and Eric Foner, *Reconstruction: America's Unfinished Revolution, 1863–1877* (New York: HarperCollins, 1988), 463.
39. See Mary Ellicott Arnold, *In the Land of the Grasshopper Song: Two Women in the Klamath River Indian Country in 1908–09* (Lincoln: University of Nebraska Press, 1957), a memoir of two white

women, in a long-term relationship, who serve as Indian matrons and live among the Karuk people.

40. For example, on May 3, 1877, the Nez Perce tribe was given thirty days to gather their stock and move onto reservations, an order that launched a major uprising.

41. A series of papal bulls obligated the conquerors to convert and "civilize" the 300,000 Indians living in Alta California. By the time Mexico won its independence from Spain in 1821, most of the tribal people between San Diego and San Francisco had already been removed from their native villages. New diseases, dietary deficiencies, poor sanitation, and lack of medical care, as well as Spanish irons, lashings, and imprisonment at the hands of the soldiers garrisoned with the missions, reduced the tribal population of California in some places by 75 percent. See Rawls, *Indians,* 18.

42. Annie E. K. Bidwell, *Rancho Chico Indians,* ed. Dorothy J. Hill (Chico, Calif.: Bidwell Mansion, 1980).

43. California Statutes, 1860, ch. 231. For information on the lives of indentured and enslaved Indians in Humboldt County from 1860 to 1863, see Robert F. Heizer and Alan F. Almquist, *The Other Californians: Prejudice and Discrimination Under Spain, Mexico, and the United States to 1920* (Berkeley: University of California Press, 1971), 54–56.

44. Najia Aarim, "Chinese Immigrants, African-Americans and the Problem of Race in the United States, 1848–1882" (Ph.D. diss., Temple University, 1996), 512–16.

45. *Weekly Antioch Ledger,* September 23, 1877.

46. Cited in Najia Aarim-Heriot, *Chinese Immigrants, African Americans, and Racial Anxiety in the United States, 1848–82* (Urbana: University of Illinois Press, 2003), 81–82.

47. The Slaughter-House Cases, 83 U.S. 36 (1873). See also Ronald Labbe, *The Slaughterhouse Cases: Regulation, Reconstruction, and the Fourteenth Amendment* (Lawrence: University Press of Kansas, 2003).

48. Li, *Imagining,* 5.

49. Aarim-Heriot, *Chinese Immigrants,* 81.

50. Newspaper accounts for the events in Butte and Nevada Counties covered in this chapter come from extensive reading of the *Auburn;* the *Placer Argus;* the *Chico Record;* the *Chico Enterprise;* and the *Butte Record,* also known as the *Weekly Butte Record,* which moved from Oroville to Chico in 1874. In 1877 it joined with the *Chronicle* to become the *Chico Chronicle-Record.* I am using the title *Butte Record.* It is cited interchangeably by historians as the *Chico Record* or the *Butte Record.* See also the *Oroville Mercury;* the *Sacramento Bee;* the *Sacramento Appeal;* the *Sacramento Daily Union;* the *San Francisco Chronicle;* the *San Francisco Morning Call;* the *Oakland Daily Transcript,* the *Placerville Mountain Democrat;* the *Truckee Republican; The Eureka Humboldt Times/Humboldt Times Standard,* the *Grass Valley Foothill Weekly Tidings;* and the *Marysville Daily Appeal.* I have relied heavily on the correspondence of John Bidwell, particularly his letters to his wife, Annie Bidwell, at the Meriam Library, Special Collections Department, California State University, Chico, and am indebted to the guidance of archivst Bill Jones and the curators at the Oroville Chinese Temple.

    See also Michelle Shover, *Chico's Lemm Ranch Murders and Anti-Chinese Campaign of 1877* (Chico: Association for Northern California Records and Research, California State University, Chico, 1998); "Chico Women," *California History* 67, no. 4 (December 1988), 226–43; "Fighting Back: The Chinese Influence on Chico Law and Politics, 1880–1886," *California History* 74, no. 4 (winter 1995–96), 409–21.

51. The Chinese first came to Butte County in the 1850s to search for gold along the Feather River, often working claims and tailings that had been abandoned by white miners. By 1860 only eleven Chinese people lived in Chico, but between 1865 and 1867, Chinese miners left the gold fields and the railroad gangs in the Sierra, and came into the valley town, taking unskilled and seasonal jobs in lumber and agriculture, and soon in gold. As Old Town, the county's first segregated Chinatown, grew, so did the hostility. By 1874 special trains carried between 7,000 and 10,000 Chinese miners to work the rich veins of gold in the lava beds discovered near Oroville, 25 miles south of Chico. Many wives of the Chinese merchants in Chico chose to live within the safety and camaraderie of San Francisco's Chinatown.

52. George C. Mansfield, *History of Butte County, California, with Biographical Sketches* (Los Angeles: Historic Record, 1918), 270–71. See also Michael J. Gillis and Michael F. Magliari, *John Bidwell and California: The Life and Writings of a Pioneer, 1841–1900* (Spokane, Wash.: A. H. Clarke, 2003).
53. Henry George, "Our Land and Land Policy," in *The Complete Works of Henry George* (New York: Doubleday, Page and Co., 1871), 68.
54. Cletus Daniels, *Bitter Harvest: A History of California Farmworkers, 1870–1941* (Ithaca, N.Y.: Cornell University Press, 1981), 27–28, 31.
55. Aarim, "Chinese Immigrants," 161–67.
56. See Susan Wiley Book, "The Chinese in Butte County, 1860–1920" (master's thesis, California State University, Chico, 1974), 19.
57. Blum, *Reforging*, 124.
58. For the information on the fabric of daily life in Chico in the last three decades of the nineteenth century and its relationship to the anti-Chinese movement, and for her detailed narrative of the arsons, murders, and trials, I am indebted to the thoughtful work of the historian Michelle Shover. I am also grateful to her for her detailed and accurate citations, which helped mark my way.
59. Book, "Chinese in Butte County," 52.
60. Mansfield, *History of Butte County*, 276.
61. Ibid., 288. As early as 1862 the Chinese emperor Tsai-ch'un honored the local Chinese by building a temple in Oroville to celebrate the anniversary of his ascension to power. Three parallel sanctuaries in one magnificent building served the Confucian, Buddhist, and Taoist communities. Nearby were four Chinese cemeteries where the dead were laid to rest until their bones were ready to be scraped clean of flesh and shipped back to China for their final burial. In Deadwood, a successful Chinese physician and herbalist, Ah Sang, opened a large hospital, seeing 100 paying patients a week. Today thousands of Chinese medicines and bottles lie buried beneath the Oro-Concow Road that passes by the site of his hospital. See Shover, *Lemm Ranch*, 13. See also the *Record, Enterprise* covering the winter through the late summer of 1876; Book, "The Chinese in Butte County"; Mansfield, *History of Butte County*.
62. Shover, *Lemm Ranch*, 15; and *Chico Butte Record*, May 13, June 24, and July 1, 1876; January 27 and February 10, 1877.
63. These included Andrew Hallet, Chico's justice of the peace, as well as merchants, carpenters, and unemployed men.
64. *Sacramento Appeal*, March 29, 1877, quoted in Shover, *Lemm*, 19.
65. Bancroft, *California Inter Pocula*, 568–69.
66. Ibid., 569.
67. Ibid., 573.
68. Shover, *Lemm Ranch*, 21.
69. *Butte Record*, March 17, 1877.
70. Ibid. Also quoted in Shover, *Lemm Ranch*, 39.
71. Bancroft, *California Inter Pocula*, 575.
72. See Sim Moak, "The Last of the Mill Creeks and Early Life in Northern California" (Chico, Calif., 1923), 29. Moak's is a settler's memoir of a well-known local Indian fighter.
73. *Butte Record*, June 2, 1877.
74. Moak, "Mill Creeks," 29. See also Bancroft, *California Inter Pocula*, 575–76.
75. *Butte Record*, June 2, 1877.
76. Moak, "Mill Creeks," 29.
77. Shover, *Lemm Ranch*, 36.
78. Ibid.
79. *Butte Record*, March 17, 1877.
80. Bancroft, *California Inter Pocula*, 576.
81. *Butte Record*, March 18, 1877.
82. Moak, "Mill Creeks," 28.
83. Transcribed as written. Bancroft, *California Inter Pocula*, 580–81.

84. *Chico Enterprise,* April 27, 1877.
85. *Butte Record,* August 11, 1877.
86. John Bidwell, Diary, John Bidwell Papers, 1844–1900, Special Collections Department, Meriam Library, California State University, Chico.
87. Quoted in Gillis and Magliari, *John Bidwell and California,* 336.
88. Quoted in *Sacramento Appeal,* March 29, 1877.
89. *Chico Enterprise,* March 30, 1877. See also Shover, *Lemm Ranch.* The author turned to the confessions themselves in her detailed, fulsome account of the events following the massacre.
90. Shover, *Lemm Ranch,* 55.
91. Ibid., 55–57. Downhill and downriver from the Sierra Nevada, Chico and the other towns in Butte County also thrived by their easy access to cut lumber. During the post–Civil War building boom in California, wagon, frame, and door factories opened in the county, many with retail outlets in San Francisco, Oakland, and Portland.
92. *Oroville Mercury,* May 24, 1878; and Book, "Chinese in Butte County," 72.
93. These figures are consistent with statewide figures that show that Chinese working males comprised one fourth of California's wage laborers at the time. Sucheng Chan, *This Bittersweet Soil: The Chinese in California Agriculture* (Berkeley: University of California Press, 1987), 48–50. Note also that in Butte County, 783 Chinese immigrants lived in Chico, 29 of whom were women. According to the 1880 census, more than 3,500 Chinese immigrants lived in the county, of whom 81 were females.
94. The *Daily Alta California* observed that the fines for violating the codes were designed not to increase the city's revenue but to decrease "the immigration of Chinese." *San Francisco Daily Alta California,* May 27, 1873. See also Ruth Ann Lum McCunn, *The Illustrated History of the Chinese in America* (San Francisco: Design Enterprises of San Francisco, 1979), 77.
95. In 1885, hundreds of Chinese resisted arrest under the Cubic Air Ordinance, rushing upon the police officers and tearing fellow Chinese prisoners away from an arresting officer, "giving him a parting shot from a revolver . . . before the other raiders could come to his assistance." Facing the resistance of the Chinese, the mass overcrowding in the jail, and Judge Sawyer's interpretation of the Fourteenth Amendment, Mayor Alvord of San Francisco began rescinding the ordinances within a month. These laws lived on elsewhere in California throughout the 1880s.
96. *Ho Ah Kow v. Nunan,* 12 F. 252 (C.C. Cal. 1879).
97. *General Orders of the Board of Supervisors . . . of the City and County of San Francisco and Ordinances of Park Commissioners* (San Francisco: W. M. Hinton, 1878).
98. Amendment to the Civil Code of California, 1880.
99. *California Statutes* (1860), 325. See also Theodore Hittell, *The General Laws of the State of California from 1850 to 1864* (San Francisco: A. L. Bancroft & Company, 1865), 998; and Aarim-Heriot, *Chinese Immigrants* (2003), 62.
100. Rudolph Lapp, *Blacks in the California Gold Rush* (New Haven, Conn.: Yale University Press, 1977), 21–22.
101. I am indebted to Najia Aarim-Heriot for an insightful and thoroughly documented discussion of the overlay of anti-Chinese and anti-black discourses and practices in the attempts to dismantle Reconstruction. Aarim-Heriot, *Chinese Immigrants,* Picket quoted 180–81.
102. The entire testimony from these hearings is collected in an invaluable volume entitled *Chinese Immigration: Its Social, Moral, and Political Effect: Reports to the California State Senate of Its Special Committee on Chinese Immigration.* U.S. House, 45th Cong., 1st sess., Mis. Doc. No. 9 (Sacramento: F. P. Thompson, 1878).
103. Quoted in Aarim-Hariot, *Chinese Immigrants,* 183.
104. See Hiroyuki Matsubara's analysis of the report in "Stratified Whiteness and Sexualized Chinese Immigrants in San Francisco: The Report of the California Special Committee on Chinese Immigration in 1876," *American Studies International* 41, no. 3 (October 2003).
105. See Ira B. Cross, *A History of the Labor Movement in California* (Berkeley: University of California Press, 1935), 79–80; and Aarim-Heriot, *Chinese Immigrants.*
106. Deborah Cooper, "A Lowly Pickaxe Handle," manuscript, Oakland Museum (2005), 1. See also *Oakland Daily Transcript,* July 26, 1877; and *Oakland Evening Tribune,* July 25, 1877.

107. *San Francisco Daily Evening Bulletin,* December 12, 1877, and January 10, 1878. See also Cross, *Labor Movement,* 107.
108. *Sacramento Daily Union,* September 28, 1877.
109. *San Francisco Chronicle,* September 16, 1877.
110. California Constitution (1879), art. 19, sec. 1.
111. Among the delegates to the constitutional convention was Charles McGlashan, who would soon lead the massive purge of the Chinese in Truckee and become a spokesman for Chinese expulsions across the state.
112. Rudolph Lapp, *Afro-Americans in California* (San Francisco: Boyd and Fraser, 1979), 24.
113. *In re Tiburcio Parrott,* 1F. 481 (C.C. Cal 1880).
114. *Statutes at Large* 57 (1943), 600.
115. Arnold Shankman, *Afro-Americans View the Immigrant* (Westport, Conn.: Greenwood Press, 1982), 13.
116. Lapp, *Blacks in the California Gold Rush,* 7.
117. Shankman, *Afro-Americans,* 4. See also David Hellwig, "Black Reactions to Chinese Immigration and the Anti-Chinese Movement: 1850–1910," *Amerasia* 6 (1979), 34.
118. Shankman, *Afro-Americans,* 4.
119. Ibid., 7.
120. *San Francisco Elevator,* May 24, 1873; and ibid., 6.
121. Ibid.
122. Philip Bell, *San Francisco Elevator,* June 19, 1866, and August 30, 1867. Also cited in Leigh Dana Johnson, "Equal Rights and the Heathen 'Chinee': Black Activism in San Francisco, 1865–1875," *Western Historical Quarterly* 11, no. 1 (January 1980), 61.
123. *San Francisco Elevator,* December 17, 1869; and Johnson, "Equal Rights," 67.
124. *San Francisco Elevator,* December 17, 1869, July 8, 1870, March 29, April 26, May 3 and 17, and June 14, 1873. See also Shankman, *Afro-Americans,* 6.
125. Hellwig, "Black Reactions," 30–38 in particular.
126. Eric Foner and Olivia Mahoney, *America's Reconstruction: People and Politics After the Civil War* (Baton Rouge: Louisiana State University Press, 1995), 74ff.
127. *San Francisco Chronicle,* September 15, 1877.
128. "Frederick A. Bee's Identification with the History of California," ms., H. H. Bancroft Collection, Bancroft Library, University of California, Berkeley.
129. See Robert G. Lee, *Orientals: Asian Americans in Popular Culture* (Philadelphia: Temple University Press, 1999), for an analysis of the representations of Chinese immigrants and the political formation and consequences of these stereotypes. For analysis of the ways these images endured and were transformed in cinema, see Peter X. Feng, *Identities in Motion: Asian American Film and Video* (Durham, N.C.: Duke University Press, 2002).
130. The *Examiner* reported that the Chinese dwellings were owned by white men who wanted them "broken up" in any case. *San Francisco Examiner,* September 20, 1877.
131. *San Francisco Chronicle,* September 20, 1877.
132. Sources for the discussion of the expulsions of Chinese from Placer County include the *San Francisco Chronicle, Sacramento Daily Union, Sacramento Bee, Chico Butte Record, Placerville Mountain Democrat,* and *El Dorado Republican.*
133. Leonard M. Davis, *Rocklin: Past, Present, Future: An Illustrated History of Rocklin, Placer County, from 1864 to 1981* (Roseville, Calif.: Rocklin Friends of the Library, 1981), 31–32.
134. Thompson and West, *History of Placer County, California, with Illustrations and Biographical Sketches of Its Prominent Men and Pioneers* (Oakland, Calif.: Thompson and West, 1882), 396.
135. *Sacramento Daily Union,* September 19, 1877.
136. *El Dorado County Republican,* October 11, 1877.
137. *San Francisco Daily Examiner,* September 20, 1877.
138. Ibid.
139. Ibid.
140. Ibid.
141. *San Francisco Daily Alta California,* September 22, 1877.
142. Newton and Newton, *Racial and Religious Violence,* 218–34.

143. McWilliams, *California,* 183.
144. Shover, *Lemm Ranch,* 10.

CHAPTER 3. THE WOMAN'S TALE

1. 1880 census lists 620 total residents for Antioch. The Bureau of the Census, *Tenth Census of the United States,* vol. 1, *Statistics of the Population of the United States, 1880* (Washington, D.C.: 1886).
2. Nayan Shah, *Contagious Divides: Epidemics and Race in San Francisco's Chinatown* (Berkeley: University of California Press, 2001), 28.
3. *History of Contra Costa County, California* (San Francisco: W. A. Slocum, 1882), 495. See also *San Francisco Chronicle,* May 2, 1876; *San Francisco Daily Alta California,* February 26, 1886; *Public Opinion,* May 6, 1876; and *Sacramento Daily Record,* May 2, 1876.
4. These contemporary sources were useful for reporting on the situation of Chinese women: *Antioch Daily Ledger, Weekly Antioch Ledger, San Francisco Chronicle, San Francisco Daily Alta California, Public Opinion, Sacramento Daily Record, Humboldt Times Standard, California Census Index, Sacramento Union.*
5. Earl Hohlmayer, "Chinese Were Treated as Lesser Human Beings," *Antioch Daily Ledger,* April 2, 1990. Other contemporary journalists and local historians of Antioch writing in the *Daily Ledger* who have contributed to this chapter include Paul Allen, Elizabeth Rimbault, and Nilda Rego.
6. George Emanuels, *California's Contra Costa County: An Illustrated History* (Fresno, Calif.: Panorama West Books, 1986), 218.
7. The Starr Flour Mill was later converted to the Spreckels California-Hawaiian Sugar Refinery, where Chinese workers refined imported sugarcane grown by Asian and Pacific Islanders on the Hawaiian Islands. See ibid.
8. *Weekly Antioch Ledger,* September 18, 1877.
9. *Humboldt Times Standard,* April 16, 1886.
10. Marlon K. Hom, *Songs of Gold Mountain: Cantonese Rhymes from San Francisco Chinatown* (Berkeley: University of California Press, 1987).
11. Herbert Asbury, *The Barbary Coast: An Informal History of Chinatown's Underworld* (New York: Alfred A. Knopf, 1933, 1944), available online at www.sfgenealogy.com/sf/history/hbtbc8.htm. See also Shah, *Contagious Divides.*
12. Benson Tong, *Unsubmissive Women: Chinese Prostitutes in Nineteenth-Century San Francisco* (Norman: University of Oklahoma Press, 1994), 14. Tong estimates that in 1870, 61 percent of Chinese women in California were prostitutes—a number considerably lower than other estimates.
13. *San Francisco Chronicle,* December 5, 1869.
14. From "Confessions of a Chinese Slave-Dealer," transcribed by Helen Grey, in Judy Yung, *Unbound Voices: A Documentary History of Chinese Women in San Francisco* (Berkeley: University of California Press, 1999), 153.
15. Tong, *Unsubmissive Women,* 12.
16. Information on Chinese prostitution in the nineteenth century is based on Shah, *Contagious Divides;* Tong, *Unsubmissive Women;* Asbury, *Barbary Coast;* Margit Stange, *Personal Property: Wives, White Slaves, and the Market in Women* (Baltimore: Johns Hopkins University Press, 1998); Helen Fletcher Collins, "An Historical Local Commerce: Prostitution," *Pacifica: Magazine of the Northcoast* (May 1972); and George Anthony Peffer, *If They Don't Bring Their Women Here: Chinese Female Immigration Before Exclusion* (Urbana: University of Illinois Press, 1999).
17. Humboldt County, *California Census Index,* 1880, 53–58.
18. Peffer, *If They Don't,* 32.
19. John D'Emilio and Estelle Freedman, *Intimate Matters: A History of Sexuality in the United States* (Chicago: University of Chicago Press, 1987).
20. Shah, *Contagious Divides,* 87.
21. Willard B. Farwell, *The Chinese at Home and Abroad* (San Francisco: A. L. Bancroft, 1885), cited in Shah, *Contagious Divides,* 80.
22. D'Emilio and Freedman, *Intimate Matters,* 146–48.

23. Physicians understood how the disease was spread long before they understood how it could be cured. It was not until 1904 that Dr. Prince Morrow described how common female complaints among young married women—sterility, congenital blindness in infants, syphilitic insanity, chronic uterine inflammation, and fatigue—"innocent infections"—could be traced "back to their original source in that irregular sexual commerce known as prostitution." Morrow blamed "masculine unchastity" rather than the female prostitute as the "chief malefactor." Ibid., 204.
24. See Susan Craddock, "Embodying Place: Pathologizing Chinese and Chinatown in Nineteenth-Century San Francisco," *Antipode* 31, no. 4 (1999), 351–371, for an astute discussion of how the pathologizing of the Chinese female in San Francisco in the mid-nineteenth century lent scientific authority to the "politics of normal" and the crucial role of medical theory in authorizing the superiority of Anglo-Saxon heritage.
25. California had rejected the model solution of the English Contagious Diseases Acts of the 1860s, which incarcerated infected prostitutes in public "lock hospitals," leaving their patrons, equally infected, free to transmit the disease to their wives or other prostitutes.
26. "Committee to Investigate Chinatown," 1880:5–6, cited in Craddock, "Embodying Place," 359.
27. D'Emilio and Freedman, *Intimate Matters,* 204.
28. Shah, *Contagious Divide,* 81.
29. San Francisco Board of Health, *S.F. Municipal Report,* 1864–65, 139. Cited in ibid., 81.
30. *Medico-Literary Journal* 5 (1878), cited in Craddock, "Embodying Place," 363.
31. Shah, *Contagious Divide,* 84.
32. Major studies of the Page Act include Shah, *Contagious Divide;* Peffer, *If They Don't;* and Judy Yung, *Unbound Feet: A Social History of Chinese Women in San Francisco* (Berkeley: University of California Press, 1995).
33. See Peffer, *If They Don't.*
34. Senate, Joint Special Committee to Investigate Chinese Immigration, in *Chinese Immigration,* 1877, p. 145.
35. Hom, *Songs of Gold Mountain,* 46.
36. Cited in Yung, *Unbound Feet,* 20–21.
37. Peffer, *If They Don't,* 4.
38. The 1870 census listed 2,157 of the 3,536 adult Chinese women as prostitutes. The 1880 census enumerators listed only 759. See "*The Chinese in California, 1850–1925,* Timeline," *American Memory* (Library of Congress), available online at http://memory.loc.gov/ammem/award99/cubhtml/chron.html. See generally Robert Takaki, *Strangers from a Different Shore: A History of Asian Americans* (Boston: Back Bay Books, 1998), 123.
39. By 1890, there were 22 Chinese men to 1 Chinese woman residing in California. See generally Geoffrey Dunn, *Santa Cruz Is in the Heart* (Capitola, Calif.: Capitola Book Company, 1983).
40. Sucheng Chan, "The Exclusion of Chinese Women," in *Entry Denied: Exclusion and the Chinese Community in America, 1882–1943,* ed. Sucheng Chan (Philadelphia: Temple University Press, 1991).
41. See Yung, *Unbound Feet,* 37–47, for a discussion of the daily life of *mui tsai* and merchants' wives.
42. There were 63 female Chinese gold miners in 1860, 29 in 1870, and 1 in 1880. Lucie Cheng Hirata, "Chinese Immigrant Women in Nineteenth-Century California," in *Women of America: A History,* eds. Carol Ruth Berkin and Mary Beth Norton (Boston: Houghton Mifflin, 1979). This trend reflects the impact of the Page Law as well as the overall decline in gold mining. In 1880, however, the census reflects 10 Chinese women railroad laborers near Truckee.
43. Yung, *Unbound Voices,* 166–67.
44. Ibid.
45. See Patricia Embrey, "Gender and Sinology: Shifting Western Interpretations of Foot Binding, 1300–1900," *Late Imperial China* 20, no. 2 (1999), 1–34.
46. Cited in Yung, *Unbound Feet,* p. 24.

47. Nancy Cott, "Marriage and Women's Citizenship in the United States, 1830–1934," *American Historical Review* 103, no. 5 (December 1999), 1457.
48. Ibid., 1456.
49. Ibid., 1444.
50. These laws also pitted a white woman's hope for suffrage and full civil rights against marriage to a Chinese man. I am indebted to Cott, "Marriage and Women's Citizenship," 1440–1474, for her astute linkages between the ideology of the family, the legal situation of late-nineteenth-century marriage, and the social and political construction of race. See in particular 1461.
51. Hirata, "Chinese Immigrant Women," 237.
52. See Doug Barrett, "The Trials and Tribulations of Ah Too," *Sierra Sun,* September 30, 1982.
53. Hirata, "Chinese Immigrant Women," 227–33.
54. Albert Dressler, *California Chinese Chatter* (San Francisco: A. Dressler, 1927), with verification letter from Milton J. Ferguson, state librarian, California State Library, Sacramento, dated March 21, 1927.
55. *Daily Humboldt Standard.*
56. A. W. Loomis, *Overland Monthly* and *Overland Weekly* 2, no. 4 (April 1869), 345–51.
57. *San Francisco Daily Alta California,* October 1, 1885. For similar reports, see January 11, 1885.
58. *Antioch Daily Ledger,* September 27, 1886.
59. *London Daily News,* May 4, 1876.
60. *Sacramento Daily Union,* June (n.d.), 1876.
61. *Sacramento Daily Record,* May 4, 1876.

CHAPTER 4. THE EUREKA METHOD

The history of the Eureka purge is based on the unpublished memoir of the Rev. Charles Huntington, *Incidents in the Life of Rev. C. A. Huntington, Discovery and Settlement of Western North America,* Collection of William Robertson Coe, Beinecke Rare Book Collection, Yale University Library, 196–203; Jerry Rohde and Gisela Rohde, *Redwood National and State Parks: Tales, Trails, and Auto Tours* (McKinleyville, Calif.: Mountain Home Books, 1994); Lynn Carranco, *The Redwood Country* (Dubuque, Iowa: Kendall/Hunt, 1971), 34; contemporary newspapers, including the *Daily Humboldt Standard,* February 7 and 9, 1885; the *Eureka Daily Times-Telephone,* February 5 and 7, 1885; the *Eureka Humboldt Times,* February 6 and 14, 1885; the *Ferndale Enterprise,* February 14, 1885; the *Weekly Times-Telephone,* February 14, 1885; and the *Blue Lake Advocate,* February 21, 1957; the extensive scrapbooks of Susie Baker Fountain, Humboldt Room, California State University, Humboldt ; mss. held at the Humboldt County Historical Society, the Humboldt County Library, and the Humboldt Room, California State University, Humboldt; David E. Gordon, "One California Town Without a Chinaman," unpublished ms. 1910, 2.; miscellaneous and undated clipping files, California State University, Humboldt; Sam Kelsey, Oral History interview by Martha Roscoe, September 16, 1961, Humboldt County Historical Society meeting at Mattole Grange, 8; Bernice Barum Cockburn interview by Lynwood Carranco, cited in Carranco, *Redwood Country;* Andrew Genzoli, *Eureka Times Standard,* January 24, 1975; and Sophie Huntington, "In Our Midst," ms., California State University, Humboldt.

1. The *San Francisco Examiner* of November 22, 1893, contains a dispatch from San Jose that may identify Kendall's murderer. It states that during the trial of a Chinese man named Ung Dong, another Chinaman, Ah Bun, stated that he was a merchant in this city when Councilman Kendall was killed, and that it was known to a number of Chinese that Ung Dong, who kept a gambling house, fired the fatal shot, which was intended for another man. Ung Dong had just been sentenced to two years at Folsom Prison for an assault upon a Chinese resident from San Jose.
2. *Daily Humboldt Standard,* February 9, 1885.
3. *San Francisco Daily Report,* as quoted by *Eureka Weekly Times-Telephone,* February 14, 1885.
4. *Eureka Daily Times-Telephone,* February 5, 1885.
5. Rohde and Rohde, *Redwood National and State Parks,* 3.

6. Ibid., 40.
7. Ibid.
8. Essential to the understanding of the role of labor in the purges are Ping Chiu, *Chinese Labor in California: An Economic Study* (Madison: State Historical Society of Wisconsin for the University of Wisconsin, 1963); Daniel Cornford, *Workers and Dissent in the Redwood Empire* (Philadelphia: Temple University Press, 1987); Daniel Cornford, ed., *Working People of California* (Berkeley: University of California Press, 1995); Lucile Eaves, *A History of California Labor Legislation* (Berkeley: University of California Press, 1910); Chris Friday, *Organizing Asian American Labor* (Philadelphia: Temple University Press, 1994); Robert Weir, *Beyond Labor's Veil: The Culture of the Knights of Labor* (Philadelphia: Penn State University Press, 1996) and *Knights Unhorsed: International Conflict in a Gilded Age Social Movement* (Detroit: Wayne State University Press, 2000).
9. D. L. Thornbury, *California's Redwood Wonderland: Humboldt County* (San Francisco: Sunset Press, 1923), 65.
10. *Humboldt Times,* March 11, 1882.
11. Records of the Humboldt County Assessor, 1884, Office of the County Assessor, Humboldt County, California.
12. *Eureka Daily Times-Telephone,* December 24, 1884.
13. Ibid., March 4, 1882.
14. *San Francisco Morning Call,* February 9, 1885.
15. Fountain scrapbooks, February 7, 1885.
16. *Eureka Daily Times-Telephone,* February 5, 1885.
17. Ibid., January 10, 1885.
18. *Eureka Weekly Times-Telephone,* January 3, 1885.
19. *Eureka Daily Times-Telephone,* February 8, 1885; Minutes of the Eureka Common Council, February 7, 1885; Carranco, *Redwood Country.*
20. *Daily Humboldt Times,* February 20, 1885, and February 13, 1886.
21. Michael J. Kellogg, "Treatment of Minority Groups in Humboldt County," ms., Humboldt Room, California State University, Arcata, 100; *Daily Humboldt Times,* February 4 and 10, 1885, and February 13, 1886.
22. *Eureka Daily Times-Telephone,* February 15, 1885.
23. *Daily Humboldt Standard,* February 19, 1885.
24. Ibid., February 14, 1885.
25. Ibid., February 9, 1885.
26. *Red Bluff Weekly People's Cause,* March 28, 1885.
27. *Daily Times-Telephone,* February 12, 1885.
28. Ibid., February 10, 1885.
29. See Stanford Lyman, "The 'Chinese Question' and American Labor Historians," *New Politics* (winter 2000), 113–48; and Andrew Gyory, *Closing the Gate: Race, Politics and the Chinese Exclusion Act* (Chapel Hill: University of North Carolina Press, 1998), for an influential debate on the role of labor, labor unions, and national politicians in provoking anti-Chinese sentiment and the Chinese Exclusion Act of 1882 in particular. See also Gyory's "A Reply to Stanford Lyman," *New Politics* (summer 2000).
30. See Elmer Sandmeyer, *The Anti-Chinese Movement in California* (1939; reprint Urbana: University of Illinois Press, 1991); and Alexander Saxton, *The Indispensable Enemy: Labor and the Anti-Chinese Movement in California* (Berkeley: University of California Press, 1995). See also Mary Roberts Coolidge, *Chinese Immigration* (New York: Henry Holt, 1909); and Gyory, *Closing the Gate.*
31. Saxton, *Indispensable Enemy,* and Carlos Schwantes, *The Pacific Northwest: An Interpretative History* (Lincoln: University of Nebraska Press, 1996).
32. Desperate attempts to drive the Chinese from California may also be understood through Gary Okihiro's notion of "commonalities in differences." Gary Okihiro, *Common Ground: Reimagining American History* (Princeton, N.J.: Princeton University Press, 2001), 27.
33. Thornbury, *Redwood Wonderland,* 65.

34. See the writings of Lisa Lowe, in particular "Discourse and Heterogeneity," in *Critical Terrains: French and British Orientalisms* (Ithaca, N.Y.: Cornell University Press, 1991).
35. *Eureka Weekly Times-Telephone,* February 14, 1885.
36. *San Francisco Chronicle,* February 8, 1885.
37. See Thomas Almaguer, *Racial Fault Lines: The Historical Origins of White Supremacy in California* (Berkeley: University of California Press, 1994).
38. Rohde and Rohde, *Redwood National and State Parks,* 11.
39. Cornford, *Workers and Dissent,* 8.
40. Ibid., 153.
41. Ibid., 33.
42. *Humboldt Times,* December 20, 1886.
43. Phil Sanders, private conversations with author, 2002–5.
44. Hubert Howe Bancroft, *History of the Pacific States of North America, California,* vol. 7 (San Francisco: History Company, 1890), 327.
45. *Northern Independent,* August 12, 1868.
46. The debts for passage were usually owed to one of the Chinese Six Companies that had arranged loans with the Pacific Mail Steamship Company.
47. Isaac Cox, *Annals of Trinity County* (San Francisco: John Henry Nash, 1858), 37.
48. Cornford, *Workers and Dissent,* 67.
49. Philip Choy, Lorraine Dong, and Marlon Hom, eds., *The Coming Man: Nineteenth Century Perceptions of the Chinese* (Seattle: University of Washington Press, 1995); Robert Lee, *Orientals: Asian Americans in Popular Culture* (Philadelphia: Temple University Press, 1999).
50. *Eureka Daily Times-Telephone,* September 23, 1884.
51. Winfield J. Davis, *History of Political Conventions in California, 1849–1892* (Sacramento: Publications of the California State Library, 1893), 416.
52. Frank Roney, *Frank Roney, Irish Rebel and California Labor Leader: An Autobiography,* ed. Ira B. Cross (Berkeley: University of California Press, 1931), 362ff.
53. See Stanford Lyman, " 'Chinese Question' "; and Gyory, *Closing the Gate.*
54. Daniel Cornford, "To Save the Republic: The California Workingmen's Party in Humboldt County," in Cornford, *Working People,* 301.
55. Minutes of the Humboldt County Board of Supervisors, vol. F, 95. See also Noel E. Harris, "Humboldt County Elections: An Account of Elections and a Survey of Election Returns from the Formation of the County to the Present Day Along with Some Contemporary and Historical Comment on these Events," California State University, Humboldt.
56. In the mid-1870s, Keller and his wife, Caroline Woodward Keller, filed a homestead claim along the Eel River in southern Humboldt. Keller had headed west to escape his overbearing and conservative father, who had opposed his service in the Union Army. In California, Keller drifted—doing construction work in the San Bernardino Mountains, renting a brewery in San Bernardino, losing a land grant to the mission in San Buenaventura, working as a waiter, and finally raising cattle along the Eel River. Keller moved back into Eureka to open a meat market "in opposition to a millionaire land and cattle owner who had driven out by underselling and later buying out everyone who had ever attempted to oppose him." Within six months the landowner "did away" with Keller's store. Charles Keller, "Autobiography," ms., University of California, Berkeley, Bancroft Library, 1–2. See also Rohde and Rohde, *Redwood National and State Parks,* 15–18.
57. *Humboldt Daily Standard,* May 19, 1880. See also Cornford, 54.
58. Ibid., 67; and *Humboldt Daily Standard,* March 24, 1883.
59. Cornford, "To Save the Republic," 68.
60. Burnette Haskell was born in Sierra County mining country, drifted through the University of California, University of Illinois, and Oberlin College, and found his political voice when he took charge of his uncle's weekly paper, *Truth,* in 1882 and turned it into a labor journal.
61. *Humboldt Times,* February 13, 1885.
62. Sandmeyer, *Anti-Chinese Movement,* 65.

63. Cited in "Holy Moses," Humboldt Room Pamphlet Collection, Humboldt State University, in Sophie Huntington, "In Our Midst," 11.
64. *Northern Independent,* June 1, 1872.
65. *Truth,* May 24, 1882.
66. Cornford, *Workers and Dissent,* 58ff.
67. Almaguer, *Racial Fault Lines.*
68. *Humboldt Standard,* May 29, 1880. I am indebted to Daniel Cornford for leading me to several early Humboldt County newspapers.
69. *Truth,* March 25, 1882.
70. Many leaders of the Knights, such as James Beith and Daniel Cronin, became leaders in the purges of Chinese people from Humboldt County. See Cornford, *Workers and Dissent,* 77ff.
71. A balanced and astute reading of historical debates about the relationship of the anti-Chinese movement in California, the emerging labor movement, and the national absorption of the West Coast into a functioning political magnet is Gary Okihiro, *The Columbia Guide to Asian American History* (New York: Columbia University Press, 2001), 75–99. For discussions of anti-Chinese violence that stresses the role of white labor, see Coolidge, *Chinese Immigration,* as well as Gyory, *Closing the Gate;* and Saxton, *Indispensable Enemy,* among others.
72. I am indebted to my teacher, the late Raymond Williams, who guided my early work on rural labor. Williams develops the concept of the "knowable community" in *The Country and the City* (New York: Oxford University Press, 1973).
73. *Eureka Weekly Times-Telephone,* January 16, 1886, names Mssrs Youill, Baird, Riddell, and Bledsoe.
74. A. J. Bledsoe, interview, *Humboldt Weekly Standard,* January 28, 1886.
75. *Eureka Daily Times-Telephone,* February 12, 1885.
76. *Daily Humboldt Standard,* February 21, 1885.
77. Byron Smith, interview by Monica Hadley, *Arcata Union,* June 28, 1963.
78. *Diary of James Beith,* vol. 7, February 8, 1885, Bancroft Library, University of California, Berkeley.
79. *Eureka Daily Times-Telephone,* February 16, 1886.
80. Ibid., February 16, 1886.
81. *Humboldt Standard,* April 27, 1886.
82. *Eureka Daily Times-Telephone,* February 16, 1886.
83. *Humboldt Standard,* April 27, 1886.
84. See Humboldt County Code, sec. 315 and 367; and *Humboldt Standard,* April 27, 1886.
85. *Eureka Daily Times-Telephone,* February 26, 1886.
86. *Humboldt Standard,* April 5 and 27, 1886.
87. *Eureka Daily Times-Telephone,* February 17, 1886.
88. Doris Chase, *They Pushed Back the Forest* (n.p., 1959), 53.
89. Ibid., 55.
90. *Eureka Daily Times-Telephone,* February 10, 1886.
91. Ibid., February 17, 1886.
92. *San Francisco Chronicle,* May 21, 1885.
93. Ibid., May 4, 1885.
94. L. E. Hamm, ed., *History and Business Directory of Humboldt County* (Eureka, Calif.: Daily Humboldt Standard, 1890), 91.
95. *Humboldt Standard,* March 3, 1886.
96. Ibid., February 20, 1886.
97. Phil Sanders, conversations with author, Orleans, California, 2002–5.
98. Cornford, *Workers and Dissent,* 58–59, fn. 38, 39.
99. California Bureau of Labor Statistics, *Second Biennial Report of the Bureau of Labor Statistics of the State of California for the Years 1885 and 1886,* ed. John Summerfield Enos, commissioner (Sacramento, 1887), 664–66.
100. *Western Watchman,* October 29, 1887.
101. I am most indebted for this analysis to Almaguer, *Racial Fault Lines;* and Okihiro, *Common Ground.*
102. This interpretation builds on Franklin Ng's analysis of Chinese immigrants as agents of cultural diffusion between China and the United States in "The Sojourner, Return Migration,

and Immigration History," in the journal *Chinese America: History and Perspectives,* published by the Chinese Historical Society in San Francisco (1987); and Gary Okihiro's notions of commonalities in differences.

103. David Roedeger, *The Wages of Whiteness: Race and the Making of the American Working Class* (London: Verso, 1991), 10. This analysis begins where Almaguer, in *Racial Fault Lines,* leaves off, when, in describing the diverse origins of white supremacy in California, he says, "Race rather than class served as the key organizing principle of hierarchical relations" (7).

CHAPTER 5. THE TRUCKEE METHOD

I am deeply grateful for my correspondence and personal conversations with local historian Wallace Hagaman, who has pioneered the history of the Chinese in Truckee, shared documents and analysis, and restored the Chinese cemetery in Nevada City. This chapter has been greatly aided by the following publications: Wallace R. Hagaman and Steve Cottrell, *The Chinese Must Go: The Anti-Chinese Boycott in Truckee, 1886* (Nevada City, Calif.: Cowboy Press, 2004); Wallace R. Hagaman, *A Short History of the Chinese Cemetery at Nevada City, California* (Nevada City, Calif.: Cowboy Press, 1998); and *Chinese Temples of Nevada City and Grass Valley, California, 1869–1938* (Nevada City, Calif.: Cowboy Press, 2001); Marilou West Ficklin, *Early Truckee Records* (Nevada City, Calif.: Cowboy Press, 1999); Guy Coates, "The Trout Creek Outrage," *Sierra Sun,* April 2, 1998; Paul A. Lord, Jr., ed., *Fire and Ice: A Portrait of Truckee* (Truckee, Calif.: Truckee Donner Historical Society, 1981, 1994); Priscilla Wegars, ed., *Hidden Heritage: Historical Archaeology of the Overseas Chinese* (Amityville, N.Y.: Baywood Publishing, 1983); Dick Wilson, *Sawdust Trails in the Truckee Basin: A History of Lumbering Operations, 1856–1936* (Nevada City, Calif.: Nevada County Historical Society, n.d.); David Beesley, "The Chinese and the Narrow Gauge Railroad," *Nevada County Historical Society Bulletin* 40, no. 4 (1986); Carmena Freeman, "The Chinese in Nevada County a Century Ago," *Nevada County Historical Society Bulletin* 33, no. 1 (1979); "Nevada County's Chinese," parts 1 and 2, *Nevada County Historical Society Bulletin* 25, no. 2 (1975); David A. Comstock and Ardis H. Comstock, *1895 Pictorial History of Nevada County, California* (reissue, Grass Valley, Calif.: Comstock Bonanza Press, 2000); Harry K. Wells, *History of Nevada County, California* (Oakland, Calif.: Thompson & West, 1880); "A Look at One of Truckee's Forgotten Murders," *Sierra Sun,* December 31, 1981; Juanita Kennedy Browne, "Nuggets of Nevada County History" (Nevada County Historical Society, 1983); "Nevada City, California: Chinese Quarter, A Walking Guide," ms.; "Chinese Culture" clippings file, Nevada County Library, History Branch; Archives of the Searls Library, Nevada City, Calif.; Minutes of the Historic Preservation and Advisory Commission, Truckee, Calif., 1998–2000; Archives of the Truckee Donner Historical Society, Truckee; "Sanburn Fire Insurance Map of Truckee, 1885"; *Truckee Republican, Nevada City Nevada Tri-Weekly Herald, Grass Valley Tidings, Grass Valley Foothill Weekly Tidings, Placerville Mountain Democrat, Sacramento Bee, Sacramento Daily Union, Grass Valley Union, Nevada City Nevada Daily Transcript, San Francisco Alta California, Eureka Times-Telephone, Red Bluff People's Cause, Sonora Democratic Banner, San Francisco Chronicle, Union/Valley Voice, Sierra Heritage, San Jose Daily Mercury;* Joanne Meschery, *Truckee: An Illustrated History of the Town and Its Surroundings* (Truckee, Calif.: Rocking Stone Press, 1978); Town of Truckee Municipal government website, available online at www.truckee2025.org.

1. See Doug Barrett, "Chinese Laborers Played a Major Role in Truckee's Past," *Sierra Sun,* June 21, 1984.
2. Pat Shui, "Truckee's Chinese," ms., 1981, collection of Truckee Historical Society, Truckee Calif.; Ralph Mann, *After the Gold Rush* (Stanford, Calif.: Stanford University Press, 1982), 53; and California Department of Parks and Recreation Historic Resources Inventory, 10/74925/4356550.
3. Doug Barrett, *Sierra Sun,* March 26, 1981.
4. M. Nona McGlashan, *Give Me a Mountain Meadow: The Life of Charles Fayette McGlashan, the Dynamic Lawyer/Editor Who Gave the World the Donner Party's True Story and Played a Dramatic Role in the Fascinating History of Truckee and California* (Fresno, Calif.: Pioneer Press, 1977). Toward the end of his life, McGlashan reportedly told his daughter, June, that he "had come to regret . . . bitterly" his support of Chinese exclusion. McGlashan's four book-length publications focus on the history of the Donner Party.

5. *Truckee Republican,* July 21, 1875.
6. Ibid., September 11, 1875.
7. *Thompson and West's History of Nevada County California, with Illustrations* (1880; reprint Berkeley, Calif.: Howell-North Books, 1970), 114.
8. Quoted in Doug Barrett, *Sierra Sun,* August 26, 1977; Meschery, *Truckee: An Illustrated History.*
9. *Sacramento Daily Union,* October 3, 1876.
10. *Reno Evening Gazette,* October 5, 1876.
11. For a discussion of the nineteenth-century Chinese in Nevada, see Sue Fawn Chung, "The Anti-Chinese Movement in Tonopah, Nevada," in *Chinese America: History and Perspectives* 17 (January 2003), 35–45.
12. *Truckee Republican,* July 17, 1878.
13. Ibid., November 2, 1878.
14. Ibid., November 6, 1878.
15. Ibid., November 16, 1878.
16. Ibid., November 23, 1878.
17. Ibid., November 13, 1878.
18. Ibid., November 9, 1878.
19. Ibid.
20. South Truckee Association, December 7, 1878. See deeds, receipts, and maps, 1890.
21. *Truckee Republican,* November 27, 1878.
22. Ibid., November 30, 1878; *Sacramento Record-Union,* November 30, 1878.
23. Ibid., September 21, 1878.
24. Meschery, *Truckee,* 73.
25. Ibid.
26. *San Francisco Daily Alta California,* December 12, 1885.
27. *Grass Valley Foothill Weekly Tidings,* January 2, 1886.
28. *San Francisco Daily Alta California,* January 3, 1886.
29. Ibid., January 6, 1886.
30. *Truckee Republican,* January 6, 1886.
31. Ibid., January 9, 1886.
32. *Placerville Mountain Democrat,* January 9, 1886.
33. *Truckee Republican,* January 13, 1886.
34. Ibid.
35. *Nevada City Nevada Tri-Weekly Herald,* January 19, 1886.
36. *San Francisco Daily Alta California,* January 19, 1886.
37. *Truckee Republican,* January 27, 1886.
38. *San Francisco Argonaut,* January 27, 1886.
39. *San Francisco Daily Alta California,* February 12, 1886.
40. *Truckee Republican,* April 7, 1886.
41. *San Francisco Times,* March 4, 1886.
42. *Truckee Republican,* February 3, 1886.
43. Ibid., February 13, 1886.
44. Ibid.
45. Ibid., February 6, 1886.
46. Ibid., February 10, 1886.
47. Ibid., March 17, 1886.
48. *Grass Valley Foothill Weekly Tidings,* March 20, 1886.
49. *Truckee Republican,* June 19, 1886.
50. McGlashan, *Give Me a Mountain,* 144.

CHAPTER 6. THE CHINESE REWRITE THE LETTER OF THE LAW

Asian American legal studies returns to the profoundly influential work of Charles J. McClain, *In Search of Equality: The Chinese Struggle Against Discrimination in Nineteenth Century America* (Berkeley: University of California Press, 1994). See in particular "Seeking Protection Against Mob Violence: The

Unusual Case of *Baldwin* v. *Franks*," 173–90. I am grateful for his telephone conversations as we shared our futile search for the attorney Thomas Riordan. See also Charles McClain, "The Chinese Struggle for Civil Rights in Nineteenth Century America: The First Phase: 1850–1870," *California Law Review* 72 (1984), 529–67; and Christian Fritz, "A Nineteenth Century 'Habeas Corpus' Mill: The Chinese Before the Federal Courts in California," in *Chinese Immigrants and American Law*, ed. Charles McClain (New York: Garland, 1994), 55–80.

My analysis of the cases discussed in this chapter is indebted to Angelo N. Ancheta, *Race, Rights, and the Asian American Experience* (New Brunswick, N.J.: Rutgers University Press, 1998), and to Derrick Bell, Jr., *Race, Racism and American Law* (Boston: Little, Brown, 1975); Richard Delgado, *The Rodrigo Chronicles: Conversations About America and Race* (New York: New York University Press, 1995); and Lucy Salyer, *Laws Harsh as Tigers: Chinese Immigrants and the Shaping of Modern Immigration Law* (Chapel Hill and London: University of North Carolina Press, 1995).

1. *Eureka Daily Times-Telephone*, February 13, 1885.
2. Ibid.
3. *Wing Hing* v. *City of Eureka*, 3948 F. (9th Cir. 1886). See File 3948, NARA.
4. James Beith, a member of the board of supervisors, predicted the town's jeopardy: "This wholesale exodus will bring Eureka in conflict with the Federal Courts." Fred Bee "will insist on damage and restitution." Diary of James Beith, vol. 7, Bancroft Library, University of California, Berkeley.
5. *Sacramento Daily Bee*, January 29, 1886.
6. *Nevada City Nevada Daily Transcript*, January 27, 1886.
7. "I do not think there will be any suits brought. The talk about actions for millions of dollars is the sheerest nonsense. The total damages maintained by the Chinese by being driven out did not exceed $2000. The people of Eureka are aware that, as a matter of law, they are liable for actual damages inflicted on the Chinese, but if Consul Bee or any one else undertakes to collect more they will have their hands full. There was just one Chinese in Eureka, working in a kitchen, when I left for this city, but he was notified by the committee at once, and the probability is that he is not there now. The citizens are as one man on this question, and not a single Chinaman will be allowed to take up his residence there in the future." A. J. Bledsoe, interview, *San Francisco Chronicle*, May 21, 1885.
8. *Eureka Daily Times-Telephone*, October 29, 1885.
9. Janna Thompson, *Taking Responsibility for the Past: Reparation and Historical Injustice* (Cambridge, U.K.: Polity Press/Blackwell Publishers, 2002).
10. Geoffrey Sayre-McCord, "Criminal Justice and Legal Reparations as an Alternative to Punishment," *Philosophical Issues* 11 (2001), 3–4; and Derrick Bell, *And We Are Not Saved: The Elusive Quest for Racial Justice* (New York: Basic Books, 1987), 123–39.
11. Gerald Gaus, "Does Compensation Restore Equality?" in *Nomos XXXIII: Compensatory Justice*, ed. John W. Chapman (New York: New York University Press, 1991), 45–81, 72.
12. Adjoa A. Aiyetoro, "Developing Legal Strategies to Advance Reparations," excerpted from "Formulating Reparations Litigation Through the Eyes of the Movement," *NYU Annual Survey of American Law* 58 (2003), 457–74.
13. *Agudo* v. *Monterey*, 13 Cal. 2d, 285, 286 (1939); *Bank of California* v. *Shaber*, 55 Cal. 2d 322, 324 (1880). This statute was codified in 1872. The complaint for *Wing Hing* v. *City of Eureka* is dated January 21, 1886. The Political Code for California, and the relevant section, 4452, was recodified in 1949 as California Government Code sec. 50140, which was later repealed altogether.
14. *Agudo* held that the California Penal Code was to provide "remedial" not "penal" redress. The Supreme Court of California said, "It seems plain from the standpoint of both legislative intention and historical interpretation that the purpose of section 4452 was to provide a compensatory remedy" to sue as "persons whose property has been injured or destroyed by mob violence." See *Agudo* v. *Monterey*, 284. The Chinese constructed reparations as a legal remedy to mob violence against racial minorities. This protection no longer exists, as became clear in the litigation following the Los Angeles riots of 2002.
15. Born in Upstate New York, Judge Lorenzo Sawyer had come in 1850, with the gold rush, to

California, where he set up private practice first in Sacramento and later in Nevada City, San Francisco, and Virginia City. He served on the California Supreme Court during the Civil War and was chief justice from 1868 to 1869, promoted by fellow Republican, Governor Leland Stanford. His biographer claims that Sawyer displayed a rare sympathy for Chinese immigrants and held an uncommon belief that the North's victory during the Civil War signaled a triumph of nationalism over states' rights, indeed, implementing through the law a concern for the civil rights of the Chinese that often went beyond what his colleague Stephen Field or other members of the supreme court would accept as doctrinally correct. For a history of the origins of the judicial system in the Pacific Northwest, see John R. Wunder, *Inferior Courts, Superior Justice: A History of the Justices of the Peace on the Northwest Frontier, 1852–1889* (Westport, Conn.: Greenwood Press, 1979).

16. *People* v. *Hall,* 4 Cal. 399 (1854); and *People* v. *Awa* 27 Cal. 638 (1865).
17. Linda C. A. Przbyszewski, "Judge Lorenzo Sawyer and the Chinese Civil Rights Decisions of the Ninth Circuit," in McClain, *Chinese Immigrants,* 345.
18. *In re Ah Chong,* 2 F. 733 (CC Cal. 1880); and ibid., 348.
19. *In re Wo Lee,* 26 F. 471 (CC Cal. 1886).
20. For detailed discussion of the legislative debate surrounding these early civil rights provisions, see Przybyszewski, "Judge Lorenzo Sawyer," 343.
21. *Yick Wo* v. *Hopkins,* 118 U.S. 356 (1886).
22. *In re Chae Chan Ping,* 36 F. 431, 436 (CCND Cal. 1888).
23. See pleadings of *Wing Hing* v. *Eureka.*
24. The Chinese plaintiffs argued that "a mob of disorderly and riotous persons assembled together . . . and created a riot" and that these rioters drove the Chinese away. *Wing Hing* v. *Eureka.*
25. Minutes of the City Council, City of Eureka, February 8, 1886.
26. Eureka denied that any of the twenty-one merchants were "transacting or doing business in the city," were "occupants of or proprietors" of any building, or owned "large or valuable quantities" of furniture, personal effects, or money. The Chinese merchants did not sustain "great or any damage by the breaking into their premises"; indeed the purge did not cause "the total destruction of their business." *Wing Hing* v. *Eureka.*
27. Minutes of the City Council, City of Eureka, February 8, 1886.
28. *Eureka Daily Times-Telephone,* January 27, 1886.
29. Ibid., January 21, 1886.
30. Ibid.
31. Lorenzo Sawyer, "Dictation to H. H. Bancroft," 38, Bancroft Library, University of California, Berkeley, C-D 321, no. 4.
32. Lorenzo Sawyer, "Dictation Concerning the Lick Trust," Bancroft Library, University of California, Berkeley, available online at http://sunsite.berkeley.edu.
33. Secretary of State Bayard to Cheng Tsao Ju, February 18, 1886, in Jules Davids, ed., *American Diplomatic and Public Papers,* series 2, *The United States, China, 1861–1893,* and *Imperial Rivalries,* vol. 12, doc. 43 (Wilmington, Del.: Scholarly Resources, 1973–1981). Hereafter cited as *ADPP: U.S., China.*
34. Report of F. A. Bee, Consul at San Francisco, inclosure, Fred Bee to Imperial Chinese Minister, Washington, D.C., November 30, 1885, *ADPP: U.S., China,* vol. 12, doc. 39.
35. Notes from the Chinese legation in the United States to the Department of State, 1868–1906, M-98, roll 1, NARA.
36. Cited in *Truckee Republican,* March 6, 1886.
37. The United States had also demanded compensation when Chinese pirates attacked American ships. According to Cheng, China's payment to the United States was not only a matter of treaty obligations but also a "desire to show its appreciation of the United States in a time of great trial." Cheng to Bayard, November 30, 1885, *ADPP: U.S., China,* vol. 12, doc. 40.
38. Bayard to Cheng, February 18, 1886, *ADPP: U.S., China,* vol. 12, doc. 43.
39. *Harper's Weekly,* October 17, 1885, 677.
40. "Crimes Against the Chinese," ibid., November 21, 1885, 755.
41. *Harper's Weekly,* April 24, 1886.

42. Ambassador Charles Denby, legation of the United States at Peking, to Secretary of State Bayard, July 16, 1886, *ADPP: U.S., China,* vol. 14, doc. 41.
43. Bayard to Cheng, February 18, 1886, *ADPP: U.S., China,* vol. 12, doc. 43.
44. Enclosures, Denby to Bayard, *ADPP: U.S., China,* vol. 12, docs. 44–47.
45. Hildebrand, Background Notes for Chinese Reconciliation Memorial Project, "The Tacoma Method," ms., Chinese Reconciliation Project Foundation, Tacoma, Washington.
46. Bayard to Denby, December 10, 1888, *ADPP: U.S., China,* vol. 12, doc. 53; *New York Times,* March 14, 1888; and Hildebrand, "Tacoma Method."
47. Cheng to Bayard, October 17, 1885, *ADPP: U.S., China,* vol. 12, doc. 30.
48. Cheng to Bayard, February 15, 1886, *ADPP: U.S., China,* vol. 12, doc. 33.
49. Ibid.
50. Cheng to Bayard, *Miscellaneous Letters of the Department of State,* 1789–1906, NARA, M-179, roll 3.
51. In September 1885, at a mass anti-Chinese meeting in Seattle, white residents agreed that the Chinese should be forced to leave the territory on or before November 1. Squire to Lamar, October 12, 1885, ibid.
52. Jules Karlin, "The Anti-Chinese Outbreak in Tacoma, 1885," *Pacific Historical Review* 23, no. 3 (August 1954), 271–83. See also *Tacoma Ledger* and *Tacoma News,* 1884–85.
53. Karlin, "Outbreak," 271.
54. Ibid., 272.
55. *Tacoma Ledger* and *Tacoma News,* February 17, 19, 20, 21, 22, 27, and 28, March 1, 8, and 15, 1885.
56. George Dudley Lawson, "The Tacoma Method," *Overland Monthly Magazine* 7, no. 39, 234–39, and "Sequel to Tacoma Method," 239–40.
57. Murray Morgan, *Puget's Sound: A Narrative of Early Tacoma and the Southern Sound* (Seattle: University of Washington Press, 1979), 244.
58. David Chesanow, "Chinese Reconciliation Project Addresses Dark Chapter in Tacoma's Past," ms., n.d., Tacoma Reconciliation Project Foundation.
59. July 17–31, 1886, *Miscellaneous Letters of the Department of State, 1789–1906,* NARA, M-179, roll 707. See also Lorraine Barker Hildebrand, *Straw Hats, Sandals and Steel: The Chinese in Washington State* (Tacoma: Washington State American Revolution Bicentennial Commission, 1977), 49–68.
60. July 17–31, 1886, *Miscellaneous Letters of the Department of State, 1789–1906,* NARA, M-179, roll 707. See also Hildebrand, *Straw Hats;* and Morgan, *Puget's Sound,* 240.
61. July 17–31, 1886, *Miscellaneous Letters of the Department of State, 1789–1906,* NARA, M-179, roll 707.
62. Affidavit of J. Roper, deputy marshal, November 3, 1886, ibid.
63. Squire to Bayard, July 17, 1886, *Miscellaneous Letters of the Department of State, 1789–1906,* NARA, M-179, roll 707.
64. *Report of the Governor of Washington Territory to the Secretary of the Interior, 1886* (Washington, D.C.: GPO, 1886), 875, Special Collections, University of Washington Library, Seattle.
65. See, for example, Affidavit of W. J. Fife, attorney, July 14, 1886, *Miscellaneous Letters of the Department of State, 1789–1906,* NARA, M-179, roll 707.
66. On Yang Ming reminded Bayard that most of the Chinese on the forced march from Tacoma were legal immigrants, yet "these people have been so suddenly and unreasonably expelled from their occupations and homes, their lives and property are in imminent danger, I therefore feel compelled to request that immediate and earnest efforts be taken to secure for them due protection, in order to restore to them the rights and privileges" of the Burlingame Treaty. As evidence he appended a desperate telegram from Wah Chang, now in Seattle, to Governor Squire: "Chinese residents of Tacoma forcibly driven out yesterday. From two to three hundred now in Seattle in imminent danger. Local authorities willing but not strong enough to protect us. We ask you to secure protection for us. Immediate action necessary." Squire replied with a vague proclamation calling for peace, self-control, and self-preservation. November 5, 1885, *Miscellaneous Letters of the Department of State, 1789–1906,* NARA, M-179, roll 3. See also affidavit of Fuke, doc. 34, *Report of the Governor.*
67. See *United States* v. *Jacob R. Weisbach et al.,* U.S. District Court Holding Terms at Vancouver, W.T., NARA, 1786 and 1787.

68. Hildebrand, "Tacoma Method," 58.
69. Weisbach et al. were also charged with conspiracy to deprive certain persons of equal protection of the laws, of equal privileges and immunities under the laws, and with insurrection and inciting insurrection under sections 5519, 5534, and 5536 of the Revised Statutes.
70. Morgan, *Puget's Sound*, 247.
71. The defendants argued that women were unqualified to serve on a grand jury because the territorial supreme court had ruled Washington's Woman Suffrage Act unconstitutional. Ibid., 251.
72. The Rev. Barnabus MacLafferty of the First Baptist Church testified that N. W. Gow, for example, was a convert in his church and regularly attended his Sabbath school. Gow, said MacLafferty, was a "very good man of correct deportment and habits, truthful in his speech," and as his "affiant" he would trust his recounting of the events and his accounting of his financial consequences. The pastor was present when Gow pleaded with the mayor for extra time to pack his store, and recalled Weisbach stating, "You ought to have been ready. You had plenty of time. You must now go with the rest." The mayor, he added, did not attempt "to protect Gow or his property, but seemed to be master of the situation." Affidavit of Barnabus MacLafferty, July 12, 1886, *Miscellaneous Letters of the Department of State, 1789–1906,* NARA, M-179, roll 707.
73. Thomas E. Stuen, "Asian Americans and Their Rights for Land Ownership," in *Asian Americans and the Supreme Court,* ed. Hyung Chan Kim (New York: Greenwood Press, 1992), 603–4.
74. "Burlingame Treaty of 1868," 16 Stat. 740, arts 5 and 6.
75. *Dred Scott* v. *Sandford,* 60 U.S. 393 (1857).
76. *United States* v. *Harris,* 106 U.S. 629 (1883), "Civil Rights Act" (1875), *Revised Statutes of 1875,* sec. 5519.
77. *U.S.* v. *Weisbach,* Brief and Argument of Defendants on Demurrer.
78. *U.S.* v. *Weisbach,* affidavit, June 16, 1886.
79. The mayor did confirm that as soon as the Chinese left, he sent the health inspector to Chinatown and he quickly reported that the Chinese houses were in such a "filthy condition" that they should be declared a nuisance. Indeed, they "could not have been rendered fit for the occupation of white people." The mayor reported, "A few minutes later I heard the fire signal, and saw the smoke arising from the wharf." Because the houses were "mere dry wooden shells . . . it was impossible to save them." He knew nothing, he added, of the fire in the Chinese section of "Old Tacoma," a half mile from the center of town. *U.S.* v. *Weisbach* affidavit, June 16, 1886.
80. *Tacoma News,* March 5, 1887.
81. Morgan, *Puget's Sound,* 249–51.
82. Karlin, "Outbreak," 283 and fn. 59–61.
83. *Republican Free Press,* August 31, 1889.
84. *Quen Hing Tong* v. *City of San Jose et al.* (9th Cir, 1894), 11282–11294, NARA, RG 21.
85. For the research on the Chinese Americans in San Jose I am greatly indebted to private conversations with the historian Connie Young Yu, and to her book *Chinatown San Jose, USA* (San Jose, Calif.: History San José, 2001); the generous assistance and outstanding archives of the San Jose Daily Historical Society; *San Jose Mercury;* San Jose *Herald;* San Jose *Evening News;* Eugene T. Sawyer, *History of Santa Clara County* (Los Angeles: Historic Record, 1922); William A. Z. Edwards, *Diaries* vol. 1–4, in possession of the author; *Golden Legacy,* Chinese Historical and Cultural Project in partnership with San Jose Historical Museum, 1994, 1999; and the analysis of Henry Wu, *Thinking Orientals: Migration, Contact, Exoticism in Modern America* (Oxford, U.K.: Oxford University Press, 2001).
86. See Sucheng Chan, *This Bittersweet Soil: The Chinese in California Agriculture, 1860–1910* (Berkeley: University of California Press, 1987), for rise in the Chinese berry and vegetable tenant farming in the Santa Clara Valley. Ping Chiu, *Chinese Labor in California: An Economic Study* (Madison: State Historical Society of Wisconsin, 1963), 67–88.
87. Edwards, *Diaries.*

88. By 1876 San Francisco's Chinatown, *Dai Fow,* housed more than 30,000 Chinese in nine city blocks. Wu, *Thinking Orientals,* 13; and Yu, *Chinatown,* 10–12.
89. Glory Anne Laffey, "The Chinatowns of San Jose," ms., San Jose Historical Museum, 1993, 22.
90. Bureau of the Census, *Tenth Census of the United States,* vol. 1, *Statistics of the Population of the United States, 1880* (Washington, D.C.: 1886).
91. Wu, *Thinking Orientals,* 13.
92. Yu, *Chinatown,* 28; and Laffey, "Chinatowns," 27.
93. The *San Jose Daily Herald* covered this issue extensively in January and February 1879.
94. *Red Bluff Weekly People's Cause,* October 31, 1885.
95. Towns across northern California were rounding up and expelling Chinese residents, and the *Daily Mercury* urged San Jose to likewise "compel the retirement of Chinatown from the central portions of town, to the outskirts, or to such isolated portions as will not endanger the lives of the white inhabitants." *San Jose Daily Mercury,* November 29, 1885.
96. Ibid.
97. *San Francisco Daily Alta California,* January 7–9, 1886. See also Yu, *Chinatown,* 28–29.
98. *Chico Enterprise,* January 15, 1886.
99. *San Jose Daily Mercury,* February 2, 1886.
100. *Truckee Republican,* February 6, 1886.
101. *Wheatland Graphic,* March 6, 1886.
102. *San Jose Daily Mercury,* January 27, 1886.
103. During these years police officers were elected by the mayor and city council, and hence were in themselves a highly political body. Between 1880 and 1900 there were six chiefs of police in San Jose, and the city ordinance prohibiting political activity by police officers was generally ignored. Between 1880 and 1890 a new mayor took office every two years. The office of chief of police, a one-year term, was also filled by a different person every two years, with the exception of Brown, who served two consecutive terms. See *San Jose Daily Mercury,* March 8, 1887.
104. Ibid.
105. *San Jose Daily Mercury,* February 23–March 22, 1887.
106. The Chinese and white losses combined amounted to about $75,000.
107. One week after the San Jose fire, a fire claimed $50,000 of property in Fresno's Chinese community. Again, there was no water to put out the fire. In October, Chico's Chinese community was also destroyed by fire, and "to cap the disaster, the fire hose was chopped in four places during the conflagration, evidently by persons who hated the Chinese." See National Park Service website, www.cr.nps.gov/history/online_books/5views/5views3e.htm, fns. 104–6.
108. Yu, *Chinatown,* 37.
109. Ibid., 36–37.
110. *San Jose Mercury,* May 18, 1887.
111. Ibid., June 30, 1888.
112. Yu, *Chinatown,* 43–44.
113. *San Jose Mercury,* June 14, 15, and 16, 1891.
114. *San Jose Daily Mercury,* August 12, 1891.
115. *San Jose Daily Mercury,* July 8, 1891.
116. Minutes of San Jose Common Council, May 16, 1881, 2, and Craig Foster et al., "The History of Municipal Policing in San Jose, California, 1880–1900," ms., December 1972 (on file with author).
117. *San Jose Daily Mercury,* November 11, 1891, and February 15, 1892.
118. Flickenger Cannery published a promotional book, *Sunshine, Fruit, and Flowers: Santa Clara and Its Resources* (1895), in which it called the new packinghouse "an immense establishment. . . . The fruit is all packed by white men and women" (200). See also Rebecca Allen et al., *Excavation of the Woolen Mills Chinatown,* vol. 1 (Ca-Scl-807H) (San Jose, Calif.: San Jose Historical Society, 2001).

119. Chan, *Bittersweet Soil.* The population of Chinese in Santa Clara was 2,695 in 1880 and 1,738 in 1900 (319).
120. *San Jose Daily Herald,* February 19, 1902.
121. *San Jose Evening News,* April 26, 1906.
122. Mae Ngai, "San Francisco's Survivors," *New York Times,* April 18, 2006.
123. This discussion is deeply indebted to Connie Yu. See Yu, *Chinatown.* In personal conversations and correspondence, in her books, her private collections, and her interviews with descendants, Yu has established the enduring role of San Jose's Chinatown.
124. Cited in John C. Lammers, "The Accommodation of Chinese Immigrants in Early California Courts," *Sociological Perspectives* 31, no. 4 (October 1988), 458.
125. Franklin Ng, "The Sojourner, Return Migration, and Immigration History," *Chinese America: History and Perpsectives* (1987), p. 56. Austin Sarat, "Going to Court: Access, Autonomy, and the Contradictions of Liberal Legality," in *The Politics of Law: A Progressive Critique,* ed. David Kairys (New York: Basic Books, 1998), 97–114; and Robert Chang, "Why We Need a Critical Asian American Legal Studies," in *Disoriented: Asian Americans, Law, and the Nation-State* (New York: New York University Press, 1999), 48–60.
126. Mari Matsuda, "Looking to the Bottom: Critical Legal Studies and Reparations," in *Critical Race Theory: The Key Writings That Formed the Movement,* eds. Kimberle Crenshaw et al. (New York: New Press, 1995), 63–79.
127. This study confirms the work of Arif Dirlik, who analyzes the relationship between the growth of global capitalism and the local as the site of "redicament" and resistance. "The Global in the Local," in *Global/Local: Cultural Production and the Transnational Imaginary,* eds. Rob Wilson and Wimal Dissanayake (Durham, N.C., Duke University Press, 1996), 22.
128. *In re Lee Sing,* 43 F. 359 (1890).
129. *Chae Chan Ping* v. *United States,* 130 U.S. 581 (1889); *Nishimura Ekiu* v. *United States,* 142 U.S. 651 (1892); *Fong Yue Ting* v. *United States,* 149 U.S. 698 (1893); *Sing Tuck* v. *United States,* 194 U.S. 161 (1904); and *Ju Toy* v. *United States,* 198 U.S. 253 (1905).
130. Stephen Field to John N. Pomeroy, April 14, 1882, Stephen Field Papers, Bancroft Library, University of California, Berkeley.
131. *The Slaughter House Cases,* 83 U.S. (16 Wall.) 36 (1872).
132. *United States* v. *Cruikshank,* 92 U.S. 542 (1875).
133. See John Hayakawa Torok, "Reconstruction and Racial Nativism: Chinese Immigrants and the Debates on the Thirteenth, Fourteenth, and Fifteenth Amendments and Civil Rights Laws," *Asian Law Journal* 55 (1966), 55–103.
134. Kairys, *Politics of Law,* 110, fn. 46.
135. *Yick Wo* v. *Hopkins;* and Sarat, "Going to Court."

CHAPTER 7. A LITANY OF HATE

1. *Grass Valley Foothill Weekly Tidings,* November 7, 1874.
2. Cited in *Wheatland Graphic,* February 13, 1886.
3. *Sonora Union Democrat,* February 20, 1886.
4. *Red Bluff Weekly People's Cause,* July 25, 1885.
5. *Weekly Shasta Courier,* March 20, 1886.
6. For an important study of racial expulsions in America, see James Loewen, *Sundown Towns: A Hidden Dimension of American Racism* (New York: New Press, 2005).
7. *Placer Herald,* October 27, 1881.
8. William Wei, "History and Memory: The Story of Denver's Chinatown," *Colorado Heritage* (autumn 2002), 3.
9. Docent Guide, "Chinese and Chinese Americans in Santa Cruz County," Monterey History Gallery, n.d. A foundational work on the Chinese in Monterey County is Sandy Lydon, *Chinese Gold: The Chinese in the Monterey Bay Region* (Capitola, Calif.: Capitola Book Company, 1985).
10. Theodore Hittel, *Supplement to the Codes and Statutes of the State of California, 1877–78 and 1880,* vol. 3, code 5069 (San Francisco: A. L. Bancroft, 1880), 209.
11. Geoffrey Dunn, *Santa Cruz Is in the Heart* (Capitola, Calif.: Capitola Book Company, 1989), 28.

12. Andrea Pugsley, "As I Kill This Chicken So May I Be Punished if I Tell an Untruth: Chinese Opposition to Legal Discrimination in Arizona Territory," *Journal of Arizona History* 44, no. 2 (2003), 181.
13. Sue Fawn Chung, "Chinese Lumbermen in the Lake Tahoe Region," *Gum Saan Journal* 25, no. 2 (December 2002), 17.
14. *Placer Herald,* April 14, 1883.
15. Ibid.
16. *Cloverdale Reveille,* May 28, 1882.
17. *State ex rel. Fook Ling* v. *C. S. Preble* (1883), in Chung, "Chinese Lumbermen," 16.
18. *Sonora Democratic Banner,* January 22, 1886.
19. Ibid., December 25, 1885.
20. *San Francisco Elevator,* May 2, 1885.
21. *Petaluma Courier,* July 15, 1885.
22. *New York Times,* October 8, 1885.
23. Ibid., September 10, 1885.
24. *Santa Cruz Daily Surf,* November 8, 1885.
25. *Sonora Democratic Banner,* December 25, 1885, and January 22, 1886.
26. *Weekly Butte Record,* October 24, 1885.
27. *San Francisco Chronicle,* April 6, 1885.
28. *New York Times,* September 10, 1885.
29. *Petaluma Courier,* July 15, 1885.
30. *Red Bluff Weekly People's Cause,* November 28, 1885.
31. *Santa Cruz Daily Sentinel,* November 8, 1885, and February 2, 1886.
32. The American Presidency Project, www.presidency.ucsb.edu/showplatforms.php?platindex=D1884.
33. *Sonora Democratic Banner,* November 6, 1885.
34. *Napa Register,* November 13, 1885.
35. *Santa Cruz Daily Sentinel,* December 22, 1885.
36. *San Francisco Daily Alta California,* March 11, 1886.
37. Julie Courtwright, "A Slave to Yellow Peril: The 1886 Ouster Attempt in Wichita, Kansas," *Great Plains Quarterly* 22, no. 1 (2001), 30. See also "War on Chinese in Wichita," *Wichita Eagle,* January 3, 1886, and *Wichita Beacon,* January 4, 1886.
38. *Marysville Daily Appeal,* February 11, 1886.
39. *Eureka Daily Times-Telephone,* May 1, 1886.
40. *San Francisco Daily Alta California,* March 11 (?), 1886.
41. *Napa Register,* April 9, 1886.
42. *Red Bluff Weekly People's Cause,* March 21, 1886.
43. *Marysville Daily Appeal,* January 30, 1886.
44. *Truckee Republican,* January 27, 1886.
45. *San Francisco Daily Alta California,* February 11, 1886.
46. *Los Angeles Times,* February 21, 1886.
47. *Marysville Daily Appeal,* February 2, 1886.
48. *Eureka Daily Times-Telephone,* February 27, 1886.
49. *Marysville Daily Appeal,* February 26, 1886.
50. *Eureka Daily Times-Telephone,* November 3, 1886.
51. *Sonora Democratic Banner,* March 5, 1886.
52. Ibid.
53. *Sonora Union Democrat,* April 3, 1886.
54. *Contra Costa Gazette,* June 26, 1886.
55. *San Francisco Daily Alta California,* July 19, 1886.
56. *San Francisco Daily Examiner,* August 12, 1886.
57. *San Francisco Daily Alta California,* August 19, 1886. Information on Yreka, Callahan, and Etna also based on *Yreka Weekly Union, Yreka Semi-Weekly Journal, Weekly Scott Valley News.*
58. State of California, Department of Parks and Recreation, Historic Resources Inventory, "Chinese American Cemetery," Yreka, Siskiyou County. n.d.

59. *Truckee Republican,* November 10, 1886.
60. *Red Bluff Weekly People's Cause,* January 23, 1886; and *Alameda Encinal,* January 27, 1886.
61. *Chico Enterprise,* February 5, 1886.
62. *Sacramento Daily Bee,* January 30, 1886.
63. *Chico Enterprise,* February 12, 1886; and *Marysville Daily Appeal,* February 13, 1886.
64. *Eureka Daily Times-Telephone,* January 26, February 2 and 3, and March 16, 1886; *Daily Humboldt Standard,* January 17, 1885, February 2, and March 16, 1886; *San Francisco Daily Alta California,* January 26, February 10, 11, and 16, and March 9, 1886; *Chico Enterprise,* May 7, 1886; and *Los Angeles Times,* January 27, 1886.
65. *Wheatland Graphic,* February 27, 1886.
66. *San Francisco Daily Alta California,* May 3, 1886; and *Mendocino Dispatch-Democrat,* March 5, 1886.
67. *Mendocino Beacon,* February 27, 1886, and March 9, 1886.
68. *San Francisco Daily Alta California,* April 24, 1886.
69. *Placerville Mountain Democrat,* February 13, 1886.
70. *Marin Journal,* February–September 1886; and Eve Armentrout Ma, in *Chinese America: History and Perspectives* (San Francisco: Chinese Historical Society of America, 1991).
71. *Eureka Daily Times-Telephone,* February 9, 1886.
72. *San Francisco Daily Alta California,* February 19, 1886.
73. Ibid., February 9, 1886.
74. *Nevada City Nevada Daily Transcript,* February 28, 1886.
75. *Red Bluff Weekly Sentinel,* February 20, 1886.
76. *Tehama Weekly Sentinel,* March 6, 1886. Other information on Stockton comes from the *Sonora Democratic Banner, San Francisco Daily Alta California, Daily Humboldt Standard,* and *San Jose Mercury.*
77. *Alameda Encinal,* January 20, 1886.
78. See, e.g., *Placer Argus,* September 23 and 30, 1886.
79. *San Francisco Daily Alta California,* March 11, 1886.
80. *Napa Register,* November 12, 1886.
81. *Sacramento Daily Record-Union,* February 13, 1886.
82. *San Joaquin Valley Argus,* from *San Francisco Post,* April 10, 1886.
83. Pugsley, "As I Kill," 90.
84. *Red Bluff Weekly Sentinel,* February 20, 1986.
85. *Eureka Daily Times-Telephone,* March 3, 1886.
86. *San Francisco Daily Alta California,* February 19, 1886.
87. *Wheatland Graphic,* March 27, 1886.
88. See Charles J. McClain, *In Search of Equality: The Chinese Struggle Against Discrimination in Nineteenth-Century America,* ch. 7, "Seeking Federal Protection Against Mob Violence: The Unusual Case of *Baldwin v. Franks*" (Berkeley: University of California Press, 1994), 173–90.
89. *Napa Register,* February 19, 1886.
90. *Weekly Shasta Courier,* December 18, 1886.
91. See *Grass Valley Weekly Tidings, Grass Valley Daily Tidings, Grass Valley Foothill Weekly Tidings.*
92. *Del Norte Record,* March 16, 1887.
93. Ibid., June 25, 1887.
94. Ibid.
95. Lydon, *Chinese Gold,* 184–87.
96. Arif Dirlik, *The Chinese on the American Frontier* (Lanham, Md.: Rowman and Littlefield, 2001); David H. Stratton, "The Snake River Massacre of Chinese Miners, 1887," in *A Taste of the West: Essays in Honor of Robert G. Athearn,* ed. Duane A. Smith (Boulder, Colo.: Pruett Publishing, 1983), 109–29.
97. *Red Bluff Weekly People's Cause,* August 27, 1887.
98. *Del Norte Record,* February 5, 1887.
99. Campbell Gibson and Kay Jung, "Historical Census Statistics on Population Totals by Race, 1790 to 1990, and by Hispanic Origin, 1970 to 1990," for the United States, Regions, Divisions, and States; Population Division, U.S. Census Bureau, Working Paper Series No. 56, September 2002.

CHAPTER 8. THE DOG TAG LAW

The research and analysis of the following have been profoundly informative and influential as I unearthed and analyzed the materials for the "Dog Tag Act"—its causes, repercussions, and implications: Kitty Calavita, *U.S. Immigration Law and the Control of Labor, 1820–1924* (New York: Academic Press, 1984); Lucie Cheng and Edna Bonacich, eds., *Labor Immigration Under Capitalism* (Berkeley: University of California Press, 1984); Sucheng Chan, ed., *Entry Denied: Exclusion and the Chinese Community in America 1882–1943* (Philadelphia: Temple University Press, 1991); Hyung-Chan Kim, ed., *Asian Americans and the Supreme Court: A Documentary History* (New York: Greenwood Press, 1992); Franklin Odo, ed., *The Columbia Documentary History of the Asian American Experience* (New York: Columbia University Press, 2002); John King Fairbank, *The United States and China* (Cambridge, Mass.: Harvard University Press, 1979); Andrew Gyory, *Closing the Gate: Race, Politics, and the Chinese Exclusion Act* (Chapel Hill: University of North Carolina Press, 1998); Bill Ong Hing, *Defining America Through Immigration Policy* (Philadelphia: Temple University Press, 2004); and *Making and Remaking Asian America Through Immigration Policy 1850–1990* (Stanford, Calif.: Stanford University Press, 1993); Madeline Yuan-yin Hsu, *Dreaming of Gold, Dreaming of Home* (Stanford, Calif.: Stanford University Press, 2000); Michael H. Hunt, *The Making of a Special Relationship: The United States and China to 1914* (New York: Columbia University Press, 1983); Peter Irons, *A People's History of the Supreme Court* (New York: Viking, 1999); Thomas LaFargue, *China's First Hundred: Educational Mission Students in the United States, 1872–1881* (Pullman: Washington State University Press, 1987); Wen Hwan Ma, *American Policy Toward China* (New York: Arno Press and New York Times, 1970); Mae M. Ngai, *Impossible Subjects: Illegal Aliens and the Making of Modern America* (Princeton, N.J.: Princeton University Press, 2004); Lynn Pan, *Sons of the Yellow Emperor: A History of the Chinese Diaspora* (Boston: Little, Brown, 1990); Anders Stephanson, *Manifest Destiny: American Expansionism and the Empire of Right* (New York: Hill and Wang, 1995); David M. Reimers, *Unwelcome Strangers: American Identity and the Turn Against Immigration* (New York: Columbia University Press, 1998); Ssu-yü Teng and John K. Fairbank, *China's Response to the West: A Documentary Survey, 1839–1923* (Cambridge, Mass.: Harvard University Press, 1954); Shi-Shan Henry Tsai, *China and the Overseas Chinese in the United States, 1868–1911* (Fayetteville: University of Arkansas Press, 1983); Kim Voss, *The Making of American Exceptionalism: The Knights of Labor and Class Formation in the Nineteenth Century* (Ithaca, N.Y.: Cornell University Press, 1993); David Wyatt, *Five Fires, Race, Catastrophe, and the Shaping of California* (New York: Addison-Wesley, 1997); Scott Wong and Sucheng Chan, eds., *Claiming America: Constructing Chinese American Identities During the Exclusion Era* (Philadelphia: Temple University Press, 1998); Liping Zhu, *A Chinaman's Chance: The Chinese on the Rocky Mountain Mining Frontier* (Boulder: University Press of Colorado, 1997); and Kil Young Zo, *Chinese Emigration into the United States 1850–1880* (New York: Arno Press, 1978).

1. Cited in Charles McClain, *In Search of Equality: The Chinese Struggle Against Discrimination in Nineteenth-Century America* (Berkeley: University of California Press, 1994), 204–5; and *San Francisco Morning Call,* September 20, 1892.
2. *Geary Act of 1892,* 52d. Cong., 1st sess. (27 Stat. 25).
3. *San Francisco Daily Evening Bulletin,* September 10, 1892.
4. McClain, *In Search,* 203.
5. *San Francisco Evening Bulletin,* September 10, 1892.
6. *New York Times,* December 17, 1892.
7. See Philip Choy, Lorraine Dong, and Marlon K. Hom, *The Coming Man: Nineteenth-Century American Perceptions of the Chinese* (Seattle: University of Washington Press, 1994). In discussing the stereotyping of Asian Americans, my thinking on the role of cultural representations, of "Orientalism" and "the yellow peril," has been influenced by the work of Robert G. Lee, *Orientals: Asian Americans in Popular Culture* (Philadelphia: Temple University Press, 1999); and Krysten R. Moon, *Yellowface: Creating the Chinese in American Popular Music and Performance, 1850s–1920s* (New Brunswick, N.J.: Rutgers University Press, 2005).
8. Ibid.
9. Chinese Equal Rights League, "The New and Monstrous Anti-Chinese Bill: The Geary Registration Act," in *Appeal of the Chinese Equal Rights League to the People of the United States for*

Equality of Manhood (New York: Chinese Equal Rights League, 1892). See also Edward P. Hutchinson, *Legislative History of American Immigration Policy, 1798–1965* (Philadelphia: University of Pennsylvania Press, 1981).

10. Ibid.
11. Quoted in McClain, *In Search.* See also Minister Ts'ui to Secretary Blaine, April 12, March 22, April 21, May 5, November 7, 1892, *Notes from the Chinese Legation;* and McClain, *In Search,* 348. The president of the Sam Yup Company in San Francisco took a train across the country to Washington, D.C., to personally alert Blaine's successor, Secretary John Foster Dulles: "I told him the bill proposed to treat Chinamen like animals. I said we would not stand it." "Foreign Relations" dispatch from Secretary of State Gresham to Ambassador Denby, *House Executive Documents, 1893–1894,* 53rd Cong., 2d sess., vol. 1 (Washington, D.C.: GPO, n.d.), 250. See also Tien-Lu Li, *Congressional Policy of Chinese Immigration or Legislation Relating to Chinese Immigration to the United States* (Nashville: Publishing House of the Methodist Episcopal Church, 1916). Extensive citations from the congressional debates are in Ma, *American Policy Toward China,* 93–104.
12. *Report of the Select Committee on Immigration and Naturalization on Chinese Immigration,* 52d Cong., 1st sess., 1891; see also *Chinese Immigration: Report from the Committee on Immigration and Naturalization to Accompany H.R. 5809,* 52d Cong., 2d sess., 1892.
13. *Rural Press,* September 16, 1893, 198–99.
14. *San Francisco Chronicle,* May 2, 1892.
15. Hudson N. Janisch, "The Chinese Exclusion Laws: Congress and the Politics of Unbridled Passion," in Kim, *Asian Americans and Congress,* 98–103.
16. *Los Angeles Times,* September 2, 1893, cited in Alexander Saxton, *The Indispensable Enemy Labor and the Anti-Chinese Movement in California* (Berkeley: University of California Press, 1975), 234. Bill Ong Hing argues that if the McCreary amendment had not passed and mass deportations occurred, there would have been dire results on California's new fruit industry. *Defining America.*
17. Henry Wu, *Thinking Orientals: Migration, Contact, Exoticism in Modern America* (Oxford, U.K.: Oxford University Press, 2001), 7–9.
18. *San Francisco Morning Call,* September 20, 1892.
19. *Congressional Record,* 52d Cong., 1st sess. April 4, 1892, 2911. Also cited in Wen Ma, *American Policy,* 94, and in "New and Monstrous."
20. *San Francisco Morning Call,* April 1, 1893.
21. Ibid., March 23, 1893.
22. Ibid., April 9, 1893.
23. *U.S. Statutes at Large* 27 (1891–1893), 590.
24. *San Francisco Chronicle,* May 6, 1886.
25. Ibid., May 5, 1893.
26. Ibid., May 4, 1893.
27. Ibid., May 3 and 4, 1893.
28. Ibid., May 5, 1893.
29. Ibid., May 3, 1893.
30. *New York Times,* October 18, 1893.
31. *San Francisco Morning Call,* May 4, 1893.
32. Janisch, "Exclusion Laws," 101. See also Kim, *Legal History,* 81.
33. *Fong Yue Ting v. United States,* 149 U.S. 698, 744 (1893).
34. Ibid., and *San Francisco Chronicle,* May 16, 1893.
35. This figure varies somewhat. Some sources put the monies remaining in the enforcement funds at $36,000 for the process of deporting the 106,000 Chinese who refused to register. See McClain, *In Search,* 350, fn. 107; House Committee on Foreign Affairs, *Report to Accompany H.R. 3687,* 53rd Cong., 1st sess., 1893, 2.
36. See McClain, *In Search,* 350, fn. 107; *Report to Accompany H.R. 3687.* According to the Department of Treasury, 13,342 Chinese had registered under the Geary Act by May 1893. See Saxton, *Indispensable Enemy,* 231, n. 5, for different numbers; and *San Francisco Chronicle,* May 30, 1893.

37. *San Francisco Chronicle,* May 25 and 26, 1893.
38. *San Francisco Morning Call,* March 30, 1893.
39. Ibid., March 31, 1893.
40. *San Francisco Chronicle,* February 8, March 1, and April 22, 1894.
41. Ibid., February 3, 1894.
42. *United States* v. *Wong Dep Ken,* 57 F. 206 (1893). See also *San Francisco Chronicle,* August 11, 1893. Wong Dep Ken was deported even as the United States insisted that China honor its treaties protecting American citizens abroad. *San Francisco Chronicle,* June 4, 1893.
43. Erika Lee has observed that the Chinese were much more successful at using the federal courts to overturn individual denials than they were at challenging the policy of exclusion itself. *At America's Gates: Chinese Immigration During the Exclusion Era, 1882–1943* (Chapel Hill: University of North Carolina Press, 2003), 123.
44. *San Francisco Chronicle,* May 18, 1893.
45. Ibid., August 2, 1893.
46. Ibid.
47. *Los Angeles Times,* August 13, 1893.
48. *San Francisco Chronicle,* August 26, 1893.
49. Ibid., August 18–20, 1893.
50. Ibid., August 20, 1893.
51. For a discussion of the various Chinese organizations in the 1890s, see L. Eve Armentrout Ma, "The Social Organization of Chinatowns in North America and Hawaii in the 1890s," in *Early Chinese Immigrant Societies: Case Studies from North America and British Southeast Asia,* ed. Lee Lai (Singapore: Heinemann Asia, 1988), 159–85.
52. *San Francisco Chronicle,* August 22, 1893.
53. *Los Angeles Saturday Times and Weekly Mirror,* September 2, 1893.
54. *San Francisco Chronicle,* September 1, 1893.
55. See *Los Angeles Times,* August 15 and 19 and September 1 and 2, 1893.
56. *Los Angeles Saturday Times and Weekly Mirror,* September 9, 1893.
57. *Los Angeles Times,* September 3 and 4, 1893.
58. Cited in Saxton, *Indispensable Enemy,* 229.
59. *Los Angeles Times,* September 3 and 4, 1893; and *Los Angeles Evening Express,* September 4, 1893.
60. *Los Angeles Evening Express,* September 7, 1893.
61. *San Francisco Chronicle,* August 31, 1893.
62. *Los Angeles Evening Express,* September 9, 1893.
63. *San Francisco Chronicle,* September 7, 1893.
64. *Los Angeles Evening Express,* September 7, 1893.
65. *San Francisco Chronicle,* September 8, 1893.
66. *Los Angeles Times,* September 26, 1893.
67. Cited in *Los Angeles Evening Express,* September 7, 1893.
68. *Los Angeles Evening Express,* September 8, 1893.
69. *San Francisco Chronicle,* September 10, 1893.
70. *San Francisco Chronicle,* May 14–15, 1893. The California Methodist Conference wrote to President Cleveland that Ross's decision placed "a new weapon in the hands of the anti-Chinese agitators now causing trouble on this coast. Wholesale arrest of the Chinese laborers has begun and hundreds of Chinese, lawful residents of this country, will be thrown in prison." *San Francisco Chronicle,* September 9, 1893. The local *Colfax Sentinel,* in turn, accused the ministers of joining the "lawless element" of working toward the same end, and neither deserves sympathy. Both the missionaries and the Chinese should "be sent back to the country which he holds in such high esteem." *Colfax Sentinel,* September 15 and October 6, 1893. See Russell Towle, *The Dutch Flat Chronicles, 1849–1906* (Dutch Flat, Calif.: Giant Gap Press, 1994), 433.
71. Edward Blum, *Reforging the White Republic: Race, Religion, and American Nationalism, 1865–1898* (Baton Rouge: Louisiana State University Press, 2005), 214.
72. Cited in *San Francisco Chronicle,* May 19, 1893.
73. *San Francisco Morning Call,* March 30, 1893.

74. *San Francisco Chronicle,* March 19, 1894.
75. Ibid., April 7, 1894.
76. Ibid., August 24, 1893.
77. *New York Times,* October 18, 1893.
78. *San Francisco Chronicle,* August 25, 1893.
79. Ibid., August 31, 1893.
80. Ibid., September 12, 1893.
81. *San Francisco Chronicle,* October 21, 25, and 27, and November 3 and 6, 1893.
82. 53rd Cong., 1st sess., doc. 78, 1893.
83. On December 8, 1893, House Resolution 88 was signed by the president and provided $50,000 for payment of salaries and expenses of additional deputy collectors of the BIR to carry out provisions of the Chinese Exclusion Act (issuing certificates of registration). On April 4, 1894, H.R. 146 was signed by the president and provided $10,000 for payment of salaries and expenses of additional deputy collectors who were issuing certificates of registration to the Chinese. 53rd Cong. 2d sess. H. Rept. 618 (53-2), 3270. The secretary of the Treasury sent a communication to the Appropriation Committee stating that the additional funds were needed in order to complete the registration process by the deadline set by the law. Additional collectors must be hired. H.R. 10238: Making Appropriations for Sundry Civil Expenses of Government for Fiscal Year Ending June 30, 1894, passed by House and Senate on March 3, 1893; 53d Cong., 1st sess.; date of presidential approval is omitted from record. I think it is less likely that this appropriation bill contained funding for registration because the one resolution (H.R. 146) appropriating funding was passed after H.R. 10238 received congressional approval. H.R. 5575: Making Appropriations for Sundry Civil Expenses of Government for Fiscal Year Ending June 30, 1895, passed by House and Senate on August 16, 1894, approved by president on August 20, 1894. 53d Cong., 2nd sess.
84. Yen Ching-Hwang, *Coolies and Mandarins: China's Protection of Overseas Chinese During the Late Ch'ing Period, 1851–1911* (Singapore: Singapore University Press, 1985), 242–48. *Coffin* v. *United States* held that the notion of innocent until proven guilty was not a constitutional protection but a valid presumption of common law. 156 U.S. 432 (1895).
85. *San Francisco Chronicle,* September 16, 1893. See also Yen, *Coolies and Mandarins;* 242–48.
86. Cited in Wen, *American Policy,* 103.
87. *U.S. Statutes at Large* 27 (1891–1893): 365, 589–90; 28 (1893–1896): 390, 932; 29 (1895–1897): 311, 431; 30 (1897–1899): 30, 616, 1093; 31 (1899–1901): 611, 1013, 1155.
88. June 9, 1894: Secretary of Treasury J. G. Carlisle sent a message to the Senate asking that an additional clause be added in the sundry civil appropriations bill for enforcement of the Chinese Exclusion Act. 53d Cong., 2d sess.
89. *San Francisco Chronicle,* September 22, 1893.
90. Ibid., September 22 and 23, 1893.
91. *Los Angeles Saturday Times and Weekly Mirror,* September 23, 1993; and *Sacramento Daily Bee,* September 13, 1893.
92. *Los Angeles Times,* August 24, 1893; see also August 15 and 19 and September 1 and 2, 1893.
93. *Sacramento Bee,* September 19, 1993; *Los Angeles Evening Express,* September 19, 1893.
94. *San Francisco Chronicle,* September 15, 1893.
95. Ibid., September 26, 1893.
96. Ibid., September 20, 1893.
97. Ibid., September 22, 1893.
98. Ibid., April 13, 1894.
99. Ibid., June 28, 1894.
100. Ibid., December 2, 1893.
101. Lee, *America's Gates,* 162–63.
102. *San Francisco Chronicle,* September 10, 1893.
103. *Los Angeles Times,* September 12, 1893.
104. *San Francisco Chronicle,* May 16, 1893.
105. *In re Tsu Tse Mee,* 81 F. 562 (D.C. Cal. 1897); *In re Wong Fock,* 81 F. 558 (D.C. Cal. 1897); *Fong Yue Ting* v. *United States.*

106. Erika Lee, "Enforcing and Challenging Exclusion in San Francisco: U.S. Immigration Officials and Chinese Immigrants, 1882–1905," in *Chinese America: History and Perspectives* (San Francisco: Chinese Historical Society, 1997), 6–7; *San Francisco Chronicle,* May 16, 1893.
107. Judith Wyman, "The Ambiguities of Chinese Anti-Foreignism: Chongqing, 1870–1900," *Late Imperial China* 18, no. 2 (1998), 92; Diana Preston, *The Boxer Rebellion: The Dramatic Story of China's War on Foreigners That Shook the World in the Summer of 1900* (New York: Walker, 2000).
108. Guanhua Wang, *In Search of Justice: The 1905–1906 Chinese Anti-American Boycott* (Cambridge, Mass.: Harvard University Press, 2001); Delber McKee, "The Chinese Boycott of 1905–1906 Reconsidered: The Role of Chinese Americans," *Pacific Historical Review* 5, no. 2 (1986), 165–91.
109. Tsai, *China and the Overseas Chinese,* 96.
110. Jules Davids, ed., *American Diplomatic and Public Papers,* series 2, *The United States, China, and Imperial Rivalries, 1861–1893* (18 vols.), vol. 3, *Chinese Immigration* (Wilmington, Del.: Scholarly Resources, 1979), 347–53. Hereafter cited as Davids, *ADPP: United States, China,* vol. 3.
111. The best resource on early Chinese American newspapers continues to be Him Mark Lai and Karl Lo, *Chinese Newspapers Published in North America, 1854–1975* (Washington, D.C.: Center for Chinese Research Materials, 1977). See also *Chinese Newspapers in Nineteenth Century California, California Newspaper Project Online MARC Catalog.* For a contemporary view, see Ednah Robinson, "Chinese Journalism in California," *OutWest Magazine* 16, no. 1 (January), 1902.
112. Davids, *ADPP: United States, China,* vol. 3.
113. Ibid., 365–76.
114. Yen, *Coolies and Mandarins,* 246.
115. *San Francisco Chronicle,* August 22, 1893.
116. *Los Angeles Evening Express,* September 9, 1893.
117. The full text of the treaty, which had been kept secret during the period of negotiations, was published with much fanfare in the *San Francisco Chronicle,* March 25, 1894.
118. See Tien-Lu Li, *Congressional Policy.*
119. Wyman, "Ambiguities," 102–3.
120. See Him Mark Lai, *Becoming Chinese Americans: A History of Communities and Institutions* (New York: Rowman and Littlefield, 2004), for a thorough history and insightful analysis of the Chinese Six Companies and the Chinese Consolidated Benevolent Association.
121. *San Francisco Chronicle,* January 20, 1894.
122. Ibid., December 29, 1893.
123. Ibid., March 19, 1894.
124. U.S. Congress, *Facts Concerning the Enforcement of the Chinese Exclusion Laws,* 59th Cong., 1st sess., 1905–06, H. Doc. 847, 76 (S.N. 4990). See also Janisch, "Exclusion Laws," 102–4.
125. Nancy Wey, *Five Views: An Ethnic Historic Site Survey for California,* National Park Service website, www.cr.nps.gov/history/online_books/5views/5views3f.htm.
126. LexisNexis Statistical Document, table C-11; United States Census, *Asians for the United States, Regions, Divisions; Appendix to the Census, Chinese in the United States,* part 2, 1882–1906, 500–1.
127. The U.S. Census of 1890 reported that 107,500 Chinese lived in the United States. Census reports are inconsistent between categories; another possible figure is that 45,753 Chinese men and women resided in California in 1890.
128. Chinese immigration historian Erika Lee argues that it is impossible to know with certainty how many Chinese men or women in fact entered the United States between 1892 and 1895. *America's Gates,* 117–19.
129. *San Francisco Chronicle,* December 12 and 14, 1893.
130. *U.S. Statutes at Large,* 27, (1891–1893), 365; 28 (1893–1896), 589; *United States Statutes at Large,* 28 (1893–1895), 390; 29 (1895–1897), 311, 423; 30 (1897–1899), 148; 1093; 616; 31 (1899–1901), 282, 316, 1053, 1013, 1155.
131. U.S. Treasury Department, Bureau of Internal Revenue, "Registration of the Chinese," *Annual Report of the Commissioner of Internal Revenue for the Fiscal Year* (Washington, D.C.: GPO, 1892, 1893, 1894, 1985, 1896, 1897, 1898, 1899, 1900, 1901, 1902, 1903). See also *San Francisco Chronicle,* March 9, 1994.
132. *San Francisco Chronicle,* April 29, May 4, 5, 7, 8, and 9, 1894.
133. Alexander Saxton suggests that the majority of the Chinese immigrants did in fact register

under the law. I have found no evidence that suggests that nearly half of the Chinese registered. *Indispensable Enemy.*

134. *San Francisco Chronicle,* February 10, 1894.
135. For the relevance of the history of photography on Chinese immigration, see Anna Pegler-Gordon, "Chinese Exclusion, Photography, and the Development of U.S. Immigration Policy," *American Quarterly* 58, no. 1 (March 2006), 51–78.
136. *San Francisco Chronicle,* May 28 and 29, 1894. See also Lee, "Enforcing and Challenging," 5–8.
137. *San Francisco Chronicle,* May 18, 1894.
138. *Port Orford Tribune,* March 27, 1894.
139. *San Francisco Chronicle,* May 18, 1894.
140. A thorough, if early, summary of the congressional debate surrounding the McCreary amendment is in Mary Roberts Coolidge, *Chinese Immigration* (New York: Henry Holt, 1909), 209–41.
141. Lucy E. Salyer, *Laws as Harsh as Tigers: Chinese Immigrants and the Shaping of Modern Immigration Law* (Chapel Hill: University of North Carolina Press, 1995), 57.
142. Immigration authorities regularly rejected more than 20 percent of Chinese who arrived with certificates, issued not only by the Chinese government identifying him as a student or merchant, thus a member of an "exempt class," but also by a United States representative in Canton or Hong Kong.

CONCLUSION: "NO PLACE FOR A CHINAMAN"

The information for this chapter was compiled from the *Daily Humboldt Times,* the *Daily Humboldt Standard,* the *Humboldt Standard,* the *Ferndale Enterprise,* the *Fortuna Advance,* the *Humboldt Beacon,* the *Eureka Daily Times-Telephone,* the *Eureka Weekly Times-Telephone,* and *The Western Watchman;* the scrapbooks of Susie Baker Fountain, Humboldt Room, California State University Humboldt; Denis P. Edeline, "Along the Banks of the Salt River" (n.p., 1983), and "Ferndale . . . The Village, 1875–1893" (n.p., 1987); Susie Van Kirk, "Newspaper References Concerning the Fisheries of the Lower Eel River, Humboldt County, California, 1854–1955" (n.p., 1996); and Alan Lufkin, "The Chinese and the Salmon Canneries."

Driven Out is a study about race, racism, and resistance. My thinking about the deep causes and potential resolutions has been profoundly shaped by many. James Loewen's important *Sundown Towns: A Hidden Dimension of American Racism* (New York: New Press, 2005) appeared as this book was in its last stages, and draws us to the modern instances of racial expulsions. Other texts that have shaped my thinking on race throughout the writing of *Driven Out* that have not been cited previously include: Russ Castronovo, *Necro Citizenship: Death, Eroticism, and the Public Sphere in the Nineteenth-Century United States* (Durham, N.C.: Duke University Press, 2001); Jacques Downs, *The Golden Ghetto: The American Commercial Community at Canton and the Shaping of American China Policy, 1784–1844* (Bethlehem, Pa.: Lehigh University Press, 1997); E. San Juan, Jr., *Racial Formations/Critical Transformations: Articulations of Power in Ethnic and Racial Studies in the United States* (Atlantic Highlands, N.J.: Humanities Press, 1992); *Nation and Narration,* ed. Homi K. Bhabka (New York: Routledge, 1990); Robert Heizer, *The Destruction of California Indians* (Santa Barbara, Calif.: Peregrine Smith, 1974); Werner Sollors, *The Invention of Ethnicity* (New York: Oxford University Press, 1989); David L. Eng, *Racial Castration: Managing Masculinity in Asian America* (Durham, N.C.: Duke University Press, 2001); George M. Fredrickson, *The Arrogance of Race: Historical Perspectives on Slavery, Racism, and Social Inequity* (Middletown, Conn.: Wesleyan University Press, 1998); David Theo Goldberg, *Racial Subjects: Writing on Race in America* (New York: Routledge, 1997); Thomas F. Gosset, *Race: The History of an Idea in America* (New York: Oxford University Press, 1997); Robert Heizer and Alan Almquist, *The Other Californians: Prejudice and Discrimination Under Spain, Mexico, and the United States to 1920* (Los Angeles: University of California Press, 1971); George L. Henderson, *California and the Fictions of Capital* (Philadelphia: Temple University Press, 2003); Noel Ignatiev, *How the Irish Became White* (New York: Routledge, 1995); Donald Lowe, *The Body in Late-Capitalist USA* (Durham, N.C.: Duke University Press, 1995); Martha Minow, *Between Vengeance and Forgiveness: Facing History After Genocide and Mass Violence* (Boston: Beacon Press, 1998) and *Making All the Difference: Inclusion, Exclusion and American Law* (Ithaca, N.Y.: Cornell University Press, 1990); David Palumbo-Liu, *Asian/American: Historical Cross-*

ings of a Racial Frontier (Stanford, Calif.: Stanford University Press, 1999); Robert Seto Quan, *Lotus Among the Magnolias: The Mississippi Chinese* (Jackson: University Press of Mississippi, 1982); C. F. Remer, *A Study of Chinese Boycotts* (Taipei: Cheng-Wen Publishing, 1966); Joseph Tilden Rhea, *Race Pride and the American Identity* (Cambridge, Mass.: Harvard University Press, 1997); David R. Roediger, *The Wages of Whiteness: Race and the Making of the American Working Class* (New York: Verso, 1991); Malini Johar Schuller, *U.S. Orientalisms: Race, Nation, and Gender in Literature, 1790–1890* (Ann Arbor: University of Michigan Press, 1998); Guanhua Wang, *In Search of Justice: The 1905–1906 Chinese Anti-American Boycott* (Cambridge, Mass.: Harvard University Asia Center, 2001); Frank H. Wu, *Yellow: Race in America Beyond Black and White* (New York: Basic Books, 2002); Henry Yu, *Thinking Orientals: Migration, Contact, and Exoticism in Modern America* (New York: Oxford University Press, 2001).

1. *Eureka Daily Times-Telephone,* September 30, 1906.
2. *Daily Humboldt Standard,* September 31 and October 1, 1906.
3. *Eureka Daily Times-Telephone,* September 30, 1906.
4. *Daily Humboldt Standard,* October 2, 1906.
5. Ibid., October 1, 1906.
6. "The Wyoming Riots," Translated from the *Shen-Pao.* See also Jules Davids, *American Diplomatic and Public Papers,* series 2, *United States, China, and Imperial Rivalries, 1861–1893* (18 vols.), vol. 12, doc. 42 (Wilmington, Del.: Scholarly Resources, 1979), 195.
7. Quoted in correspondence from Secretary of State Bayard to Cheng Tsao Ju, Chinese minister, February 18, 1886, Washington, D.C., in ibid., 196.
8. Madeline Yuan-yin Hsu, *Dreaming of Gold, Dreaming of Home: Transnationalism and Migration Between the United States and South China, 1882–1943* (Stanford, Calif.: Stanford University Press, 2000), 4–15.
9. Him Mark Lai and Karl Lo, *Chinese Newspapers, Published in North America, 1854–1975* (Washington, D.C.: Center for Chinese Research Materials, 1977).
10. Jack Norton, *Genocide in Northwestern California: When Our Worlds Cried* (San Francisco: Indian Historian Press, 1979), 91.
11. Cited in ibid., 89; and *New York Century,* June 1860.
12. Norton, *Genocide,* 92.
13. Him Mark Lai, *Becoming Chinese American: A History of Communities and Institutions* (New York: Rowman and Littlefield, 2004), 21.

INDEX

ABOUT THE AUTHOR

JEAN PFAELZER is a professor of English, East Asian studies, and women's studies at the University of Delaware. She is the author of *Rebecca Harding Davis and the Origins of Social Realism* and *The Utopian Novel in America* as well as two other books and more than thirty articles in the areas of nineteenth-century American history, American studies, American literature, feminist theory, utopian fiction, and cultural theory. She was the executive director of the National Labor Law Center of the National Lawyers Guild, and worked as a senior legislative analyst to Congressman Frank McCloskey on immigration, labor, and women's legislation. She was appointed to the Washington, D.C., Commission for Women and was a consultant for the Coal Employment Project, the organization of women coal miners. A longtime Californian, she now lives near Washington, D.C., with her family.

ABOUT THE TYPE

This book was set in Requiem, a typeface designed by the Hoefler Type Foundry. It is a modern typeface inspired by inscriptional capitals in Ludovico Vicentino degli Arrighi's 1523 writing manual, *Il modo de temperare la penne.* An original lowercase, a set of figures, and an italic in the "chancery" style that Arrighi helped popularize were created to make this adaptation of a classical design into a complete font family.